IRISH
Country Cooking

pil

Publications International, Ltd.

Photography on pages 19, 107, 119, 133, 145, 151, 161, 163, 181, 187, 205, 211, 219, 225, 249, 273, 295, 299, 303 and 311 by PIL Photo Studio North.

Recipe development on pages 132, 210, 218, 224, 272, 294, 298 and 302 by Sandra Wu.

Pictured on the front cover: Bacon and Stout Braised Short Ribs *(page 126)*.

Pictured on the back cover *(left to right):* Shepherd's Pie *(page 234)*, Glazed Cornish Hens *(page 136)* and Scotch Eggs *(page 210)*.

ISBN: 978-1-4508-9664-1

Library of Congress Control Number: 2014950502

Manufactured in China.

8 7 6 5 4 3 2 1

Publications International, Ltd.

TABLE OF CONTENTS

BREAKFAST

Bacon and Potato Quiche

  1 refrigerated pie crust (half of 15-ounce package)
12 ounces thick-cut bacon, cut crosswise into ½-inch pieces
  ½ medium onion, chopped
  ½ pound Yukon Gold potatoes, peeled and cut into ¼-inch pieces
  ½ teaspoon chopped fresh thyme
1½ cups half-and-half
  4 eggs
  ½ teaspoon salt
  ½ teaspoon black pepper
  ¾ cup (3 ounces) shredded Dubliner cheese
  2 tablespoons chopped fresh chives

1. Preheat oven to 450°F. Line baking sheet with foil.

2. Roll out pie crust into 12-inch circle on floured surface. Line 9-inch pie plate with crust, pressing firmly against bottom and up side of plate. Trim crust to leave 1-inch overhang; fold under and flute edge. Prick bottom of crust with fork. Bake about 8 minutes or until lightly browned. Remove to wire rack to cool slightly. *Reduce oven temperature to 375°F.*

3. Cook bacon in large skillet over medium heat about 10 minutes or until crisp, stirring occasionally. Drain on paper towel-lined plate. Drain all but 1 tablespoon drippings from skillet. Add onion, potatoes and thyme to skillet; cook about 10 minutes or until vegetables are tender, stirring occasionally.

4. Place pie plate on prepared baking sheet. Whisk half-and-half, eggs, salt and pepper in medium bowl until well blended. Sprinkle cheese evenly over bottom of crust; top with vegetable mixture. Pour in egg mixture; sprinkle with chives.

5. Bake 35 to 40 minutes or until quiche is set and knife inserted into center comes out clean. Let stand 10 minutes before slicing.

MAKES 8 SERVINGS

Apple Date Nut Muffins

1½ cups all-purpose flour
⅔ cup packed brown sugar
½ cup old-fashioned oats
1 tablespoon baking powder
1 teaspoon ground cinnamon
½ teaspoon salt
⅛ teaspoon ground nutmeg
⅛ teaspoon ground ginger
   Dash ground cloves
1 cup coarsely chopped peeled apples
½ cup chopped walnuts
½ cup chopped pitted dates
½ cup (1 stick) butter, melted
2 eggs
¼ cup milk

1. Preheat oven to 400°F. Line 12 standard (2½-inch) muffin cups with paper baking cups.

2. Combine flour, brown sugar, oats, baking powder, cinnamon, salt, nutmeg, ginger and cloves in large bowl. Stir in apples, walnuts and dates.

3. Whisk butter, eggs and milk in small bowl until blended. Add to flour mixture; stir just until moistened. Spoon batter evenly into prepared muffin cups.

4. Bake 20 to 25 minutes or until toothpick inserted into centers comes out clean. Cool in pan 5 minutes; remove to wire rack to cool completely.

MAKES 12 MUFFINS

Irish Whiskey Cured Salmon

1 skin-on salmon fillet (1¾ pounds), pin bones removed
2 tablespoons Irish whiskey
⅓ cup packed dark brown sugar
3 tablespoons salt
  Black bread or Irish soda bread (optional)
  Fresh dill, crème fraîche, thinly sliced red onion and/or capers (optional)

1. Line rimmed baking sheet with plastic wrap. Rinse salmon and pat dry with paper towels. Arrange salmon, skin side down, on prepared baking sheet; brush with whiskey.

2. Combine brown sugar and salt in small bowl; rub mixture over salmon. Wrap plastic wrap securely around salmon. Top with another sheet of plastic wrap.

3. Place second baking sheet on top of salmon, then place heavy skillet or several cans on top to weigh it down. Refrigerate salmon at least 48 hours and up to 72 hours.

4. Remove top baking sheet. Unwrap salmon and rinse under cold water to remove any remaining salt mixture. Pat dry with paper towels. Cut salmon into very thin slices; serve with bread and assorted toppings, if desired. Refrigerate leftover salmon up to 2 days.

MAKES 6 TO 8 SERVINGS

tip Ask your fishmonger to remove the pin bones when purchasing the salmon. (Often this is already done, or you can remove the pin bones at home with tweezers.)

Irish Porridge with Berry Compote

4 cups plus 1 tablespoon water, divided

½ teaspoon salt

1 cup steel-cut oats

½ teaspoon ground cinnamon

⅓ cup half-and-half

¼ cup packed brown sugar

1 cup fresh strawberries, hulled and quartered

1 container (6 ounces) fresh blackberries

1 container (6 ounces) fresh blueberries

3 tablespoons granulated sugar

1. Bring 4 cups water and salt to a boil in medium saucepan over medium-high heat. Whisk in oats and cinnamon. Reduce heat to medium; simmer, uncovered, about 40 minutes or until water is absorbed and oats are tender. Remove from heat; stir in half-and-half and brown sugar.

2. Meanwhile, combine strawberries, blackberries, blueberries, granulated sugar and remaining 1 tablespoon water in small saucepan; bring to a simmer over medium heat. Cook 8 to 9 minutes or until berries are tender but still hold their shape, stirring occasionally.

3. Divide porridge among four bowls; top with berry compote.

MAKES 4 SERVINGS

Apple Breakfast Cake

3 cups all-purpose flour
1 teaspoon baking soda
1 teaspoon salt
1 teaspoon ground cinnamon
1 cup chopped walnuts
1 ½ cups granulated sugar
1 cup vegetable oil
2 eggs
2 teaspoons vanilla
2 medium tart apples, peeled and chopped
Powdered sugar (optional)

1. Preheat oven to 325°F. Grease 10-inch tube pan.

2. Sift flour, baking soda, salt and cinnamon into large bowl. Stir in walnuts.

3. Combine granulated sugar, oil, eggs and vanilla in medium bowl. Stir in apples. Add to flour mixture; stir just until moistened. Spoon batter into prepared pan.

4. Bake 1 hour or until toothpick inserted near center comes out clean. Cool in pan on wire rack 10 minutes. Loosen edges with metal spatula, if necessary. Remove to wire rack to cool completely.

5. Sprinkle with powdered sugar, if desired, just before serving.

MAKES 12 SERVINGS

Smoked Salmon and Spinach Frittata

2 tablespoons vegetable oil, divided
1 medium red onion, diced
1 clove garlic, minced
6 ounces baby spinach
10 eggs
1 teaspoon dried dill weed
¼ teaspoon salt
¼ teaspoon black pepper
4 ounces smoked salmon, chopped
4 ounces Dubliner cheese, cut into ¼-inch cubes

1. Position oven rack in upper-middle position. Preheat broiler.

2. Heat 1 tablespoon oil in large ovenproof nonstick skillet. Add onion; cook 7 to 8 minutes or until softened, stirring occasionally. Add garlic; cook and stir 1 minute. Add spinach; cook 3 minutes or just until wilted. Transfer mixture to small bowl.

3. Whisk eggs, dill, salt and pepper in large bowl until blended. Stir in salmon, cheese and spinach mixture.

4. Heat remaining 1 tablespoon oil in same skillet over medium heat. Add egg mixture; cook about 3 minutes, stirring gently to form large curds. Cook without stirring 5 minutes or until eggs are just beginning to set.

5. Transfer skillet to oven. Broil 2 to 3 minutes or until frittata is puffed, set and lightly browned. Let stand 5 minutes; carefully slide frittata onto large plate or cutting board. Cut into wedges.

MAKES 6 TO 8 SERVINGS

Oatmeal Pecan Pancakes

1 1/4 to 1 1/2 cups milk, divided
1/2 cup old-fashioned oats
2/3 cup all-purpose flour
1/3 cup whole wheat flour
2 1/2 tablespoons packed brown sugar
2 teaspoons baking powder
1/2 teaspoon baking soda
1/4 teaspoon salt
1 egg
2 tablespoons melted butter
1/2 cup chopped toasted pecans
Additional butter and golden syrup (optional)

1. Bring 1/2 cup milk to a simmer in small saucepan. Stir in oats. Remove from heat; let stand 10 minutes.

2. Combine all-purpose flour, whole wheat flour, brown sugar, baking powder, baking soda and salt in large bowl.

3. Whisk egg and melted butter in medium bowl until blended. Stir in oatmeal and 3/4 cup milk. Add to flour mixture; stir just until blended. *Do not overmix.* If mixture is too thick, thin with remaining 1/4 cup milk, 1 tablespoon at a time. Stir in pecans.

4. Lightly grease large skillet or griddle; heat over medium heat. Pour batter into skillet by 1/4 cupfuls; flatten slightly. Cook 2 minutes or until tops are bubbly and bottoms are golden brown. Turn and cook 2 minutes or until golden brown. Serve with additional butter and syrup, if desired.

MAKES 4 SERVINGS

 tip To toast pecans, spread them in a single layer in a small heavy skillet. Cook and stir over medium heat 2 to 3 minutes or until the pecans are lightly browned. Immediately remove them from the skillet and cool before using.

Sausage and Apple Quiche

  1 unbaked deep-dish 9-inch pie crust
  8 ounces bulk pork sausage
  ½ cup chopped onion
  ¾ cup shredded peeled tart apple
  1 tablespoon lemon juice
  1 tablespoon sugar
  ⅛ teaspoon red pepper flakes
  1 cup (4 ounces) shredded Cheddar cheese
1½ cups half-and-half
  3 eggs
  ¼ teaspoon salt
   Dash black pepper

1. Preheat oven to 450°F. Line crust with foil; partially fill with uncooked beans or rice. Bake 10 minutes. Remove foil and beans; bake crust 5 minutes or until lightly browned. Set aside to cool. *Reduce oven temperature to 375°F.*

2. Crumble sausage into large skillet. Add onion; cook and stir over medium heat until sausage is browned and onion is tender. Spoon off and discard pan drippings. Add apple, lemon juice, sugar and red pepper flakes; cook and stir 4 minutes or until apple is barely tender and liquid is evaporated. Cool to room temperature. Spoon sausage mixture into crust; sprinkle with cheese.

3. Whisk half-and-half, eggs, salt and black pepper in medium bowl until well blended. Pour over sausage mixture in crust.

4. Bake 35 to 45 minutes or until filling is puffed and knife inserted in center comes out clean. Let stand 10 minutes before serving.

MAKES 6 SERVINGS

Raisin Oat Scones >

        2 cups all-purpose flour
        2 teaspoons baking powder
        ½ teaspoon baking soda
        ¼ teaspoon salt
        1 cup old-fashioned oats
        ½ cup (1 stick) cold butter, cut into pieces
        1 cup raisins
        1 cup buttermilk

1. Preheat oven to 425°F. Line baking sheet with parchment paper.

2. Sift flour, baking powder, baking soda and salt into medium bowl. Stir in oats. Cut in butter with pastry blender or two knives until mixture resembles coarse crumbs. Stir in raisins. Stir in just enough buttermilk to make soft dough.

3. Turn out dough onto lightly floured surface; knead several times until smooth. Pat dough into 12×10-inch rectangle. Cut into 2-inch squares; arrange on prepared baking sheet.

4. Bake about 15 minutes or until browned. Remove to wire rack to cool slightly

MAKES 30 SCONES

Bacon and Egg Breakfast Strata

        8 to 10 slices sandwich bread, cut into ½-inch cubes (about 6 cups)
        2 cups (8 ounces) shredded sharp Cheddar cheese
        1 package (8 ounces) bacon, crisp-cooked and crumbled
        6 eggs
        2 cups milk
        ½ teaspoon salt
        ½ teaspoon black pepper

1. Preheat oven to 350°F. Spray 13×9-inch baking dish with nonstick cooking spray.

2. Arrange bread cubes in prepared baking dish. Top with cheese and bacon.

3. Beat eggs in large bowl; gradually whisk in milk, salt and pepper. Pour over bread cubes, pressing down lightly until evenly coated.

4. Bake 35 to 40 minutes or until golden brown and knife inserted into center comes out clean.

MAKES 8 SERVINGS

Corned Beef Hash

2 large russet potatoes, peeled and cut into ½-inch cubes
½ teaspoon salt
¼ teaspoon black pepper
¼ cup (½ stick) butter
1 cup chopped onion
½ pound corned beef, finely chopped
1 tablespoon horseradish
4 eggs

1. Place potatoes in large skillet; add water to cover. Bring to a boil over high heat. Reduce heat to low; simmer 6 minutes. (Potatoes will be firm.) Remove potatoes from skillet; drain well. Sprinkle with salt and pepper.

2. Melt butter in same skillet over medium heat. Add onion; cook and stir 5 minutes. Stir in corned beef, horseradish and potatoes; mix well. Press mixture with spatula to flatten.

3. Reduce heat to low; cook 10 to 15 minutes. Turn hash in large pieces; pat down and cook 10 to 15 minutes or until bottom is well browned.

4. Meanwhile, bring 1 inch of water to a simmer in small saucepan. Break 1 egg into shallow dish; carefully slide into water. Cook 5 minutes or until white is opaque. Remove with slotted spoon to plate; keep warm. Repeat with remaining eggs.

5. Top each serving of hash with 1 egg. Serve immediately.

MAKES 4 SERVINGS

Hot Cross Buns

1 package (¼ ounce) active dry yeast
1 cup warm milk, divided
2¼ cups all-purpose flour
1 cup currants
½ cup whole wheat flour
¼ cup granulated sugar
¼ teaspoon salt
¼ teaspoon ground nutmeg
2 eggs, beaten
¼ cup (½ stick) butter, melted
½ cup powdered sugar
1 to 2 tablespoons milk or cream

1. Sprinkle yeast over ¼ cup warm milk in small bowl; stir to dissolve yeast. Let stand 10 minutes or until bubbly. Meanwhile, combine all-purpose flour, currants, whole wheat flour, granulated sugar, salt and nutmeg in medium bowl. Whisk eggs, butter and remaining ¾ cup warm milk in large bowl until blended.

2. Stir yeast mixture into egg mixture. Gradually beat in flour mixture until well blended. (Dough will be sticky.) Cover and let rise in warm place 1 hour.

3. Preheat oven to 400°F. Grease 12 standard (2½-inch) muffin cups. Vigorously stir down dough with wooden spoon. Spoon about ¼ cup dough into each muffin cup; smooth tops.

4. Bake 20 minutes or until golden brown. Cool buns in pan 5 minutes; remove to wire rack to cool completely.

5. For icing, whisk powdered sugar and milk in small bowl until smooth. Spoon into small resealable food storage bag. Cut off small corner of bag; pipe cross on center of each bun.

MAKES 12 BUNS

Date-Nut Granola >

2 cups old-fashioned oats
2 cups barley flakes
1 cup sliced almonds
⅓ cup vegetable oil
⅓ cup honey
1 teaspoon vanilla
1 cup chopped dates

1. Preheat oven to 350°F. Grease 13×9-inch baking pan.

2. Combine oats, barley flakes and almonds in large bowl. Whisk oil, honey and vanilla in small bowl until blended. Pour honey mixture over oat mixture; stir until well blended. Pour into prepared pan.

3. Bake about 25 minutes or until toasted, stirring frequently after 10 minutes. Stir in dates while granola is still hot. Cool completely in pan. Store tightly covered.

MAKES 6 CUPS

Scrambled Eggs with Smoked Salmon

8 eggs
¼ teaspoon salt
⅛ teaspoon black pepper
1 tablespoon butter
2 tablespoons sliced green onions
1 ounce cold cream cheese, cut into ¼-inch cubes
2 ounces smoked salmon, flaked

1. Whisk eggs, salt and pepper in large bowl. Melt butter in large nonstick skillet over medium-low heat, swirling butter around skillet to coat bottom.

2. Add egg mixture; cook without stirring 2 minutes or just until mixture begins to set around edge. Gently stir, lifting cooked portions and letting uncooked mixture flow underneath. Cook 3 minutes, stirring occasionally.

3. Gently fold in green onions, cream cheese and salmon; cook and stir about 3 minutes or just until eggs are cooked through but still slightly moist.

MAKES 4 SERVINGS

Caramelized Bacon >

12 slices (about 12 ounces) applewood-smoked bacon
½ cup packed brown sugar
2 tablespoons water
¼ teaspoon ground red pepper

1. Preheat oven to 375°F. Line 15×10-inch jelly-roll pan with heavy-duty foil. Spray wire rack with nonstick cooking spray; place in prepared pan.

2. Cut bacon in half crosswise, if desired; arrange in single layer on prepared wire rack. Combine brown sugar, water and red pepper in small bowl; mix well. Brush generously over bacon.

3. Bake 20 to 25 minutes or until bacon is well browned. Immediately remove to serving platter; cool completely.

MAKES 6 SERVINGS

Baked Oatmeal

1 cup old-fashioned oats
1 teaspoon ground cinnamon, divided
¼ teaspoon salt
1½ cups milk
1 egg
2 tablespoons honey
2 tablespoons butter, melted
1 teaspoon vanilla
1 cup chopped peeled apple
3 tablespoons finely chopped dried fruit
¼ cup chopped nuts (optional)

1. Preheat oven to 350°F. Grease 1½- to 2-quart baking dish.

2. Combine oats, ½ teaspoon cinnamon and salt in large bowl. Whisk milk, egg, honey, butter and vanilla in medium bowl; stir into oat mixture. Stir in apple and dried fruit. Pour mixture into prepared baking dish. Sprinkle with remaining ½ teaspoon cinnamon.

3. Bake 40 to 45 minutes or until knife inserted into center comes out clean. Let stand 5 minutes before serving. Sprinkle with nuts, if desired.

MAKES 4 SERVINGS

Cheddar and Leek Strata

8 eggs

2 cups milk

½ cup porter or stout

2 cloves garlic, minced

½ teaspoon salt

¼ teaspoon black pepper

1 loaf (16 ounces) sourdough bread, cut into ½-inch cubes

2 small leeks, coarsely chopped

1 red bell pepper, chopped

1½ cups (6 ounces) shredded Swiss cheese

1½ cups (6 ounces) shredded sharp Cheddar cheese

1. Spray 13×9-inch baking dish with nonstick cooking spray. Whisk eggs, milk, porter, garlic, salt and black pepper in large bowl until well blended.

2. Spread half of bread cubes in prepared baking dish. Sprinkle with half of leeks and half of bell pepper. Top with half of Swiss cheese and half of Cheddar cheese. Repeat layers. Pour egg mixture evenly over top.

3. Cover tightly with plastic wrap or foil. Weigh down top of strata with slightly smaller baking dish. Refrigerate at least 2 hours or overnight.

4. Preheat oven to 350°F. Bake, uncovered, 40 to 45 minutes or until center is set. Serve immediately.

MAKES 12 SERVINGS

SOUPS

Cock-A-Leekie Soup

    4 cups water
    4 cups reduced-sodium chicken broth
2½ pounds chicken thighs (with bones and skin)
    3 stalks celery, sliced
    2 bay leaves
    5 to 6 large leeks (about 2½ pounds)
    ½ cup uncooked pearl barley
    1 teaspoon salt
    1 teaspoon ground allspice
  12 pitted prunes, halved
    Additional salt and black pepper

1. Combine water, broth, chicken, celery and bay leaves in large saucepan or Dutch oven; bring to a boil over high heat. Reduce heat to low; cover and simmer 30 minutes or until chicken is tender. Remove chicken to cutting board to cool.

2. Meanwhile, trim leeks. Cut off roots, any damaged leaves and very tough tops. Cut in half lengthwise, then cut crosswise into ¾-inch pieces. Wash well in several changes of water.

3. Add leeks, barley, 1 teaspoon salt and allspice to saucepan; cover and simmer 40 minutes or until leeks and barley are tender.

4. Remove skin and bones from chicken; cut into bite-size pieces. Add to soup with prunes; simmer 3 minutes or until prunes soften. Remove and discard bay leaves. Season with additional salt and pepper.

MAKES 6 TO 8 SERVINGS

Double Pea Soup

1 tablespoon vegetable oil
1 onion, finely chopped
3 cloves garlic, minced
6 cups water
2 cups dried split peas
1 bay leaf
1 teaspoon ground mustard
1½ cups frozen green peas
1 teaspoon salt
¼ teaspoon black pepper
Sour cream (optional)

1. Heat oil in large saucepan or Dutch oven over medium-high heat. Add onion; cook 5 minutes or until tender, stirring occasionally. Add garlic; cook and stir 1 minute.

2. Add water, split peas, bay leaf and mustard; bring to a boil over high heat. Reduce heat to medium-low; cover and simmer 45 minutes or until split peas are tender, stirring occasionally.

3. Add green peas, salt and pepper; cover and simmer 10 minutes or until green peas are tender. Remove and discard bay leaf. Working in batches, blend soup in blender or food processor until smooth.

4. Top each serving with sour cream, if desired.

MAKES 6 SERVINGS

Cod Chowder

2 tablespoons vegetable oil
1 pound red potatoes, diced
2 medium leeks, halved and thinly sliced
2 stalks celery, diced
1 bulb fennel, diced
½ yellow or red bell pepper, diced
2 teaspoons chopped fresh thyme
¾ teaspoon salt
½ to ¾ teaspoon black pepper
2 tablespoons all-purpose flour
2 cups clam juice
1 cup water
1 cup half-and-half
1½ pounds cod, cut into 1-inch pieces
1 cup frozen corn
¼ cup finely chopped fresh Italian parsley

1. Heat oil in Dutch oven or large saucepan over medium heat. Add potatoes, leeks, celery, fennel, bell pepper, thyme, salt and pepper; cover and cook about 8 minutes or until vegetables are slightly softened, stirring occasionally. Add flour; cook and stir 1 minute.

2. Add clam juice and water; bring to a boil over high heat. Reduce heat to medium-low; cover and simmer about 10 minutes or until potatoes are tender. Remove from heat.

3. Transfer 1½ cups soup to blender; add half-and-half and blend until smooth.

4. Add cod, corn and parsley to saucepan; bring to a simmer over medium-high heat. Stir in blended soup mixture; cover and cook over medium heat about 3 minutes or until fish is firm and opaque, stirring occasionally. Serve immediately.

MAKES 6 TO 8 SERVINGS

Oxtail Soup

2½ pounds oxtails (beef or veal)
1 large onion, sliced
4 carrots, cut into 1-inch pieces, divided
3 stalks celery, cut into 1-inch pieces, divided
2 sprigs fresh parsley
5 whole black peppercorns
1 bay leaf
4 cups beef broth
1 cup dark beer
2 cups diced baking potatoes
1 teaspoon salt
2 tablespoons chopped fresh parsley (optional)

1. Combine oxtails, onion, half of carrots, one third of celery, parsley sprigs, peppercorns and bay leaf in large saucepan. Add broth and beer; bring to a boil over high heat. Reduce heat to low; cover and simmer 3 hours or until meat is falling off bones.

2. Remove oxtails to plate; set aside. Strain broth and return to saucepan; skim fat. Add remaining carrots, celery and potatoes; bring to a simmer. Cook 10 to 15 minutes or until vegetables are tender.

3. Remove meat from oxtails; discard bones. Stir meat and salt into soup; cook until heated through. Remove and discard bay leaf. Sprinkle with chopped parsley, if desired.

MAKES 4 SERVINGS

Curried Parsnip Soup

3 pounds parsnips, peeled and cut into 2-inch pieces
1 tablespoon olive oil
2 tablespoons butter
1 medium yellow onion, chopped
2 stalks celery, diced
3 cloves garlic, minced
1 tablespoon salt
1 to 2 teaspoons curry powder
½ teaspoon grated fresh ginger
½ teaspoon black pepper
8 cups reduced-sodium chicken broth
   Toasted bread slices (optional)
   Chopped fresh chives (optional)

1. Preheat oven to 400°F. Line large baking sheet with foil.

2. Combine parsnips and oil in large bowl; toss to coat. Spread in single layer on prepared baking sheet. Bake 35 to 45 minutes or until parsnips are tender and lightly browned around edges, stirring once halfway through cooking.

3. Melt butter in large saucepan or Dutch oven over medium heat. Add onion and celery; cook and stir about 8 minutes or until vegetables are tender and onion is translucent. Add garlic, salt, curry powder, ginger and pepper; cook and stir 1 minute. Add parsnips and broth; bring to a boil over medium-high heat. Reduce heat to medium-low; cover and simmer 10 minutes.

4. Working in batches, blend soup in blender or food processor until smooth. Serve with toasted bread, if desired; garnish with chives.

MAKES 6 TO 8 SERVINGS

Mulligatawny Soup

1 tablespoon olive oil

1 pound boneless skinless chicken breasts, cooked and cut into ½-inch pieces

2 cups finely chopped carrots

1 cup chopped green bell pepper

2 stalks celery, thinly sliced

½ cup finely chopped onion

3 cloves garlic, minced

¼ cup all-purpose flour

1 to 2 teaspoons curry powder

¼ teaspoon ground nutmeg

3 cups reduced-sodium chicken broth

1 cup milk

1 cup chopped seeded tomato

1 medium apple, cored, peeled and sliced

¼ cup uncooked converted rice

½ teaspoon salt

⅛ teaspoon black pepper

1. Heat oil in large saucepan over medium heat. Add chicken, carrots, bell pepper, celery, onion and garlic; cook and stir 5 minutes. Sprinkle with flour, curry powder and nutmeg; cook and stir 1 to 2 minutes.

2. Add broth, milk, tomato, apple, rice, salt and black pepper; bring to a boil over medium-high heat. Reduce heat to low; cover and simmer 20 minutes or until rice is tender.

MAKES 8 SERVINGS

Hearty Beef Soup

1 tablespoon vegetable oil

¾ pound boneless beef round steak, cut into ½-inch pieces

1 large onion, chopped

2 medium carrots, sliced

2 stalks celery, diced

5 cups beef broth

1 bottle (12 ounces) Irish stout or dark ale

¾ teaspoon dried oregano

½ teaspoon salt

⅛ teaspoon black pepper

1 can (about 15 ounces) kidney beans, rinsed and drained

1 small zucchini, cut into ½-inch cubes

4 ounces mushrooms, sliced

1. Heat oil in large saucepan or Dutch oven over medium heat. Add beef, onion, carrots and celery; cook and stir until beef is no longer pink and carrots and celery are crisp-tender.

2. Add broth, stout, oregano, salt and pepper; bring to a boil over high heat. Reduce heat to medium-low; simmer, uncovered, 45 minutes or until beef is fork-tender.

3. Add beans, zucchini and mushrooms; bring to a boil over high heat. Reduce heat to medium-low; simmer, uncovered, 5 minutes or until zucchini is tender.

MAKES 6 SERVINGS

Potato and Leek Soup

4 cups chicken broth

3 potatoes, peeled and diced

1½ cups chopped cabbage

1 leek, diced

1 onion, chopped

2 carrots, diced

1 teaspoon salt

½ teaspoon caraway seeds

½ teaspoon black pepper

1 bay leaf

½ cup sour cream

1 pound bacon, crisp-cooked and crumbled

¼ cup chopped fresh parsley

SLOW COOKER DIRECTIONS

1. Combine broth, potatoes, cabbage, leek, onion, carrots, salt, caraway seeds, pepper and bay leaf in slow cooker; mix well.

2. Cover; cook on LOW 8 to 10 hours or on HIGH 4 to 5 hours.

3. Remove and discard bay leaf. Whisk ½ cup hot liquid from slow cooker into sour cream in small bowl until blended. Add sour cream mixture and bacon to slow cooker; mix well. Sprinkle with parsley.

MAKES 6 TO 8 SERVINGS

Chicken, Barley and Vegetable Soup

8 ounces boneless skinless chicken breasts, cut into ½-inch pieces

8 ounces boneless skinless chicken thighs, cut into ½-inch pieces

¾ teaspoon salt

¼ teaspoon black pepper

1 tablespoon olive oil

½ cup uncooked pearl barley

4 cans (about 14 ounces each) chicken broth

2 cups water

1 bay leaf

2 cups whole baby carrots

2 cups diced peeled potatoes

2 cups sliced mushrooms

2 cups frozen peas

3 tablespoons sour cream

1 tablespoon chopped fresh dill *or* 1 teaspoon dried dill weed

1. Sprinkle chicken with salt and pepper. Heat oil in large saucepan or Dutch oven over medium-high heat. Add chicken; cook without stirring 2 minutes or until golden. Turn and cook 2 minutes. Remove chicken to plate.

2. Add barley to saucepan; cook and stir 1 to 2 minutes or until barley begins to brown, adding 1 tablespoon broth if necessary to prevent burning. Add remaining broth, water and bay leaf; bring to a boil. Reduce heat to low; cover and simmer 30 minutes.

3. Add chicken, carrots, potatoes and mushrooms to saucepan; cook 10 minutes or until vegetables are tender. Add peas; cook 2 minutes. Remove and discard bay leaf.

4. Top with sour cream and dill; serve immediately.

MAKES 6 SERVINGS

Oyster Chowder

    4 slices thick-cut bacon, diced
1¼ cups chopped onions
    1 can (about 14 ounces) chicken or vegetable broth
1¼ cups diced peeled potatoes
    1 pint fresh shucked oysters, drained and liquor reserved
    1 cup whipping cream or half-and-half
      Salt and black pepper
      Sliced green onions (optional)

1. Cook bacon in large saucepan over medium heat until crisp, stirring frequently. Drain on paper towel-lined plate.

2. Drain all but 2 tablespoons drippings from saucepan. Add onions to saucepan; cook and stir 5 minutes or until tender. Add broth, potatoes and reserved oyster liquor; bring to a boil over high heat. Reduce heat to medium-low; cover and simmer 5 minutes or until potatoes are tender but firm.

3. Add oysters and cream; cook 5 minutes or until edges of oysters begin to curl. Season with salt and pepper. Top with bacon and green onions, if desired.

MAKES 4 SERVINGS

Pork and Cabbage Soup

8 ounces pork loin, cut into ½-inch cubes

1 medium onion, chopped

2 slices bacon, finely chopped

2 cups reduced-sodium beef broth

2 cups reduced-sodium chicken broth

1 can (about 28 ounces) whole tomatoes, drained and coarsely chopped

2 medium carrots, sliced

1 bay leaf

1 teaspoon salt

¾ teaspoon dried marjoram

⅛ teaspoon black pepper

¼ medium cabbage, chopped

2 tablespoons chopped fresh parsley

1. Heat large saucepan or Dutch oven over medium heat. Add pork, onion and bacon; cook and stir until pork is no longer pink and onion is slightly tender. Drain fat.

2. Add beef broth, chicken broth, tomatoes, carrots, bay leaf, salt, marjoram and pepper; bring to a boil over high heat. Reduce heat to medium-low; simmer, uncovered, about 30 minutes. Remove and discard bay leaf. Skim off fat.

3. Add cabbage; bring to a boil over high heat. Reduce heat to medium-low; simmer, uncovered, about 15 minutes or until cabbage is tender. Stir in parsley.

MAKES 6 SERVINGS

Two-Cheese Potato and Cauliflower Soup

   1 tablespoon butter
   1 cup chopped onion
   2 cloves garlic, minced
   5 cups whole milk
   1 pound Yukon Gold potatoes, diced
   1 pound cauliflower florets
1½ teaspoons salt
  ⅛ teaspoon ground red pepper
1½ cups (6 ounces) shredded sharp Cheddar cheese
  ⅓ cup crumbled blue cheese

1. Melt butter in large saucepan or Dutch oven over medium-high heat. Add onion; cook and stir 4 minutes or until translucent. Add garlic; cook and stir 30 seconds. Add milk, potatoes, cauliflower, salt and red pepper; bring to a boil. Reduce heat to low; cover and simmer 15 minutes or until potatoes are tender. Cool slightly.

2. Working in batches, blend soup in blender or food processor until smooth. Return to saucepan; cook and stir over medium heat just until heated through. Remove from heat; stir in cheeses until melted.

MAKES 4 TO 6 SERVINGS

 tip One pound of trimmed cauliflower will yield about 1½ cups of florets. You can also substitute 1 pound of frozen cauliflower florets for the fresh florets.

Beef Barley Soup

    1 tablespoon vegetable oil
12 ounces boneless beef top round steak, cut into ½-inch pieces
    3 cans (about 14 ounces each) reduced-sodium beef broth
    2 cups unpeeled cubed potatoes
    1 can (about 14 ounces) diced tomatoes
    1 cup chopped onion
    1 cup sliced carrots
    ½ cup uncooked pearl barley
    1 tablespoon cider vinegar
    2 teaspoons caraway seeds
    2 teaspoons dried marjoram
    2 teaspoons dried thyme
    ½ teaspoon salt
    ½ teaspoon black pepper
1 ½ cups sliced green beans (½-inch slices)

1. Heat oil in large saucepan or Dutch oven over medium heat. Add beef; cook and stir until browned on all sides.

2. Add broth, potatoes, tomatoes, onion, carrots, barley, vinegar, caraway seeds, marjoram, thyme, salt and pepper; bring to a boil over high heat. Reduce heat to low; cover and simmer 1 ½ hours. Add green beans; cook, uncovered, 30 minutes or until beef is fork-tender.

MAKES 4 SERVINGS

Split Pea Soup with Ham and Ale

1 tablespoon olive oil

1 cup chopped onion

½ cup chopped carrot

½ cup chopped celery

3 cloves garlic, minced

1 bay leaf

¼ teaspoon dried thyme

1 bottle (12 ounces) India Pale Ale

4 cups reduced-sodium chicken broth

1 package (16 ounces) dried split peas, picked over and rinsed

1 pound smoked ham hocks

2 cups water

1. Heat oil in large saucepan or Dutch oven over medium heat. Add onion, carrot, celery, garlic, bay leaf and thyme; cook 4 to 5 minutes or until vegetables begin to soften, stirring occasionally. Add ale; bring to boil over medium-high heat. Cook 6 to 7 minutes or until liquid is reduced by half.

2. Add broth, split peas, ham hocks and water; bring to a boil. Reduce heat to medium-low; cover and simmer about 1 hour or until split peas are tender, stirring occasionally.

3. Remove ham hocks to cutting board; let stand until cool enough to handle. Remove ham from hocks. Chop ham and stir into saucepan. Remove and discard bay leaf.

MAKES 6 SERVINGS

FISH & SHELLFISH

Roasted Salmon Fillets with Irish Whiskey Sauce

4 salmon fillets (about 6 ounces each)
½ teaspoon salt, divided
⅛ teaspoon black pepper
⅓ cup Irish whiskey
¼ cup finely chopped shallots
1 tablespoon white wine vinegar
½ cup whipping cream
1½ teaspoons Dijon mustard
2 tablespoons butter, cut into small pieces
2 tablespoons chopped fresh chives

1. Position rack in center of oven. Preheat oven to 425°F. Spray large rimmed baking sheet with nonstick cooking spray.

2. Place salmon on prepared baking sheet; sprinkle with ¼ teaspoon salt and pepper. Roast 8 to 10 minutes or until fish begins to flake when tested with fork.

3. Meanwhile, combine whiskey, shallots and vinegar in small saucepan; bring to a boil over medium-high heat. Cook about 4 minutes or until liquid nearly evaporates and mixture looks like wet sand. Stir in cream and mustard; cook and stir 2 minutes or until slightly thickened. Remove from heat; whisk in butter, chives and remaining ¼ teaspoon salt.

4. Spoon sauce over fish. Serve immediately.

MAKES 4 SERVINGS

Traditional Mussels in Cream

2 tablespoons butter
1 medium onion, chopped
4 cloves garlic, minced
1 sprig fresh thyme
1 bay leaf
¾ cup whipping cream
¼ teaspoon salt
2 pounds mussels, scrubbed and debearded
1 tablespoon lemon juice
　Crusty bread for serving

1. Melt butter in large saucepan over medium-high heat. Add onion and garlic; cook and stir about 2 minutes or until garlic begins to brown slightly. Add thyme and bay leaf; cook 30 seconds. Stir in cream and salt; bring to a boil and cook 1 minute.

2. Add mussels to saucepan; cover and bring to a boil. Cook 4 to 5 minutes or until mussels open. Uncover saucepan; cook 1 minute. Remove from heat; stir in lemon juice. Discard any unopened mussels. Serve immediately in bowls with bread.

MAKES 4 APPETIZER OR 2 MAIN-DISH SERVINGS

Simple Baked Cod >

4 cod fillets (about 6 ounces each)
½ teaspoon salt
¼ teaspoon black pepper
¼ cup (½ stick) butter
1 teaspoon chopped fresh thyme
2 teaspoons grated lemon peel
3 tablespoons chopped fresh parsley

1. Position rack in center of oven. Preheat oven to 425°F. Spray large rimmed baking sheet with nonstick cooking spray.

2. Arrange cod on prepared baking sheet; sprinkle with salt and pepper. Bake 12 to 14 minutes or until fish just begins to flake when tested with fork.

3. Melt butter in small saucepan over medium heat. Stir in thyme and lemon peel; cook 1 minute. Remove from heat; stir in parsley. Spoon butter mixture over fish. Serve immediately.

MAKES 4 SERVINGS

Dilled Salmon in Parchment

2 skinless salmon fillets (4 to 6 ounces each)
2 tablespoons butter, melted
1 tablespoon lemon juice
1 tablespoon chopped fresh dill
1 tablespoon chopped shallots
Salt and black pepper

1. Preheat oven to 400°F. Cut two pieces of parchment paper into 12-inch squares; fold squares in half diagonally and cut into half heart shapes. Open parchment; place salmon fillet on one side of each heart.

2. Combine butter and lemon juice in small bowl; drizzle over fish. Sprinkle with dill and shallots; season with salt and pepper.

3. Fold parchment hearts in half. Beginning at top of heart, fold edges together, 2 inches at a time. At tip of heart, fold parchment over to seal.

4. Bake fish about 10 minutes or until parchment pouch puffs up. To serve, cut an "X" through top layer of parchment and fold back points to display contents.

MAKES 2 SERVINGS

Pan-Seared Scallops with Mushrooms and Leeks

   3 tablespoons butter, divided

1 ½ pounds sea scallops, patted dry

   ½ teaspoon salt, divided

   ¼ teaspoon black pepper, divided

   1 package (8 ounces) sliced mushrooms

   3 medium leeks, white and light green parts only, cut in half crosswise and
      very thinly sliced lengthwise

   2 cloves garlic, minced

   ½ cup vermouth or dry white wine

   ⅓ cup whipping cream

   ¼ cup (1 ounce) shredded Dubliner cheese

1. Melt 1 tablespoon butter in large nonstick skillet over medium-high heat. Sprinkle scallops with ¼ teaspoon salt and ⅛ teaspoon pepper. Add to skillet; cook 2 to 3 minutes per side or until browned and opaque. (Cook in batches if necessary to prevent overcrowding.) Remove scallops to plate; keep warm.

2. Melt remaining 2 tablespoons butter in same skillet over medium-high heat. Add mushrooms; cook 3 to 4 minutes or just until mushrooms begin to brown slightly. Add leeks and garlic; cook and stir 3 to 4 minutes or until leeks are tender. Add vermouth; cook about 2 minutes or until almost evaporated. Stir in cream; bring to a boil and cook 1 minute. Add cheese, remaining ¼ teaspoon salt and ⅛ teaspoon pepper; cook and stir about 30 seconds or until cheese melts.

3. Return scallops to skillet; cook 1 to 2 minutes or until heated through. Serve immediately.

MAKES 4 SERVINGS

Hazelnut-Coated Salmon

¼ cup hazelnuts

4 salmon steaks (about 5 ounces each)

1 tablespoon apple butter

1 tablespoon Dijon mustard

¼ teaspoon dried thyme

⅛ teaspoon black pepper

1. Preheat oven to 375°F. Spread hazelnuts on ungreased baking sheet; bake 8 minutes or until lightly browned. Immediately transfer nuts to clean kitchen towel. Fold towel over nuts; rub vigorously to remove as much of skins as possible. Finely chop hazelnuts in food processor or with knife.

2. *Increase oven temperature to 450°F.* Place salmon in single layer in baking dish. Combine apple butter, mustard, thyme and pepper in small bowl; brush over fish. Top with hazelnuts, pressing to adhere.

3. Bake 14 to 16 minutes or until fish begins to flake when tested with fork.

MAKES 4 SERVINGS

Pan-Fried Oysters

¼ cup all-purpose flour

½ teaspoon salt

¼ teaspoon black pepper

2 eggs

½ cup plain dry bread crumbs

5 tablespoons chopped fresh parsley, divided

2 containers (8 ounces each) shucked fresh oysters, rinsed, drained and patted dry
  or 1 pound fresh oysters, shucked and patted dry

  Canola oil for frying

5 slices Irish bacon, crisp-cooked and chopped

  Lemon wedges

1. Combine flour, salt and pepper in shallow dish. Beat eggs in shallow bowl. Combine bread crumbs and 4 tablespoons parsley in another shallow bowl.

2. Working with one oyster at a time, coat with flour mixture, shaking off excess. Dip in eggs, shaking off excess; roll in bread crumb mixture to coat. Place coated oysters on clean plate.

3. Heat ½ inch of oil in large skillet over medium-high heat until very hot but not smoking (about 370°F). Add one third of oysters; cook about 2 minutes per side or until golden brown. Drain on paper towel-lined plate. Repeat with remaining oysters.

4. Toss oysters with bacon and remaining 1 tablespoon parsley in large bowl. Serve immediately with lemon wedges.

MAKES 4 APPETIZER SERVINGS

Trout with Mushrooms and Potato-Parsnip Mash

    4 medium potatoes, peeled and cut into chunks
    4 medium parsnips, peeled and cut into chunks
    ¼ cup all-purpose flour
    ½ teaspoon dried thyme
    ¼ teaspoon salt
    ¼ teaspoon black pepper
    2 fresh whole trout (about 12 ounces each), filleted
    4 tablespoons (½ stick) butter, divided
    12 ounces cremini mushrooms, sliced
       Additional salt and black pepper
    ¼ cup dry white or rosé wine
    1 tablespoon minced fresh sage

1. Place potatoes and parsnips in large saucepan; add cold water to cover. Bring to a boil over high heat. Reduce heat to medium-low; simmer until vegetables are fork-tender.

2. Meanwhile, combine flour, thyme, ¼ teaspoon salt and ¼ teaspoon pepper in shallow dish. Coat trout with flour mixture, shaking off excess. Heat 2 tablespoons butter in large skillet over medium-high heat. Add fish to skillet in single layer; cook 1 to 2 minutes per side or until fish begins to flake when tested with fork. Remove from skillet; keep warm.

3. Add mushrooms to skillet; cook and stir 3 minutes, adding additional butter if necessary to prevent scorching. Season with additional salt and pepper. Add wine; cook and stir until most of liquid has evaporated.

4. Drain potatoes and parsnips; return to saucepan and mash. Stir in remaining 2 tablespoons butter and sage; season with salt and pepper. Serve trout over mashed vegetables; top with mushrooms.

MAKES 4 SERVINGS

Dill-Crusted Salmon

4 salmon fillets (about 5 ounces each)
½ cup panko bread crumbs
½ cup finely chopped fresh dill
3 tablespoons mayonnaise
2 tablespoons olive oil
1 teaspoon salt

1. Preheat oven to 400°F. Spray rack in roasting pan with nonstick cooking spray. Place salmon on rack.

2. Combine panko, dill, mayonnaise, oil and salt in medium bowl; mix well. Mound mixture evenly on top of fish, pressing to adhere.

3. Bake 20 to 25 minutes or until topping is browned and fish begins to flake when tested with fork.

MAKES 4 SERVINGS

 tip Look for bunches of fresh dill with vibrant green color, firm stems and a fresh fragrance; avoid any with browning or discoloration. Store fresh dill in the refrigerator, loosely wrapped in a slightly damp paper towel in a resealable food storage bag. It can last up to a week, but it's best to use it as soon as possible for maximum flavor.

Mussels in Beer Broth

2 tablespoons olive oil

⅓ cup chopped shallots

4 cloves garlic, minced

2 cups pale ale or other light-colored beer

1 can (about 14 ounces) seasoned diced tomatoes

¼ cup chopped fresh parsley

1 tablespoon chopped fresh thyme

½ teaspoon salt

¼ teaspoon red pepper flakes

3 pounds mussels, scrubbed and debearded

   French bread (optional)

1. Heat oil in large saucepan or Dutch oven over medium-high heat. Add shallots and garlic; cook and stir 3 minutes or until tender. Add beer, tomatoes, parsley, thyme, salt and red pepper flakes; bring to a boil.

2. Add mussels. Reduce heat to low; cover and simmer 5 to 7 minutes or until mussels open. Discard any unopened mussels. Serve with French bread, if desired.

MAKES 4 SERVINGS

Pan-Seared Sole with Lemon-Butter Caper Sauce

¼ cup all-purpose flour
½ teaspoon plus ⅛ teaspoon salt, divided
¼ teaspoon black pepper
1 pound Dover sole fillets
2 tablespoons vegetable oil
3 tablespoons butter
2 tablespoons lemon juice
2 teaspoons capers, rinsed, drained and chopped
2 tablespoons finely chopped fresh chives

1. Combine flour, ½ teaspoon salt and pepper in shallow dish. Coat sole with flour mixture, shaking off excess.

2. Heat oil in large nonstick skillet over medium heat. Add half of fish; cook 2 to 3 minutes per side or until golden brown. Remove to plate; keep warm. Repeat with remaining fish.

3. Wipe out skillet with paper towels. Add butter and remaining ⅛ teaspoon salt; cook 20 to 30 seconds or until melted and lightly browned. Remove from heat; stir in lemon juice and capers.

4. Drizzle sauce over fish; sprinkle with chives. Serve immediately.

MAKES 2 SERVINGS

Baked Cod with Tomatoes and Olives

1 tablespoon olive oil, plus additional for pan
1 pound cod fillets (about 4 fillets), cut into 2-inch pieces
  Salt and black pepper
1 can (about 14 ounces) diced tomatoes
2 tablespoons chopped pitted black olives
1 teaspoon minced garlic
2 tablespoons chopped fresh parsley

1. Preheat oven to 400°F. Brush 13×9-inch baking dish with oil. Place cod in baking dish; season with salt and pepper.

2. Combine tomatoes, olives, 1 tablespoon oil and garlic in medium bowl; mix well. Spoon over fish.

3. Bake 20 minutes or until fish begins to flake when tested with fork. Sprinkle with parsley.

MAKES 4 SERVINGS

 tip Cod is a mild-flavored fish with a dense, flaky white flesh. It's versatile, easy to prepare and adapts well to a variety of recipes—it can be roasted, broiled, steamed, poached or fried and will take on the flavors of the ingredients it is cooked with.

Salmon Patties

1 can (12 ounces) pink salmon, undrained
1 egg, lightly beaten
¼ cup minced green onions
1 tablespoon chopped fresh dill
1 clove garlic, minced
½ cup all-purpose flour
1½ teaspoons baking powder
1½ cups vegetable oil

1. Drain salmon, reserving 2 tablespoons liquid. Place salmon in medium bowl; break apart with fork. Add reserved liquid, egg, green onions, dill and garlic; mix well.

2. Combine flour and baking powder in small bowl; add to salmon mixture. Stir until well blended. Shape mixture into six patties.

3. Heat oil in large skillet to 350°F. Add salmon patties; cook until golden brown on both sides. Drain on paper towel-lined plate. Serve warm.

MAKES 6 PATTIES

 tip Pink and red canned salmon are interchangeable in recipes, although they come from two different species of salmon. The pink (humpback salmon) is more abundant and less expensive; it has a milder flavor and is lighter in color and lower in fat. Red salmon, known as sockeye salmon, has a more intense flavor and deeper color. For dishes that include a number of additional flavorful ingredients (herbs, spices, etc.), it makes sense to choose the more economical option since the flavor of the fish itself is not as critical to the recipe.

Pan-Roasted Pike with Buttery Bread Crumbs

6 tablespoons butter, divided

2 cloves garlic, minced

⅓ cup plain dry bread crumbs

½ teaspoon salt, divided

4 tablespoons chopped fresh parsley

4 pike fillets or other medium-firm white fish (about 6 ounces each)

⅛ teaspoon black pepper

2 tablespoons lemon juice

1. Preheat oven to 400°F.

2. Melt 2 tablespoons butter in small nonstick skillet over medium-high heat. Add garlic; cook and stir 1 minute or just until lightly browned. Add bread crumbs and ⅛ teaspoon salt; cook and stir 1 minute. Transfer to small bowl; stir in parsley.

3. Melt 1 tablespoon butter in large ovenproof skillet over medium-high heat. Sprinkle pike with ¼ teaspoon salt and pepper. Add to skillet, flesh side down; cook 1 minute. Remove from heat; turn fish and top with bread crumb mixture.

4. Place skillet in oven; roast 8 to 10 minutes or until fish begins to flake when tested with fork.

5. Wipe out small skillet with paper towel; heat over medium heat. Add remaining 3 tablespoons butter; cook 3 to 4 minutes or until melted and lightly browned, stirring occasionally. Stir in lemon juice and remaining ⅛ teaspoon salt. Spoon mixture over fish just before serving.

MAKES 4 SERVINGS

Roast Dill Scrod with Asparagus

1 bunch (12 ounces) asparagus spears, ends trimmed

1 tablespoon olive oil

4 scrod or cod fillets (about 5 ounces each)

1 tablespoon lemon juice

1 teaspoon dried dill weed

½ teaspoon salt

¼ teaspoon black pepper

Paprika (optional)

1. Preheat oven to 425°F.

2. Place asparagus in 13×9-inch baking dish; drizzle with oil. Roll asparagus to coat lightly with oil; push to edges of dish, stacking asparagus into two layers.

3. Arrange scrod in center of dish; drizzle with lemon juice. Combine dill, salt and pepper in small bowl; sprinkle over fish and asparagus. Sprinkle with paprika, if desired.

4. Roast 15 to 17 minutes or until asparagus is crisp-tender and fish is opaque in center and begins to flake when tested with fork.

MAKES 4 SERVINGS

Seared Scallops with Spinach

1 tablespoon olive oil

1 pound sea scallops* (approximately 12)

¼ teaspoon salt

⅛ teaspoon black pepper

2 cloves garlic, minced

1 shallot, minced

1 bag (6 ounces) baby spinach leaves, washed

1 tablespoon fresh lemon juice

Lemon wedges

Make sure scallops are dry before adding to pan to ensure a golden crust.

1. Heat oil in large nonstick skillet over medium-high heat. Add scallops; sprinkle with salt and pepper. Cook 2 to 3 minutes per side or until golden. Remove to large plate; keep warm.

2. Add garlic and shallot to skillet; cook and stir 45 seconds or until fragrant. Add spinach; cook 2 minutes or until spinach just begins to wilt, stirring occasionally. Remove from heat; stir in lemon juice.

3. Serve scallops over spinach. Serve with lemon wedges.

MAKES 4 SERVINGS

Broiled Tilapia with Mustard Cream Sauce

4 tilapia fillets, ¾ inch thick (about 4 ounces each)
½ teaspoon salt, divided
⅛ teaspoon black pepper
½ cup sour cream
2 tablespoons chopped fresh dill
4 teaspoons Dijon mustard
2 teaspoons lemon juice
⅛ teaspoon garlic powder
    Fresh dill sprigs (optional)

1. Preheat broiler. Lightly spray rack of broiler pan with nonstick cooking spray. Place tilapia on rack; sprinkle with ¼ teaspoon salt and pepper.

2. Broil 4 to 5 inches from heat 5 to 8 minutes or until fish begins to flake when tested with fork.

3. Meanwhile, combine sour cream, chopped dill, mustard, lemon juice, remaining ¼ teaspoon salt and garlic powder in small bowl; mix well. Serve sauce over fish; garnish with dill sprigs.

MAKES 4 SERVINGS

 tip When purchasing fresh fish, make sure the fillets have a moist appearance, firm texture and a mild, fresh odor. (They should not smell fishy.) When purchasing raw frozen fish, make sure the fillets are completely frozen; there should be no dark, white or dry spots that might indicate the fish has been thawed and refrozen. Frozen fish can be stored in the freezer for up to 6 months.

Poached Salmon with Dill-Lemon Sauce

4 cups water

1 cup white wine

Peel of 1 lemon

4 whole black peppercorns

2 sprigs fresh parsley

2 sprigs fresh dill

1 shallot, sliced

2 salmon fillets, about 1 inch thick (6 ounces each)

DILL-LEMON SAUCE

2 tablespoons mayonnaise

½ tablespoon lemon juice

1 teaspoon vegetable oil

2 tablespoons milk

1 teaspoon chopped fresh dill

Additional fresh dill sprigs (optional)

1. Combine water, wine, lemon peel, peppercorns, parsley, 2 dill sprigs and shallot in medium saucepan; bring to a simmer. Simmer gently 15 minutes; do not boil.

2. Reduce heat to just below simmering. Place salmon in liquid; cook 4 to 5 minutes or until fish begins to flake when tested with fork.

3. Meanwhile, whisk mayonnaise, lemon juice and oil in small bowl. Whisk in milk, 1 teaspoon at a time, until well blended. Stir in chopped dill just before serving.

4. Remove salmon from liquid; place on serving plates. Top with sauce; garnish with additional dill sprigs.

MAKES 2 SERVINGS

MEAT

Sirloin with Mushrooms and Whiskey-Cream Sauce

2 tablespoons butter

1 tablespoon vegetable oil

8 ounces cremini mushrooms, sliced

1½ pounds sirloin steak

½ teaspoon salt

¼ teaspoon black pepper

½ cup Irish whiskey

½ cup whipping cream

½ cup reduced-sodium beef broth

Chopped fresh chives

1. Heat butter and oil in large skillet over medium-high heat. Add mushrooms; cook and stir 8 minutes or until liquid evaporates. Remove to bowl.

2. Sprinkle both sides of steak with salt and pepper. Add to skillet; cook about 3 minutes per side or to desired doneness. Remove to serving plate; keep warm.

3. Add whiskey to skillet; cook and stir 2 minutes, scraping up browned bits from bottom of skillet. Add cream and broth; cook and stir 3 minutes. Stir in any accumulated juices from steak.

4. Return mushrooms to skillet; cook and stir 2 minutes or until sauce thickens. Pour sauce over steak; sprinkle with chives.

MAKES 4 SERVINGS

Stuffed Pork Tenderloin with Apple Relish

6 tablespoons (¾ stick) butter

1 onion, chopped

3 cloves garlic

1 cup dry bread crumbs

1 tablespoon chopped fresh parsley

2 teaspoons minced fresh thyme

1 teaspoon minced fresh sage

½ teaspoon salt, divided

¼ teaspoon black pepper

1 egg, lightly beaten

3 to 4 tablespoons dry white wine or apple cider

2 pork tenderloins (about 1 pound each)

Apple Relish (recipe follows)

1. Preheat oven to 450°F. Place rack in large roasting pan; spray with nonstick cooking spray.

2. Melt butter in large skillet. Add onion and garlic; cook and stir 2 to 3 minutes or until translucent. Add bread crumbs, parsley, thyme, sage, ¼ teaspoon salt and pepper; mix well. Stir in egg. Add enough wine to moisten stuffing.

3. Trim fat from pork. Cut each tenderloin in half horizontally about halfway through and open flat. Cover with plastic wrap; pound to ½-inch thickness.

4. Sprinkle pork with remaining ¼ teaspoon salt. Spoon half of stuffing down center of each tenderloin. Close pork around stuffing; tie with kitchen string every 3 or 4 inches to secure. Place in prepared pan.

5. Bake 15 minutes. *Reduce heat to 350°F;* bake 45 minutes or until cooked through (145°F). Meanwhile, prepare Apple Relish. Serve with pork.

MAKES 8 SERVINGS

Apple Relish: Combine 3 large apples, cut into ½-inch pieces, ½ cup chopped green onions, ½ cup golden raisins, ¼ cup chopped crystalized ginger, ¼ cup cider vinegar, 3 tablespoons sugar and 1 tablespoon Irish whiskey in medium saucepan. Cook, partially covered, over medium heat 20 to 30 minutes or until apples are tender but not falling apart. Let cool. Stir in 1 tablespoon chopped fresh mint. Serve warm or cold.

Mint Marinated Racks of Lamb

2 whole racks (6 ribs each) lamb rib chops, well trimmed (about 3 pounds)

1 cup dry red wine

½ cup plus 2 tablespoons chopped fresh mint, divided

3 cloves garlic, minced

¼ cup Dijon mustard

⅔ cup plain dry bread crumbs

1. Place lamb in large resealable food storage bag. Combine wine, ½ cup mint and garlic in small bowl; pour over lamb. Seal bag; turn to coat. Marinate in refrigerator at least 2 hours or up to 4 hours, turning occasionally.

2. Prepare grill for indirect cooking.

3. Drain lamb; discard marinade. Pat dry with paper towels. Place lamb in large shallow dish. Combine mustard and remaining 2 tablespoons mint in small bowl; spread over meaty side of lamb. Pat bread crumbs evenly over mustard mixture.

4. Place lamb, crumb side down, on grid. Grill lamb, covered, over medium heat 10 minutes. Turn and grill, covered, 20 minutes until medium or to desired doneness. Remove to cutting board; let stand 5 minutes. Cut lamb between ribs into individual chops.

MAKES 4 SERVINGS

Smoked Sausage and Cabbage >

1½ tablespoons olive oil, divided
1 pound smoked sausage, cut into 2-inch pieces
6 cups coarsely chopped cabbage
1 yellow onion, cut into ½-inch wedges
2 cloves garlic, minced
¾ teaspoon sugar
¼ teaspoon caraway seeds
¼ teaspoon salt
¼ teaspoon black pepper

1. Heat ½ tablespoon oil in large skillet over medium-high heat. Add sausage; cook and stir 3 minutes or until browned. Remove to plate.

2. Heat remaining 1 tablespoon oil in same skillet. Add cabbage, onion, garlic, sugar, caraway seeds, salt and pepper; cook and stir 5 minutes or until onion begins to brown. Add sausage; cover and cook 5 minutes. Remove from heat; let stand 5 minutes.

MAKES 4 SERVINGS

Pork Chops with Creamy Mustard Sauce

4 center-cut pork chops, ¾ inch thick
Salt and black pepper
1 tablespoon olive oil
⅓ cup water
½ cup coarse-grain mustard
¼ cup whipping cream

1. Season pork chops with salt and pepper. Heat oil in large skillet over medium heat. Add pork; cook about 5 minutes per side or until barely pink in center. Remove to plate; keep warm.

2. Add water to skillet; bring to a boil, scraping up browned bits from bottom of skillet. Reduce heat to low; simmer 1 to 2 minutes. Add mustard and cream; cook and stir just until sauce begins to simmer. Serve over pork.

MAKES 4 SERVINGS

Herbed Standing Rib Roast

2 teaspoons coarse salt

1 (4-rib) bone-in standing rib roast (about 9 pounds)

2 tablespoons olive oil, plus additional for pan

4 cloves garlic, minced

2 teaspoons grated lemon peel

2 tablespoons chopped fresh rosemary

2 tablespoons chopped fresh thyme

2 tablespoons chopped fresh Italian parsley

2 tablespoons chopped fresh oregano

2 teaspoons black pepper

⅛ teaspoon red pepper flakes

1. Sprinkle salt over entire roast. Wrap with plastic wrap and refrigerate at least 2 hours or up to 2 days.

2. Combine 2 tablespoons oil, garlic, lemon peel, rosemary, thyme, parsley, oregano, black pepper and red pepper flakes in small bowl; mix well. Rub paste over all sides of roast; let stand at room temperature 1 hour.

3. Preheat oven to 450°F. Brush large roasting pan with oil. Place roast, bone side down, in prepared pan.

4. Roast 25 minutes. *Reduce oven temperature to 350°F.* Roast 1½ to 2 hours or until beef is 120° to 125°F (rare) or 130° to 140°F (medium-rare). Remove beef to cutting board; cover loosely with foil. Let stand 15 to 20 minutes before slicing.

MAKES ABOUT 16 SERVINGS

Sage-Roasted Pork with Rutabaga

1 bunch fresh sage

4 cloves garlic, minced

1½ teaspoons coarse salt, divided

1 teaspoon coarsely ground black pepper, divided

5 tablespoons extra virgin olive oil, divided

1 boneless pork loin roast (2 to 2½ pounds)

2 medium or 1 large rutabaga (1 to 1½ pounds)

4 carrots, cut into 1½-inch pieces

1. Chop enough sage to measure 2 tablespoons; reserve remaining sage. Mash chopped sage, garlic, ½ teaspoon salt and ½ teaspoon pepper in small bowl to form paste. Stir in 2 tablepoons oil.

2. Score fatty side of pork roast with sharp knife, making cuts about ¼ inch deep. Rub herb paste into cuts and over all sides of pork. Place pork on large plate; cover and refrigerate 1 to 2 hours.

3. Preheat oven to 400°F. Spray large roasting pan with nonstick cooking spray. Cut rutabaga into halves or quarters; peel and cut into 1½-inch pieces. Combine rutabaga and carrots in large bowl. Drizzle with remaining 3 tablespoons oil and sprinkle with remaining 1 teaspoon salt and ½ teaspoon pepper; toss to coat.

4. Arrange vegetables in single layer in prepared pan. Place pork on top of vegetables, scraping any remaining herb paste from plate into roasting pan. Tuck 3 sprigs of remaining sage into vegetables.

5. Roast 15 minutes. *Reduce oven temperature to 325°F.* Roast 45 minutes to 1 hour 15 minutes or until pork is 145°F and barely pink in center, stirring vegetables once or twice during cooking time. Remove pork to cutting board; let stand 10 minutes before slicing.

MAKES 4 TO 6 SERVINGS

 tip Rutabagas can be difficult to cut—they are a tough vegetable and slippery on the outside because they are waxed. Cutting them into large pieces (halves or quarters) before peeling and chopping makes them easier to manage.

Irish Lamb Stew

½ cup all-purpose flour

2 teaspoons salt, divided

½ teaspoon pepper, divided

3 pounds boneless lamb stew meat, cut into 1½-inch cubes

3 tablespoons vegetable oil

1 cup chopped onion

1 can (about 15 ounces) Irish stout, divided

1 teaspoon sugar

1 teaspoon dried thyme

1 pound small new potatoes, quartered

1 pound carrots, peeled and cut into ½-inch pieces

½ cup water

1 cup frozen peas

¼ cup chopped fresh parsley

1. Combine flour, 1 teaspoon salt and ¼ teaspoon pepper in large bowl. Add lamb; toss to coat, shaking off excess. Discard any remaining flour mixture.

2. Heat oil in Dutch oven over medium heat. Cook lamb in batches about 7 minutes or until browned on all sides. Remove to bowl.

3. Add onion and ¼ cup stout to Dutch oven; cook 10 minutes, stirring to scrape up browned bits from bottom of pan. Return lamb to Dutch oven; stir in remaining stout, sugar, thyme, remaining 1 teaspoon salt and ¼ teaspoon pepper. If necessary, add enough water so liquid just covers lamb. Bring to a boil over medium-high heat. Reduce heat to low; cover and simmer 1½ hours or until lamb is tender.

4. Add potatoes, carrots and ½ cup water; cover and cook 30 minutes or until vegetables are tender. Stir in peas and parsley; cook 5 to 10 minutes or until heated through.

MAKES 8 SERVINGS

Sunday Dinner Roast

1 tablespoon vegetable oil

1 boneless beef eye of round roast (about 3 pounds), trimmed

1 can (about 14 ounces) beef broth

2 cloves garlic, minced

¾ teaspoon dried thyme

¼ teaspoon dried rosemary

¼ teaspoon dried sage

4 small turnips, peeled and cut into wedges

12 ounces fresh brussels sprouts (about 10 medium), trimmed

8 ounces baby carrots (about 2 cups)

4 ounces pearl onions (about 1 cup), skins removed

1 tablespoon water

2 teaspoons cornstarch

1. Heat oil in Dutch oven over medium-high heat. Add roast; cook until browned on all sides.

2. Add broth, garlic, thyme, rosemary and sage to Dutch oven; bring to a boil. Reduce heat to low; cover and simmer 1½ hours.

3. Add turnips, brussels sprouts, carrots and onions; cover and cook over medium heat 25 to 30 minutes or until vegetables are tender. Remove beef and vegetables to serving platter; keep warm.

4. Strain broth; return to Dutch oven. Stir water into cornstarch in small bowl until smooth; whisk mixture into broth. Bring to a boil over medium-high heat; cook and stir 1 minute or until thick and bubbly. Serve with beef and vegetables.

MAKES 6 SERVINGS

Spiced Honey Glazed Ham

1 smoked bone-in spiral-cut ham (8 pounds)
½ cup clover honey or other mild honey
2 tablespoons spicy brown mustard
2 tablespoons cider vinegar
1 teaspoon finely grated orange peel
¼ teaspoon black pepper
⅛ teaspoon ground cloves

1. Position rack in lower third of oven. Preheat oven to 325°F.

2. Line large rimmed baking sheet with heavy-duty foil; place wire rack over foil. Place ham on rack; cover loosely with foil. Pour 2 cups water into pan. Bake 1½ hours.

3. Meanwhile, prepare glaze. Combine honey, mustard, vinegar, orange peel, pepper and cloves in small saucepan; bring to a boil over medium-high heat. Remove from heat; set aside to cool.

4. Remove ham from oven. *Increase oven temperature to 400°F.* Brush ham with glaze; bake, uncovered, 40 minutes or until shiny golden brown crust has formed, brushing with glaze every 10 minutes. Remove ham to cutting board; let stand 10 minutes before slicing.

MAKES 12 TO 14 SERVINGS

Roasted Dijon Lamb with Herbs and Vegetables

20 cloves garlic, peeled (about 2 medium heads)

¼ cup Dijon mustard

2 tablespoons water

2 tablespoons fresh rosemary leaves

1 tablespoon fresh thyme

1¼ teaspoons salt, divided

1 teaspoon black pepper

4½ pounds boneless leg of lamb, trimmed

1 pound parsnips, cut diagonally into ½-inch pieces

1 pound carrots, cut diagonally into ½-inch pieces

2 large onions, cut into ½-inch wedges

3 tablespoons extra virgin olive oil, divided

1. Combine garlic, mustard, water, rosemary, thyme, ¾ teaspoon salt and pepper in food processor; process until smooth. Place lamb in large bowl or baking pan. Spoon mixture over lamb; cover and refrigerate at least 8 hours.

2. Preheat oven to 500°F. Line broiler pan with foil; place broiler rack over foil. Spray rack with nonstick cooking spray. Combine parsnips, carrots, onions and 2 tablespoons oil in large bowl; toss to coat. Spread evenly on broiler rack; top with lamb.

3. Roast 15 minutes. *Reduce oven temperature to 325°F.* Roast 1 hour 20 minutes or until lamb is 155°F (medium) or to desired doneness. Remove lamb to cutting board; let stand 10 minutes before slicing. Continue roasting vegetables 10 minutes.

4. Spoon vegetables into large bowl. Add remaining 1 tablespoon oil and ½ teaspoon salt; toss to coat. Slice lamb; serve with vegetables.

MAKES 8 TO 10 SERVINGS

Cider Pork and Onions

2 to 3 tablespoons vegetable oil

4 to 4½ pounds bone-in pork shoulder roast (pork butt)

4 to 5 medium onions, sliced (about 4 cups)

1 teaspoon salt, divided

4 cloves garlic, minced

3 sprigs fresh rosemary

½ teaspoon black pepper

2 to 3 cups apple cider

1. Preheat oven to 325°F. Heat 2 tablespoons oil in Dutch oven over medium-high heat. Add pork; cook until browned on all sides. Remove to plate.

2. Add onions and ½ teaspoon salt to Dutch oven; cook and stir 10 minutes or until translucent, adding additional oil if necessary to prevent scorching. Add garlic; cook and stir 1 minute. Add pork and rosemary; sprinkle with remaining ½ teaspoon salt and pepper. Add cider to come about halfway up sides of pork.

3. Cover and bake 2 to 2½ hours or until very tender. (Meat should be almost falling off bones.) Remove to large platter and keep warm.

4. Remove rosemary sprigs from Dutch oven. Boil liquid in Dutch oven over medium-high heat about 20 minutes or until reduced by half; skim fat. Season with additional salt and pepper, if desired. Cut pork; serve with sauce.

MAKES 8 SERVINGS

Lamb in Dill Sauce

2 large boiling potatoes, peeled and cut into 1-inch cubes

½ cup chopped onion

1½ teaspoons salt

½ teaspoon black pepper

½ teaspoon dried dill weed *or* 4 sprigs fresh dill

1 bay leaf

2 pounds lamb stew meat, cut into 1-inch cubes

1 cup plus 3 tablespoons water, divided

2 tablespoons all-purpose flour

1 teaspoon sugar

2 tablespoons lemon juice

Fresh dill sprigs (optional)

SLOW COOKER DIRECTIONS

1. Layer potatoes, onion, salt, pepper, dried dill, bay leaf, lamb and 1 cup water in slow cooker. Cover; cook on LOW 6 to 8 hours.

2. Remove lamb and potatoes to bowl with slotted spoon; cover and keep warm. Remove and discard bay leaf. Stir remaining 3 tablespoons water into flour in small bowl until smooth. Add ½ cup cooking liquid and sugar; mix well. Whisk into slow cooker. *Turn slow cooker to HIGH.* Cook, uncovered, 15 minutes or until thickened.

3. Stir in lemon juice. Return lamb and potatoes to slow cooker. Cover; cook 15 minutes or until heated through. Garnish with fresh dill.

MAKES 6 SERVINGS

Dublin Coddle

8 ounces Irish bacon*

8 pork sausages, preferably Irish bangers

3 onions, sliced

   Black pepper

2 pounds potatoes, peeled and thickly sliced

2 carrots, peeled and cut into 1½-inch pieces

¼ cup chopped fresh parsley, plus additional for garnish

2 sprigs fresh thyme

3 cups chicken broth or water

Or substitute Canadian bacon or pancetta if Irish bacon is not available.

1. Cook bacon in Dutch oven over medium heat until crisp. Drain on paper towel-lined plate; cut into 1-inch pieces. Drain all but 1 tablespoon drippings. Add sausages to Dutch oven; cook about 10 minutes or until browned on all sides. Drain on paper towel-lined plate; cut into 1-inch pieces.

2. Add onions to Dutch oven; cook and stir about 8 minutes or until translucent. Return bacon and sausages to Dutch oven; sprinkle with pepper. Add potatoes, carrots, ¼ cup parsley and thyme; sprinkle generously with pepper. Pour broth over vegetables; bring to a boil.

3. Reduce heat to low; partially cover and simmer about 1 hour 20 minutes or until vegetables are tender. Sprinkle with additional parsley

MAKES 6 SERVINGS

Steak and Mushroom Pie

3 tablespoons butter, divided

1½ pounds boneless beef chuck steak, cut into 1-inch cubes

2 medium onions, chopped

3 stalks celery, cut into ½-inch slices

1 package (8 ounces) sliced mushrooms

½ teaspoon dried thyme

½ cup red wine

¼ cup all-purpose flour

1 cup reduced-sodium beef broth

2 tablespoons tomato paste

1 tablespoon Dijon mustard

½ teaspoon salt

¼ teaspoon black pepper

1 refrigerated pie crust (half of 15-ounce package)

1 egg, lightly beaten

1. Spray deep-dish pie plate or 1½-quart baking dish with nonstick cooking spray. Melt 2 tablespoons butter in large saucepan over medium-high heat. Add half of beef; cook 4 to 5 minutes or until browned, turning occasionally. Remove to plate; repeat with remaining beef.

2. Melt remaining 1 tablespoon butter in same saucepan over medium-high heat. Add onions, celery, mushrooms and thyme; cook and stir 4 to 5 minutes or until vegetables begin to soften. Add wine; cook and stir 3 to 4 minutes or until almost evaporated. Add flour; cook and stir 1 minute. Stir in broth, tomato paste and mustard; bring to a boil. Reduce heat to medium-low; cover and simmer 1 hour to 1 hour 10 minutes or until beef is very tender, stirring occasionally. Remove from heat; stir in salt and pepper. Spoon into prepared pie plate; let cool 20 minutes.

3. Preheat oven to 400°F. Roll out pie crust on lightly floured surface to fit top of pie plate. Place crust over filling; decoratively flute or crimp edges. Brush crust with egg; cut several small slits in top of crust with tip of knife.

4. Bake 23 to 25 minutes or until crust is golden. Let stand 5 minutes before serving.

MAKES 4 TO 6 SERVINGS

Braised Lamb Shanks

2 tablespoons all-purpose flour

1 teaspoon salt

½ teaspoon ground black pepper

4 lamb shanks (about 4 to 5 pounds total)

2 to 3 tablespoons olive oil

1 tablespoon butter

1 large onion, chopped

4 cloves garlic, minced

1 cup beef or chicken broth

1 cup dry red wine

2 tablespoons chopped fresh rosemary leaves *or* 2 teaspoons dried rosemary

1. Combine flour, salt and pepper in large resealable food storage bag. Add lamb shanks, one at a time, to bag; shake to coat lightly with seasoned flour. (Be sure to use all of flour mixture.)

2. Heat 2 tablespoons oil and butter in Dutch oven over medium heat. Add lamb in batches; cook until browned on all sides. Remove to plate.

3. Add remaining 1 tablespoon oil to Dutch oven, if necessary. Add onion and garlic; cook and stir 5 minutes. Add broth, wine and rosemary; bring to a boil over high heat.

4. Return lamb and any accumulated juices from plate to Dutch oven. Cover and cook 1½ to 2 hours over low heat or until lamb is fork-tender. Remove lamb to serving platter; keep warm.

5. Skim off and discard fat from liquid in Dutch oven. Boil until liquid is reduced to 2 cups and slightly thickened. (Depending on amount of remaining liquid, this could take from 2 to 10 minutes.) Pour sauce over lamb.

MAKES 4 SERVINGS

Rosemary Roast Pork and Vegetables

¼ cup chicken broth

2 tablespoons olive oil

1 teaspoon salt, divided

3 large parsnips, peeled and cut diagonally into ½-inch slices

2 cups baby carrots

1 medium onion, cut into wedges

1 red bell pepper, cut into ¾-inch pieces

2 pork tenderloins (12 ounces each)

2 tablespoons Dijon mustard

2 teaspoons dried rosemary

½ teaspoon black pepper

1. Preheat oven to 400°F. Combine broth, oil and ¼ teaspoon salt in small bowl; mix well.

2. Combine parsnips, carrots and 3 tablespoons broth mixture in large shallow roasting pan; toss to coat. Roast vegetables 10 minutes.

3. Add onion, bell pepper and remaining broth mixture to pan; toss to coat. Push vegetables to edges of pan. Place pork in center of pan; spread with mustard. Sprinkle pork and vegetables with rosemary, remaning ¾ teaspoon salt and black pepper.

4. Roast 25 to 30 minutes or until vegetables are tender and pork is 145°F. Remove pork to cutting board; let stand 10 minutes before slicing. Serve with vegetables and any juices from pan.

MAKES 4 TO 6 SERVINGS

Bacon and Stout Braised Short Ribs

4 pounds bone-in beef short ribs, well trimmed

   Salt and black pepper

1 tablespoon vegetable oil

6 ounces thick-cut bacon, chopped

1 large onion, halved and sliced

2 tablespoons all-purpose flour

2 tablespoons Dijon mustard

1 tablespoon tomato paste

1 teaspoon salt

½ teaspoon ground black pepper

1 bottle (12 ounces) Irish stout

1 cup beef broth

1 bay leaf

2 tablespoons finely chopped parsley

   Hot mashed potatoes (optional)

SLOW COOKER DIRECTIONS

1. Season short ribs with salt and pepper. Heat oil in large skillet over medium-high heat until almost smoking. Cook ribs in batches until browned on all sides. Place in slow cooker. Wipe out skillet with paper towels.

2. Cook bacon in same skillet over medium heat about 4 minutes or until crisp, stirring occasionally. Drain on paper towel-lined plate. Drain all but 1 tablespoon drippings from skillet.

3. Add onion to skillet; cook and stir about 6 minutes or until translucent. Add flour, mustard, tomato paste, 1 teaspoon salt and ½ teaspoon pepper; cook and stir 1 minute. Remove from heat. Add stout, stirring to scrape up browned bits from bottom of skillet. Pour mixture over short ribs in slow cooker. Add bacon, broth and bay leaf.

4. Cover; cook on LOW 8 hours. Skim off and discard fat from cooking liquid. Remove and discard bay leaf. Stir in parsley. Serve with mashed potatoes, if desired.

MAKES 4 TO 6 SERVINGS

Tip: This recipe only gets better if made ahead and refrigerated overnight. It is also easier to skim any fat from the surface.

Lamb and Potato Hot Pot

   3 tablespoons canola oil, divided
1½ pounds boneless leg of lamb, cut into 1-inch cubes
   4 medium onions, thinly sliced
   3 carrots, thinly sliced
   1 teaspoon chopped fresh thyme
   2 tablespoons all-purpose flour
1¼ cups reduced-sodium chicken broth
  ¾ teaspoon salt, divided
  ¼ teaspoon black pepper
   3 medium russet potatoes (12 ounces), peeled and thinly sliced
   1 tablespoon butter, cut into small pieces

1. Preheat oven to 350°F. Spray 2-quart casserole with nonstick cooking spray.

2. Heat 2 tablespoons oil in large saucepan over medium-high heat. Add half of lamb; cook 4 to 5 minutes or until browned, turning occasionally. Remove to plate; repeat with remaining lamb.

3. Add remaining 1 tablespoon oil to saucepan; heat over medium-high heat. Add onions, carrots and thyme; cook 10 to 12 minutes or until onions are golden, stirring occasionally. Add in lamb and any accumulated juices; cook 1 minute. Add flour; cook and stir 1 minute. Add broth, ½ teaspoon salt and pepper; bring to a boil. Cook and stir about 1 minute or until mixture begins to thicken. Spoon into prepared casserole.

4. Arrange potato slices in overlapping layer over lamb mixture, starting from side of casserole and working in towards center. Sprinkle potatoes with remaining ¼ teaspoon salt; dot with butter. Cover tightly with foil.

5. Bake 1 hour. Uncover; bake 15 to 20 minutes or until potatoes begin to brown and lamb is tender.

MAKES 4 TO 6 SERVINGS

Apple Stuffed Pork Loin Roast

2 cloves garlic, minced

1 teaspoon coarse salt

1 teaspoon dried rosemary

½ teaspoon dried thyme

½ teaspoon black pepper

1 boneless center cut pork loin roast (4 to 5 pounds)

1 tablespoon butter

2 large tart apples, peeled, cored and thinly sliced (about 2 cups)

1 medium onion, cut into thin strips (about 1 cup)

2 tablespoons packed brown sugar

1 teaspoon Dijon mustard

1 cup apple cider or juice

1. Preheat oven to 325°F. Combine garlic, salt, rosemary, thyme and pepper in small bowl. Cut lengthwise down roast almost to, but not through, bottom and open flat. Rub half of garlic mixture onto cut sides of pork.

2. Melt butter in large skillet over medium-high heat. Add apples and onion; cook and stir 5 to 10 minutes or until tender. Stir in brown sugar and mustard. Spread mixture evenly over one cut side of roast. Close halves; tie roast with kitchen string at 2-inch intervals. Place roast on rack in shallow roasting pan; pour cider over roast. Rub outside of roast with remaining garlic mixture.

3. Roast, uncovered, 2 to 2½ hours or until pork is 145°F, basting frequently with pan drippings. Cover loosely with foil; let stand 15 minutes before slicing.

MAKES 12 TO 14 SERVINGS

Corned Beef and Cabbage

3½ to 4 pounds packaged corned beef brisket

3 carrots, peeled and cut into 1½-inch pieces

2 small onions, peeled and quartered

3 stalks celery, cut into 1½-inch pieces

1 bunch fresh parsley

2 large sprigs fresh thyme

1 head green cabbage (about 2 pounds), cut into 8 wedges

1½ pounds small red potatoes

1 cup sour cream

2 tablespoons prepared horseradish

½ teaspoon coarse salt

1. Combine corned beef, carrots, onions and celery in Dutch oven. Tie parsley and thyme together with kitchen string; add to Dutch oven. Add water to cover beef by 1 inch; bring to a boil over high heat. Reduce heat to medium-low; cover and cook about about 2½ hours or until almost tender.

2. Add cabbage and potatoes; cover and cook about 30 minutes or until beef, cabbage and potatoes are tender.

3. Meanwhile, combine sour cream, horseradish and ½ teaspoon salt in medium bowl; mix well. Refrigerate until ready to serve.

4. Remove herbs from Dutch oven and discard. Remove beef to cutting board; let stand 10 minutes. Slice beef across the grain. Arrange on serving platter with vegetables; season vegetables with additional salt to taste. Serve with horseradish sauce.

MAKES 8 SERVINGS

Lamb Chops with Mustard Sauce >

  1 teaspoon dried thyme

  ½ teaspoon salt

  ¼ teaspoon black pepper

  4 lamb loin chops (about 6 ounces each)

  2 tablespoons canola or vegetable oil

  ¼ cup finely chopped shallots or sweet onion

  ¼ cup beef or chicken broth

  2 tablespoons Worcestershire sauce

1½ tablespoons Dijon mustard

     Fresh thyme sprigs (optional)

1. Sprinkle dried thyme, salt and pepper over lamb chops. Heat oil in large skillet over medium heat. Add lamb; cook 4 minutes per side. Remove to plate.

2. Add shallots to skillet; cook 3 minutes, stirring occasionally. Add broth, Worcestershire sauce and mustard; simmer over medium-low heat 5 minutes or until sauce thickens slightly, stirring occasionally.

3. Return lamb to skillet; cook 2 minutes or until medium-rare, turning once. Garnish with fresh thyme.

MAKES 4 SERVINGS

Pork Chops with Cider Glaze

  4 center-cut pork chops (¾ inch thick)

    Salt and black pepper

  1 tablespoon vegetable oil

  1 onion, cut into thin wedges

  ½ cup apple cider or juice

1. Season pork chops with salt and pepper. Heat oil in large skillet over medium heat. Add pork; cook about 3 minutes per side or until browned. Remove to plate.

2. Add onion to skillet; cook and stir 3 minutes. Add cider; bring to a boil, scraping up browned bits from bottom of skillet. Simmer 4 to 5 minutes or until liquid begins to thicken. Return pork to skillet; cook until pork is barely pink in center. Remove pork to serving platter.

3. Cook liquid in skillet until reduced to syrupy texture, stirring occasionally. Serve over pork.

MAKES 4 SERVINGS

POULTRY

Glazed Cornish Hens

2 fresh or thawed frozen Cornish hens (1½ pounds each)
3 tablespoons lemon juice
1 clove garlic, minced
¼ cup orange marmalade
1 tablespoon coarse grain or country-style mustard
2 teaspoons grated fresh ginger

1. Remove giblets from cavities of hens; reserve for another use or discard. Split hens in half with sharp knife or poultry shears, cutting through breastbones and backbones. Place hens in large resealable food storage bag.

2. Combine lemon juice and garlic in small bowl; pour over hens. Seal bag; turn to coat. Marinate in refrigerator 30 minutes.

3. Prepare grill for direct cooking.

4. Drain hens; discard marinade. Grill hens, skin side up, covered, over medium-high heat 20 minutes.

5. Meanwhile, combine marmalade, mustard and ginger in small bowl. Brush half of marmalade mixture evenly over hens. Grill, covered, 10 minutes. Brush with remaining mixture. Grill, covered, 5 to 10 minutes or until cooked through (165°F).

MAKES 4 SERVINGS

Lemon Rosemary
Chicken and Potatoes

4 bone-in skin-on chicken breasts
½ cup lemon juice
6 tablespoons olive oil, divided
6 cloves garlic, minced, divided
2 tablespoons plus 1 teaspoon chopped fresh rosemary leaves, divided
1½ teaspoons salt, divided
2 pounds small red potatoes, cut into quarters
1 large onion, cut into 2-inch chunks
¼ teaspoon black pepper

1. Place chicken in large resealable food storage bag. Combine lemon juice, 3 tablespoons oil, 3 cloves garlic, 1 tablespoon rosemary and ½ teaspoon salt in small bowl; pour over chicken. Seal bag; turn to coat. Marinate in refrigerator several hours or overnight.

2. Preheat oven to 400°F. Combine potatoes and onion in roasting pan. Combine remaining 3 tablespoons oil, 3 cloves garlic, 1 tablespoon rosemary, 1 teaspoon salt and pepper in small bowl; mix well. Pour over vegetables; toss to coat.

3. Drain chicken; discard marinade. Arrange chicken in pan with vegetables; sprinkle with remaining 1 teaspoon rosemary.

4. Roast about 50 minutes or until chicken is cooked through (165°F) and potatoes are tender. Sprinkle with additional salt and pepper to taste.

MAKES 4 SERVINGS

Roasted Chicken Thighs with Mustard-Cream Sauce

8 bone-in skin-on chicken thighs

¾ teaspoon black pepper, divided

¼ teaspoon plus ⅛ teaspoon salt, divided

2 teaspoons vegetable oil

2 shallots, thinly sliced

½ Granny Smith apple, peeled and cut into ¼-inch pieces

½ cup chicken broth

½ cup whipping cream

1 tablespoon spicy brown mustard

½ teaspoon chopped fresh thyme

1. Preheat oven to 400°F.

2. Sprinkle both sides of chicken with ½ teaspoon pepper and ¼ teaspoon salt. Heat oil in large ovenproof skillet over medium-high heat. Add chicken, skin side down; cook 8 to 10 minutes or until skin is golden brown. Remove chicken to plate; drain excess fat from skillet.

3. Return chicken to skillet, skin side up. Transfer skillet to oven; roast about 25 minutes or until cooked through (165°F). Remove chicken to clean plate; keep warm.

4. Drain all but 1 tablespoon fat from skillet; heat over medium heat. Add shallots and apple; cook and stir about 8 minutes or until tender. Add broth; cook over medium-high heat about 1 minute or until reduced by half, scraping up browned bits from bottom of skillet. Add cream, mustard, thyme, remaining ¼ teaspoon pepper and ⅛ teaspoon salt; cook and stir about 2 minutes or until slightly thickened. Spoon sauce over chicken. Serve immediately.

MAKES 4 SERVINGS

Pan-Roasted Chicken Breasts

4 boneless skin-on chicken breasts (about 6 ounces each)
   Salt and black pepper
2 tablespoons vegetable oil
1 medium shallot, finely chopped (about ¼ cup)
1 tablespoon all-purpose flour
½ cup India Pale Ale
½ cup reduced-sodium chicken broth
¼ cup whipping cream
1 teaspoon Dijon mustard
½ teaspoon finely chopped fresh thyme
¼ teaspoon salt
⅛ teaspoon black pepper
½ cup (2 ounces) shredded Gruyère or Emmental cheese

1. Preheat oven to 375°F.

2. Season both sides of chicken breasts with salt and pepper. Heat oil in large ovenproof skillet over medium-high heat until almost smoking. Add chicken, skin side down; cook 8 to 10 minutes or until until skin is golden brown. Turn chicken; transfer skillet to oven. Roast about 15 minutes or until no longer pink in center. Remove chicken to plate; keep warm.

3. Add shallot to skillet; cook and stir over medium heat until softened. Add flour; cook and stir 1 minute. Add ale; cook until reduced by half, scraping up browned bits from bottom of skillet. Add broth, cream, mustard, thyme, ¼ teaspoon salt and ⅛ teaspoon pepper; cook until slightly thickened.

4. Remove from heat; whisk in cheese until melted and smooth. Spoon sauce over chicken. Serve immediately.

MAKES 4 SERVINGS

Duck Breasts with Balsamic Honey Sauce

3 tablespoons balsamic vinegar

3 tablespoons honey

2 tablespoons lemon juice

4 boneless duck breasts (6 to 8 ounces each)

   Salt and black pepper

1 shallot, minced

1. Combine vinegar, honey and lemon juice in small bowl; mix well.

2. Score skin on duck breasts with tip of sharp knife in crosshatch pattern, being careful to cut only into the fat and not the meat. Season both sides of duck with salt and pepper. Place duck breasts skin side down in large skillet over medium heat; cook without turning 10 to 12 minutes or until skin is crisp and golden brown. Turn and cook about 8 minutes or until medium-rare (130°F). Remove duck to plate; let stand 10 minutes before slicing.

3. Meanwhile, drain all but 1 tablespoon fat from skillet. Add shallot to skillet; cook and stir over medium heat 2 to 3 minutes or until translucent. Add vinegar mixture; cook and stir about 5 minutes or until slightly thickened. Season with additional salt and pepper.

4. Slice duck; drizzle with sauce.

MAKES 4 SERVINGS

Chicken Scallopini with Swiss Chard

2 slices bacon, chopped

1 cup chopped onion

1 pound Swiss chard, trimmed and coarsely chopped (6 cups packed)

1 egg white

1 teaspoon water

¼ cup plain dry bread crumbs

1 pound chicken cutlets*

1 tablespoon olive oil

Lemon wedges (optional)

Chicken cutlets are fresh boneless skinless chicken breasts that have been sliced about ⅓ inch thick. If they aren't available, pound four 4-ounce chicken breasts to ⅓-inch thickness.

1. Cook bacon and onion in large saucepan over medium heat 6 to 8 minutes or until onion is golden brown. Add Swiss chard; cover and cook 2 minutes to wilt. Stir mixture; cook, uncovered, 10 minutes or until chard is tender, stirring occasionally.

2. Meanwhile, beat egg white and water in shallow dish. Place bread crumbs in another shallow dish. Dip each chicken cutlet in egg white, letting excess drip off, then in bread crumbs, coating both sides lightly and using all crumbs.

3. Heat oil in large nonstick skillet over medium-high heat. Add chicken; cook 3 minutes or until golden brown on bottom. Turn and cook over medium heat 3 to 4 minutes or until golden brown and no longer pink in center. (Watch carefully to avoid burning.) Serve over chard mixture; garnish with lemon wedges.

MAKES 4 SERVINGS

Crispy Mustard Chicken >

  4 bone-in chicken breasts
    Salt and black pepper
⅓ cup Dijon mustard
½ cup panko bread crumbs or coarse dry bread crumbs

1. Preheat oven to 350°F. Spray rack of broiler pan or shallow baking pan with nonstick cooking spray.

2. Remove skin from chicken. Season chicken with salt and pepper; place on prepared rack. Bake 20 minutes.

3. Brush chicken generously with mustard. Sprinkle with panko and gently press panko into mustard. Bake 20 to 25 minutes or until chicken is cooked through (165°F).

MAKES 4 SERVINGS

Herb Roasted Chicken

  1 whole chicken (3 to 4 pounds)
1¼ teaspoons salt, divided
  ½ teaspoon black pepper, divided
  1 lemon, cut into quarters
  4 sprigs fresh rosemary, divided
  4 sprigs fresh thyme, divided
  4 cloves garlic, peeled
  2 tablespoons olive oil

1. Preheat oven to 425°F. Place chicken, breast side up, in shallow roasting pan. Season cavity with ½ teaspoon salt and ¼ teaspoon pepper. Fill cavity with lemon quarters, 2 sprigs rosemary, 2 sprigs thyme and garlic cloves.

2. Chop remaining rosemary and thyme leaves; combine with oil, remaining ¾ teaspoon salt and ¼ teaspoon pepper in small bowl. Brush mixture over chicken.

3. Roast 30 minutes. *Reduce oven temperature to 375°F;* roast 35 to 45 minutes or until cooked through (165 °F). Let stand 10 to 15 minutes before carving.

MAKES 4 TO 5 SERVINGS

Honey Lemon Garlic Chicken

2 lemons, divided

2 tablespoons butter, melted

2 tablespoons honey

3 cloves garlic, chopped

2 sprigs fresh rosemary, leaves removed from stems

1 teaspoon coarse salt

½ teaspoon black pepper

3 pounds chicken (4 bone-in skin-on chicken thighs and 4 drumsticks)

1¼ pounds potatoes, cut into halves or quarters

1. Preheat oven to 375°F. Grate peel and squeeze juice from one lemon. Cut remaining lemon into slices.

2. Combine lemon peel, lemon juice, butter, honey, garlic, rosemary, salt and pepper in small bowl; mix well. Combine chicken, potatoes and lemon slices in large bowl. Pour butter mixture over chicken and potatoes; toss to coat. Arrange chicken and potatoes in single layer on large rimmed baking sheet or in shallow roasting pan.

3. Bake about 1 hour or until potatoes are tender and chicken is cooked through (165°F). Cover loosely with foil if chicken skin is becoming too dark.

MAKES 4 SERVINGS

Kale and Mushroom Stuffed Chicken Breasts

2 tablespoons olive oil, divided
1 cup coarsely chopped mushrooms
2 cups thinly sliced kale
1 tablespoon lemon juice
½ teaspoon salt, divided
4 boneless skinless chicken breasts (about 4 ounces each)
¼ cup crumbled goat or feta cheese
¼ teaspoon black pepper

1. Heat 1 tablespoon oil in large skillet over medium-high heat. Add mushrooms; cook and stir 5 minutes or until mushrooms begin to brown. Add kale; cook and stir 8 minutes or until wilted. Sprinkle with lemon juice and ¼ teaspoon salt. Remove to small bowl; let stand 5 to 10 minutes to cool slightly.

2. Meanwhile, place each chicken breast between sheets of plastic wrap. Pound to ½-inch thickness with meat mallet or rolling pin.

3. Gently stir cheese into mushroom and kale mixture. Spoon ¼ cup mixture down center of each chicken breast. Roll up to enclose filling; secure with toothpicks. Sprinkle with remaining ¼ teaspoon salt and pepper.

4. Wipe out same skillet with paper towel. Add remaining 1 tablespoon oil to skillet; heat over medium heat. Add chicken; cook until browned on all sides. Cover and cook 5 minutes per side or until no longer pink. Remove toothpicks before serving.

MAKES 4 SERVINGS

Chicken and Herb Stew

½ cup all-purpose flour
½ teaspoon salt
¼ teaspoon black pepper
¼ teaspoon paprika
4 chicken drumsticks
4 chicken thighs
2 tablespoons olive oil
12 ounces new potatoes, quartered
2 carrots, quartered lengthwise and cut into 3-inch pieces
1 green bell pepper, cut into thin strips
¾ cup chopped onion
2 cloves garlic, minced
1¾ cups water
¼ cup dry white wine
2 cubes chicken bouillon
1 tablespoon chopped fresh oregano
1 teaspoon chopped fresh rosemary leaves
2 tablespoons chopped fresh Italian parsley (optional)

1. Combine flour, salt, black pepper and paprika in shallow dish; mix well. Coat chicken with flour mixture; shake off excess.

2. Heat oil in large skillet over medium-high heat. Add chicken; cook 8 minutes or until browned on both sides, turning once. Remove to plate.

3. Add potatoes, carrots, bell pepper, onion and garlic to same skillet; cook and stir 5 minutes or until lightly browned. Add water, wine and bouillon; cook 1 minute, stirring to scrape up browned bits from bottom of skillet. Stir in oregano and rosemary.

4. Place chicken on top of vegetable mixture, turning several times to coat. Cover and simmer 45 to 50 minutes or until chicken is cooked through (165°F), turning occasionally. Garnish with parsley.

MAKES 4 SERVINGS

Roast Duck with Apple Stuffing

1 duck (about 5 pounds)
Coarse salt and black pepper
2 tablespoons butter
1 small onion, chopped
2 stalks celery, chopped
3 apples, peeled and cut into bite-size pieces
½ cup chopped mixed dried fruit (prunes, apricots, etc.)
5 to 6 fresh sage leaves (tear large leaves in half)
1 cup dried bread cubes (¼- to ½-inch pieces)
Juice of 1 lemon
1 cup plus 1 tablespoon chicken broth, divided
⅔ cup dry white wine

1. Discard neck, giblets and liver from duck (or reserve for another use); trim fat. Rinse duck thoroughly under cold water; pat dry with paper towels. Generously season outside of duck and cavity with salt and pepper. Place duck on rack in roasting pan. Refrigerate, uncovered, 1 to 3 hours until ready to cook.

2. For stuffing, melt butter in medium skillet over medium-high heat. Add onion and celery; cook and stir 2 minutes. Add apples, dried fruit and sage; cook and stir 10 minutes or until apples and vegetables are softened. Combine apple mixture and bread cubes in medium bowl; season with ½ teaspoon salt and ¼ teaspoon pepper. Stir in lemon juice. If stuffing seems dry, add 1 tablespoon broth.

3. Preheat oven to 350°F. Spoon stuffing into duck cavity, packing tightly. Tie legs together with kitchen string. Cut through duck skin in crisscross pattern over breast and legs, being careful to only cut though skin and fat layer (about ¼ inch thick), but not into duck flesh. (Cuts will help render duck fat and make skin crisp.)

4. Roast 1½ to 2 hours or until juices run clear and thermometer inserted into leg joint registers 175°F, rotating pan every 20 minutes. (Temperature of stuffing should reach 165°F.) Remove duck to serving platter. Pour off fat from pan; refrigerate or freeze for another use or discard.

5. For sauce, place roasting pan over medium-high heat. Add wine; cook and stir 5 minutes or until wine is reduced by half, scraping up browned bits from bottom of pan. Add remaining 1 cup broth; cook and stir 2 minutes. Strain sauce; serve with duck and stuffing.

MAKES 4 SERVINGS

Tip: Ducks' looks are deceiving—they are large birds, but have very little meat for their size. One duck can serve four, provided there are side dishes (and all four people don't want a duck leg). For a bigger group, double the stuffing recipe and roast two ducks.

Irish Stout Chicken

2 tablespoons vegetable oil

1 medium onion, chopped

2 cloves garlic, minced

1 whole chicken (3 to 4 pounds), cut into serving pieces

5 carrots, sliced

2 parsnips, peeled and sliced

1 teaspoon dried thyme

¾ teaspoon salt

½ teaspoon black pepper

¾ cup Irish stout

8 ounces sliced mushrooms

¾ cup frozen peas

1. Heat oil in large skillet over medium heat. Add onion and garlic; cook and stir 3 minutes or until tender. Remove to small bowl.

2. Add chicken to same skillet in single layer; cook over medium-high heat 5 minutes per side or until lightly browned.

3. Add onion mixture, carrots, parsnips, thyme, salt and pepper to skillet. Add stout; bring to a boil over high heat. Reduce heat to low; cover and simmer 35 minutes.

4. Add mushrooms and peas to skillet; cover and cook 10 minutes. Uncover; cook over medium heat 10 minutes or until sauce is slightly thickened and chicken is cooked through (165°F).

MAKES 4 SERVINGS

Herb Roasted Turkey

½ cup coarse-grain or Dijon mustard
¼ cup chopped fresh sage
2 tablespoons chopped fresh thyme
2 tablespoons chopped fresh chives
1 small (8- to 10-pound) turkey, thawed if frozen
Salt and black pepper

1. Preheat oven to 450°F. Combine mustard, sage, thyme and chives in small bowl; mix well.

2. Rinse turkey under cold water; pat dry with paper towels. Carefully insert fingers under skin, beginning at neck cavity and sliding down over breast to form pocket between skin and turkey breast. Spoon mustard mixture into pocket; massage outside of skin to spread mixture into even layer.

3. Place turkey, breast side up, on rack in shallow roasting pan. Tie legs together with kitchen string. Season with salt and pepper.

4. Place turkey in oven. *Reduce oven temperature to 325°F.* Roast turkey 18 minutes per pound or until cooked through (165°F). Once turkey browns, tent with foil for remainder of roasting time. Remove turkey to cutting board; reserve pan drippings for gravy, if desired. Loosely tent turkey with foil; let stand 20 minutes before carving.

MAKES 8 TO 10 SERVINGS

Blue Cheese Stuffed Chicken Breasts

½ cup (2 ounces) crumbled blue cheese

2 tablespoons butter, softened, divided

¾ teaspoon dried thyme

Salt and black pepper

4 bone-in skin-on chicken breasts

1 tablespoon lemon juice

1. Preheat oven to 400°F. Combine blue cheese, 1 tablespoon butter and thyme in small bowl; mix well. Season with salt and pepper.

2. Loosen chicken skin by pushing fingers between skin and meat, taking care not to tear skin. Spread blue cheese mixture under skin; massage skin to spread mixture evenly over breast. Place chicken breasts in shallow roasting pan.

3. Melt remaining 1 tablespoon butter in small bowl; stir in lemon juice until blended. Brush over chicken.

4. Roast chicken about 50 minutes or until cooked through (165°F).

MAKES 4 SERVINGS

SIDE DISHES

Haggerty

8 slices bacon (about 8 ounces)
3 onions, thinly sliced
1½ cups (6 ounces) shredded Irish Cheddar cheese, divided
2 tablespoons butter, divided
5 medium red potatoes (about 1¼ pounds), very thinly sliced
Salt and black pepper

1. Preheat oven to 375°F.

2. Cook bacon in large ovenproof skillet until crisp. Drain on paper towel-lined plate; crumble into medium bowl. Drain all but 1 tablespoon drippings from skillet.

3. Add onions to skillet; cook and stir over medium heat about 8 minutes or until translucent but not browned. Drain on paper towel-lined plate. Remove to bowl with bacon; mix well.

4. Reserve ¼ cup cheese; set aside. Melt 1 tablespoon butter in same skillet or 8- to 9-inch baking dish. Arrange one quarter of potato slices to cover bottom of skillet. Season with salt and pepper. Top with one third of bacon-onion mixture; sprinkle with one third of remaining cheese. Repeat layers twice. Top with remaining one quarter of potato slices; dot with remaining 1 tablespoon butter.

5. Cover with foil and bake 50 minutes. Uncover and bake 10 minutes or until potatoes are tender. *Turn oven to broil.* Broil 2 to 3 minutes or until lightly browned. Sprinkle with reserved ¼ cup cheese. Serve warm.

MAKES 6 TO 8 SERVINGS

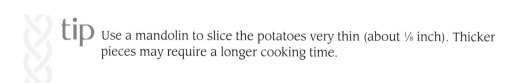 tip Use a mandolin to slice the potatoes very thin (about ⅛ inch). Thicker pieces may require a longer cooking time.

Classic Irish Salad

DRESSING

- 3 tablespoons mayonnaise
- 1 tablespoon Dijon mustard
- 1 tablespoon canola oil
- 1 tablespoon cider vinegar
- 2 teaspoons sugar
- ¼ teaspoon salt
- ⅛ teaspoon black pepper

SALAD

- 6 cups torn romaine lettuce
- 2 cups baby arugula
- 1 large cucumber, halved lengthwise and sliced
- 4 radishes, thinly sliced
- 3 tablespoons chopped fresh chives
- 2 hard-cooked eggs, cut into wedges
- 2 bottled pickled beets, quartered

1. For dressing, whisk mayonnaise, mustard, oil, vinegar, sugar, salt and pepper in small bowl until well blended.

2. For salad, toss romaine, arugula, cucumber, radishes and chives in large bowl. Divide among four plates; top with egg wedges and beet quarters. Serve dressing separately or drizzle over salads just before serving.

MAKES 4 SERVINGS

Roasted Cauliflower with Cheddar Beer Sauce

1 large head cauliflower (about 2½ pounds), trimmed and cut into ½-inch florets
2 tablespoons vegetable oil, divided
½ teaspoon salt, divided
½ teaspoon black pepper
2 medium shallots, finely chopped
2 teaspoons all-purpose flour
½ cup Irish ale
1 tablespoon spicy brown mustard
1 tablespoon Worcestershire sauce
1½ cups (6 ounces) shredded Cheddar cheese

1. Preheat oven to 450°F. Line large baking sheet with foil.

2. Combine cauliflower, 1 tablespoon oil, ¼ teaspoon salt and pepper in medium bowl; toss to coat. Spread in single layer on prepared baking sheet.

3. Roast 25 minutes or until cauliflower is tender and lightly browned, stirring occasionally.

4. Meanwhile, heat remaining 1 tablespoon oil in medium saucepan over medium heat. Add shallots; cook and stir 3 to 4 minutes or until tender. Add flour and remaining ¼ teaspoon salt; cook and stir 1 minute. Add ale, mustard and Worcestershire sauce; bring to a simmer over medium-high heat. Reduce heat to medium-low; add cheese by ¼ cupfuls, stirring until cheese is melted before adding next addition. Cover and keep warm over low heat, stirring occasionally.

5. Transfer roasted cauliflower to large serving bowl; top with cheese sauce. Serve immediately.

MAKES 4 TO 6 SERVINGS

Colcannon with Spinach and Parsnips >

3 medium russet potatoes (1½ pounds), peeled and cut into 1-inch pieces

3 parsnips (12 ounces), peeled and cut into 1-inch pieces

⅔ cup milk

5 tablespoons butter, plus additional for serving

¾ teaspoon salt

¼ teaspoon ground black pepper

3 cups baby spinach

1. Combine potatoes and parsnips in large saucepan; add cold water to cover by 2 inches. Bring to a boil over medium-high heat; cook 18 to 20 minutes or until tender. Drain vegetables; return to saucepan.

2. Heat milk in small saucepan over medium-high heat until hot. Add 5 tablespoons butter, salt and pepper; stir until butter is melted.

3. Pour three-fourths of milk mixture into saucepan with vegetables; mash until smooth. Stir in spinach until well combined. Add remaining milk mixture as needed to reach desired consistency. Spoon into serving dish; top with additional butter, if desired.

MAKES 4 TO 6 SERVINGS

Chutney Glazed Carrots

2 cups chopped carrots (1½-inch pieces)

3 tablespoons mango chutney

1 tablespoon Dijon mustard

2 teaspoons butter

2 tablespoons chopped pecans, toasted*

To toast pecans, spread in single layer in heavy skillet. Cook over medium heat 2 minutes or until lightly browned, stirring frequently.

1. Place carrots in medium saucepan; add cold water to cover. Bring to a boil over high heat. Reduce heat to medium-low; simmer 6 to 8 minutes or until carrots are tender.

2. Drain carrots; return to saucepan. Add chutney, mustard and butter; cook and stir over medium heat 2 minutes or until carrots are glazed. Sprinkle with pecans just before serving.

MAKES 4 SERVINGS

Braised Leeks

3 to 4 large leeks (1½ to 2 pounds)
¼ cup (½ stick) butter
¼ teaspoon salt
¼ teaspoon black pepper
¼ cup dry white wine
¼ cup reduced-sodium chicken or vegetable broth
3 to 4 sprigs fresh parsley

1. Trim green stem ends of leeks; remove any damaged outer leaves. Slice leeks lengthwise up to, but not through, root ends to hold leeks together. Rinse leeks under cold water, separating layers to remove embedded dirt. Cut leeks crosswise into 3-inch lengths; cut off and discard root ends.

2. Melt butter in skillet large enough to hold leeks in single layer. Arrange leeks in skillet in crowded layer, keeping pieces together as much as possible. Cook over medium-high heat about 8 minutes or until leeks begin to color and soften, turning with tongs once or twice. Sprinkle with salt and pepper.

3. Add wine, broth and parsley; bring to a simmer. Cover and cook over low heat 20 minutes or until leeks are very tender. Remove parsley sprigs before serving.

MAKES 4 SERVINGS

Serving Suggestion: Top the braised leeks with toasted bread crumbs, cheese or crisp crumbled bacon for an extra-rich side dish.

 tip Leeks often contain a lot of embedded dirt between their layers, so they need to be washed thoroughly. It's easiest to slice up to—but not through—the root ends before slicing or chopping so the leeks hold together while washing them.

Roasted Asparagus with
Shallot Vinaigrette >

    1 pound fresh asparagus

    4 tablespoons olive oil, divided

    1 shallot, minced

    1 tablespoon balsamic or white wine vinegar

    ¼ teaspoon salt

    ¼ teaspoon black pepper

1. Preheat oven to 425°F. Place asparagus in shallow baking pan or jelly-roll pan. Drizzle with 1 tablespoon oil; toss to coat.

2. Roast asparagus 10 minutes or until tender and lightly browned.

3. Meanwhile, whisk remaining 3 tablespoons oil, shallot, vinegar, salt and pepper in small bowl until well blended. Let stand at least 5 minutes to allow flavors to blend.

4. Arrange asparagus on serving plate; drizzle with dressing.

MAKES 4 SERVINGS

Green Cabbage Salad

    2 tablespoons extra virgin olive oil

    1 tablespoon cider vinegar

    1 clove garlic, minced

    ½ teaspoon sugar

    ¼ teaspoon salt

    ⅛ teaspoon black pepper

    2 cups thinly sliced green cabbage

1. Combine oil, vinegar, garlic, sugar, salt and pepper in small jar with tight-fitting lid. Cover and shake untill well blended.

2. Place cabbage in medium bowl; add dressing and toss gently to coat. Let stand at least 10 minutes before serving. For milder flavor, refrigerate 1 hour.

MAKES 2 SERVINGS

Stovies with Bacon

3 medium russet potatoes (about 1½ pounds), peeled
6 slices bacon
2 large onions, halved vertically and sliced
4 teaspoons butter
½ teaspoon salt
⅛ teaspoon black pepper
⅓ cup water

1. Place potatoes in large saucepan; add cold water to cover by 2 inches. Bring to a boil over medium-high heat; cook 15 minutes or until partially cooked. Drain; let stand until cool enough to handle. Cut potatoes into ½-inch-thick slices.

2. Cook bacon in large skillet over medium-high heat 6 to 7 minutes or until crisp, turning occasionally. Drain on paper towel-lined plate. Chop bacon; set aside.

3. Drain all but 2 tablespoons drippings from skillet; heat over medium heat. Add onions; cook 8 to 9 minutes or until softened but not browned, stirring occasionally. Remove onions to small bowl.

4. Add butter to skillet; heat over medium heat until melted. Add potatoes; sprinkle with salt and pepper. Top with onions and pour in ⅓ cup water; cover and cook 5 minutes. Stir in bacon; cook, uncovered, 10 to 12 minutes or until potatoes are tender and browned, stirring occasionally.

MAKES 4 SERVINGS

Cider Vinaigrette-Glazed Beets

6 medium beets with tops
1 tablespoon olive oil
1 tablespoon cider vinegar
½ teaspoon prepared horseradish
½ teaspoon Dijon mustard
¼ teaspoon packed brown sugar
⅓ cup crumbled blue cheese

1. Cut tops off beets, leaving at least 1 inch of stems. Scrub beets with soft vegetable brush, being careful not to break skins. Place beets in large saucepan; add cold water to cover. Bring to a boil over high heat. Reduce heat to low; simmer 30 minutes or until just barely firm when pierced with fork. Remove to plate to cool slightly.

2. Meanwhile, whisk oil, vinegar, horseradish, mustard and brown sugar in medium bowl until well blended.

3. When beets are cool enough to handle, peel off skins and trim off root end. Cut beets into halves, then into wedges. Add warm beets to vinaigrette; toss gently to coat. Sprinkle with cheese. Serve warm or at room temperature.

MAKES 8 SERVINGS

Potato and Leek Gratin

5 tablespoons butter, divided

2 large leeks, sliced

2 tablespoons minced garlic

2 pounds baking potatoes, peeled (about 4 medium)

1 cup whipping cream

1 cup milk

3 eggs

2 teaspoons salt

¼ teaspoon white pepper

2 to 3 slices dense day-old white bread, such as French or Italian

2 ounces grated Parmesan cheese

1. Preheat oven to 375°F. Generously grease shallow 10-cup baking dish with 1 tablespoon butter.

2. Melt 2 tablespoons butter in large skillet over medium heat. Add leeks and garlic; cook and stir 8 to 10 minutes or until leeks are softened. Remove from heat.

3. Cut potatoes crosswise into ¹⁄₁₆-inch-thick slices. Layer half of potato slices in prepared baking dish; top with half of leek mixture. Repeat layers. Whisk cream, milk, eggs, salt and white pepper in medium bowl until well blended; pour evenly over leek mixture.

4. Tear bread slices into 1-inch pieces. Place in food processor; process until fine crumbs form. Measure ¾ cup crumbs; place in small bowl. Stir in Parmesan cheese. Melt remaining 2 tablespoons butter; stir into crumb mixture. Sprinkle evenly over vegetables in baking dish.

5. Bake 60 to 75 minutes or until top is golden and potatoes are tender. Let stand 5 to 10 minutes before serving.

MAKES 6 TO 8 SERVINGS

Bacon-Roasted Brussels Sprouts >

1 pound brussels sprouts
3 slices bacon, cut into ½-inch pieces
2 teaspoons packed brown sugar
Salt and black pepper

1. Preheat oven to 400°F. Trim ends from brussels sprouts; cut in half lengthwise.

2. Combine brussels sprouts, bacon and brown sugar in glass baking dish.

3. Roast 25 to 30 minutes or until golden brown, stirring once. Season with salt and pepper.

MAKES 4 SERVINGS

Onions Baked in Their Papers

4 medium yellow onions with skins intact (about 2½ inches in diameter)
1½ teaspoons mixed dried herbs such as thyme, sage and tarragon
1 teaspoon sugar
½ teaspoon salt
¼ cup (½ stick) butter, melted
½ cup fresh bread crumbs

1. Preheat oven to 400°F. Line 8- or 9-inch square baking pan with foil.

2. Cut off stem and root ends of onions. Cut 1½-inch cone-shaped indentation in top of each onion with paring knife. Arrange onions on root ends in prepared pan.

3. Stir herbs, sugar and salt into melted butter in small bowl. Add bread crumbs; mix well. Spoon mixture evenly into indentations in onions.

4. Bake about 1 hour or until onions are fork-tender. Serve immediately.

MAKES 4 SIDE-DISH SERVINGS

Roasted Potatoes and Pearl Onions >

3 pounds red potatoes, cut into 1½-inch pieces
1 package (10 ounces) pearl onions, peeled
2 tablespoons olive oil
2 teaspoons dried basil or thyme
¾ teaspoon salt
¾ teaspoon dried rosemary
¾ teaspoon black pepper

1. Preheat oven to 400°F.

2. Combine potatoes and onions in large shallow roasting pan. Drizzle with oil; toss to coat. Combine basil, salt, rosemary and pepper in small bowl; mix well. Sprinkle over vegetables; toss gently.

3. Roast 20 minutes. Stir vegetables; roast 20 minutes or until potatoes are browned and fork-tender.

MAKES 8 SERVINGS

Yorkshire Pudding

1 cup milk
2 eggs
½ teaspoon salt
1 cup all-purpose flour
¼ cup reserved drippings from roast or melted butter

1. Combine milk, eggs and salt in blender or food processor; blend 15 seconds. Add flour; blend 2 minutes. Let batter stand in blender at room temperature 30 minutes to 1 hour.

2. Preheat oven to 450°F. Place meat drippings in 9-inch square baking pan. Heat in oven 5 minutes.

3. Blend batter 10 seconds; pour into hot drippings. Do not stir. Immediately return pan to oven. Bake 20 minutes. *Reduce oven temperature to 350°F;* bake 10 minutes or until pudding is golden brown and puffed. Cut into squares. Serve warm.

MAKES 6 TO 8 SERVINGS

Sautéed Kale with Mushrooms and Bacon >

  1 slice bacon, chopped
½ cup sliced shallots
  1 package (4 ounces) sliced mixed mushrooms *or* 2 cups sliced button mushrooms
10 cups (8 ounces) loosely packed torn fresh kale leaves (tough stems removed)*
  2 tablespoons water
½ teaspoon black pepper
¼ teaspoon salt

Look for 16-ounce bags of ready-to-cook fresh kale leaves in the produce section of the supermarket.

1. Cook bacon in large heavy skillet over medium heat 5 minutes. Add shallots; cook and stir 3 minutes. Add mushrooms; cook and stir 8 minutes.

2. Add kale and water; cover and cook 5 minutes. Uncover; cook and stir 5 minutes or until kale is crisp-tender. Season with pepper and salt.

MAKES 4 SERVINGS

Cabbage Colcannon

  1 pound new red potatoes, halved
  1 tablespoon vegetable oil
  1 small onion, thinly sliced
½ small head green cabbage, thinly sliced
  Salt and black pepper
  3 tablespoons butter

1. Place potatoes in medium saucepan; add cold water to cover. Bring to a boil over medium heat; cook 20 minutes or until tender. Drain well.

2. Heat oil in large nonstick skillet over medium-high heat. Add onion; cook and stir 8 minutes or until lightly browned. Add cabbage; cook and stir 5 minutes or until softened.

3. Add potatoes to skillet; cook until heated through. Slightly mash potatoes; season to taste with salt and pepper. Place ½ tablespoon slice of butter on each portion just before serving.

MAKES 6 SERVINGS

Mashed Carrots and Parsnips >

1 medium russet potato (8 ounces), peeled and cut into 1-inch pieces
3 parsnips (12 ounces), peeled and cut into 1-inch pieces
3 carrots (12 ounces), cut into 1-inch pieces
1 tablespoon honey
¼ cup (½ stick) butter, softened
½ teaspoon salt
¼ teaspoon black pepper

1. Place potato in large saucepan; add cold water to cover by 3 inches. Bring to a boil over medium-high heat; cook about 7 minutes or until potato is partially cooked.

2. Add parsnips, carrots and honey to saucepan; return to a boil. Cook 16 to 18 minutes or until vegetables are tender. Drain vegetables; return to saucepan. Add butter, salt and pepper; mash until smooth. Serve hot.

MAKES 4 TO 6 SERVINGS

Leeks with Dijon Vinaigrette

4 medium leeks
1 tablespoon extra virgin olive oil
2 to 3 teaspoons red wine vinegar
¼ teaspoon Dijon mustard
⅛ teaspoon salt
   Pinch black pepper

1. Trim leek roots; cut leeks lengthwise in half to about ½-inch from root end, leaving root ends intact. Rinse thoroughly under cold water; drain well. Arrange in single layer in steamer basket. Steam leeks in large saucepan over boiling water, covered, 10 minutes or until tender when tested with tip of knife. Cool to room temperature or chill.

2. Whisk oil, vinegar, mustard, salt and pepper in small bowl until well blended. Spoon over leeks.

MAKES 4 SERVINGS

Tip: The smaller the leek, the more tender it will be. Leeks more than 1½ inches in diameter can be tough and woody. Choose leeks with firm bright green stalks and white blemish-free bases. Avoid leeks with split or oversized bases.

Boxty Pancakes

2 medium russet potatoes (1 pound), peeled, divided

⅔ cup all-purpose flour

1 teaspoon baking powder

½ teaspoon salt

⅔ cup buttermilk

3 tablespoons butter

1. Cut 1 potato into 1-inch chunks; place in small saucepan and add cold water to cover by 2 inches. Bring to a boil over medium-high heat; cook 14 to 18 minutes or until tender. Drain potato; return to saucepan and mash. Transfer to medium bowl.

2. Shred remaining potato on large holes of box grater; add to bowl with mashed potato. Stir in flour, baking powder and salt until blended. Stir in buttermilk.

3. Melt 1 tablespoon butter in large nonstick skillet over medium heat. Drop four slightly heaping tablespoonfuls of batter into skillet; flatten into 2½-inch circles. Cook about 4 minutes per side or until golden and puffed. Remove to plate; cover to keep warm. Repeat with remaining batter and butter. Serve immediately.

MAKES 4 SERVINGS (16 TO 20 PANCAKES)

Serving Suggestion: Serve with melted butter or sour cream.

Mixed Greens with Pear and Goat Cheese

DRESSING

   ¼ cup balsamic vineger

   2 tablespoons olive oil

   2 tablespoons honey

   1 small clove garlic, minced

   ½ teaspoon salt

   ¼ teaspoon black pepper

SALAD

   1 package (5 ounces) spring greens salad mix

   1 cup chopped cooked chicken (about 5 ounces)

   2 pears, thinly sliced

   ½ cup chopped celery

   ⅓ cup crumbled goat cheese

   2 tablespoons slivered almonds (optional)

1. Whisk vinegar, oil, honey, garlic, salt and pepper in small bowl until well blended.

2. Combine greens, chicken, pears, celery and goat cheese in large bowl. Drizzle dressing over salad; toss gently to coat. Top with almonds, if desired.

MAKES 4 SERVINGS

Kale with Lemon and Garlic >

2 bunches kale or Swiss chard (1 to 1¼ pounds)
1 tablespoon olive or vegetable oil
3 cloves garlic, minced
½ cup chicken or vegetable broth
½ teaspoon salt
¼ teaspoon black pepper
1 lemon, cut into 8 wedges

1. Trim any tough stems from kale. Stack and thinly slice leaves. Heat oil in large saucepan over medium heat. Add garlic; cook 3 minutes, stirring occasionally. Add chopped kale and broth; cover and simmer 7 minutes. Stir kale; cover and simmer over medium-low heat 8 to 10 minutes or until tender.

2. Stir in salt and pepper. Squeeze wedge of lemon over each serving.

MAKES 8 SERVINGS

Potato and Blue Cheese Salad

8 new or fingerling potatoes (about 1 pound), scrubbed
½ teaspoon salt
½ cup shredded radicchio
¼ cup pitted kalamata or niçoise olives, halved
¼ cup (1 ounce) crumbled blue cheese
2½ tablespoons olive oil
1 teaspoon white wine vinegar
1 teaspoon Dijon mustard
¼ teaspoon black pepper

1. Place potatoes and salt in medium saucepan; add cold water to cover. Bring to a boil over medium heat; cook about 20 to 25 minutes or until tender. Drain well; cut into bite-size pieces.

2. Combine potatoes, radicchio, olives and cheese in large bowl. Whisk oil, vinegar, mustard and pepper in small bowl until well blended. Pour over potato mixture; toss gently to coat. Let stand 30 minutes to allow flavors to blend. Serve at room temperature.

MAKES 4 TO 6 SERVINGS

Roasted Parsnips, Carrots and Red Onion

2 carrots (9 ounces), cut into 2-inch-long pieces

2 parsnips (9 ounces), peeled and cut into 2-inch-long pieces

¾ cup vertically sliced red onion (¼-inch slices)

1 tablespoon extra virgin olive oil

1 tablespoon balsamic vinegar

¼ teaspoon salt

⅛ teaspoon black pepper

1. Preheat oven to 425°F. Line large baking sheet with foil.

2. Combine carrots, parsnips, onion, oil, vinegar, salt and pepper in large bowl; toss to coat. Spread in single layer on prepared baking sheet.

3. Roast 25 minutes or until vegetables are tender, stirring occasionally.

MAKES 2 TO 4 SERVINGS

 tip Choose parsnips that are firm, unblemished and small or medium in size (about 8 inches long). Rinse and scrub parsnips with a vegetable brush to remove embedded soil. Peel parsnips with a swivel-bladed vegetable peeler or paring knife.

Potato Cakes with Brussels Sprouts

2½ pounds Yukon Gold potatoes, peeled and cut into 1-inch cubes
6 tablespoons butter, melted
⅓ cup milk, warmed
2 teaspoons salt
½ teaspoon black pepper
3 tablespoons vegetable oil, divided
12 ounces brussels sprouts, ends trimmed, thinly sliced
4 green onions, thinly sliced on the diagonal

1. Place potatoes in large saucepan or Dutch oven; add cold water to cover by 2 inches. Bring to a boil over high heat. Reduce heat to medium-low; cover and simmer about 10 minutes or until potatoes are tender.

2. Drain potatoes; return to saucepan and mash with potato masher until slightly chunky. Stir in butter, milk, salt and pepper until well blended; set aside.

3. Heat 1 tablespoon oil in large nonstick skillet over medium-high heat. Add brussels sprouts; cook about 8 minutes or until tender and lightly browned, stirring occasionally. Stir brussels sprouts and green onions into potato mixture. Wipe out skillet with paper towel.

4. Heat 1 tablespoon oil in skillet over medium heat. Drop potato mixture into skillet by ½ cupfuls, spacing about ½ inch apart. (Use spoon to remove mixture from cup if necessary.) Cook about 3 minutes per side or until cakes are browned and crisp, pressing down lightly with spatula. Remove to platter; keep warm. Repeat with remaining 1 tablespoon oil and potato mixture.

MAKES 12 CAKES

Tangy Red Cabbage
with Apples and Bacon

8 slices Irish or thick-cut bacon

1 large onion, sliced

½ small head red cabbage (1 pound), thinly sliced

1 tablespoon sugar

1 Granny Smith apple, peeled and sliced

2 tablespoons cider vinegar

½ teaspoon salt

¼ teaspoon black pepper

1. Heat large skillet over medium-high heat. Add bacon; cook 6 to 8 minutes or until crisp, turning occasionally. Drain on paper towel-lined plate. Coarsely chop bacon.

2. Drain all but 2 tablespoons drippings from skillet. Add onion; cook and stir over medium-high heat 2 to 3 minutes or until onion begins to soften. Add cabbage and sugar; cook and stir 4 to 5 minutes or until cabbage wilts. Add apple; cook and stir 3 minutes or until crisp-tender. Stir in vinegar; cook 1 minute or until absorbed.

3. Stir in bacon, salt and pepper; cook 1 minute or until heated through. Serve hot or at room temperature.

MAKES 4 SERVINGS

Leek and Chive Champ

3 medium russet potatoes (1½ pounds), peeled and cut into 1-inch pieces
6 tablespoons butter, divided
2 large leeks, halved and sliced
½ cup milk
¼ cup chopped fresh chives
½ teaspoon salt
¼ teaspoon black pepper
½ cup prepared French fried onions (optional)

1. Place potatoes in large saucepan; add cold water to cover by 2 inches. Bring to a boil over medium-high heat; cook 16 to 18 minutes or until tender. Drain and return to saucepan.

2. Meanwhile, melt 2 tablespoons butter in small skillet over medium heat. Add leeks; cook 5 to 6 minutes or until tender, stirring occasionally.

3. Heat milk in small saucepan over medium-high heat until hot. Add 2 tablespoons butter; cook until melted. Pour milk mixture into saucepan with potatoes; mash until smooth. Add leeks, chives, salt, and pepper; mix well.

4. Spoon into serving bowl; make large indentation in top of potatoes. Melt remaining 2 tablespoons butter; pour into indentation. Sprinkle with fried onions, if desired.

MAKES 4 TO 6 SERVINGS

Rhubarb Chutney >

1 cup coarsely chopped peeled apple
½ cup sugar
¼ cup water
¼ cup dark raisins
1 teaspoon grated lemon peel
2 cups sliced rhubarb (½-inch pieces)
3 tablespoons coarsely chopped pecans
2 to 3 teaspoons white vinegar
¾ teaspoon ground cinnamon (optional)

1. Combine apple, sugar, water, raisins and lemon peel in medium saucepan; heat over medium heat until sugar is dissolved, stirring constantly. Reduce heat to low; simmer, uncovered, about 5 minutes or until apple is almost tender.

2. Stir in rhubarb and pecans; bring to a boil over high heat. Reduce heat to low; simmer 8 to 10 minutes or until slightly thickened, stirring occasionally. Stir in vinegar and cinnamon, if desired, during last 2 to 3 minutes of cooking.

3. Remove from heat; cool to room temperature. Cover and refrigerate until ready to serve. Serve with cheese and crackers, chicken, duck or pork.

MAKES ABOUT 2 CUPS

Potato-Cauliflower Mash

3 cups water
2 cups cubed unpeeled Yukon Gold potatoes (about 12 ounces)
10 ounces cauliflower florets
¼ cup milk
2 tablespoons butter
¾ teaspoon salt
¼ teaspoon black pepper

1. Bring water to a boil in large saucepan over high heat. Add potatoes and cauliflower; return to a boil. Reduce heat to medium-low; cover and simmer 10 minutes or until potatoes are tender.

2. Drain vegetables; place in blender with milk, butter, salt and pepper. Blend until smooth.

MAKES 4 SERVINGS

PUB FARE

Pub-Style Fish and Chips

¾ cup all-purpose flour, plus additional for dusting fish

½ cup flat beer

Vegetable oil

3 large or 4 medium russet potatoes

1 egg, separated

1 pound cod fillets

Salt

Prepared tartar sauce

Lemon wedges

1. Combine ¾ cup flour, beer and 2 teaspoons oil in small bowl; mix well. Cover and refrigerate 30 minutes to 2 hours.

2. Peel and cut potatoes into ¾-inch sticks. Place in large bowl of cold water. Pour at least 2 inches of oil into deep heavy saucepan or deep fryer; heat over medium heat to 320°F. Drain and thoroughly dry potatoes. Fry in batches 3 minutes or until slightly softened but not browned. Drain on paper towel-lined plate.

3. Stir egg yolk into cold flour mixture. Beat egg white in medium bowl with electric mixer at medium-high speed until soft peaks form. Fold egg white into flour mixture. Season batter with pinch of salt.

4. Preheat oven to 200°F. Heat oil to 365°F. Cut cod into pieces about 6 inches long and 2 to 3 inches wide; remove any pin bones. Dust fish with flour; dip fish into batter, shaking off excess. Lower carefully into oil; cook 4 to 6 minutes or until batter is browned and fish is cooked through, turning once. Cook fish in batches; do not crowd saucepan. (Allow temperature of oil to return to 365°F between batches.) Drain on paper towel-lined plate; keep warm in oven.

5. Return potatoes to hot oil; cook in batches 5 minutes or until browned and crisp. Drain on paper towel-lined plate; sprinkle with salt. Serve fish with potatoes, tartar sauce and lemon wedges.

MAKES 4 SERVINGS

Emerald Isle Lamb Chops

2 tablespoons vegetable or olive oil, divided

2 tablespoons coarse Dijon mustard

1 tablespoon Irish whiskey

1 tablespoon minced fresh rosemary

2 teaspoons minced garlic

1½ pounds loin lamb chops (about 6 chops)

½ teaspoon salt

½ teaspoon black pepper

¾ cup dry white wine

2 tablespoons black currant jam

1 to 2 tablespoons butter, cut into pieces

1. Whisk 1 tablespoon oil, mustard, whiskey, rosemary and garlic in small bowl to form paste. Season lamb chops with salt and pepper; spread paste over both sides. Cover and marinate 30 minutes at room temperature or refrigerate 2 to 3 hours.

2. Heat remaining 1 tablespoon oil in large skillet over medium-high heat. Add lamb chops in single layer; cook 2 to 3 minutes per side or to desired doneness. Remove to serving plate; keep warm.

3. Drain excess fat from skillet. Add wine; cook and stir about 5 minutes, scraping up browned bits from bottom of skillet. Stir in jam until well blended. Remove from heat; stir in butter until melted. Serve sauce over lamb chops.

MAKES 4 TO 6 SERVINGS

Scotch Eggs

10 eggs, divided
2 tablespoons vegetable oil
1½ cups panko bread crumbs
1 pound bulk breakfast sausage
¼ cup thinly sliced green onions
¾ cup all-purpose flour
2 tablespoons whole grain mustard

1. Preheat oven to 400°F. Line large baking sheet with foil.

2. Place 8 eggs in large saucepan filled with cold water; cover and bring to a boil over medium-high heat, Turn off heat; let stand 10 minutes. Run eggs under cool water to stop cooking. When cool enough to handle, carefully crack and peel eggs.

3. Meanwhile, heat oil in medium skillet over medium heat. Add panko; cook about 8 minutes or until toasted and golden brown, stirring occasionally. Remove to medium bowl; let cool.

4. Combine sausage and green onions in medium bowl. Place flour in shallow bowl. Lightly beat remaining 2 eggs and mustard in another shallow bowl.

5. Scoop out one eighth of sausage mixture; press flat in palm of your hand. Place 1 cooked egg in center of mixture and wrap sausage around it. Gently roll between your hands until sausage completely encloses egg. Coat sausage-wrapped egg in flour, shaking off excess. Dip in egg-mustard mixture; roll in panko to coat. Place on prepared baking sheet. Repeat with remaining eggs and sausage.

6. Bake 16 to 18 minutes or until sausage is cooked through. Drain well on paper towel-lined plate. Serve immediately.

MAKES 8 SERVINGS

Guinness Beef Stew

3 tablespoons vegetable oil, divided
3 pounds boneless beef chuck roast, cut into 1-inch pieces
2 medium onions, chopped
2 stalks celery, chopped
3 tablespoons all-purpose flour
1 tablespoon minced garlic
1 tablespoon tomato paste
2 teaspoons chopped fresh thyme
1½ teaspoons salt
½ teaspoon black pepper
1 bottle (about 11 ounces) Guinness
1 cup reduced-sodium beef broth
3 carrots, cut into 1-inch pieces
4 small turnips (12 ounces), peeled and cut into 1-inch pieces
4 medium Yukon Gold potatoes (1 pound), peeled and cut into 1-inch pieces
¼ cup finely chopped fresh parsley

1. Preheat oven to 350°F. Heat 2 tablespoons oil in Dutch oven over medium-high heat until almost smoking. Cook beef in two batches about 10 minutes or until browned on all sides. Remove beef to large plate.

2. Add remaining 1 tablespoon oil to Dutch oven; heat over medium heat. Add onions and celery; cook about 10 minutes or until softened and onions are translucent, stirring occasionally. Add flour, garlic, tomato paste, thyme, salt and pepper; cook and stir 1 minute. Add Guinness; use wooden spoon to scrape up browned bits from bottom of Dutch oven. Return beef to Dutch oven; stir in broth.

3. Cover and bake 1 hour. Stir in carrots, turnips and potatoes; cover and bake about 1 hour 20 minutes or until beef and vegetables are tender. Stir in parsley.

MAKES 6 SERVINGS

Spicy Ale Shrimp

Dipping Sauce (recipe follows)
3 bottles (12 ounces each) pilsner beer, divided
1 tablespoon seafood boil seasoning blend
1 teaspoon mustard seeds
1 teaspoon red pepper flakes
2 lemons, quartered and divided
1 pound large raw shrimp, peeled and deveined (with tails on)

1. Prepare Dipping Sauce; set aside. Pour 1 bottle of beer into large bowl half-filled with ice; set aside.

2. Fill large saucepan half full with water. Add remaining 2 bottles of beer, seafood seasoning, mustard seeds and red pepper flakes. Squeeze 4 lemon quarters into saucepan and add lemon quarters. Bring to a boil over medium-high heat.

3. Add shrimp to saucepan; cover and remove from heat. Let stand 3 minutes or until shrimp are pink and opaque. Drain shrimp; transfer to bowl of chilled beer and ice. Cool. Remove shrimp from bowl; arrange on platter. Serve with Dipping Sauce and remaining lemon quarters.

MAKES 15 TO 20 SHRIMP

Dipping Sauce

1 cup ketchup
1 tablespoon chili-garlic paste
1 tablespoon prepared horseradish
Juice of 1 lemon

Combine ketchup, chili-garlic paste, horseradish and lemon juice in small bowl; mix well. Cover and refrigerate 1 hour.

MAKES ABOUT 1 CUP SAUCE

Lamb and Vegetable Pie

2 tablespoons vegetable oil

1 ½ pounds boneless leg of lamb, cut into 1-inch cubes

3 medium russet potatoes (about 12 ounces), peeled and cut into 1-inch cubes

16 frozen pearl onions (about 1 cup)

1 cup frozen peas and carrots

3 tablespoons all-purpose flour

1 ½ cups reduced-sodium beef broth

3 tablespoons chopped fresh parsley

2 tablespoons tomato paste

2 teaspoons Worcestershire sauce

½ teaspoon salt

¼ teaspoon black pepper

1 refrigerated pie crust (half of 15-ounce package)

1 egg, lightly beaten

1. Spray 9-inch deep-dish baking dish or pie plate with nonstick cooking spray. Heat oil in large saucepan over medium-high heat. Add half of lamb; cook 4 to 5 minutes or until browned, turning occasionally. Remove lamb to plate; repeat with remaining lamb.

2. Add potatoes, onions and peas and carrots to saucepan; cook 2 minutes, stirring occasionally. Stir in lamb and any accumulated juices; cook 2 minutes. Add flour; cook and stir 1 minute. Stir in broth, parsley, tomato paste, Worcestershire sauce, salt and pepper; bring to a boil. Reduce heat to medium-low; cover and simmer about 30 minutes or until lamb and potatoes are tender, stirring occasionally. Spoon mixture into prepared baking dish; let cool 20 minutes.

3. Preheat oven to 400°F. Top lamb mixture with pie crust; flute edge. Brush crust with egg; cut several small slits in crust with tip of knife.

4. Bake about 25 minutes or until crust is golden brown and filling is thick and bubbly. Cool 5 minutes before serving.

MAKES 4 TO 6 SERVINGS

Sausage Rolls

8 ounces ground pork
¼ cup finely chopped onion
½ teaspoon coarse salt
1 teaspoon minced garlic
½ teaspoon dried thyme
½ teaspoon dried basil
¼ teaspoon dried marjoram
¼ teaspoon black pepper
1 sheet puff pastry, thawed (half of 17-ounce package)
1 egg, beaten

1. Preheat oven to 400°F. Line large baking sheet with parchment paper.

2. Combine pork, onion, salt, garlic, thyme, basil, marjoram and pepper in medium bowl; mix well.

3. Place puff pastry on floured surface; cut into three strips at seams. Roll each third into 10×4½-inch rectangle. Shape one third of pork mixture into 10-inch log; arrange log along top edge of one pastry rectangle. Brush bottom ½ inch of rectangle with egg. Roll pastry down around pork; press to seal. Cut each roll crosswise into four pieces; place seam side down on prepared baking sheet. Repeat with remaining puff pastry and pork mixture. Brush top of each roll with egg.

4. Bake 22 to 25 minutes or until sausage is cooked through and pastry is golden brown and puffed. Remove to wire rack to cool 10 minutes. Serve warm.

MAKES 4 SERVINGS

Roasted Garlic and Stout Mac and Cheese

1 head garlic
1 tablespoon olive oil
6 tablespoons butter, divided
1 ¼ teaspoons salt, divided
1 cup panko bread crumbs
¼ cup all-purpose flour
½ teaspoon black pepper
2 cups whole milk
¾ cup Irish stout
2 cups (8 ounces) shredded sharp Cheddar cheese
2 cups (8 ounces) shredded Dubliner cheese
1 pound cellentani pasta,* cooked and drained

Or substitute elbow macaroni, penne or other favorite pasta shape.

1. Preheat oven to 375°F. Butter 4-quart shallow baking dish.

2. Place garlic on 10-inch piece of foil; drizzle with oil and crimp shut. Place on small baking sheet; bake 30 minutes or until tender. Cool 15 minutes; squeeze cloves into small bowl. Mash into smooth paste.

3. Melt 2 tablespoons butter in medium bowl; stir in ¼ teaspoon salt until dissolved. Stir in panko until well blended.

4. Melt remaining 4 tablespoons butter in large saucepan over medium heat. Add flour; cook and stir until light brown. Stir in roasted garlic paste, remaining 1 teaspoon salt and pepper. Slowly whisk in milk and stout. Simmer until thickened, whisking constantly. Remove from heat; whisk in cheeses, ½ cup at a time, until melted.

5. Combine cheese mixture and pasta in large bowl. Spoon into prepared baking dish; sprinkle with panko mixture.

6. Bake 40 minutes or until bubbly and topping is golden brown. Let stand 10 minutes before serving.

MAKES 8 TO 10 SERVINGS

Beef Pot Pie

½ cup all-purpose flour

1 teaspoon salt, divided

½ teaspoon black pepper, divided

1½ pounds lean beef stew meat (1-inch pieces)

2 tablespoons olive oil

1 pound new red potatoes, cubed

2 cups baby carrots

1 cup frozen pearl onions, thawed

1 parsnip, peeled and cut into 1-inch pieces

1 cup Irish stout

¾ cup beef broth

1 teaspoon chopped fresh thyme *or* ½ teaspoon dried thyme

1 refrigerated pie crust (half of 15-ounce package)

1. Preheat oven to 350°F. Combine flour, ½ teaspoon salt and ¼ teaspoon pepper in large resealable food storage bag. Add beef; shake to coat.

2. Heat oil in large skillet over medium-high heat. Add beef; cook until browned on all sides. Do not crowd beef; cook in batches if necessary. Transfer to 2½- to 3-quart casserole. Stir in potatoes, carrots, onions and parsnip.

3. Add stout, broth, thyme, remaining ½ teaspoon salt and ¼ teaspoon pepper to same skillet. Bring to a boil, scraping up browned bits from bottom of skillet. Pour into casserole; mix well.

4. Cover and bake 2½ to 3 hours or until beef is fork-tender, stirring once. Uncover; let stand at room temperature 15 minutes.

5. *Increase oven temperature to 425°F.* Place pie crust over casserole and press edges to seal. Cut slits in crust to vent. Bake 15 to 20 minutes or until crust is golden brown. Cool slightly before serving.

MAKES 4 TO 6 SERVINGS

Individual Beef Pot Pies: Instead of a refrigerated pie crust, use 1 sheet puff pastry (half of 17-ounce package). Divide beef filling among six individual ovenproof serving dishes. Cut puff pastry to fit, press over moistened edges and crimp to seal. Brush tops with 1 egg yolk, lightly beaten. Bake in preheated 400°F oven 15 to 20 minutes or until crust is puffed and golden.

Bangers and Mash

2 pounds bangers or fresh mild pork sausages

2 tablespoons vegetable oil, divided

2¼ pounds Yukon Gold potatoes, cut into 1-inch pieces

¾ cup milk, heated

3 tablespoons butter, melted

1½ teaspoons coarse salt

2 yellow onions, halved and thinly sliced (about 2 cups)

1 tablespoon butter

1 tablespoon flour

¼ cup red wine

1¼ cups reduced-sodium beef broth

Additional salt and black pepper

1. Preheat oven to 400°F. Line baking sheet with foil. Combine sausages and 1 tablespoon oil in large bowl; toss to coat. Place on prepared baking sheet; bake about 20 minutes or until cooked through and golden brown, turning once halfway through cooking.

2. Meanwhile, place potatoes in large saucepan; add cold water to cover by 2 inches. Bring to a boil over high heat. Reduce heat to medium-low; cook about 12 minutes or until tender. Drain well and press through ricer or mash with potato masher. Stir in warm milk, melted butter and 1½ teaspoons salt until well blended. Set aside and keep warm.

3. Heat remaining 1 tablespoon oil in medium saucepan over medium heat. Add onions; cover and cook about 20 minutes or until caramelized, adding ½ cup water halfway through cooking and stirring occasionally. Add 1 tablespoon butter; cook and stir until melted. Add flour; cook and stir 1 minute. Add wine; cook about 30 seconds or until almost evaporated. Add broth; cook over medium-high heat about 6 minutes or until thickened, stirring occasionally. Season with salt and pepper.

4. Serve bangers with mashed potatoes and onion gravy.

MAKES 4 TO 6 SERVINGS

Lamb Shanks Braised in Stout

4 lamb shanks, about 1 pound each*

¼ cup all-purpose flour

¼ cup vegetable oil, plus additional as needed

1 large onion, chopped (about 2 cups)

4 cloves garlic, minced

   Salt and black pepper

3 sprigs fresh rosemary

3 sprigs fresh thyme

1 bottle (about 11 ounces) Irish stout

2 to 3 cups reduced-sodium chicken broth

   Smashed Chat Potatoes (recipe follows)

1 tablespoon chopped fresh mint

For a more attractive presentation, ask butcher to "french" chops by removing flesh from last inch of bone end.

1. Preheat oven to 325°F. Trim excess fat from lamb. (Do not remove all fat or shanks will fall apart while cooking.) Dust lamb shanks with flour. Heat ¼ cup oil in large roasting pan or Dutch oven. Add lamb in batches; cook until browned on all sides. Remove to bowl.

2. Add oil to pan, if necessary, to make about 2 tablespoons. Add onion; cook and stir 2 minutes. Add garlic; cook and stir 2 minutes. Return lamb shanks and any accumulated juices to pan; sprinkle generously with salt and pepper. Tuck rosemary and thyme sprigs around lamb. Add stout to pan; pour in broth to almost cover lamb.

3. Cover and bake 2 hours or until lamb is very tender and almost falling off bones. Prepare Smashed Chat Potatoes.

4. Remove lamb shanks to plate; keep warm. Skim fat from juices in pan; boil until reduced by half. Strain sauce. Serve lamb over potatoes; sprinkle with mint.

MAKES 4 SERVINGS

Smashed Chat Potatoes

1 ½ to 2 pounds unpeeled small white potatoes
1 tablespoon butter
   Salt and black pepper

Place potatoes in large saucepan; add cold water to cover by 2 inches. Bring to a boil over high heat. Reduce heat to medium-low; simmer about 20 minutes or until fork-tender. Drain potatoes; return to saucepan and stir in butter until melted. Partially smash potatoes with fork or potato masher. Season with salt and pepper.

Note: In Irish dialect, "chat potatoes" are small white potatoes most often served whole and unpeeled after steaming or boiling. Any small potato may be substituted.

Beet and Goat Cheese Salad

1 pound whole beets with greens
3 quarts water
2⅛ teaspoons salt, divided
    Spring greens (optional)
2 tablespoons red wine vinegar
1 teaspoon Dijon mustard
¼ teaspoon black pepper
¼ cup extra virgin olive oil
¼ cup vegetable oil
½ cup chopped hazelnuts
4 ounces goat cheese

1. Cut off beet greens and set aside. Bring water and 2 teaspoons salt to a boil in large saucepan. Add beets; cook 20 to 25 minutes or until crisp-tender. Drain beets; peel under running water to help prevent staining fingers. Cut each beet into 8 pieces; place in large bowl.

2. Thoroughly wash beet greens; remove and discard tough stems. Tear greens into large pieces. Add spring greens, if necessary, to make 6 cups. Add greens to bowl with beets.

3. Whisk vinegar, mustard, pepper and remaining ⅛ teaspoon salt in medium bowl until blended. Slowly drizzle in olive oil and vegetable oil, whisking constantly.

4. Toast hazelnuts in small skillet over medium heat 5 minutes or until golden brown. Transfer to medium bowl; cool slightly. Stir in cheese. Form teaspoonfuls of cheese mixture into balls. Toss beets and greens with dressing; top with cheese balls.

MAKES 4 SERVINGS

 tip The beets, dressing and cheese balls can be all prepared in advance. Assemble the salad just before serving.

Mussels Steamed in Guinness >

    5 tablespoons butter, divided
    ½ cup chopped shallots
    2 stalks celery, chopped
    1 medium carrot, chopped
    8 sprigs fresh parsley
    ⅔ cup Guinness
    2 pounds mussels, scrubbed and debearded
        Crusty bread

1. Melt 1 tablespoon butter in large saucepan over medium-high heat. Add shallots, celery, carrot and parsley; cook and stir 2 to 3 minutes or until vegetables begin to soften.

2. Add Guinness; bring to a boil and cook 2 minutes. Add mussels; cover and return to a boil. Cook 4 to 5 minutes or until mussels open. Uncover and cook 1 minute.

3. Remove from heat; discard any unopened mussels. Stir in remaining 4 tablespoons butter. Serve immediately in bowls with bread.

MAKES 4 APPETIZER OR 2 MAIN-DISH SERVINGS

Cheese and Beer Fondue

    ¾ cup lager
    1 teaspoon mustard
    ¼ teaspoon Worcestershire sauce
    ⅛ teaspoon ground red pepper
    2 cups (8 ounces) shredded sharp Cheddar cheese
  1½ tablespoons all-purpose flour
        Sliced bread

1. Whisk lager, mustard, Worcestershire sauce and red pepper in large saucepan; bring to a boil over high heat. Reduce heat to medium-low.

2. Combine cheese and flour in medium bowl. Add to beer mixture, 1 cup at a time, whisking after each addition until smooth. Gently boil 2 minutes, stirring constantly. Serve with bread.

MAKES 6 SERVINGS

Beef Wellington

6 center-cut beef tenderloin steaks, 1 inch thick (about 2½ pounds)
¾ teaspoon salt, divided
½ teaspoon black pepper, divided
2 tablespoons butter
8 ounces cremini or button mushrooms, finely chopped
¼ cup finely chopped shallots
2 tablespoons ruby port or sweet Madeira wine
1 package (about 17 ounces) frozen puff pastry, thawed
1 egg, separated
½ cup (4 ounces) prepared liver pâté*
2 teaspoons water

Pâté can be found in the gourmet or deli section of most supermarkets or in specialty food stores.

1. Sprinkle beef with ½ teaspoon salt and ¼ teaspoon pepper. Heat large skillet over medium-high heat until hot. Cook beef in batches about 3 minutes per side or until well browned and beef is 110°F (very rare). Remove to plate; set aside to let cool.

2. Melt butter in same skillet over medium heat. Add mushrooms and shallots; cook and stir 5 minutes or until mushrooms are tender. Add port, remaining ¼ teaspoon salt and ¼ teaspoon pepper; bring to a boil. Reduce heat to low; simmer 10 minutes or until liquid evaporates, stirring frequently. Remove from heat; cool completely.

3. Roll out each pastry sheet to 18×10-inch rectangle on lightly floured surface with lightly floured rolling pin. Cut each sheet into 3 (10×6-inch) rectangles. Cut small amount of pastry from corners to use for decoration, if desired.

4. Whisk egg white in small bowl until foamy; brush over each pastry rectangle. Place one cooled steak on each pastry rectangle. Spread pâté over beef, dividing evenly. Top with mushroom mixture and press lightly to adhere.

5. Fold pastry over beef; press edges to seal. Cut pastry scraps into shapes and use to decorate; if desired. Place on ungreased baking sheet.

6. Whisk egg yolk and water in small bowl. Brush pastry with egg yolk mixture. Cover loosely with plastic wrap; refrigerate 1 to 4 hours before baking.

7. Preheat oven to 400°F. Bake 20 to 25 minutes or until pastry is puffed and golden brown and beef is 145°F (medium). Let stand 10 minutes before serving.

MAKES 6 SERVINGS

Shepherd's Pie

3 medium russet potatoes (1½ pounds), peeled and cut into 1-inch pieces
½ cup milk
5 tablespoons butter, divided
1 teaspoon salt, divided
½ teaspoon black pepper, divided
2 medium onions, chopped
2 medium carrots, finely chopped
½ teaspoon dried thyme
1½ pounds ground lamb
3 tablespoons tomato paste
1 tablespoon Worcestershire sauce
1½ cups reduced-sodium beef broth
½ cup frozen peas

1. Preheat oven to 350°F. Spray 1½-quart baking dish with nonstick cooking spray.

2. Place potatoes in large saucepan; add cold water to cover by 2 inches. Bring to a boil over medium-high heat; cook 16 to 18 minutes or until tender. Drain potatoes; return to saucepan.

3. Heat milk in small saucepan over medium-high heat until hot. Add 3 tablespoons butter, ½ teaspoon salt and ¼ teaspoon pepper; stir until butter is melted. Pour milk mixture into saucepan with potatoes; mash until smooth. Set aside.

4. Melt remaining 2 tablespoons butter in large skillet over medium heat. Add onions, carrots and thyme; cook 8 to 10 minutes or until vegetables are softened but not browned, stirring occasionally. Add lamb; cook over medium-high heat 4 minutes or until no longer pink. Drain excess fat. Return skillet to heat; cook 5 to 6 minutes or until lamb is lightly browned. Add tomato paste and Worcestershire sauce; cook 1 minute. Stir in broth; bring to a boil and cook 7 to 8 minutes or until nearly evaporated. Stir in peas, remaining ½ teaspoon salt and ¼ teaspoon pepper; cook 30 seconds. Spoon mixture into prepared baking dish.

5. Spread mashed potatoes in even layer over lamb mixture; use spatula to swirl potatoes or fork to make crosshatch design on top.

6. Bake about 35 minutes or until filling is hot and bubbly and potatoes begin to brown.

MAKES 4 TO 6 SERVINGS

Sausage and Cabbage Skillet

2 tablespoons olive oil

1 pound pork sausage, cut in half lengthwise then cut diagonally into ¾-inch slices

1 onion, thinly sliced

2 teaspoons fennel seeds

1 teaspoon caraway seeds

1 clove garlic, minced

½ cup water

1 pound cabbage (6 cups or ½ head), thinly sliced

2 pounds (5 medium) red potatoes, cut into ¾-inch pieces

1 bottle (12 ounces) lager or ale

½ teaspoon salt

¼ teaspoon black pepper

1. Heat oil in large skillet over medium heat. Add sausage; cook 5 minutes or until browned, stirring occasionally. Remove to plate.

2. Add onion, fennel seeds, caraway seeds and garlic to skillet; cook and stir 3 minutes or until onion is translucent. Add ½ cup water, scraping up browned bits from bottom of skillet. Add cabbage and potatoes; cook 10 minutes or until cabbage is wilted, stirring occasionally.

3. Stir in lager; cover and cook over medium-low heat 15 minutes or until potatoes are tender. Season with salt and pepper; cook over medium heat 15 minutes until liquid has reduced to sauce consistency. Return sausage to skillet; cook until heated through.

MAKES 6 SERVINGS

Ham with Dark Beer Gravy

1 fully cooked bone-in ham (about 6 pounds)
1 tablespoon Dijon mustard
2 cans (6 ounces each) pineapple juice
1 bottle (12 ounces) dark beer, such as porter
   Dark Beer Gravy (recipe follows)

1. Line large roasting pan with foil.

2. Remove skin and excess fat from ham. Score ham in diamond pattern.

3. Place ham in prepared pan. Spread mustard over ham. Pour pineapple juice and beer over ham. Cover and refrigerate 8 hours.

4. Preheat oven to 350°F. Cook ham 1½ hours or until 140°F, basting every 30 minutes. Remove ham to cutting board. Cover loosely with foil; let stand 15 minutes before slicing.

5. Meanwhile, pour drippings from pan into 4-cup measuring cup. Let stand 5 minutes; skim off and discard fat. Prepare Dark Beer Gravy; serve with ham.

MAKES 10 TO 12 SERVINGS

Dark Beer Gravy

¼ cup (½ stick) butter
¼ cup all-purpose flour
½ cup dark beer, such as porter
2 cups drippings from roasting pan
   Salt and black pepper

Melt butter in small saucepan over medium heat. Whisk in flour until blended. Cook 1 to 2 minutes, whisking constantly. Add beer to drippings; whisk into flour mixture. Cook until mixture is thickened and bubbly, whisking constantly. Season with salt and pepper.

MAKES 2½ CUPS

Blue Cheese Stuffed Sirloin Patties

1½ pounds ground beef sirloin

½ cup (2 ounces) shredded sharp Cheddar cheese

¼ cup crumbled blue cheese

¼ cup finely chopped fresh parsley

2 teaspoons Dijon mustard

1 teaspoon Worcestershire sauce

1 clove garlic, minced

¼ teaspoon salt

2 teaspoons olive oil

1 medium red bell pepper, cut into thin strips

1. Shape beef into eight patties, about 4 inches in diameter and ¼ inch thick.

2. Combine cheeses, parsley, mustard, Worcestershire sauce, garlic and ¼ teaspoon salt in small bowl; toss gently.

3. Mound one fourth of cheese mixture on each of four patties (about 3 tablespoons per patty). Top with remaining four patties; pinch edges of patties to seal completely.

4. Heat oil in large skillet over medium-high heat until hot. Add bell pepper; cook and stir 5 minutes or until edges begin to brown. Sprinkle with additional salt. Remove to plate; keep warm.

5. Add beef patties to same skillet; cook 5 minutes. Turn patties; top with peppers. Cook 4 minutes or until medium (160°F) or to desired doneness.

MAKES 4 SERVINGS

Lamb and Mint Hand Pies

2 cups plus 1 tablespoon all-purpose flour, divided
1 teaspoon salt, divided
10 tablespoons cold butter, cut into small pieces
7 to 8 tablespoons ice water
1 pound ground lamb
1 small onion, finely chopped
1 carrot, finely chopped
½ cup reduced-sodium beef broth
1 teaspoon Dijon mustard
¼ teaspoon black pepper
1 tablespoon chopped fresh mint
½ cup (2 ounces) shredded Irish Cheddar cheese
1 egg, lightly beaten

1. Combine 2 cups flour and ½ teaspoon salt in medium bowl. Cut in butter with pastry blender or two knives until mixture resembles coarse crumbs. Add water, 1 tablespoon at a time, stirring with fork until loose dough forms. Knead dough in bowl 1 to 2 times until it comes together. Divide dough into four pieces; press each into 4-inch disc. Wrap dough with plastic wrap; freeze 15 minutes.

2. Meanwhile, prepare filling. Heat large skillet over medium-high heat. Add lamb; cook 7 to 8 minutes or until lightly browned, stirring occasionally. Drain well; remove to plate. Add onion and carrot to skillet; cook 2 to 3 minutes or until vegetables begin to soften, stirring occasionally. Stir in lamb; cook 1 minute. Add remaining 1 tablespoon flour; cook and stir 1 minute. Add broth, mustard, remaining ½ teaspoon salt and pepper; cook over medium heat about 2 minutes or until thickened. Remove from heat; stir in mint. Cool 10 minutes. Stir in cheese.

3. Position rack in center of oven. Preheat oven to 400°F. Line large baking sheet with parchment paper or spray with nonstick cooking spray.

4. Working with one disc at a time, roll out dough into 9-inch circle on lightly floured surface. Cut out four circles with 4-inch round cookie cutter (16 circles total). Place 8 dough circles on prepared baking sheet. Top each with one eighth of lamb filling, leaving ½-inch border around edge of circle. Top with remaining dough circles, pressing edges to seal. Press edges again with tines of fork. Brush tops with egg; cut 1-inch slit in top of each pie with tip of knife.

5. Bake 28 to 30 minutes or until golden brown. Serve hot or at room temperature.

MAKES 4 MAIN-DISH OR 8 APPETIZER SERVINGS

Tip: Pies can be made 1 day ahead and refrigerated, then reheated before serving.

BREADS

Irish Soda Bread

2½ cups all-purpose flour

1¼ cups whole wheat flour

1 cup currants

¼ cup sugar

4 teaspoons baking powder

2 teaspoons caraway seeds (optional)

1 teaspoon salt

½ teaspoon baking soda

½ cup (1 stick) butter, cut into small pieces

1⅓ to 1½ cups buttermilk

1. Preheat oven to 350°F. Grease large baking sheet.

2. Combine all-purpose flour, whole wheat flour, currants, sugar, baking powder, caraway seeds, if desired, salt and baking soda in large bowl.

3. Cut in butter with pastry blender or two knives until mixture resembles coarse crumbs. Add buttermilk; mix until slightly sticky dough forms. Place dough on prepared baking sheet; shape into 8-inch round.

4. Bake 50 to 60 minutes or until bread is golden and crust is firm. Cool on baking sheet 10 minutes; remove to wire rack to cool completely.

MAKES 1 LOAF

Honey Scones

Cherry Compote (optional, recipe follows)
2 cups all-purpose flour
½ cup old-fashioned oats
2 tablespoons packed brown sugar
1 tablespoon granulated sugar
1 tablespoon baking powder
½ teaspoon salt
6 tablespoons butter, melted
1 egg
¼ cup whipping cream
¼ cup milk
3 tablespoons honey

1. Prepare Cherry Compote, if desired.

2. Preheat oven to 425°F. Line baking sheet with parchment paper.

3. Combine flour, oats, brown sugar, granulated sugar, baking powder and salt in large bowl. Whisk butter, egg, cream, milk and honey in medium bowl until well blended. Add to flour mixture; stir just until dough forms. Turn out dough onto lightly floured surface. Pat into 8-inch round about ¾ inch thick. Cut into eight triangles; place 1 to 2 inches apart on prepared baking sheet.

4. Bake 12 to 15 minutes or until golden brown. Remove to wire rack to cool 15 minutes. Serve warm with Cherry Compote, if desired.

MAKES 8 SCONES

Cherry Compote

1 pound fresh Bing cherries, pitted and halved
¼ cup sugar
¼ cup water
2 tablespoons lemon juice

1. Combine cherries, sugar, water and lemon juice in medium heavy saucepan; bring to a boil over medium heat, stirring frequently. Boil 2 minutes. Remove cherries with slotted spoon; set aside.

2. Reduce heat to medium-low; simmer 2 to 4 minutes or until liquid thickens. Return cherries to saucepan; remove from heat. Cool 1 hour before serving.

MAKES ABOUT 2 CUPS

Rhubarb Bread

2 cups all-purpose flour

1 cup sugar

1 tablespoon baking powder

1 teaspoon salt

¼ teaspoon ground cinnamon

1 cup milk

2 eggs

⅓ cup butter, melted

2 teaspoons grated fresh ginger (about 1 inch)

10 ounces chopped fresh rhubarb (¼-inch pieces, about 2¼ cups total)

¾ cup chopped walnuts, toasted*

To toast walnuts, spread in single layer on ungreased baking sheet. Bake in preheated 350°F oven 6 to 8 minutes or until lightly browned, stirring frequently.

1. Preheat oven to 350°F. Generously grease 9×5-inch loaf pan.

2. Combine flour, sugar, baking powder, salt and cinnamon in large bowl. Whisk milk, eggs, butter and ginger in medium bowl until well blended. Add to flour mixture; stir just until dry ingredients are moistened. Add rhubarb and walnuts; stir just until blended. Pour batter into prepared pan.

3. Bake 60 to 65 minutes or until toothpick inserted into center comes out clean. Cool in pan on wire rack 15 minutes; remove to wire rack to cool completely.

MAKES 12 SERVINGS

Beer and Bacon Muffins

6 slices bacon, chopped

2 cups chopped onions

3 teaspoons sugar, divided

¼ teaspoon dried thyme

1½ cups all-purpose flour

¾ cup grated Parmesan cheese

2 teaspoons baking powder

½ teaspoon salt

¾ cup lager or other light-colored beer

2 eggs

¼ cup extra virgin olive oil

1. Preheat oven to 375°F. Grease 12 standard (2½-inch) muffin cups.

2. Cook bacon in large skillet over medium heat until crisp, stirring occasionally. Drain on paper towel-lined plate. Add onions, 1 teaspoon sugar and thyme to skillet; cook 12 minutes or until onions are golden brown, stirring occasionally. Cool 5 minutes; stir in bacon.

3. Combine flour, cheese, baking powder, salt and remaining 2 teaspoons sugar in large bowl. Whisk lager, eggs and oil in medium bowl until well blended. Add to flour mixture; stir just until dry ingredients are moistened. Gently stir in onion mixture. Spoon batter evenly into prepared muffin cups.

4. Bake 15 minutes or until toothpick inserted into centers comes out clean. Cool in pan 5 minutes; remove to wire rack. Serve warm or at room temperature.

MAKES 12 MUFFINS

Treacle Bread (Brown Soda Bread)

2 cups all-purpose flour

1 cup whole wheat flour

1 teaspoon baking soda

½ teaspoon salt

½ teaspoon ground ginger

1¼ cups buttermilk, plus additional as needed

3 tablespoons dark molasses (preferably blackstrap)

1. Preheat oven to 375°F. Line baking sheet with parchment paper.

2. Combine all-purpose flour, whole wheat flour, baking soda, salt and ginger in large bowl. Whisk 1¼ cups buttermilk and molasses in small bowl until well blended.

3. Stir buttermilk mixture into flour mixture. Add additional buttermilk by tablespoonfuls if necessary to make dry, rough dough. Turn out dough onto floured surface; knead 8 to 10 times or just until smooth. (Do not overknead.) Shape dough into round loaf about 1½ inches thick. Place on prepared baking sheet.

4. Use floured knife to cut halfway through dough, scoring into quarters (called farls in Ireland). Sprinkle top of dough with additional flour, if desired.

5. Bake about 35 minutes or until bread sounds hollow when tapped. Remove to wire rack to cool slightly. Serve warm.

MAKES 6 TO 8 SERVINGS

Note: Treacle Bread can be sliced or pulled apart into farls.

Irish-Style Scones

3 eggs, divided
½ cup whipping cream
1½ teaspoons vanilla
2 cups all-purpose flour
2 teaspoons baking powder
¼ teaspoon salt
¼ cup (½ stick) cold butter, cut into small pieces
¼ cup finely chopped pitted dates
¼ cup golden raisins or currants
1 teaspoon water
Orange marmalade
Crème fraîche or whipped cream

1. Preheat oven to 375°F. Line large baking sheet with parchment paper.

2. Whisk 2 eggs, cream and vanilla in medium bowl until well blended. Combine flour, baking powder and salt in large bowl. Cut in butter with pastry blender or two knives until mixture resembles coarse crumbs. Stir in dates and raisins. Add cream mixture; mix just until dry ingredients are moistened.

3. Turn out dough onto lightly floured surface; knead 4 times with floured hands. Place dough on prepared baking sheet; pat into 8-inch circle. Gently score dough into six wedges with sharp wet knife, cutting three-fourths of the way through dough. Beat remaining egg and water in small bowl; brush lightly over dough.

4. Bake 18 to 20 minutes or until golden brown. Remove to wire rack to cool 5 minutes. Cut into wedges; serve warm with marmalade and crème fraîche.

MAKES 6 SCONES

Oatmeal Honey Bread

1½ to 2 cups all-purpose flour

1 cup plus 1 tablespoon old-fashioned oats, divided

½ cup whole wheat flour

1 package (¼ ounce) rapid-rise active dry yeast

1 teaspoon salt

1⅓ cups plus 1 tablespoon water, divided

¼ cup honey

2 tablespoons butter

1 egg

1. Combine 1½ cups all-purpose flour, 1 cup oats, whole wheat flour, yeast and salt in large bowl.

2. Heat 1⅓ cups water, honey and butter in small saucepan over low heat until honey dissolves and butter melts. Let cool to 130°F (temperature of very hot tap water). Add to flour mixture; beat with electric mixer at medium speed 2 minutes. Add additional flour by tablespoonfuls until dough begins to cling together. Dough should be shaggy and very sticky, not dry. (Dough should not form a ball and/or clean side of bowl.)

3. Attach dough hook to mixer; knead at medium-low speed 4 minutes. Place dough in large greased bowl; turn to grease top. Cover and let rise in warm place 45 minutes or until doubled in size.

4. Spray 8×4-inch loaf pan with nonstick cooking spray. Punch down dough; turn out onto floured surface. Flatten and stretch dough into 8-inch-long oval. Bring long sides together and pinch to seal; fold over short ends and pinch to seal. Place seam side down in prepared pan. Cover and let rise in warm place 20 to 30 minutes or until dough reaches top of pan.

5. Preheat oven to 375°F. Beat egg and remaining 1 tablespoon water in small bowl. Brush top of loaf with egg mixture; sprinkle with remaining 1 tablespoon oats.

6. Bake 30 to 35 minutes or until bread sounds hollow when tapped (about 190°F). Remove to wire rack to cool completely.

MAKES 1 LOAF

Bacon-Cheddar Muffins

    2 cups all-purpose flour
    ¾ cup sugar
    2 teaspoons baking powder
    ½ teaspoon baking soda
    ½ teaspoon salt
    ¾ cup plus 2 tablespoons milk
    ⅓ cup butter, melted
    1 egg
    1 cup (4 ounces) shredded Cheddar cheese
    ½ cup crumbled crisp-cooked bacon (about 6 slices)

1. Preheat oven to 350°F. Grease 12 standard (2½-inch) muffins cups or line with paper baking cups.

2. Combine flour, sugar, baking powder, baking soda and salt in medium bowl. Whisk milk, butter and egg in small bowl until blended. Add to flour mixture; stir just until dry ingredients are moistened. Fold in cheese and bacon. Spoon batter evenly into prepared muffin cups.

3. Bake 15 to 20 minutes or until toothpick inserted into centers comes out clean. Cool in pan 2 minutes; remove to wire rack. Serve warm or at room temperature.

MAKES 12 MUFFINS

Barm Brack

4 to 4½ cups all-purpose flour
½ cup plus 1 teaspoon sugar, divided
1 package (¼ ounce) rapid-rise active dry yeast
1 teaspoon salt
½ teaspoon ground cinnamon
¼ teaspoon ground nutmeg
¾ cup plus 1 tablespoon water, divided
¾ cup milk
¼ cup (½ stick) butter, softened
1 egg
1 cup golden raisins (optional)
½ cup chopped dried or candied fruit (apricots, cherries, prunes, etc.)

1. Place 4 cups flour in large bowl. Stir in ½ cup sugar, yeast, salt, cinnamon and nutmeg. Combine ¾ cup water, milk and butter in small saucepan; heat over low heat until butter melts and temperature reaches 120° to 130°F. Add to flour mixture; beat with electric mixer at medium speed 2 minutes or until well blended. Beat in egg.

2. Gradually add additional flour, if necessary, until slightly sticky dough forms. Attach dough hook to mixer; knead at low speed 4 minutes or knead by hand 8 minutes on lightly floured surface. Place in greased bowl; turn to grease top. Cover and let rise in warm place 45 minutes to 1 hour or until doubled in size.

3. Spray two 8×4-inch loaf pans with nonstick cooking spray. Punch down dough; turn out onto floured surface. Knead in raisins, if desired, and dried fruit. Divide dough into two balls; cover and let rest 5 minutes. To shape loaves, flatten and stretch each ball of dough into oval shape. Bring long sides together and pinch to seal; fold over short ends and pinch to seal. Place seam side down in prepared pans. Cover and let rise 45 minutes or until dough almost reaches tops of pans.

4. Preheat oven to 375°F. Bake 35 to 40 minutes or until browned. (Cover loosely with foil if loaves begin to overbrown.) Dissolve remaining 1 teaspoon sugar in 1 tablespoon water in small bowl. Brush over loaves; bake 2 minutes. Cool in pans 2 minutes; remove to wire rack to cool slightly. Serve warm.

MAKES 2 LOAVES

Note: This fruity loaf is traditionally served on Halloween. Charms are baked into the bread to predict the future. If your piece of barm brack contains a ring, you will get married within the year; if you find a coin, you'll become rich. If you wish to add charms to the recipe, wrap them in parchment paper (to avoid eating them accidentally). Knead the charms into the dough along with the dried fruit.

Buttermilk Biscuits

2 cups all-purpose flour
1 tablespoon baking powder
2 teaspoons sugar
½ teaspoon salt
½ teaspoon baking soda
⅓ cup shortening
⅔ cup buttermilk*

Or substitute soured fresh milk. To sour milk, combine 2½ teaspoons lemon juice plus enough milk to equal ⅔ cup. Stir; let stand 5 minutes before using.

1. Preheat oven to 450°F.

2. Combine flour, baking powder, sugar, salt and baking soda in medium bowl. Cut in shortening with pastry blender or two knives until mixture resembles coarse crumbs. Make well in center of dry ingredients. Add buttermilk; stir until mixture forms soft dough that clings together and forms a ball.

3. Turn out dough onto well-floured surface; knead gently 10 to 12 times. Roll or pat dough to ½-inch thickness. Cut out dough with floured 2½-inch biscuit cutter. Place 2 inches apart on ungreased baking sheet.

4. Bake 8 to 10 minutes or until golden brown. Serve warm.

MAKES ABOUT 9 BISCUITS

Drop Biscuits: Prepare Buttermilk Biscuits as directed in step 2, increasing buttermilk to 1 cup. Stir batter with wooden spoon about 15 strokes. *Do not knead.* Drop dough by heaping tablespoonfuls 1 inch apart onto greased baking sheets. Bake as directed in step 4. Makes about 18 biscuits.

Sour Cream Dill Biscuits: Prepare Buttermilk Biscuits as directed in step 2, omitting buttermilk. Combine ½ cup sour cream, ⅓ cup milk and 1 tablespoon chopped fresh dill in small bowl until well blended. Stir into dry ingredients and continue as directed. Makes about 9 biscuits.

Oatmeal Raisin Nut Bread

  3 cups bread flour, divided
  1 cup old-fashioned oats
  1 package (¼ ounce) rapid-rise active dry yeast
1½ teaspoons salt
1½ teaspoons ground cinnamon
  1 cup plus 2 tablespoons warm water (130°F)
  ¼ cup honey
  2 tablespoons canola oil
  1 cup raisins
  ¾ cup chopped pecans

1. Combine 1 cup flour, oats, yeast, salt and cinnamon in large bowl of electric stand mixer. Whisk water, honey and oil in medium bowl until well blended. Add to flour mixture; beat 3 minutes with paddle attachment.

2. Replace paddle attachment with dough hook; beat in enough remaining flour until soft dough forms. Knead at medium-low speed 6 to 8 minutes or until dough is smooth and elastic. Add raisins and pecans; knead until well incorporated. Place dough in greased bowl; turn to grease top. Cover and let rise in warm place about 40 minutes or until doubled in size.

3. Spray 9×5-inch loaf pan with nonstick cooking spray. Punch down dough. Roll out dough into 14×8-inch rectangle on lightly floured surface. Starting with short side, roll up tightly jelly-roll style; pinch seam to seal. Place seam side down in prepared pan. Cover and let rise about 30 minutes or until doubled in size. Preheat oven to 375°F.

4. Bake 30 to 40 minutes or until top is browned and loaf sounds hollow when tapped.

MAKES 1 LOAF

Orange-Currant Scones

1 ½ cups all-purpose flour

¼ cup plus 1 teaspoon sugar, divided

1 teaspoon baking powder

¼ teaspoon salt

¼ teaspoon baking soda

⅓ cup currants

1 tablespoon grated orange peel

6 tablespoons (¾ stick) cold butter, cut into small pieces

½ cup buttermilk, yogurt or sour cream

1. Preheat oven to 425°F. Line large baking sheet with parchment paper.

2. Combine flour, ¼ cup sugar, baking powder, salt and baking soda in large bowl. Stir in currants and orange peel. Cut in butter with pastry blender or two knives until mixture resembles coarse crumbs. Add buttermilk; stir until mixture forms soft sticky dough that clings together.

3. Shape dough into a ball; pat into 8-inch round on prepared baking sheet. Cut dough into 8 wedges with floured knife. Sprinkle with remaining 1 teaspoon sugar.

4. Bake 18 to 20 minutes or until lightly browned. Remove to wire rack to cool 5 minutes. Serve warm.

MAKES 8 SCONES

DESSERTS

Bread and Butter Pudding

3 tablespoons butter, softened, plus addtional for baking dish
1 pound egg bread or firm white bread, sliced
⅔ cup golden raisins
¾ cup sugar, divided
1 teaspoon ground cinnamon
¼ teaspoon ground nutmeg
2 cups half-and-half
2 cups whole milk
6 eggs
1½ teaspoons vanilla

1. Preheat oven to 350°F. Butter 1½-quart or 13×9-inch baking dish.

2. Lightly butter both sides of bread slices. Cut into 1½-inch pieces. Combine bread and raisins in prepared baking dish. Combine ¼ cup sugar, cinnamon and nutmeg in small bowl; sprinkle over bread mixture and toss to coat.

3. Whisk half-and-half, milk, eggs, remaining ½ cup sugar and vanilla in large bowl until well blended. Pour over bread mixture; let stand 10 minutes.

4. Bake about 1 hour or until pudding is set, puffed and golden brown. Serve warm or at room temperature.

MAKES 8 TO 10 SERVINGS

Strawberry-Rhubarb Crisp

4 cups sliced rhubarb (1-inch pieces)

3 cups sliced strawberries (about 1 pint)

¾ cup granulated sugar

⅓ cup plus ¼ cup all-purpose flour, divided

1 tablespoon grated lemon peel

1 cup quick oats

½ cup packed brown sugar

1 teaspoon ground cinnamon

½ teaspoon salt

⅓ cup butter, melted

1. Preheat oven to 375°F. Combine rhubarb and strawberries in large bowl.

2. Combine granulated sugar, ¼ cup flour and lemon peel in small bowl. Sprinkle over fruit; toss to coat. Spoon into 9-inch square baking pan.

3. Combine oats, brown sugar, remaining ⅓ cup flour, cinnamon and salt in medium bowl. Stir in butter until mixture is crumbly. Sprinkle over rhubarb mixture.

4. Bake 45 to 50 minutes or until filling is bubbly and topping is lightly browned. Serve warm or at room temperature.

MAKES 8 SERVINGS

Porter Cake

3½ cups all-purpose flour, plus additional for pan

1½ teaspoons pumpkin pie spice

1 teaspoon baking powder

½ teaspoon salt

1 cup (2 sticks) butter

1 (10-ounce) bottle porter or stout

1 cup packed brown sugar

1½ cups golden raisins

1½ cups raisins

Finely grated peel of 1 orange

2 eggs, lightly beaten

¼ chopped candied citrus peel

¼ cup candied cherries

1. Preheat oven to 350°F. Grease 9-inch springform pan; line bottom with parchment paper. Grease parchment paper; dust bottom and side of pan with flour, tapping out excess. Line baking sheet with foil.

2. Combine 3½ cups flour, pumpkin pie spice, baking powder and salt in large bowl. Combine butter, porter and brown sugar in large saucepan; cook over medium heat about 7 minutes or until butter is melted and sugar is dissolved, stirring occasionally. Remove from heat; stir in raisins and orange peel. Let cool about 15 minutes or until just warm.

3. Add porter mixture and eggs to flour mixture; stir just until combined. Fold in candied citrus peel and cherries. Pour batter into prepared pan; place on prepared baking sheet.

4. Bake 60 to 65 minutes or until toothpick inserted into center comes out clean. Cool in pan on wire rack 15 minutes; remove side of pan and cool completely on wire rack.

MAKES 10 SERVINGS

Oatmeal Brûlée with Raspberry Sauce

4 cups water

½ teaspoon salt

3 cups old-fashioned oats

1 cup whipping cream

½ teaspoon vanilla

¾ cup granulated sugar, divided

3 egg yolks

2 tablespoons packed brown sugar

6 ounces frozen raspberries, thawed

¼ cup water

1. Preheat oven to 300°F. Line baking sheet with foil.

2. Bring 4 cups water and salt to a boil in medium saucepan over high heat. Add oats; cook over low heat 3 to 5 minutes or until water is absorbed and oats are tender, stirring occasionally. Divide oatmeal among four large ramekins or ovenproof bowls. Place on prepared baking sheet.

3. Bring cream to a simmer in small saucepan over medium heat. *Do not boil.* Remove from heat; stir in vanilla. Whisk ¼ cup granulated sugar and egg yolks in medium bowl until blended. Slowly pour about ½ cup hot cream into egg mixture, whisking constantly. Stir egg mixture back into saucepan with cream, whisking until well blended. Pour cream mixture evenly over oatmeal in ramekins.

4. Bake 35 minutes or until nearly set. Remove from oven; *turn oven to broil.*

5. Meanwhile, combine raspberries, remaining ½ cup granulated sugar and water in blender or food processor; blend until smooth. Strain sauce.

6. Sprinkle ½ tablespoon brown sugar evenly over each cup. Broil 3 to 5 minutes or until sugar melts and browns slightly. Cool 5 to 10 minutes before serving. Serve with raspberry sauce.

MAKES 4 SERVINGS

Rustic Apple Tart

Rustic Tart Dough (recipe follows)
2 pounds Golden Delicious apples, peeled and cut into ½-inch wedges
2 tablespoons lemon juice
½ cup plus 2 tablespoons sugar, divided
½ cup raisins
2 tablespoons plus 1½ teaspoons apple brandy,* divided
1 teaspoon ground cinnamon
3 tablespoons butter, cut into small pieces
1 cup apricot jam
Whipped cream or crème fraiche (optional)

*Any brandy or cognac can be substituted.

1. Prepare Rustic Tart Dough.

2. Preheat oven to 400°F. Combine apples and lemon juice in large bowl. Add ½ cup sugar, raisins, 2 tablespoons brandy and cinnamon; toss gently to coat.

3. Cut piece of parchment paper to fit 15×10-inch jelly-roll pan. Place parchment on counter; sprinkle with flour. Place dough on parchment; sprinkle lightly with flour. Roll dough into 18×16-inch oval about ¼ inch thick. Transfer parchment and dough to baking sheet.

4. Spread apple mixture over dough, leaving 2-inch border. Dot apple mixture with butter. Fold edge of dough up and over filling, overlapping as necessary. Press gently to adhere to filling. Sprinkle edge of dough with remaining 2 tablespoons sugar.

5. Bake 50 to 55 minutes or until crust is browned and apples are tender. Cool slightly.

6. Meanwhile, strain jam through sieve into small saucepan; cook and stir over low heat until smooth. Stir in remaining 1½ teaspoons brandy. Brush warm tart with jam mixture. Serve with whipped cream, if desired.

MAKES 8 SERVINGS

Rustic Tart Dough

    2 cups all-purpose flour
    1 teaspoon sugar
    1 teaspoon grated lemon peel
    ½ teaspoon salt
    ½ teaspoon ground cinnamon
    ½ cup cold shortening, cut into small pieces
    ½ cup (1 stick) cold butter, cut into small pieces
    ⅓ cup ice water

1. Combine flour, sugar, lemon peel, salt and cinnamon in food processor; process until blended.

2. Add shortening; pulse until mixture forms pea-sized chunks. Add butter; pulse until dough resembles coarse crumbs. Add water; process just until dough begins to come together. Shape dough into 6-inch disc; wrap with plastic wrap. Refrigerate at least 1 hour or overnight.

Gingerbread with Lemon Sauce

2½ cups all-purpose flour

1½ teaspoons ground cinnamon

1 teaspoon ground ginger

½ teaspoon baking soda

½ teaspoon salt

½ cup (1 stick) butter, softened

¾ cup packed brown sugar

⅓ cup light molasses

1 egg

¾ cup stout, at room temperature

Lemon Sauce (recipe follows)

Grated lemon peel (optional)

1. Preheat oven to 350°F. Spray bottom of 9-inch square baking pan with nonstick cooking spray.

2. Combine flour, cinnamon, ginger, baking soda and salt in medium bowl. Beat butter and brown sugar in large bowl with electric mixer at medium speed until light and fluffy. Add molasses and egg; beat until blended. Add flour mixture alternately with stout, beating until blended after each addition. Pour batter evenly into prepared pan.

3. Bake 35 to 40 minutes or until toothpick inserted into center comes out clean. Cool completely in pan on wire rack. Prepare Lemon Sauce.

4. Serve cake with sauce; sprinkle with lemon peel, if desired.

MAKES 9 SERVINGS

Lemon Sauce

1 cup granulated sugar

¾ cup whipping cream

½ cup (1 stick) butter

1 tablespoon lemon juice

2 teaspoons grated lemon peel

Combine granulated sugar, cream and butter in small saucepan; cook and stir over medium heat until butter is melted. Reduce heat to low; simmer 5 minutes. Stir in lemon juice and lemon peel. Cool slightly.

Irish Soda Bread Cookies >

2 cups all-purpose flour
½ teaspoon baking soda
¼ teaspoon salt
½ cup (1 stick) butter, softened
½ cup sugar
1 egg
¾ cup currants
1 teaspoon caraway seeds
⅓ cup buttermilk

1. Preheat oven to 350°F. Line cookie sheets with parchment paper.

2. Combine flour, baking soda and salt in medium bowl. Beat butter and sugar in large bowl with electric mixer at medium speed until fluffy. Add egg; beat 1 minute until combined. Add flour mixture; beat on low speed until combined. Add currants and caraway seeds; mix well. Add buttermilk; mix until combined. Drop dough by tablespoonfuls 1 inch apart on prepared cookie sheets.

3. Bake 12 to 15 minutes or until edges begin to brown. Remove to wire rack to cool slightly. Serve warm.

MAKES ABOUT 3 DOZEN COOKIES

Poached Dried Fruit Compote

1½ cups water
8 ounces mixed dried fruit, such as apricots, pears, apples and prunes
½ cup Riesling or other white wine
2 cinnamon sticks
4 whole cloves

1. Combine water, dried fruit, wine, cinnamon sticks and cloves in medium saucepan; bring to a boil over high heat.

2. Reduce heat to low; simmer, uncovered, 12 to 15 minutes or until fruit is tender. Cool slightly. Discard cinnamon sticks and cloves. Serve warm, at room temperature or chilled.

MAKES 6 SERVINGS

Pecan Bread Pudding with Caramel Whiskey Sauce

8 cups cubed egg bread or brioche (about 10 ounces)

½ cup coarsely chopped pecans, toasted*

1⅔ cups sugar, divided

3 eggs

3 egg yolks

3 cups whole milk

1 teaspoon vanilla

¼ teaspoon salt

¼ teaspoon ground nutmeg

1 teaspoon ground cinnamon

2 tablespoons butter, cut into pieces

⅓ cup whipping cream

2 to 3 tablespoons Irish whiskey

To toast pecans, spread in single layer on baking sheet. Bake in preheated 350°F oven 6 to 8 minutes or until lightly toasted, stirring occasionally.

1. Grease 13×9-inch baking dish or 2-quart shallow casserole. Combine bread cubes and pecans in prepared baking dish.

2. Beat ¾ cup sugar, eggs and egg yolks in large bowl until blended. Add milk, vanilla, salt and nutmeg; beat until well blended. Pour egg mixture over bread mixture. Let stand 15 to 20 minutes, pressing down on bread occasionally.

3. Preheat oven to 350°F. Combine ¼ cup sugar and cinnamon in small bowl; sprinkle over bread mixture.

4. Bake 45 to 50 minutes or until puffed and golden brown. Cool on wire rack 15 minutes.

5. For sauce, place butter in small heavy saucepan. Add remaining ⅔ cup sugar; shake pan to make even layer but do not stir. Cook over medium heat 5 minutes or until golden and bubbly. Stir mixture; cook 2 minutes or until deep golden brown. Gradually stir in cream. (Mixture will sizzle.) Cook and stir until smooth. Remove from heat; stir in whiskey, 1 tablespoon at a time. Serve bread pudding warm or at room temperature topped with warm sauce.

MAKES 8 SERVINGS

Tip: The sauce may be prepared up to 2 days in advance and refrigerated. Reheat the sauce just before serving.

Rhubarb Tart >

1 refrigerated pie crust (half of 15-ounce package)
4 cups sliced rhubarb (½-inch pieces)
1¼ cups sugar
¼ cup all-purpose flour
2 tablespoons butter, cut into small pieces
¼ cup old-fashioned oats

1. Preheat oven to 450°F. Line 9-inch pie plate with crust. Trim excess crust; flute or crimp edge.

2. Combine rhubarb, sugar and flour in medium bowl; mix well. Pour into pie crust. Dot with butter; sprinkle with oats.

3. Bake 10 minutes. *Reduce oven temperature to 350°F.* Bake 40 minutes more or until bubbly.

MAKES 8 SERVINGS

Baked Apples in Whiskey-Cider Sauce

2 large baking apples such as Jonagold, McIntosh or Rome Beauty
1 cup apple cider
2 tablespoons Irish whiskey or additional apple cider
½ teaspoon cinnamon
⅛ teaspoon ground nutmeg
⅛ teaspoon ground cloves
1 tablespoon butter
Whipped cream (optional)

1. Preheat oven to 375°F. Peel apples; cut in half through stem ends. Place apple halves, cut sides up, in shallow baking dish.

2. Pour apple cider and whiskey over apples; sprinkle with cinnamon, nutmeg and cloves.

3. Bake 10 minutes. Baste apples with juices in dish; bake 15 to 20 minutes or until apples are tender. Remove to serving plates; let stand 10 minutes.

4. Meanwhile, pour juices in baking dish into small saucepan. Cook over medium-high heat about 8 minutes or until reduced to ¼ cup. Remove from heat; stir in butter until melted. Spoon sauce over apples; serve warm with whipped cream, if desired.

MAKES 2 SERVINGS

Apricot Oatmeal Bars >

1½ cups old-fashioned oats
1¼ cups all-purpose flour
½ cup packed brown sugar
1 teaspoon ground ginger, divided
½ teaspoon salt
½ teaspoon baking soda
½ teaspoon ground cinnamon
¾ cup (1½ sticks) butter, melted
1¼ cups apricot preserves

1. Preheat oven to 350°F. Line 8-inch square baking pan with foil.

2. Combine oats, flour, brown sugar, ½ teaspoon ginger, salt, baking soda and cinnamon in large bowl. Add butter; stir just until moistened and crumbly. Reserve 1½ cups oat mixture. Press remaining oat mixture evenly onto bottom of prepared pan.

3. Combine preserves and remaining ½ teaspoon ginger in small bowl. Spread preserves evenly over crust. Sprinkle with reserved oat mixture.

4. Bake 30 minutes or until golden brown. Cool completely in pan on wire rack. Cut into bars.

MAKES 9 SERVINGS

Lemon Curd

6 tablespoons butter
1 cup sugar
6 tablespoons lemon juice
2 teaspoons grated lemon peel
3 eggs, lightly beaten

1. Melt butter in double boiler set over simmering water. Stir in sugar, lemon juice and lemon peel.

2. Stir in eggs until blended. Cook and stir 15 to 20 minutes or until mixture is thick and smooth.

3. Remove from heat; let cool. Cover and refrigerate 2 hours or until cold. (Lemon curd will thicken as it cools.) Serve chilled. Store in refrigerator up to 3 weeks.

MAKES 1¾ CUPS

Chocolate Stout Cake

2 cups all-purpose flour

¾ cup unsweetened cocoa powder

1 teaspoon baking soda

¼ teaspoon salt

1 cup packed brown sugar

¾ cup (1½ sticks) butter, softened

½ cup granulated sugar

1 teaspoon vanilla

3 eggs

1 cup Irish stout, at room temperature

   Cream Cheese Frosting (recipe follows)

1. Preheat oven to 350°F. Spray 13×9-inch baking pan with nonstick cooking spray.

2. Combine flour, cocoa, baking soda and salt in medium bowl. Beat brown sugar, butter and granulated sugar in large bowl with electric mixer at medium speed until light and fluffy. Beat in vanilla. Add eggs, one at a time, beating well after each addition. Add flour mixture alternately with stout, beating until blended after each addition. Pour batter evenly into prepared pan.

3. Bake 35 to 40 minutes or until toothpick inserted into center comes out clean. Cool completely in pan on wire rack.

4. Prepare Cream Cheese Frosting. Spread frosting over cake.

MAKES 12 SERVINGS

Cream Cheese Frosting

1 package (8 ounces) cream cheese, softened

¼ cup (½ stick) butter, softened

4 cups powdered sugar

1 teaspoon vanilla

1 to 2 tablespoons milk

Beat cream cheese and butter in large bowl with electric mixer at medium speed until creamy. Gradually beat in powdered sugar and vanilla until smooth. Add enough milk to make spreadable frosting; beat until smooth.

MAKES 2½ CUPS

Apple-Buttermilk Pie

     2 medium Granny Smith apples
     3 eggs
  1 ½ cups sugar, divided
     1 cup buttermilk
   ⅓ cup butter, melted
     2 tablespoons all-purpose flour
     2 teaspoons vanilla
     2 teaspoons ground cinnamon, divided
   ¾ teaspoon ground nutmeg, divided
     1 (9-inch) unbaked pie shell
       Whipped cream and additional ground cinnamon (optional)

1. Preheat oven to 350°F. Peel and core apples; cut into small pieces. Place apples in medium bowl; add cold water to cover.

2. Beat eggs in large bowl with electric mixer at low speed until blended. Add all but 1 teaspoon sugar, buttermilk, butter, flour, vanilla, 1 teaspoon cinnamon and ½ teaspoon nutmeg; beat at low speed until well blended.

3. Drain apples well; place in unbaked pie shell. Pour buttermilk mixture over apples. Combine remaining 1 teaspoon sugar, 1 teaspoon cinnamon and ¼ teaspoon nutmeg in small bowl; sprinkle over top.

4. Bake 50 to 60 minutes or until knife inserted into center comes out clean. Serve warm or at room temperature. Garnish with whipped cream and additional cinnamon.

MAKES 8 SERVINGS

Traditional Fruit Cake

3 cups walnut halves

1 package (8 ounces) candied cherries

1 package (8 ounces) chopped dates

1 package (4 ounces) candied pineapple

¾ cup sifted all-purpose flour

¾ cup sugar

½ teaspoon baking powder

½ teaspoon salt

3 eggs, lightly beaten

3 tablespoons Irish whiskey or brandy

1 tablespoon grated orange peel

1 teaspoon vanilla

1. Preheat oven to 300°F. Line 9×5-inch loaf pan with parchment paper; spray with nonstick cooking spray.

2. Combine walnuts and fruit in large bowl. Combine flour, sugar, baking powder and salt in medium bowl. Sift into walnut mixture; toss gently to coat. Stir in eggs, whiskey, orange peel and vanilla. Spread batter evenly in prepared pan.

3. Bake 1 hour 45 minutes or until golden brown. Cool completely in pan on wire rack.

MAKES 1 LOAF

Irish Sherry Trifle

SPONGE CAKE

> 4 eggs
> ⅔ cup sugar
> 1½ teaspoons vanilla
> 1 cup all-purpose flour
> ¼ teaspoon baking powder
> ¼ teaspoon salt

CUSTARD

> 4 eggs
> ⅓ cup sugar
> 1 teaspoon vanilla
> 3 cups milk
> ½ cup seedless raspberry jam
> ¼ cup cream sherry
> 1¾ cups fresh raspberries, divided

SWEETENED WHIPPED CREAM

> 1 cup whipping cream
> 2 tablespoons sugar
> 1 teaspoon vanilla
> ½ cup sliced almonds, toasted

1. Preheat oven to 350°F. Grease and flour two 8-inch round cake pans.

2. For cake, beat 4 eggs, ⅔ cup sugar and 1½ teaspoons vanilla in large bowl with electric mixer and whisk attachment at medium-high speed about 6 minutes or until thick and tripled in volume. Combine flour, baking powder and salt in small bowl. Gently fold into egg mixture in two additions until blended. Pour batter evenly into prepared pans. Bake 15 to 17 minutes or until toothpick inserted into centers comes out clean. Cool in pans 10 minutes; remove to wire racks to cool completely.

3. Meanwhile, for custard, whisk 4 eggs, ⅓ cup sugar and 1 teaspoon vanilla in medium heatproof bowl. Bring milk to a simmer in medium saucepan over medium-high heat. Slowly whisk milk into egg mixture; return mixture to saucepan and cook over medium-low heat 4 to 5 minutes or until slightly thickened and mixture coats back of wooden spoon, stirring frequently. Return custard to bowl; let cool to room temperature. Place plastic wrap directly on top of custard and refrigerate until completely chilled.

4. To assemble, spread jam evenly over top of each cake layer. Cut each layer into 16 (2-inch) pieces. Line bottom of trifle bowl with half of cake squares; drizzle with 2 tablespoons sherry. Pour half of custard over cake; sprinkle with 1 cup raspberries. Repeat layers with remaining cake, sherry and custard. Cover and refrigerate 6 to 8 hours.

5. Just before serving, beat cream, 2 tablespoons sugar and 1 teaspoon vanilla in large bowl with electric mixer and whisk attachment at medium speed about 2 minutes or until medium peaks form. Spoon whipped cream over custard; top with remaining ¾ cup raspberries and almonds.

MAKES 10 TO 12 SERVINGS

Lemon Tart

1 refrigerated pie crust (half of 15-ounce package)
5 eggs
1 tablespoon cornstarch
1 cup sugar
½ cup (1 stick) butter
½ cup lemon juice

1. Position rack in center of oven. Preheat oven to 450°F.

2. Line 9-inch tart pan with pie crust, pressing to fit securely against side of pan. Trim off any excess crust. Prick bottom and side of crust with fork. Bake 9 to 10 minutes or until golden brown. Cool completely. *Reduce oven temperature to 350°F.*

3. Meanwhile, whisk eggs and cornstarch in medium bowl. Combine sugar, butter and lemon juice in small saucepan; cook and stir until over medium-low heat just until butter melts. Whisk in egg mixture; cook 8 to 10 minutes or until thickened, stirring constantly. (Do not let mixture come to a boil.) Pour into medium bowl; stir 1 minute or until cooled slightly. Let stand 10 minutes.

4. Pour cooled lemon curd into baked crust. Bake 25 to 30 minutes or until set. Cool completely before cutting. Store leftovers in refrigerator.

MAKES 8 TO 10 SERVINGS

Plum Rhubarb Crumble

1½ pounds plums, each plum pitted and cut into 8 wedges (4 cups)

1½ pounds rhubarb, cut into ½-inch pieces (5 cups)

1 cup granulated sugar

1 teaspoon finely grated fresh ginger

¼ teaspoon ground nutmeg

3 tablespoons cornstarch

¾ cup old-fashioned oats

½ cup all-purpose flour

½ cup packed brown sugar

½ cup sliced almonds, toasted*

¼ teaspoon salt

½ cup (1 stick) cold butter, cut into small pieces

*To toast almonds, spread in single layer on ungreased baking sheet. Bake in preheated 350°F oven 5 minutes or until golden brown, stirring frequently.

1. Combine plums, rhubarb, granulated sugar, ginger and nutmeg in large bowl; cover and let stand at room temperature 2 hours.

2. Preheat oven to 375°F. Spray 9-inch round or square baking dish with nonstick cooking spray. Line baking sheet with foil.

3. Pour juices from fruit into small saucepan; bring to a boil over medium-high heat. Cook about 12 minutes or until reduced to syrupy consistency, stirring occasionally. Stir in cornstarch until well blended. Stir mixture into bowl with fruit; pour into prepared baking dish. Place dish on prepared baking sheet.

4. Combine oats, flour, brown sugar, almonds and salt in medium bowl. Add butter; mix with fingertips until butter is evenly distributed and mixture is clumpy. Sprinkle evenly over fruit.

5. Bake about 50 minutes or until filling is bubbly and topping is golden brown. Cool 1 hour before serving.

MAKES 6 TO 8 SERVINGS

Tip: If the fruit is not very juicy after standing for 2 hours, it may require less time to reduce the liquid and/or less cornstarch to thicken it.

Classic Apple Cake

  4 medium apples, cut into ¼-inch slices (4 cups)
    Juice of ½ lemon
  3 cups all-purpose flour
  1 cup plus 1 tablespoon sugar, divided
  ¾ cup chopped almonds
  1½ teaspoons baking soda
  1 teaspoon ground cinnamon
  ½ teaspoon salt
  ½ teaspoon ground nutmeg
  1 cup vegetable oil
  1 teaspoon vanilla

1. Preheat oven to 350°F. Spray 13×9-inch baking pan with nonstick cooking spray.

2. Place apples in medium bowl. Drizzle with lemon juice and sprinkle with 1 tablespoon sugar; toss to coat. Let stand 20 minutes or until juice forms.

3. Combine flour, remaining 1 cup sugar, almonds, baking soda, cinnamon, salt and nutmeg in large bowl. Add oil and vanilla; stir until well blended. Stir in apple mixture. Spread batter evenly in prepared pan.

4. Bake about 35 minutes or until browned and toothpick inserted into center comes out clean. Cool in pan on wire rack 10 minutes. Serve warm.

MAKES 16 SERVINGS

Note: Either whole skin-on almonds or sliced almonds can be used.

Sticky Toffee Pudding

CAKE

1 cup pitted chopped dates (5 ounces)

⅔ cup water

½ teaspoon baking soda

1 cup all-purpose flour

1 teaspoon baking powder

¼ teaspoon salt

¾ cup packed brown sugar

5 tablespoons butter, softened, plus additional for greasing ramekins

1 egg

½ teaspoon vanilla

TOFFEE SAUCE

¼ cup (½ stick) butter

½ cup packed brown sugar

½ cup whipping cream

½ teaspoon vanilla

⅛ teaspoon salt

1. Preheat oven to 350°F. Butter six 4-ounce ramekins; place on parchment paper-lined baking sheet.

2. Combine dates and water in medium saucepan; bring to a boil over medium-high heat. Remove from heat; stir in baking soda. Set aside to cool.

3. Combine flour, baking powder and ¼ teaspoon salt in small bowl. Beat ¾ cup brown sugar and 5 tablespoons butter in large bowl with electric mixer at medium-high speed about 3 minutes or until light and fluffy. Scrape down side of bowl. Add egg and ½ teaspoon vanilla; beat 1 minute or until well blended. Stir in date mixture with spatula until blended. Add flour mixture; stir just until blended. Divide batter evenly among prepared ramekins.

4. Bake about 25 minutes or until toothpick inserted into centers comes out clean. Meanwhile, prepare sauce. Melt ¼ cup butter in heavy medium saucepan over medium heat. Add ½ cup brown sugar, cream, ½ teaspoon vanilla and ⅛ teaspoon salt; cook over medium-high heat about 5 minutes or until brown sugar is dissolved and sauce is reduced to 1 cup, stirring frequently. Remove from heat; cover to keep warm.

5. Poke top of puddings with skewer at ½-inch intervals. Gradually pour half of sauce over puddings; let stand about 15 minutes or until all of sauce is absorbed. Run sharp knife around edge of ramekins; invert onto serving plates. Reheat remaining sauce over medium-low heat; pour over top of puddings. Serve immediately.

MAKES 6 SERVINGS

Ginger Stout Cake

    2 cups all-purpose flour
    2 teaspoons ground ginger
1 ½ teaspoons baking powder
1 ½ teaspoons baking soda
    ¾ teaspoon ground cinnamon
    ½ teaspoon salt
    ¼ teaspoon ground cloves
    ½ cup (1 stick) butter, softened
    1 tablespoon grated fresh ginger *or* 1 teaspoon ground ginger
    1 cup granulated sugar
    ½ cup packed brown sugar
    3 eggs
    1 bottle (11 ounces) Irish stout
    ½ cup molasses
       Whipped cream and additional ground cinnamon (optional)

1. Preheat oven to 350°F. Grease 13×9-inch baking pan.

2. Combine flour, ground ginger, baking powder, baking soda, ¾ teaspoon cinnamon, salt and cloves in medium bowl. Beat butter and grated ginger in large bowl with electric mixer at medium speed until creamy. Add granulated sugar and brown sugar; beat 3 minutes or until light and fluffy. Add eggs, one at a time, beating well after each addition.

3. Whisk stout and molasses in medium bowl until blended. Alternately add flour mixture and stout mixture to butter mixture, beating well after each addition. Pour batter evenly into prepared pan.

4. Bake 45 minutes or until toothpick inserted into center comes out clean. Cool completely in pan on wire rack. Garnish with whipped cream and additional cinnamon.

MAKES 12 TO 15 SERVINGS

Molded Shortbread >

1½ cups all-purpose flour

¼ teaspoon salt

¾ cup (1½ sticks) butter, softened

⅓ cup sugar

1 egg

1. Preheat oven to temperature recommended by shortbread mold manufacturer. Spray 10-inch ceramic shortbread mold with nonstick cooking spray.

2. Combine flour and salt in medium bowl. Beat butter and sugar in large bowl with electric mixer at medium speed until light and fluffy. Add egg; beat until well blended. Gradually add flour mixture; beat at low speed until blended. Press dough firmly into mold.

3. Bake, cool and remove from mold according to manufacturer's directions.

MAKES 1 SHORTBREAD MOLD

Note: If shortbread mold is not available, preheat oven to 350°F. Shape dough into 1-inch balls. Place 2 inches apart on ungreased cookie sheets; press with fork to flatten. Bake 18 to 20 minutes or until edges are lightly browned. Cool on cookie sheets 2 minutes; remove to wire racks to cool completely. Makes 2 dozen cookies.

Irish Coffee

6 ounces freshly brewed strong black coffee

2 teaspoons packed brown sugar

2 ounces Irish whiskey

¼ cup whipping cream

Combine coffee and brown sugar in Irish coffee glass or mug. Stir in whiskey. Pour cream over back of spoon into coffee.

MAKES 1 SERVING

Apple Blackberry Crisp

4 cups sliced peeled apples
  Juice of ½ lemon
2 tablespoons granulated sugar
2 tablespoons Irish cream liqueur
1 teaspoon ground cinnamon, divided
1 cup old-fashioned oats
6 tablespoons (¾ stick) cold butter, cut into pieces
⅔ cup packed brown sugar
¼ cup all-purpose flour
1 cup fresh blackberries
  Irish Whipped Cream (recipe follows, optional)

1. Preheat oven to 375°F. Grease 9-inch oval or 8-inch square baking dish.

2. Place apples in large bowl; drizzle with lemon juice. Add granulated sugar, liqueur and ½ teaspoon cinnamon; toss to coat.

3. Combine oats, butter, brown sugar, flour and remaining ½ teaspoon cinnamon in food processor; pulse until combined, leaving some some chunks remaining.

4. Gently stir blackberries into apple mixture. Spoon into prepared baking dish; sprinkle with oat mixture.

5. Bake 30 to 40 minutes or until filling is bubbly and topping is golden brown. Prepare Irish Whipped Cream, if desired; serve with crisp.

MAKES 6 SERVINGS

Irish Whipped Cream: Beat 1 cup whipping cream and 2 tablespoons Irish cream liqueur in large bowl with electric mixer at high speed until slightly thickened. Add 1 to 2 tablespoons powdered sugar; beat until soft peaks form.

 tip This crisp can also be made without the blackberries; just add an additional 1 cup sliced apples.

Classic Bread Pudding

14 slices day-old, firm-textured white bread (about 12 ounces), crusts trimmed
1½ cups milk
⅓ cup butter, softened
⅓ cup packed brown sugar
1 teaspoon ground cinnamon
¼ teaspoon ground nutmeg
¼ teaspoon ground cloves
1 medium apple, peeled and chopped
1 package (6 ounces) mixed dried fruit, chopped
1 egg
⅓ cup chopped nuts
 Whipped cream and additional ground nutmeg (optional)

1. Tear bread into pieces; place in large bowl. Pour milk over bread; let stand 30 minutes.

2. Preheat oven to 350°F. Lightly grease 9×5-inch loaf pan.

3. Add butter, brown sugar, cinnamon, ¼ teaspoon nutmeg and cloves to bowl with bread mixture. Beat with electric mixer at low speed about 1 minute or until smooth. Beat in apple, dried fruit and egg until blended. Stir in nuts. Pour into prepared pan.

4. Bake 1 hour 15 minutes to 1 hour 30 minutes or until toothpick inserted into center comes out clean. Cool in pan 10 minutes. Remove to wire rack to cool slightly. Serve warm; top with whipped cream and additional nutmeg, if desired.

MAKES 6 TO 8 SERVINGS

METRIC CONVERSION CHART

VOLUME MEASUREMENTS (dry)

$\frac{1}{8}$ teaspoon = 0.5 mL
$\frac{1}{4}$ teaspoon = 1 mL
$\frac{1}{2}$ teaspoon = 2 mL
$\frac{3}{4}$ teaspoon = 4 mL
1 teaspoon = 5 mL
1 tablespoon = 15 mL
2 tablespoons = 30 mL
$\frac{1}{4}$ cup = 60 mL
$\frac{1}{3}$ cup = 75 mL
$\frac{1}{2}$ cup = 125 mL
$\frac{2}{3}$ cup = 150 mL
$\frac{3}{4}$ cup = 175 mL
1 cup = 250 mL
2 cups = 1 pint = 500 mL
3 cups = 750 mL
4 cups = 1 quart = 1 L

VOLUME MEASUREMENTS (fluid)

1 fluid ounce (2 tablespoons) = 30 mL
4 fluid ounces ($\frac{1}{2}$ cup) = 125 mL
8 fluid ounces (1 cup) = 250 mL
12 fluid ounces (1$\frac{1}{2}$ cups) = 375 mL
16 fluid ounces (2 cups) = 500 mL

WEIGHTS (mass)

$\frac{1}{2}$ ounce = 15 g
1 ounce = 30 g
3 ounces = 90 g
4 ounces = 120 g
8 ounces = 225 g
10 ounces = 285 g
12 ounces = 360 g
16 ounces = 1 pound = 450 g

DIMENSIONS

$\frac{1}{16}$ inch = 2 mm
$\frac{1}{8}$ inch = 3 mm
$\frac{1}{4}$ inch = 6 mm
$\frac{1}{2}$ inch = 1.5 cm
$\frac{3}{4}$ inch = 2 cm
1 inch = 2.5 cm

OVEN TEMPERATURES

250°F = 120°C
275°F = 140°C
300°F = 150°C
325°F = 160°C
350°F = 180°C
375°F = 190°C
400°F = 200°C
425°F = 220°C
450°F = 230°C

BAKING PAN SIZES

Utensil	Size in Inches/Quarts	Metric Volume	Size in Centimeters
Baking or Cake Pan (square or rectangular)	8×8×2	2 L	20×20×5
	9×9×2	2.5 L	23×23×5
	12×8×2	3 L	30×20×5
	13×9×2	3.5 L	33×23×5
Loaf Pan	8×4×3	1.5 L	20×10×7
	9×5×3	2 L	23×13×7
Round Layer Cake Pan	8×1½	1.2 L	20×4
	9×1½	1.5 L	23×4
Pie Plate	8×1¼	750 mL	20×3
	9×1¼	1 L	23×3
Baking Dish or Casserole	1 quart	1 L	—
	1½ quart	1.5 L	—
	2 quart	2 L	—

The
ENTREPRENEUR'S
COMPLETE
SOURCEBOOK

ALEXANDER WATSON HIAM ♦ KAREN WISE OLANDER

PRENTICE HALL
Englewood Cliffs, New Jersey 07632

Library of Congress Cataloging-in-Publication Data

Hiam, Alexander.
    The entrepreneur's complete sourcebook / by Alexander Watson Hiam
& Karen Wise Olander.
        p. cm.
    Includes index.
    ISBN 0-13-591421-3 (cloth)
    1. Small business—Management. 2. Entrepreneurship. I. Olander, Karen.
II. Title.
HD62.7.H5 1996
658.02'2—dc20   96-20413
                                                           CIP

Previous books by Alexander Hiam

The Vest Pocket Marketer

The Vest Pocket CEO: Decision-Making Tools for Executives

Closing the Quality Gap

Printed in the United States of America

10 9 8 7 6 5 4 3 2 1

ISBN 0-13-591421-3

ATTENTION: CORPORATIONS AND SCHOOLS

Prentice Hall books are available at quantity discounts with bulk purchase for educational, business, or sales promotional use. For information, please write to: Prentice Hall Career & Personal Development Special Sales, 113 Sylvan Avenue, Englewood Cliffs, NJ 07632. Please supply: title of book, ISBN number, quantity, how the book will be used, date needed.

PRENTICE HALL
Career & Personal Development
Englewood Cliffs, NJ 07632
A Simon & Schuster Company

On the World Wide Web at http://www.phdirect.com

Prentice Hall International (UK) Limited, *London*
Prentice Hall of Australia Pty. Limited, *Sydney*
Prentice Hall Canada, Inc., *Toronto*
Prentice Hall Hispanoamericana, S.A., *Mexico*
Prentice Hall of India Private Limited, *New Delhi*
Prentice Hall of Japan, Inc., *Tokyo*
Simon & Schuster Asia Pte. Ltd., *Singapore*
Editora Prentice Hall do Brasil, Ltda., *Rio de Janeiro*

Table of Contents

PART II
Start-Up Alternatives: Franchising, Acquisition, and Innovating in Existing Businesses 67

PART III
The Business Plan 107

Broome's Caveats for a Business Plan / 134   *Working Woman*'s Business Plan "Musts" / 134

PART IV
Marketing and Sales   137

twelve   Improve Your Marketing   139

Customer Service / 139   Customer Analysis / 141   Why Customer Service Is So Important / 143   ECCO's Customer-Complaint Tracking System / 144   ECCO's Customer-Complaint Form / 144   Gordon's Six Steps to Finding Prospective Customers / 146

thirteen   Increase Sales Success   148

Gitomer's Ways to Create an Excellent Sales Staff / 149   Ladin's Tips for Commercial Success / 152   Turitz's Sales-Planning Guide / 153   Gordon's Checklist for Presentations / 155   Gordon's Guidelines for Successful Sales Meetings / 157   Key Medical Supply's One-Minute Sales Presentation / 160

fourteen   Write a Marketing Plan   162

Marketing Plan Models / 163   Winer's Annual Marketing Plan / 163   SWOT Analysis / 165   Marketing Segmentation, Targeting, and Positioning / 166   The Four P's / 170   Product Tactics / 170   Pricing Tactics / 174   Pricing for Service Firms / 180   Promotion Tactics / 181   Promotion Tactics for Service Firms / 184   Placement Tactics / 184   Placement Tactics for Service Firms / 185   Implementation and Controls / 186   Sales Analysis / 186   Profitability Analysis / 187

PART V
General Management   189

fifteen   Hire and Manage Employees   191

Benchmarking to Set Salaries / 191   Raises / 192   SBA's Employee Handbook Topics / 192   Use Alternative Staffing Methods to Save Money / 194   Other Ways to Handle Changing Staffing Needs / 198   Performance Assessment / 199

sixteen   Control Inventories   201

Weinstein's Six Tips for Tracking Inventory / 201

PART VI
Strategic Management for Growth 229

PART VII
Funding and Financial Management 257

PART VIII
Resources 317

Introduction

Why the Risks and Rewards of Entrepreneurship and Small Business Management Are Higher than Ever Before— and What to do About It

Why entrepreneurship and small business management? Because this is where the growth is in the U.S. economy, this is where jobs are, this is where export growth comes from, this is where opportunities for everyone exist. A record number of new businesses are being created in the nineties—approximately 700,000 each year! And small businesses account for the vast majority of new job creation. They produce most of the export growth the U.S. economy experiences. They attract and enrich a diverse cross section of Americans, offering far more opportunity for minorities and women than big business does. And small business's share of total jobs keeps growing at the same time that big business shrinks.

In short, there is tremendous potential for almost everyone in the small-business and start-ups sector of the economy. That is why more and more readers are searching for ideas and methods to help them become entrepreneurs or small-business managers, and if they already work in this vital sector, it explains why they are seeking new and better methods and ideas. At least, it is one reason.

The other reason people seek help in starting and running businesses is that *the risks have increased along with the rewards*. The rate of business failures has doubled in the last decade. Traditionally, fewer than five of every thousand businesses fail in the United States each year. Lately, the figure has been ten or above. The conclusion is obvious: Doing business in the United States is about twice as risky as it used to be. Why? Markets are volatile, technological breakthroughs are more frequent and quickly commercialized, and competition is global. Most businesses compete against five to ten times as many other companies as they would have in the seventies, for example.

Rise in Annual Failure Rate

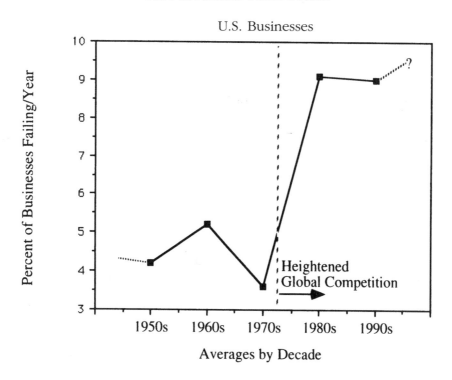

U.S. Businesses

Traditionally, 4-5% of businesses have failed each year, but since the 1970s the rate has doubled. Now 9-10% fail per year.

(Sources: Department of Commerce and Dun & Bradstreet Corp., in Economic Report of the President, 1993, p. 454)

A recent research project revealed 13 trends reshaping the U.S. economy into one that is faster changing and more challenging for business (Alexander Hiam, *The Portable Conference on Change Management,* HRD Press 1996). Here are these key trends:

Trends Re-Shaping the Business Environment in the United States

1. A goods-to-services shift
2. An increasingly global economy
3. A truly global labor market

4. More and more new products
5. Speedier scientific innovation
6. Speedier commercialization of innovations
7. An increase in disruptive technologies
8. An increase in the number of competitors
9. More and more mergers and acquisitions
10. Increased rate of business failure
11. A price squeeze on supplier businesses
12. Lower brand loyalty
13. A management innovation race

Some of these trends are more self-explanatory than others. Let's review some of the less obvious ones. As an entrepreneur or small-business manager, you might think that trend 3 is irrelevant, for example. While Nike follows the global labor market to make sure its shoes are stitched at the lowest possible rates, the average small business cannot operate on such a global scale. However, most small businesses now must compete against products and companies that *are* operating in the global labor market, and so must be prepared to cope with severe price competition—suggesting the need for a significant quality or service advantage. In the new economy, entrepreneurs should not base their business strategy on a lowcost position alone, as their low prices are likely to be undercut by an unexpected competitor.

Another trend that is nonobvious is trend 11, a price squeeze on supplier businesses. If you look at national price trends for suppliers of raw materials, parts, or services, you find that these companies have, on average, experienced slower price increases than have their customers, the businesses that sell products and services to the end consumer. A majority of businesses sell to other businesses, and the competition among these business-to-business providers has increased, squeezing their profit margins and forcing them to adopt new and challenging management techniques and production methods.

Lower brand loyalty, trend number 12, means that the majority of end consumers are no longer faithful to individual brand names. That is good news for the entrepreneur trying to enter a new market, as it means consumers are more willing to try something new. But it is also bad news, since it means consumers will not be faithful to your product just because they used it before. Today, marketers have to reenlist customers with every sale and usage cycle.

Trend 13, a management innovation race, means that today's businesses compete in part on the basis of how well and quickly they can implement the latest management fads and methods. Even the smallest businesses are forced to adopt total quality management or reengineering techniques, for example, when their customers or larger rivals do. Innovating to improve your management methods is the price of admission in today's markets.

What these trends all add up to is a more demanding environment for the entrepreneur or small business manager. To survive, let alone thrive, entrepreneurs certainly must run a far tighter ship than was the case when we started our first business, almost two decades ago. Being small or new no longer excuses you from the pursuit of excellence. If you are not striving to learn more and perform better, in everything from marketing and finance to bookkeeping and employee management, then you are doomed to join the 85,000 businesses that will fail in the United States this year! And that means you need this book.

This book offers reference material as well as a total entrepreneurial process, and both are adapted to the demands of the more rigorous business environment of the nineties. To illustrate this important point, let me run you briefly through the new entrepreneurial process we developed and are introducing in this book. Entrepreneurship, so the conventional wisdom has it, should start with a systematic, written business plan. But that formula is an old one and no longer represents the best approach to starting or expanding a business. It leads to a textbook approach that lacks innovation and excitement. It produces me-too businesses benchmarked on yesterday's successes. It fails to produce the innovations and breakthrough thinking needed to rise to the top in today's turbulent business waters.

A far better way to pursue entrepreneurship, whether when founding a business or working to improve or expand one, is to start with a systematic effort to generate business ideas. This is the subject of the first chapter of this book, and we guarantee you will be surprised at the number of opportunities you discover if you work through this part with care.

Successful start-up and growth businesses are based on great ideas. Not just any ideas, but *great* ideas. So the next step has to be a thoughtful screening of all your wild ideas in order to identify those that have the most potential and are best aligned with your personal goals and constraints as well. Therefore, the second step in the new entrepreneurial process is a systematic screening of ideas, the subject of Chapter 2 of this book.

Third, successful businesses today are based on a clear, compelling vision. This is the secret to flexibility and opportunism, because it gives the business a strong, durable focus and drive that unifies the varied efforts and strategies of its people. How do you establish and implement a vision for your business? That is the topic of Chapter 3.

Fourth, successful businesses are built on the strength of healthy business networks. The connections and contacts of the entrepreneur or small business manager make an immense difference in the prospects for success. In the challenging business environment of the nineties, you need to devote time and resources to building and utilizing a business network suited to the business you wish to start or grow. That is the topic of Chapter 4.

Finally, you need to form the business, adopting a legal and strategic form for it that best suits your vision and goals. This is the subject of Chapter 5.

These five activities combine to create the foundations upon which a successful business can be built. Without these foundations, the business is at high risk of failure. That is why these five chapters are organized into Part 1 of our book, entitled Foundations. We urge you to build these foundations carefully, not only when you first start a business, but periodically when you step outside the daily demands of management to renew that business through improvements or growth. The business that neglects its foundations will fail. The business that strengthens its foundations will be able to support continued growth and prosperity.

There is more than one way to participate in the entrepreneurship and small-business sector of our economy. And in today's difficult markets, many entrepreneurs seek lower-risk entry paths through franchising, acquisitions, and other alternatives. These are explored in depth in the chapters that make up Part II. Especially valuable are the materials in this part concerning ways to apply new total-quality management methods and advanced product development techniques to smaller businesses.

Part III of the book walks you through the business planning process, showing you how to craft a winning business plan. It also includes some helpful aids, such as templates and outlines for various kinds of plans, in order to help you through those inevitable writer's blocks. Finally, it includes an innovative chapter that helps you add an improvement loop to the plan-writing process. This chapter asks, and helps you answer, critical questions that will differentiate your plan from the mediocre majority: Does the plan address its audience and purpose? Will your plan impress a banker?

Once you have conceptualized, formed, and planned your business, the most important thing you can do to ensure success is to build a customer base. Too often, consultants, workshops and how-to books encourage entrepreneurs to avoid the difficult chores of marketing and sales until long after they have raised and spent start-up funds and gone into production. An old friend of ours who started several businesses back in Silicon Valley's heyday used to say, "You don't have a business until you have a customer." He was right. And that's why the entrepreneurship process must next move on to marketing and sales, covered in depth in Part IV of the book. An essential component of this step is the creation of a marketing plan—something most entrepreneurs neglect. But by writing a marketing plan, you will ensure that your offerings are better suited to your customers' needs and preferences and that it is easier and cheaper for you to reach your customers. Every business should write a marketing plan, even if it takes up no more space than the back of a large napkin. You will profit many times over from this investment in understanding your customers.

Now that the entrepreneurship process has lined up customers for your business, the next critical success factor is how well you perform the tasks of general management. From inventories to employees, from production to invoicing, your management performance will determine how effectively and productively your business can pursue the opportunities you have identified for it. This is the subject of Part V.

Part VI addresses strategic management, which is usually left completely out of the training provided entrepreneurs and small-business managers. That is a big mistake, because the field of strategy offers powerful tools and techniques for growing and expanding your business. In this part you will see how to make the most of your business's potential. In the current business environment, those who don't grow are doomed to fail, so we also recommend this activity highly.

Part VII gets to the bottom line: how you raise and manage the money your business needs. Fundraising is key to the success of many new businesses as well as growth plans for established businesses. But fundraising is not as simple (or as difficult) as conventional wisdom has it. Most books advise you to write a plan, then send it to venture capital firms. In reality, research indicates that *fewer than one percent of new businesses are funded by venture capital firms*. That means the conventional wisdom about fundraising is most likely wrong for you and your firm. In this book, you will find many alternative approaches to raising the capital you need. How to milk your business network for financing, how to base growth on bank loans, where to go if your business is minority- or woman-owned, and other issues are covered in Part VII. And the reality is that most entrepreneurs and small-business managers do not have advanced degrees in finance and accounting. So this part of the book starts out with a chapter that demystifies financial statements and basic accounting and record keeping.

At the end of the book, Part VIII gives you access to a wide variety of resources for entrepreneurs and small business managers, from organizations that can help out to useful publications. And a glossary of the most important technical terms you are likely to need in planning and managing a business is included in the end matter as well.

Let's review the new entrepreneurship process briefly, contrasting it with the traditional approach, in order to make sure you obtain the maximum benefit from it and from this book.

Traditional Entrepreneurship Process	*New Entrepreneurship Process*
1. Form a business (i.e., incorporate)	1. Generate many business ideas
2. Write a formal business plan	2. Screen ideas to select best
3. Submit it to venture capital firms	3. Establish a vision for the business
4. Wait	4. Build an active business network
5. If funded, invest in business	5. Form the business using the minimum seed financing or "kitchen" capital or . . .
6. Scale up production and hire employees	6. Choose one of the startup alternatives
7. Begin marketing and sales activities	7. Write a business plan
8. Wait it out to see if sales grow fast enough to avoid cash crisis	8. Check and improve the business plan
	9. Talk to customers! Make sales.
END	10. Write a marketing plan
	11. Establish general management methods
	12. Do strategic planning to identify growth opportunities
	13. Adopt formal record-keeping and accounting methods
	14. Identify all possible sources of financing
	15. Use your network to obtain financing if needed for further growth
	REPEAT periodically to renew business

The new process is longer, for a good reason. Business just isn't that simple anymore. To minimize the ever higher risks of entrepreneurship and small-business management, and to maximize the returns, you need to build strong foundations, including more and better business ideas, and you need to back carefully into the kind of large-scale formal investment that used to be the starting point. The business that can bootstrap its way through the first few years of its plan is far more likely to succeed. You also need to take more time and care in building a durable relationship with a well-defined group of customers—hence the need for a formal marketing plan as well as a business plan.

Finally, you need to take advantage of the many fresh new ideas and methods that have been developed over the last five or ten years. You will notice as you use this book that many of the good ideas in it are *not* the work of this author team. No one team could possibly come up with so many great ideas or test them so thoroughly in the school of hard knocks.

We are particularly proud of the hundreds of experts upon which we relied in the development of this handbook. You will see their names in every chapter. Thanks to them for pioneering so many great methods and ideas. And a word of advice to you: If you find one that is particularly useful and relevant in your current circumstances, go ahead and look up our source. We have documented our sources carefully so that you can easily find the name and title needed to request a book from your local bookstore or to call up a magazine publisher for a reprint. Successful entrepreneurs and small business managers are usually voracious readers, eager to pursue new ideas and to expand their knowledge of business at a rapid rate. We trust this book will contribute to that quest. And we wish you the best of luck with all your business endeavors.

Good fortune!

Alexander Watson Hiam
Karen Wise Olander
Amherst, Mass

P A R T   I

Foundations

Introduction

As we argued in the introduction to this book, there is a great need for a new approach to entrepreneurship. The business environment is different—more challenging, fast-changing, and competitive—and the traditional approaches to entrepreneurship and small-business management virtually doom a business to failure today. Nowhere is the need for a new approach greater than in the beginning of the entrepreneurship process, the subject of this part of the book.

Whether you are starting a new business or renewing an existing business, you need to build strong foundations for future growth by investing in five key activities: generation of business ideas (the more and crazier the better), screening of those ideas to choose the best, establishing a compelling vision for your business, building a rich business network to ensure access to all the resources and expertise you will need, and forming (or re-forming) your business to make sure it has the best legal and practical structure for your purposes. In the five chapters of Part 1, you will find detailed instructions for each of these vital activities, as well as hundreds of ideas and suggestions for improving your performance as an entrepreneur or small-business manager.

One more word of advice before we let you turn the page and begin your journey through this book. The first chapter is named for *the single most important activity of any entrepreneur or small-business manager: to generate business ideas.* Today, your customers, competition, and business environment in general change so rapidly that you must *lead* the changes in order to survive and thrive.

This calls for a more creative approach to management than ever before. The entrepreneurs and businesses that succeed over the long run will be those who achieve and maintain idea leadership by establishing new and better ways of doing their work, by generating creative new products and services, by implementing insights into how to redefine their customer base, and so forth. If you have time to study only one chapter in depth today, make it Chapter 1. And the same thing goes for tomorrow. And the next day. If you gain nothing else from this handbook (which is admittedly unlikely), please be sure that you learn how to be a more creative entrepreneur and manager, capable of establishing idea leadership in any market you enter.

one
Generate Business Ideas

The first thing you will do when you are considering starting a business of your own is to come up with ideas for a business. And if you already manage a small or growing business, you will need to keep thinking of ways to innovate in order to stay competitive. Small businesses thrive on ideas—and wilt without them. Thus, idea leadership, as we call it, is the most important job of any small business manager or entrepreneur, which is why this book starts with idea generation.

Many consultants and business advisers emphasize systematic business planning, careful cash-flow management, and sound marketing. These are important and will be covered in later chapters. However, good ideas are at the root of all successful businesses. Today's fast-paced business environment makes innovation the key to business success. The mom-and-pop stationery story cannot do what it has always done once a Staples discount store opens nearby. And a new software company cannot hope to introduce its software in the same way Bill Gates of Microsoft did. New formulas are required.

All readers, regardless of the stage their business is in, will be well advised to start with a focused effort to generate novel business ideas. And whenever they experience difficulties, they ought to revisit this chapter in search of creative solutions.

Ideas may be related to products you might want to make and sell, or to services you may want to provide. Generating ideas is an innovative, creative process and one that will take some time, not just in the beginning stages of going into business, but throughout the life of the business. You will need to constantly stay alert to potential innovations, product changes, and possible new products, always scanning the environment for ways to improve your product or service.

In previous times, the life cycle of a product might be expected to be 10 or 15 years. But today providers of goods are lucky if a product lasts more than 3 to 5 years. So, as you can see, innovation and creative ways of looking at the world are essential for the entrepreneur and small business owner. (We discuss other aspects of innovation in other sections of this book, in particular in the section on strategic management.)

Further, because competition tends to move into an area rapidly when there is a new product, you cannot simply rely on profit as the guiding principle for your business. The product or service itself has to be superior to make it stand out from its competitors. And this means continuing innovation—if you do not introduce new ideas, your competitors will. The reality is that every small business must be creative and entrepreneurial in today's competitive environment.

When you are brainstorming for business ideas, remember the old adage that several heads are better than one. To generate as many ideas as possible—unless you have already figured out the product that will make it big—get some help from others.

At the end of this chapter we detail a number of brainstorming methods that you may want to use with your group. To help release your creativity, use methods such as those described in *A Whack on the Side of the Head* (Roger von Oech, New York: Warner Books, 1983) or use the *Creative Whack Pack* also written by von Oech. We will review other techniques that may be of help later in this chapter.

If yours is already a going concern and you are looking for new ideas to improve it, encourage curiosity in your employees. Let people play around with ideas, explore possibilities. Let yourself go, too, and see what happens. Suggestion boxes may sound old-fashioned, but you may get some good ideas from them. Reward the people whose ideas you use and see if you do not get seven more suggestions.

Ever hear of skunk works? It is a phrase from Tom Peters (*In Search of Excellence*, 1982) that describes a small group of workers who are allowed to work on a project together and who often outproduce the larger, more structured groups in a company. Often, new product ideas arise from such groups, so you may want to encourage such work at your business.

Allow people to tinker with products and ideas. Support and encourage creative ideas and solutions. In a later section we will discuss how management can help workers in these endeavors.

There are two broad perspectives from which you can approach new products or services: Either you can design a product and find a niche for it, or you can take a need that you see and design the product or service to fit the situation. The person who designed Silly Putty, for example, first discovered the product and then looked for an appropriate market for it. Who better than kids? Even adults had fun with it.

An example of the second approach (seeing the need and designing the product to fit) is to look at a growing market segment such as the over-50 population and design a product to fit a need there, for example, a gadget to help open screw-top bottles.

You may also find that you see a business problem that needs a solution and then you will need to brainstorm or generate ideas to solve that problem.

In this chapter we will first examine sources of new business ideas and ways to find ideas. This leads to formulating appropriate strategies, which will be discussed. Then we will explore in-depth ideas for home-based businesses and other small-business start-up ideas.

We will examine the increasing importance of service businesses and list some ideas for you to consider. There is also a list of the top ten cities for new businesses that you may want to think about.

Finally, we will explore techniques for generating new and better ideas, whether for starting a business, growing it, or coping with the many challenges and puzzles that businesses encounter.

Where to Look for Business Ideas

There are numerous resources available to you when you are trying to come up with an idea for a business or for a new product, or even for a product to add to your current line. In addition to the printed word as a resource (magazines, books, newspapers), personal brainstorming can be helpful. (We take up group brainstorming later in this section.) Just looking around at your environment and observing it closely can be a helpful way to get started.

Draw from personal interests or hobbies. These are the things that you enjoy, and perhaps others enjoy. Do you like working on cars? Are you a good cook? Do you enjoy working closely with other people? Perhaps you are skilled at a particular craft. It will be easier to sustain a long-term interest in something you love and are committed to.

Look around for limitations in existing products or services. See if something is missing. Can you fill the need? For example, a resume service may offer copies only of the completed resume, but you could add as part of a resume "package" an update a year later to enhance the "product."

Make a wish list. What would you love to have that is not available on the market at the present time? A particular type of clothing that you cannot find anywhere? A knife that would cut perfect slices of homemade bread?

Think of new and different ways to use existing products. Come up with a new slant on a service. Some massage therapists have brought their services ("chair massage") to businesses, so that employees do not even have to leave the office for an appointment.

Take a close look at the social scene and how it is changing. Is there a product or service that would fill a need here? Nonalcoholic teen "clubs" became popular for the under-18 or under-21 set. Specialized types of dating services have been successful in providing people with a way of meeting people in a fast-paced society.

Consider technological advances and how they affect currently available products. Or think about how new technology could be harnessed to provide new and different products. Or how technology could be used to provide a different way of obtaining products: There are "stores" on the Internet now, where people can look at product descriptions and lists and order books, products, and so forth, directly on-line.

Think of possible spin-offs from existing products or services that might be developed. When bread machines became popular, a number of companies developed their own special blends of bread ingredients, packaged in sizes appropriate for the bread machine requirements.

Look at currently established businesses. How could they be changed to improve their services? For example, what if you could get clothes dry cleaned in one hour instead of a few days? Or, what if someone needed a car repair but could not do without the car for a day?

Consider the features of particular products. Could additional features be added to provide more benefit to the consumer? Could the product be improved? Should other related products be added to the existing line? Laundry detergents and breakfast cereals are notorious for being "new and improved" on a regular basis. Hair-care products are usually sold as a line, with complementary shampoo, conditioner, and styling gels, for example. Scott's provides a four-step lawn care product for which you need all four components if you want to have a beautiful lawn.

You will discover that the ideas you generate through this sort of brainstorming will fall into one of the four basic categories of innovation:

1. An existing product or service in an existing market
2. A new product or service in an existing market
3. An existing product or service in a new market
4. A new product or service in a new market

These embody the four strategies in H. Igor Ansoff's representation of strategies for diversification, published in 1957. (See page 8.)

Depending upon the combination of markets (new or existing) and products (new or existing), you will need to use different strategies in the market, as follows:

A *penetration strategy* is used for current products in the current market. The risk here is low, since both aspects are known and therefore manageable. You will have information on both products and consumers, so there will be less research to do and, therefore, less risk.

A *market-development strategy* is used when you take current products into new markets. Here the risk is moderate because of the unknowns in the new markets. (It would be high if the products were also new.) This strategy will require good, solid research on the potential markets and customers.

A *product-development strategy* is used for new products in current markets. The risk here is moderate, because, while the products are new, the markets are known and so will not need to be researched. The research and devel-

Product Market Grid

Markets

	Current	New
Current	Penetration Strategy Risk = L	Market Development Strategy Risk = M
New	Product Development Strategy Risk = M	Diversification Strategy Risk = H

Products

(Source: H. Igor Ansoff, "Strategies for Diversification," *Harvard Business Review*, September-October 1957, pp. 113-124.)

opment will center around the new products, although it will still be important to test market with potential customers.

A *diversification strategy* is used for new products in new markets. As you can imagine, diversification is the most risky of the four strategies. It requires full-blown research into all the aspects: customers, product, market. It also requires creativity in finding possibilities for diversification. A diversification strategy has the potential for the most new business, so it can be very appealing, yet it is the least familiar territory for those undertaking it and therefore is high risk.

Consider the business suggestions in the pages that follow. Let them be a starting point for your thought process, but let yourself go during this research. You may come up with a new idea or one that captures your imagination.

Income Opportunity Magazine's Guides to Business Ideas

The service sector is appealing because I would not have to think up and manufacture a product to sell to customers, but what should I do? I want to start a home-based business, and I want it to be service-oriented. But all I can think of is pumping septic tanks. There must be something better!

Income Opportunities magazine has made the process of idea development easier by compiling a series of easy-to-start business ideas in such business categories as products, services, and repair and maintenance. They also offer a list of part-time businesses that you can start.

Use these lists to help you brainstorm for ideas for start-ups that meet your basic requirements. And remember, the more ideas you screen, the more likely you will be to find a new business concept that really works for you. If none of these ideas inspire you, leaf through a copy of the Yellow Pages for New York City, Los Angeles, or Chicago. You will be amazed at the number of business categories you never imagined existed, and unless you live in a big city, many of them may not yet exist in your market area.

Home-Based Businesses

(Source: *32 Low-Cost Home-based Businesses*, editors of *Income Opportunities* magazine, Englewood Cliffs, NJ: Prentice Hall, 1992.)

Product-based Businesses

photography

customer catering

handmade pillows

homemade jewelry

kids' sports cards

lunch service

mail order

sign painting

specialty advertising

stained glass

swap sheet

Service-based Businesses

bed and breakfast

bookkeeping

desktop publishing

entertainment service

freelance research

pet services/pet sitting

photo agent

income tax preparation

typing services

wedding consulting

Repair and Maintenance Businesses

bicycle repair
carpet repair
glass installation
home repair

landscape maintenance
mobile sharpening service
phone installation
small-engine repair

Part-Time Businesses

(Source: *33 Profitable Part-time Businesses*, editors of *Income Opportunities* magazine, Englewood Cliffs, NJ: Prentice Hall, 1992.)

Part-time Product-based Businesses

crafts home parties
firewood delivery
flea markets
local cookbook
photo buttons
potpourri

shopping-mall booth (e.g., candles, gifts, Christmas ornaments)
silk flowers
tag sales
wooden toys

Part-time Service-based Businesses

calligraphy
court transcriber
driving instructor
delivery services
freelance bar tending
garden consulting

genealogy
limousine service
mobile disk jockey
outdoor guide
resume writing
tutoring

Part-time Repair and Maintenance Businesses

aquarium maintenance
auto striping

handyman, odd jobs
lot cleaning

American Entrepreneurs Association's Top 33 Businesses

(Source: *Small Business Development Catalog* from EntrepreneurGroup, Boulder, CO 80321.)

The American Entrepreneurs Association (AEA) publishes a catalog of business guides and other tools for the small-business owner and entrepreneur, including books, magazines, software, and tapes. In a recent catalog they offer business guides for 144 different businesses. Based on the demand for specific business guides, the AEA catalog lists the following as the top businesses. That means your fellow entrepreneurs find these the most appealing ideas for start-ups. That might be good news or bad, depending upon whether there are already too many of these businesses in your market area. Check the Yellow Pages.

Top Businesses (in alphabetical order)

Auto Detailing
Coffeehouse
Collectibles Broker
Consulting Service
Desktop Publishing
Event Planning Service
Financial Aid Service
Food Delivery Service
Gift Basket Service
Herb Farming
Home Computer
Home Inspection Service
Home Health Agency
Import/Export Management
Information Broker
Janitorial Service
Maid Service
Mail Order Business

Medical Claims Processing
Microbrewery or Brewpub
Mobile Frozen Yogurt
Operating a "900" Number for Profit
Personal Shopper
Private Investigator
Property Tax Consultant
Recycling Consultant
Restaurant
Secretarial/Word Processing Service
Seminar Promoting
Travel Agency
Utility/Telephone Bill Auditing
Vending Machine Business
Wedding Planning Service

Note that these are likely to be small, perhaps even home-based, businesses. This group's members are often looking for low-cost start-ups and ones that can be run after hours without giving up a regular job. Other entrepreneurs may have greater ambitions. There is no reason you cannot found the next Microsoft Corporation; in fact, software start-ups are quite popular with entrepreneurs. However, software businesses may have difficulty obtaining financing, as we will see in the section on financing your business.

Some readers will wish to start or grow manufacturing firms and other potentially large enterprises. It still pays to take a creative approach, however, making sure you consider all sorts of alternatives to and variations on your concept. If the lists we provide do not help, obtain more specific lists at the library. *Thomas's Register of Manufacturers*, a business-to-business phone directory, and the membership lists of trade associations are all good sources.

To contact the American Entrepreneurs Association, call 1-800-421-2300. They will be happy to sell you their plans for any of these businesses.

Burstiner's Service Sector Businesses

(Source: Irving Burstiner, *Start & Run Your Own Profitable Service Business*, Englewood Cliffs, NJ: Prentice Hall, 1993, pp. 25; 35-38.)

"The service sector is where the jobs are," say many experts, including Irving Burstiner in his book *Start & Run Your Own Profitable Service Business*. Burstiner is a business professor who has owned businesses, including one that grew into a national chain of company-owned stores, franchised outlets, and agencies. He feels that start-ups should consider the service sector rather than manufacturing. Here's why.

Services account for approximately 37 percent of our total GNP and are growing rapidly. Over the last 18 years, the jobs in the service sector expanded more than 7 times, according to the U.S. Department of Commerce's Bureau of Economic Analysis. From the early 1970s to the late 1980s the number of people employed in service positions doubled, from 11.4 million to 25 million. The U.S. Department of Commerce predicts that the number in the service sector may be up to 33.7 million by the turn of the century. Manufacturing, on the other hand, has increased very little in the same time period. The government predicts a small decrease in manufacturing jobs by the year 2000.

If you want to participate in this growth, what area of the service sector should you consider for a potential business? The three service industries where employment is growing the most are legal services, business services, and health services. This does not necessarily mean that these would be the best niche for you. In fact, if these are growing rapidly, you may find too much competition in your area and prefer to find a smaller niche. But in many regions there are good opportunities in these areas.

One major advantage of a service business is that start-up costs may be lower than those for a product-oriented business. Many service businesses do not require investment in expensive equipment. However, you may find other costs such as staffing, advertising, or rent, for example, that can make the start-up somewhat expensive. Be sure you look carefully at *all* the costs.

Burstiner separates services into categories based on initial investment (low, moderate, and high) and level of expertise required to run the business (low, medium, and high). Some examples of consumer and business services in these various categories follow.

Consumer Services

Low initial investment; low level of expertise
house cleaning, bicycle repair, lawn care, personal shopping, sewing, wedding planning

Low initial investment; medium level of expertise
appliance repair, tax form preparation, sharpening service

Low initial investment; high level of expertise
career counseling, interior decorating, music instruction, tutoring, video-taping

Moderate initial investment; low level of expertise
bed and breakfast, carpet cleaning, delivery service, telephone answering service

Moderate initial investment; medium level of expertise
hair styling, catering, seminars, travel agency

Moderate initial investment; high level of expertise
car repair, TV repair, furniture refinishing

High initial investment; low level of expertise
campgrounds, car wash, employment agency, self-storage warehouse, taxi service

High initial investment; medium level of expertise
art gallery, barber shop, dry-cleaning service, movie theater, restaurant

High initial investment; high level of expertise
dance studio, fitness center, hotel/motel, lube shop, printing services, shoe repair shop

Business

Low initial investment; low level of expertise
carpet cleaning, messenger service, painting, typing

Low initial investment; medium level of expertise
bookkeeping, secretarial, sign painting

Low initial investment; high level of expertise
fax machine repair, management consultant, marketing consultant

Medium initial investment; low level of expertise
copying services, delivery service, telephone answering service

Medium initial investment; medium level of expertise
maintenance service, newsletter publication

Medium initial investment; high level of expertise
accounting services, commercial photography, computer programming,
   desktop publishing

High initial investment; low level of expertise
car rental or lease, equipment rental and lease, mailing services, security
   service

High initial investment; medium level of expertise
hotel, motel, temporary personnel agency

High initial investment; high level of expertise
ad agency, printing, photo processing

These suggestions are offered as ideas to stimulate your thoughts for
potential service businesses. You may also find Burstiner's book helpful. It
includes a lengthy bibliography at the end of each chapter, as well as a sample tax return in the Appendix.

The premise of Burstiner's analysis is important for any business start-up,
acquisition, or expansion. It is always helpful to analyze both costs and expertise. They represent the tangible investment requirements—time, money,
equipment—and intangibles—technical knowledge, management skills, customer and industry experience, and so forth. You need to assess investment
requirements on both dimensions.

For every idea you write down, show on your list whether investment is
low, medium, or high. Also indicate the amount of expertise required—low,

medium, or high. If both are high, bear in mind that the riskiness of the business is likely to be higher.

In considering the relationship between investment and return, have a realistic view of your current investment capabilities on both dimensions.

As you rate potential businesses on the factors important to you, comparing your opportunities in terms of investment required and expertise required, you will also want to consider the potential return versus the risk. (We discuss risk in Section 4 in the segment on writing a marketing plan.)

Top Ten Cities for Setting Up Shop

(Source: "Best Places Smart Companies," *Forbes ASAP*, February 27, 1995, pp. 46-55.)

Site selection is an important issue for certain businesses and some entrepreneurs are willing to go where opportunities are best. In their February issue of ASAP, an add-on to *Forbes* magazine, Forbes lists the 100 best places in the United States to locate companies, based on a rating of 11 characteristics, including computer savvy, general education, high-end brains, airports, taxes, regulations, cost of housing, cost of living, quality of life, immigration, and entrepreneurial zest.

The top ten cities were as follows:

Salt Lake City	Seattle
Houston	Phoenix
Dallas	Minneapolis-St. Paul
Denver	Omaha
Portland	San Francisco

If you have some flexibility in where you locate your business, you may want to consider one of these sites for your new venture.

For the rest of the list, take a look at the magazine.

How to Generate Ideas

Generating new and innovative ideas is not unique to starting a business. In fact, it should be the basis of thinking throughout all stages of a business operation. Innovation can insure better product development, promote creative distribution strategies (such as introducing a software game as shareware), and provide imaginative solutions to production and sourcing problems.

Managing the Creative Process. A number of people have discovered methods by which to unlock and release creative ideas, but all are based on John Dewey's original three-step process, described in his book *How We Think* (New York: D. C. Heath, 1933). First, you must define the problem. Then, you need to identify the alternatives. Finally, you select the best solution from among the alternatives.

Other writers, such as Alex Osborn and Sidney J. Parnes, have expanded on Dewey's basic model. (Source: Alexander Hiam, *The Vest-Pocket CEO*, Englewood Cliffs, NJ: Prentice Hall, 1990, pp. 456-458, and Hanley Norins, *The Young & Rubicam Traveling Creative Workshop*, Prentice Hall, 1990, pp. 45-46.) Alex Osborn, the developer of modern creative problem solving and considered to be the father of the brainstorming process, suggested the following model to use for strategic planning, product development and innovation, and human resource development:

1. Define the problem.
2. Gather data.
3. Analyze the data.
4. Generate ideas.
5. Let it rest.
6. Synthesize the information and select a solution.
7. Evaluate the solution.

Perhaps the most important feature here is step 5, to let the process have a rest time, when the ideas generated can simmer and bubble and perhaps lead to even more creative thinking. Brainstorming is hard work, and should not be rushed.

Sidney Parnes (S. J.Parnes, R. B. Noller, and A. M. Biondi, eds., *Guide to Creative Action*, New York: Charles Scribner's Sons, 1977) expanded Osborn's process into the "Osborn-Parnes Creative Problem-Solving (CPS) Process"

(James Evans, *Creative Thinking in the Decision and Management Sciences*, South Western, 1991, pp. 90-92), as follows:

1. Mess-finding
2. Fact-finding
3. Problem-finding
4. Idea-finding
5. Solution-finding
6. Acceptance-finding

Mess-finding involves discovering challenges and opportunities in the current situation and clarifying the goals for the problem solving.

Fact-finding is the process of gathering information that will illuminate the understanding of the mess. When the data is analyzed, it may be possible to define the problem(s).

Problem-finding is the phase when you focus on developing and refining problem statements that define the mess. Clearly defining the problem is a large part of solving the problem.

Idea-finding involves coming up with as many potential ideas for solutions as possible. This is the stage when various brainstorming techniques will be helpful. (We enumerate some of the many techniques later.)

Solution-finding is the stage when you evaluate possible solutions, and select the best one(s).

Acceptance-finding follows the selection of a solution. It focuses on making sure the solution can be implemented.

In the next section we offer a variety of methods for creative thinking and brainstorming. Try these techniques with groups or alone (although they are usually most effective with groups) to help with the process of finding new ideas. Note that each method, though somewhat different, is based on the original model of problem solving: Define the problem, generate ideas, select a solution.

Brainstorming for Fun and Profit

Nominal Group Technique.

(Source: Alexander Hiam, *The Vest-Pocket CEO*, Englewood Cliffs, NJ: Prentice Hall, 1990, pp. 454-456.)

Nominal group technique is a good method to use because it is simple and can make the decision-making process shorter, especially if the group is large and you do not have time for every member to make a presentation of his or her ideas. Although this technique may reduce the group interaction, it does not eliminate all discussion.

The first step is to state the problem. (Of course, this means that you have to have a clearly defined problem!)

Then members of the group write down their ideas on paper, usually for about five to ten minutes. They write down whatever they think of.

Next, each person reads his or her ideas to the group, and a "recorder" writes them on a chalkboard or flip chart. However, there is no discussion at this time. Each idea should be numbered for convenience of identification later.

When all the ideas have been recorded, they may be discussed as necessary in order to clarify the content.

After the discussion, a vote is taken, either by show of hands or private ballot, as appropriate. If several ideas are to be selected, then each person can assign a ranking to the ideas, 1 for top preference, 2 for next, and so forth.

Votes can be tallied on the spot, or the leader can take the information as advisory and announce the results later, if appropriate.

Osborn's Brainstorming

(Source: Alexander Hiam, *The Vest-Pocket CEO*, Englewood Cliffs, NJ: Prentice Hall, 1990, pp. 456-458, and Hanley Norins, *The Young & Rubicam Traveling Creative Workshop*, Prentice Hall, 1990, pp. 45-46.)

Osborn's brainstorming can be used for strategic planning, product development and innovation, and human resource management. Brainstorming is simple and easy and can usually provide immediate results. You will need someone to record the ideas as they are suggested, either on a flip chart or a chalkboard, where everyone can see them.

Start with a clear problem statement. Then state the rules for everyone in the group: There may be as many ideas as possible, none are to be criticized, they can be as wild as possible. The objective is quantity, not quality—you want as long a list as possible. (What happens, usually, is that as the process gets going, people are first restrained in their suggestions, then as they get into it, the ideas may be crazy, but then the really creative ideas start to appear.) Piggybacking ideas onto previous ones is all right, too.

After the list has been generated, you can review the ideas, either with the current group, or perhaps with another (to get more ideas.)

Idea circle.

(Source: Arthur H. Bell, *Business Communication and Practice*, Glenview, IL: Scott, Foresman, and Company, 1987, pp. 55-57.)

One variant of brainstorming is the idea circle. This technique could be used singly or with a group. For a group, draw a large circle on a flip chart or chalkboard. Mark it with segments like pie slices. Then have members of the group suggest ideas to fill in the segments. This limits the number of suggestions to the number of pie slices you have drawn, but pushes the group to come up with as many ideas as there are segments.

Classic Questions.

(Source: Arthur H. Bell, *Business Communication and Practice*, Glenview, IL: Scott, Foresman, and Company, 1987, pp. 54-57.)

Classic Questions are based on rhetorical questions asked by the ancient Greek orators to promote ideas. Arthur Bell in *Business Communication and Practice* lists ten questions in updated form that can be used to guide brainstorming. Fill in the blanks in these questions with the words appropriate to your undertaking. For example, if you are working on solutions for widgets, the first question would be "Why should we even care about widgets?"

1. Why should we even care about _____ ?
2. How might _____ be divided into stages?
3. What led to _____ ?
4. What type of person would be interested in _____ ?

5. If _____ did not exist, how would that change things?
6. What aspect of _____ do I like best, least?
7. What larger movement, field, or situation provides background for _____ ?
8. What are _____ 's principal benefits?
9. If _____ does not succeed, what were the barriers?

10. How could _____ be explained to a ten-year old child?

Obviously, you will not use all of these in one session. But they may be useful in guiding the thought process.

Advanced Brainstorming Techniques.

(Source: Michael Pacanowsky, "Team Tools for Wicked Problems," *Organizational Dynamics*, Winter 1995, AMA, pp. 40-41.)

Here are three more ways to come up with ideas.

Question brainstorming. Question brainstorming is basically like regular brainstorming, except that you brainstorm for questions instead of answers. You follow the usual brainstorming rules—that is, to record all questions and to avoid judging any questions. It is acceptable to associate a question with a previous question. And there should be a stated time limit to the process.

The point of this technique is to consider the questions that need to be looked at, rather than to try for answers. This is a good approach for strategic planning, new-product development, and similar endeavors.

Color questioning. Color questioning is an extension of question brainstorming. It was devised by Jerry Rhodes for managers at Phillips Corporation. Basically, the types of questions that might be generated are assumed to be in one of three categories, and are assigned a color to represent that category as follows:

green - imagination and ingenuity
red - description of fact
blue - judgments and opinions of value and need

As a question is suggested during a brainstorming session, it is written on the chart or board in the appropriate color and in one of three color-coded columns. This helps everyone sort out what is being accomplished. For example, every question denoting a fact will be written in red in the "fact" column.

By looking at the color-coded list, the group can see whether the questions are primarily in one category or if a category needs to be better addressed with more questions. For example, if there are only a few green questions, there are few creative questions being suggested. The facilitator can point this out and ask for more "green" (i.e., creative) questions.

TQR (Thinker-Questioner-Reflector). TQR is a useful approach to idea generation if the members of the group are having difficulty understanding someone's idea or if a member of the group is having trouble expressing an idea. Three different tasks are assigned in this technique. The person with the idea is designated as the Thinker. Another person is selected as the Questioner. The rest of the group become Reflectors. A time limit is set.

Then the Thinker is directed to think out loud, prompted by questions from the Questioner. The Reflectors can make suggestions.

This process can allow members of the group to overcome an impasse in thinking.

Reverse Assumptions

(Source: Michael Michalko, *Thinkertoys*, Berkeley, CA, Ten Speed Press, 1991, pp. 46-49.)

Challenging or reversing assumptions can open a whole new view of a problem. Michael Michalko, author of *Thinkertoys*, says, "Many creative thinkers get their most original ideas when they challenge and reverse the obvious." Michalko points out that Henry Ford pioneered the idea of the assembly line because instead of trying to get the workers to the material, he got the material to the workers.

Another of Michalko's examples of reversing assumptions is that of a CEO who gives his employees bonuses before the busiest time of the year, rather than after the crunch. The upshot: The company's production has risen 50 percent during the bonus period.

So you reverse your assumptions about a situation, then what? The next step is to consider how to accomplish the reversals. How may not be a single answer, but an array of them—multiple ways to solve the problem. And the answers may not be the exact opposite of the original problem; they may just provide you with a different view of the problem.

People always go to the grocery store to buy their food, right? Well, what if the grocery store or parts of it came to them? Years ago you had the bread truck and the milk truck. Nowadays, people are at work. Yet there are businesses that will deliver all your frozen goods, for example, or cases of soda or spring water. The product comes to the consumer instead of the other way around.

Assumption reversal allows you to stop looking at something in the traditional way. It offers you new information that may be combined in new and different ways. The process allows you to think in a new way, and to find new solutions. It gives you an opportunity to make a breakthrough in your thinking.

Listening Harder

(Source: Michael Pacanowsky, "Team Tools for Wicked Problems," *Organizational Dynamics*, Winter 1995, AMA, pp. 36-50.)

In future chapters we will discuss the traits of good managers and leaders, but for the moment let us look briefly at two examples of good management that enables effective problem-solving.

In his article "Team Tools for Wicked Problems," Michael Pacanowsky describes qualities of good managers. One quality is the ability to jump into a project, even an ongoing one, and be able to discern where the problems lie, then ask the "right questions to get the project rolling again." In other words, such managers are good listeners—in fact, deep listeners.

Bob Gore, president of W. L. Gore which produces Gore-Tex™. is an example of a good listener. He has a reputation for asking the right questions to help guide teams in problem solving. How does he know what questions to ask? He listens very carefully.

We will see in later chapters that good leaders are good listeners.

two
Screen for Success

After you have done extensive brainstorming and soul searching, you will probably be eager to decide what business (or other idea) is best for you. Do not jump on the first appealing idea; screen all your concepts carefully to minimize risk, maximize return, and ensure a close match with personal requirements. Part of any screening is to test your idea on potential customers. But there are many factors to consider beyond the actual product or service you want to market. For example, you will want to think about the environment in which you want to work—whether the business could be out of your home, for example, or a small office elsewhere. You need to take into account whether the work will fit in with your lifestyle, or whether your lifestyle will fit with the work. And you must make sure you can handle the capital requirements and management demands of the business.

Personal Considerations

Do you have the capabilities for the work you select? Starting a business is very different from starting a new job. You will be the decision maker, and your personal characteristics will figure in a large way in this business venture. We tend to be least objective about ourselves, so this is the hardest part of idea screening.

As your decisions may not always result in a positive outcome, you will need the ability to bounce back after a setback. You will need to have lots of determination and perseverance to see your business through the inevitable ups and downs.

Creativity, important at the outset, will also be a necessity all along the way, from start-up through stages of growth and into maturity. Innovative ideas will enable you to set yourself apart from the crowd. Indeed, innovation is a business's lifeblood. Staying on top of technological changes is important, but is only part of successful business innovation. New approaches to customer service or quality, new distribution methods or packaging concepts, and many other options also exist for the innovator.

Your business will need to be able to move quickly in response to a changing market and customer needs. How flexible are you? How resilient to threats and changes? If you find change threatening, then a stable, low-risk concept is preferable, but good luck finding one!

Another skill you will need as an entrepreneur is setting goals and following through in order to accomplish them. Some people prefer to follow the rules that others set for them. They should probably not undertake to start a business themselves.

While all this introspection may seem frivolous when you are eager to get started, you should, nevertheless, be aware of your personal assets and shortcomings. Intense scrutiny of your skills, abilities, and characteristics will help you plan for any contingencies.

Are you ready to be an entrepreneur? You can evaluate your own, or someone else's, entrepreneurial capacity and capability by rating them on the characteristics of entrepreneurs. Here we have listed four basic characteristics that pop up in almost all studies of entrepreneurs, plus a dozen more that studies or entrepreneurship indicate may also increase your chances of success.

Rate yourself on a 1 = "Definitely Not" to 5 = "Definitely" scale for each of the following:

Checklist of Personal Traits

(Source: Based on literature review in Donald Kuratko and Richard Hodgetts, *Entrepreneurship: A Contemporary Approach*, Third Edition, The Dryden Press, 1995, pp. 40-43. Developed by Alex Hiam for Ken Blanchard, Charles Schewe, Robert Nelson and Alexander Hiam, *Exploring the World of Business*, Worth Publishers, in press for 1996.)

	Scale				
Core characteristics:					
Creative, innovative	1	2	3	4	5
Moderate risk taker	1	2	3	4	5
Independent	1	2	3	4	5
Determined to achieve success	1	2	3	4	5
Additional characteristics:					
Good health	1	2	3	4	5
Realistic attitude	1	2	3	4	5
Superior conceptual ability	1	2	3	4	5
Self-confidence	1	2	3	4	5
Need to control or direct	1	2	3	4	5
Attracted to challenges	1	2	3	4	5
Emotionally stable	1	2	3	4	5
Self-controlled	1	2	3	4	5
Tend to take the initiative	1	2	3	4	5
Balanced	1	2	3	4	5
Self-reliant	1	2	3	4	5
Confident	1	2	3	4	5

Readiness Score:
Add all your individual ratings
   and divide by 16   1   2   3   4   5

Anything below a "4" means you do not have the personal characteristics associated with high levels of entrepreneurship in most studies. However, if you score higher on the core characteristics you may wish to discount the importance of your overall score. And remember, these attributes represent the average entrepreneur—there may be alternative profiles that are also associated with success.

Fair Warning

(Sources: George Tunick, "Tough Truths for Start-Ups," *Executive Female*, Sept.-Oct. 1994, p. 82; Jerry W. Moorman and James W. Halloran, *Entrepreneurship*, Cincinnati, OH: South-Western Publishing Company, 1993, p. 4.)

Although it looks easy and like fun from the outside, starting a business is a great deal of work. Journalist George Tunick, Professor Jerry Moorman, and James Halloran, director of a small-business development center, all have experience with entrepreneurs, albeit in different settings. They can recount success stories as well as failures. And the failures, they would tell you, are because the would-be entrepreneur did not keep his or her eyes wide open going into the situation.

Observers of the entrepreneurial challenge would offer cautions to anyone intending to start a business of his or her own. These cautions would include the following "truths." In an effort to be realistic about your new business, be sure to consider these points as you think about starting a business.

1. Be prepared emotionally. It is tough to get a company up and running and to keep it going. Be ready for a challenge. Be sure you have the stamina and attitude to see you through the tough times. If you anticipate other emotionally draining projects, perhaps you should postpone your business—or them. Starting a business and coping with a personal crisis are incompatible activities. Be sure to factor in personal considerations when screening business ideas (see Checklist of Personal Traits).

2. Be prepared for rejection and failure. Many start-up businesses fail. According to the Small Business Administration (SBA), 24 out of 100 businesses close within two years. Twenty-seven more close within four years. And within six years, more than 60 will fail. Starting a business is not for the fainthearted. But the quality of your ideas and the screening process by which you choose one can help you beat these odds.

3. Be ready to work hard. Beginning entrepreneurs usually put in long hours to get their businesses underway. Your situation is not likely to be different. It will take a lot of hard work, especially at the beginning. A good screening exercise is to identify and list every task a business will require in its first month. Then estimate and total the hours these tasks will take. Now allocate the hours to your management team—and you have a fair estimate of your first month's time demands. It's hoped that it comes out to less than 24 hours per day!

4. Have a realistic picture of the business's potential. Analysts find that new business plans usually overestimate sales and underestimate the costs of start-up. To hedge against this, add 50 percent to your estimate of the costs and you will probably be closer to the actual costs. Similarly, assume sales will grow more slowly than you initially project and that you will need to cover the resulting cash flow gap. Can you afford to? (See our discussion of business planning in Part III.)

5. Know how to get financing. Sources of financing include the family, vendors, customers, partners, friends, banks, insurance companies, venture capitalists, angels, and government agencies. The ones who know you are more likely to loan money than those who are not emotionally involved in your venture and prefer to have profit guarantees. In order to obtain financing, you will need to have a solid business plan. Both business plans and financing are discussed in separate sections of this book. In addition, you will find an array of related resources in the resource section.

6. Be willing to do financial analysis. We are adding this sixth point to the list based on long, sad experience as consultants. Many times, entrepreneurs or small-business managers have come to one or the other of us with serious financial problems that we had to fix—but that should have been easy to foresee and prevent.

For example, one successful restaurant owner decided to sell two restaurants to franchisees, with the ultimate goal of franchising across the country. Her business continued to make and supply much of the food from a central wholesale kitchen she ran. But she had fallen deeply behind on payroll taxes, rents, loan payments, and supplier bills since switching to the franchise system. Why? Her wholesale kitchen did not operate at low enough cost to allow for profitability once she had to sell at wholesale prices to franchisors instead of the retail prices she used to obtain when she ran the stores herself. A careful cost analysis and simple projection of costs and revenues under the new plan would have revealed this problem in advance. But the owner was more interested in running restaurants than in crunching numbers.

As an entrepreneur and manager, you must be willing to roll up your sleeves, power up the spread sheet on your PC, and create realistic financial models to support decisions. Otherwise, you will eventually blunder into a financial problem you should have foreseen and avoided. (We also cover financial analysis later, under both The Business Plan and Funding and Financial Management.)

American Express's Six Success Factors for New Businesses

(Source: Based on *Profiles of Success: An American Express Study of New Business*, Beverly Wettenstein, October 10, 1989, American Express: NY)

Contrary to the Small Business Administration sample in which many new businesses failed, American Express's three-year study found a success rate much higher than expected. "Profiles of Success" reports that of 3,000 new businesses in the United States, 77 percent succeeded. What's more, 90 percent of the entrepreneurs polled said they would do it again. Why? The sample may have been different, but we think it is representative of the kinds of businesses typically started by entrepreneurs today.

The American Express study went on to define six factors that are key ingredients for the success of new businesses: self-confidence, size, service emphasis, hard work, full attention, and product knowledge. If you want your new business to succeed, you will want to pay attention to these six areas. That means your idea screening and selection should be based in part on whether these factors are present in specific businesses under consideration.

1. Self Confidence. Confidence about the business helps start-ups succeed. The confidence comes from having a good business plan and knowing the potential risks. In addition, it is important to have expertise in the business you plan to launch, or in a related business—any background that provides you with needed skills for the new undertaking. In short, those who have done their homework, and have done it thoroughly and accurately, seem to do well with their small businesses.

Ask yourself, "Do I know the ropes of this business I plan to start, or can I find someone who does?" "Can the needed skills be learned?" "Have I informed myself of the risks involved?" "Are they insurmountable, or will I be able to handle them?" Note that the answers may differ for each business concept considered—and for different entrepreneurs as well. The right match between personal and business concept is needed in order for there to be realistic self-confidence.

2. Size of Initial Investment. Sufficient initial investment is key to the success of a business. Since investment is based on the size of the company, it should not be a surprise that larger firms with greater investments (in the $50,000 range) tend to do better than do smaller firms with smaller investments (around $20,000). Likewise, companies with more employees (six or more) tend to do better than very small ones with only one or two people.

Ask yourself whether you have provided sufficiently for eventualities. For example, do you have sufficient backers to provide a cushion in the event that the business gets off to a slow start? Have you been too optimistic about your profit potential? Such mistakes lead entrepreneurs to start too small, without all the capital and people needed to make start-up easy.

Note that the size of initial investment also varies among opportunities. Most obviously, some require more funding than others. Less obviously, your resources may also vary from one opportunity to another. Your Uncle Fred may be happy to lend you money for a restaurant because he loves good food, but may have no interest in a 7-Eleven franchise. And you may be better able to obtain credit from vendors for one kind of start-up than for another, and so on. So you need to estimate both your available financial assets and the start-up costs for each opportunity you screen, then try to pick one where your resources are generous compared to the likely needs of the business.

3. Emphasis on service rather than on price. There is a better survival rate among companies that focus on customer service than among those focused primarily on low prices. Good customer service, associated with a product, tends to enhance the qualities of that product and to generate customer loyalty and repeat sales. Wal-Mart and Home Depot, evidently mindful of the impersonality of large discount/warehouse-type stores, offer exceptional customer service in order to keep their customers returning to their stores.

Similarly, a quality advantage is a safer bet than a low price. Ask yourself, "Do I offer obviously better quality or service than is now available to my target customer?" While bargains may appeal to some customers in the short run, you are more likely to have repeat customers because of the quality you

Initial Investment Screening Matrix

Plot each opportunity on this matrix and try to pick ones in the upper left. Create your own scale to fit the size of your project; just be sure you use the same scale for both axes.

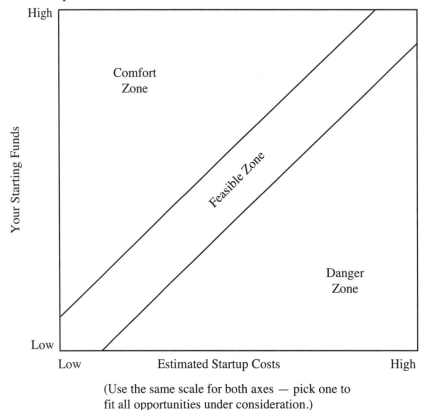

(Use the same scale for both axes — pick one to fit all opportunities under consideration.)

offer. Be sure to ask potential customers too; they may not agree with your perception of what quality is.

4. Working hard but knowing when to stop. The American Express study discovered an interesting phenomenon: Although commitment to one's own business means longer hours than one might expect in direct employment, the companies that did not take it to an extreme did just as well at survival as those who did:

Time spent	*Survival Rate*
60-69 hours	80%
59 hours and under	76%
70 hours and over	75%

So, while you need to expect to put in long hours at the outset, you also need to bear in mind that burning the candle at both ends will not necessarily make your business any more successful than if you put in fairly reasonable hours. Keep the demands on your time realistic by avoiding opportunities that require you to be a workaholic.

5. Devoting full time to the business. There is some validity to the idea that one should test the waters slowly and perhaps hang on to a current job as protection while starting a new business. However, once the start-up business is underway, you'll need to pay attention to the business and not be distracted by another job. The American Express study found that the survival rate of new businesses was 8 percent higher when the business was the entrepreneur's only job. Holding another job at the same time tended to lower the success rate of a new business.

Job	*Survival Rate*
New business is only job	78%
Person holds another job also	70%

If you need to maintain a current job, know when your new business will need your full attention and plan your time line (and your finances) accordingly. Ask yourself, "When will I be reasonably financially comfortable with shifting all my attention to the new business?" The answer will vary among opportunities. Perhaps you should avoid those that are unlikely to allow a swift and easy transition to full-time entrepreneurship.

6. Product knowledge. Knowledge is a powerful thing. Because risk can be a major factor in the success or failure of a business, prior experience with a product or process helps reduce the risk and improves the success rate. Potential investors, who tend to be risk-averse, will be more likely to be interested in your business if you can show that you are experienced in the field.

The American Express study found that when personnel in the start-up business had worked with the same products or services in previous jobs, the success rate for the business was likely to be higher:

Products in New Business	*Success Rate*
Same as in prior job	80%
Different	72%

Ask yourself, "What are the skills I bring to this business?" "What other skills would be important?" Consider partners who can fill any skills gaps you see. This is also important to bear in mind when you begin hiring for your business. Consider carefully how the backgrounds of potential employees can be complementary to those already represented by the management. Use the Skills Matrix table to help you plan for your management team and employees.

Skills Matrix

	People:			
Tasks:	*You*	*Partner*	*Employee 1*	*Missing Skills*
Bookkeeping	banking, checkbook management	same	none	cash flow analysis, taxes, payroll
Sales	no— hate personal selling!	prospecting and sales	sales support, desktop publishing, brochures	none
etc.				

Enter key tasks on rows, then list applicable skills by column for each member of the start-up team. Next, brainstorm to list any missing skills. When the matrix is complete, develop a plan to fill the skills gaps—that is, hire a tax accountant, buy cash-flow management software, and use ADP's payroll service to fill the skills gaps for the bookkeeping tasks above.

Incidentally, having prior *supervisory* experience did not seem to make a lot of difference in the success rate for new businesses.

How to Minimize the Risk of Failure

The findings of the American Express study suggest that entrepreneurs should take certain precautions to risk-proof their businesses.

1. Have a well-thought-out business plan.
2. Be sure you have enough cash.
3. Emphasize service.
4. Work hard but don't overdo it.
5. Give your full attention to the business.
6. Remember that knowledge is a powerful tool. If you don't have the direct knowledge yourself, be sure you have someone on your team who does.

Issues for Women- and Minority-Owned Businesses

There is no question about it—firms owned by women or minorities are at higher risk than those owned by white males. Why? Because of the discrimination that women and minorities experience in accessing money, customers, and other business resources. Minority and women entrepreneurs may be trading in the glass ceiling of corporate employment for a cement floor of entrepreneurship. Careful analysis and planning is needed to avoid businesses that are likely to produce a hard landing.

The National Federation of Independent Business and American Express Small Business Services study of the three-year success rates of 3,000 firms revealed these facts for women and minorities:

6% of the firms were minority-owned
22% of the firms were female-owned

78% of the male-owned firms survived
71% of the female-owned firms survived

78% of the non-minority-owned firms survived
66% of the minority-owned firms survived

30% of the minority-owned firms failed

18% of the nonminority firms failed

Minority-owned firms are 67% more likely to fail in three years than are nonminority firms.

Female-owned firms are 28% more likely to fail than are male-owned firms.

How You Can Help Yourself

So what do these statistics mean for you if your business is woman- or minority-owned? First, be sure you make a very careful assessment of your risk, allowing for the differences in access to resources.

Next, if you are looking for investment, develop a plan to overcome the limitations imposed by the business environment. Your access plan should focus on ways of obtaining funding, credit, and any other resources that are generally harder for minorities and women to obtain. With careful planning, you can overcome biases in lending and other limits to resource access. (In the financing and resources sections of this book you will find material geared specifically to women and minorities.)

Funding and resource problems are not too big to overcome, but they need attention if you want to avoid failure.

Network, network, network

Develop and use networking systems for all aspects of your business. These will serve you well when you are looking for resources, financial or otherwise. Associations of minority owners or women in business can be found in many cities. They may be listed under Women Business Owners or may be part of a local Chamber of Commerce program. Networks can help you find vendors, lenders, and other businesses that are also owned by minorities or women and therefore unlikely to discriminate against your business. Ask colleagues about the professional organizations to which they belong.

Check State and Federal Programs

In some states you can obtain minority- or women-owned business certification if you are qualified, with the help of your state Economic Development Program.

The Small Business Administration (SBA) of the federal government has a new "microloan" program to fund businesses that need $25,000 or less. It is encouraging to note that 43 percent of the funds have gone to women-owned businesses. In addition, there is a Women's Pre-Qualification Pilot Loan Program that helps women to get qualification from the SBA *before* they go to the bank.

The SBA also licenses specialized small business investment companies— SSBICs—that focus on socially and economically disadvantaged business owners.

(See the financing and resources sections of this book for more information on these topics.)

Investigate the Banks in Your Area

Harris Trust and Savings Bank in Chicago offers educational programs designed to help women prepare financial analyses of their businesses. Executive Vice President Cheryl Reich says, "We teach [women] how to connect to other entrepreneurs, and we introduce them to the financial and investment communities." This is a good example of organized networking, which helps entrepreneurs with equity financing and bank loans.

If you live near a large city, you may have a better chance of finding such a program. But even if you do not, you can develop your own network through which you can share a variety of information.

Venture Capital

Venture capital, difficult to obtain at best, is even more elusive for women- and minority-owned businesses. About 1 percent of this type of capital goes to women-owned businesses. But there are some groups open to investing in such businesses. *Working Woman* lists the following, so you could try them first:

Inroads Capital Partners. Jerrold Carrington, general partner in this Chicago-based firm, is an African American. He reports that this new firm has begun to target women- and minority-owned companies.

New Era Capital Partners. This Los Angeles firm invests in women-owned ventures in the areas of information technology, interactive-media, broadcast and cable delivery systems, and health care.

Capital Rose Perpetual Fund. This Malvern, Pennsylvania-based firm is currently raising capital through $10 donations. When they have reached their goal, they hope to be able to finance more women-owned businesses that have lower capital needs.

Women's Equity Fund. This firm, based in Boulder, Colorado, serves businesses within the state, but eventually hopes to expand. They specialize in investments of $50,000 or less in women-owned manufacturing and service businesses.

UNC Ventures. Located in Boston, Massachusetts, this is the oldest private venture-capital firm in the United States devoted to investing in minority-owned enterprises.

Other Organizations. The American Woman's Economic Development Corporation (AWED) is a national nonprofit organization based in New York City. It offers low-cost training and business consultation to women.

The Office of Women's Business Ownership (OWBO) is part of the U.S. Small Business Administration. It has its own office at 1441 L Street, N.W., Room 414, Washington, DC 20416, 202-653-8000.

(Sources: "Profiles of Success: An American Express Study of New Business" - commissioned by American Express Small Business Services and the National Federation of Independent Business (NFIB), 1989, American Express: New York; Ilyce R. Glink, "Where to Look for Money Now," *Working Woman*, October 1994, pp. 56-62.)

Screening Is Key!

The bottom line for minority and women entrepreneurs is that they may face higher risk than other entrepreneurs. So their idea screening needs to be better managed and more careful than even that of the average entrepreneur.

Evaluate the risk factors in any business concept carefully, avoid those that pose high personal risks, and plan carefully to mitigate the risks associated with the idea you do choose to pursue. But do not give up! The three-year survival rates for women- and minority-owned businesses are still two-thirds better than most people expect, and for many of us are better odds than we would give to a salaried job over the same three-year period.

three
Establish Your Vision

Why You Need to Chart Your Course with a Vision and Revision

There is a reason you want to make a new product or service to give to the world. As you define your product and do your research you have probably thought "I won't do that," or "This other is really important to me." These are your values, and they will figure strongly into your concept of your business. In addition to the fairly simple Who, What, Why, When, Where, and How of your business, there are components of your vision that are somewhat more intangible but are nevertheless important.

For example, think about what you value: professionalism, excellence of product or service, growth, economic rewards, psychological rewards, quality, diversity, ethics, goodwill, long-term relationships, enthusiasm, creativity, cooperation, teamwork. You may value some or all of these things. Those values that are important should be part of your vision and will therefore likely be part of your goal or vision statement. They may be included in a charter if you decide to write one.

It is important to give some thought to your values before you set up shop and begin to hire employees and make decisions about suppliers, customers, and the like. You need to have a good sense of your values so that you can set your goals and be aware of your limits in accomplishing them.

Personal and Business Values

There are two levels on which values need to be defined by entrepreneurs or small business managers. First, they need to clarify their personal values, the convictions and ethics that should guide their own decisions as they select, screen, develop, or manage any business. It is important to articulate your own values as an entrepreneur and to make sure your business is consistent with them. If you, like most of us, do not think often about personal values on a daily basis, you may want to take a few minutes to use the Personal Value Clarification Worksheet that follows. And if you have partners or employees who should be part of key business decisions, encourage them to complete their own copies, then compare and discuss the results. Major differences need to be resolved or compensated for so they do not create problems in the future.

Personal Value Clarification Worksheet

(Source: Alex Hiam and Susan Angle, *Adventure Careers*, Franklin Lakes, NJ: Career Press, 1995.)

Step 1: Make a list of values, ideals, and principles you consider most important in your life. These may be in the context of your personal experience, as well as in broader world terms. What is important to you? What governs how you work? List as many of these ideals as you can. They may include some or all of the following (and this list is not by any means exhaustive): honesty, compassion, kindness, steadfastness, love, charity, achievement, loyalty, family, financial success, consistency.

Step 2: From the list you made in step 1, select four to six of the most important values. Write each one, followed by a definition of what the meaning of that particular value is for you. Perhaps, for example, honesty is important to you. That may mean that you expect to be honest in all your dealings with others, especially in business, and that you expect others to do the same for you.

So your list will be filled in as below:

1. Value:

   Meaning:

2. Value:

   Meaning:

   etc., until you have four to six defined.

Step 3: Now expand on the meaning of these values for you personally. Take the six and write down what these values mean to you. Which of these values influence your actions most? Which ones affect how you go about making decisions?

1. Value:

   Its meaning in my life and work:

   and so on.

Step 4: Now select two or three of the values and describe how you want to express each one in your life.

1. Value:

   I am committed to expressing it in my life and work by:

   and so on.

After clarifying personal values, the entrepreneur is ready to look at the issue of business values. Common values provide a direction and sense of purpose to any organization and help unify and motivate its employees. The traditional start-up or small business ignores the issue of value entirely and thereby overlooks a potentially powerful success factor. But you cannot just "adopt" values by writing something down one day and assuming you or your employees will somehow be changed by it. Business values have to flow from personal values and will take root only when the entrepreneur or managers "walk the talk."

Consultant Robin Buchanan (a managing partner with Bain & Co. in London) and Andrew Campbell, Jr. (of the Ashridge Strategic Management Centre) explain:

Values are the beliefs and moral principles that lie behind the company's culture and give meaning to its norms and behaviors. Management cannot change values through mission statements or company songs. But the change CAN be accomplished through management behavior (Lance Berger, Martin Sikora, and Dorothy Berger, *The Change Management Handbook*, Burr Ridge, IL, Irwin, 1994, p. 130).

The easiest way to ensure that your behavior as owner and/or manager is aligned with appropriate business values is to set out business values that are (a) consistent with your personal values and connections, and (b) appropriate to and beneficial for your business enterprise. That is why values are given an early position in this book; they should be well thought out before you go into the details of business planning. Here is an example of a well-defined set of business values from the Managing by Values Management training module offered by Blanchard Training and Development of San Diego, California (Source: Unpublished ms. from Michael O'Connor and Ken Blanchard, dated 3/3/94):

Our Operating Values

1. Ethical

- Ensure fair and equitable treatment with *employees*.
- Conduct our business fairly and with integrity with *customers* and in the marketplace.
- Provide complete and accurate information for *shareholders*.
- Provide leadership and practice our values in the *community*.

2. Responsive

- Demonstrate respect for all *employees* and their ideas.
- Identify *customer* expectations and deliver on commitments in a timely manner.
- Deliver on commitments to *shareholders*.
- Encourage employee participation in *community* service.

3. Profitable

- Encourage personal initiative and opportunity for *employees*.
- Provide cost-effective, technologically superior products for *customers*.
- Produce a reasonable return on equity for *shareholders*.
- Make contributions that strengthen the *community*.

And here is a second example, this one from successful start-up The Body Shop, in which the company's commitment to environmentalism is translated in value in action:

A Brief Summary of Our Environmental Policy

1. *Think globally* as a constant reminder of our obligation to protect the environment.
2. *Achieve excellence* by setting clear targets and time scales within which to meet them.
3. *Search for sustainability* by using renewable resources wherever possible and conserving natural resources where renewable options aren't available.
4. *Manage growth* by letting our business decisions be guided as much by their environmental implications as by economics.
5. *Manage energy* by using the absolute minimum and working toward replacing what we must use with renewable resources.
6. *Manage waste* by adopting a four-tier approach: reduce, reuse, recycle and, as a last resort, dispose by the safest means possible.
7. *Contol pollution* by avoiding contamination, reducing emissions, and taking extra care with all potentially damaging processes and products.
8. *Operate safely* by minimizing risk at every level of our operations: for staff, for customers, and for the community in which the business operates.
9. *Obey the law* by complying with environmental laws at all times.
10. *Raise awareness* by continuously educating our staff and our customers.
    (Source: "A Brief Summary of our Enviromental Policy," This Is The Body Shop—Spring 1994.)

Following is an excellent activity for developing meaningful, actionable business values such as the above examples.

Using the Charter Exercise

(Source: *Cases in Strategic Management for the Smaller Business*, ed. Stuart St. P. Slatter. Oxford, England: Basil Blackwell Ltd, 1988, pp. 371-396.)

Consider writing a charter for your organization. Although it is not a requirement of incorporation or other business forms, a charter can be a valuable tool for your business. Your business may be guided by an unwritten philosophy and a system of values, but sometimes it helps to quantify your goals by putting them on paper. Just going through the process of writing a charter may help clarify values for management and employees alike. As time passes, the charter can be a reference document to check whether you are still aiming at your original goals and whether you are achieving them.

A charter does not have to be long or complicated, nor does it have to be written upon start-up. Take the case of F International (FI), an association of freelance computer programmers, started in England in 1962. It was not until the 1980s, when the company was experiencing significant growth, that the company charter was written. The board of directors was increasingly concerned about poor profit levels, strained management resources, and a changing computer industry. They wanted to be sure that FI retained the unique characteristics that its founder, Steve Shirley, had instilled from the start.

Ms. Shirley wanted a way for women to be able to continue working (at home primarily) after having children. She had started the business of computer consulting when she had been in that situation herself. Her approach to the business was to provide a centralized management that was personal and informal. She felt that although profit was important, quality work was also important and that it would best come from employees who felt a personal commitment to their jobs. To that end, she tried to foster growth, support, and flexibility.

As the company grew, some of these values could potentially be lost, especially as competition in computer consulting and programming increased and technology improved. Hence, the need for a charter in which to formalize the values Ms. Shirley cherished. It is interesting to note that Ms. Shirley's company is staffed and run primarily by women.

Contents of a Charter

What goes into a charter and how long should it be? Each part of the charter can be short and concise. One or two sentences for each heading may suffice. FI's charter included the following sections:

> *Description of the company.*
> Who are you? What do you do? Why do you do it?

> *Mission.*
> What do you plan to do? Do you want to be a leader in the market, fill a new niche? How will you do this?

> *Strategy.*
> What methods will you use to differentiate yourself from the competition? For example, will your focus be on cost or quality?

> *Values.*
> What does your company value—employees, knowledge, creativity, productivity, professionalism—and how are these values demonstrated?

> In the values section, FI's charter enumerated seven specific values:

1. Professional excellence, which includes professional knowledge and development, along with quality product.
2. Growth of the firm, as the market grows and in terms of market share. FI is also committed to growing locally, nationally, and internationally. (Obviously, some firms may prefer to remain local or national.)
3. Economic and psychological rewards for the firm, the employees, and investors such as shareholders. This includes not only profits but other less tangible rewards such as the good feeling generated by producing a quality product.
4. Integrated diversity, which would allow for appropriate growth in the country in which the company is operating. FI's aim here is to be con-

sistent from country to country, yet to conduct the business in a manner appropriate to the particular location's standards and regulations.

5. Universal ethics as related to the area the business serves. This means respecting local laws and regulations but also valuing the higher good of all.

6. Goodwill with colleagues, clients, and vendors, which will help promote long-term relationships.

7. Enthusiasm, which FI felt would promote creativity, cooperation, and ultimately, greater profit potential.

This charter is presented not as the only model for a charter, but to stir up ideas for you as you consider the content of your own charter. Perhaps other issues and values are more important to you and your organization. The charter, in process, can provide a vehicle for the management team to clarify the company's values and mission. The completed charter offers a document by which you can periodically measure the success of your organization.

four
Build Your Network

We mentioned networks and networking in the discussion of issues for women and minorities. But we cannot mention networking enough. It is an essential tool for everyone in business, and particularly for someone starting out. You need to "plug into" the industry and market, the sources of support and funding, and the intellectual capital and other so-called soft assets that do not show up in most business plans, but are vital to success nonetheless.

Networking can be a valuable tool for individuals, groups, and organizations. It is especially useful to the small-business entrepreneur who needs access to advice, information, and resources (both economic and noneconomic) for starting a business. Networking can lead to new customers, suppliers, business advice, supplies, and other things of value that can make the business valuable enough that others will want to invest in it.

One way to connect with others in business is to join professional groups. There you may find others with similar small businesses who are willing to share information and resources. A good example of this is the chamber of commerce in the town or city where you do business. Even personal connections can serve as networks, for friends may have experience or connections in their businesses that can be instructive and supportive to you.

Building Entrepreneurial Networks

(Sources: Andrea Larson and Jennifer A. Starr, "A Network Model of Organization Formation," *Entrepreneurship Theory and Practice*, Winter 1993, pp. 5-12; and Alex Hiam et al., [textbook].)

Networking is a skill that all businesses, but particularly small ones, need to have and use. If you are new to the scene, how can you develop a network? We use a three-stage model to describe the development of a successful network. It starts with developing a personal network and contacts, then converts them into business relationships, and finally develops interdependent links to form a free-standing business network. This model, illustrated in Figure 4-1, seems to work well for entrepreneurs or small business managers who wish to grow their businesses.

Step 1. Identify and Build Personal Contacts. The first step is to identify the resources you need for your business. For example, you will need physical and capital resources (inventory, products, loans), sales and social support, and business contacts. You will need suppliers. You will need customers.

Sources of networking relationships can be people from previous working or other relationships, friends, family, community acquaintances. You may have a very large list at first, but remember that not all of the relationships will become networking ones, and you will narrow down your list over time and as your needs become more apparent or change.

The second part of this stage is to explore the potential networking relationships to see if they can be mutually rewarding. This process will weed out your list also.

Step 2. Convert the Relationships. In the second stage of networking, you convert the relationships you have identified into formal business relationships. The connections will begin to develop and the parties will learn to trust one another and to develop a sense of give and take. You will look for common goals. You will develop and strengthen open lines of communication.

Over time, you will see whether the relationship is a committed one and whether it has an ethical basis. If not, weed it out and concentrate on developing the networking relationships that have mutual benefits.

Building an Entrepreneurial Network

Step 1. Build A Personal Network

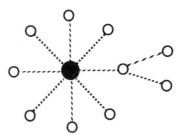

Step 2. Convert Key Relationships to Business Contacts

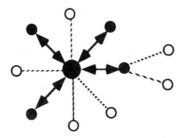

Step 3. Extend and Network your Contacts

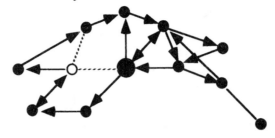

(Source: Developed by Alexander Hiam & Associates, 1995, to illustrate Andrea Larson and Jennifer Starr's network model of organization (*Entrepreneurship Theory and Practice,* Winter 1993).

Step 3. Develop Interdependence Among Your Contacts.   In the third stage links begin to develop among other members of the network. For example, your company might have several suppliers, two of whom decide to get together to collaborate on a product for you. Or two members of a networking group may agree to do joint research. These cooperative endeavors will strengthen the networking links. As interdependence grows, there will be less personal exchange and more organizational exchange. The originator of the network is no longer the key element, as the interrelationships develop on their own.

It is in the longer-term relationship that true commitment develops and there is stabilization and predictability. The relationship grows. The networkers will be able to mobilize critical resources to generate revenues via the network.

Hiring Experienced Networkers

(Source: Statistics compiled by James E. Challenger, president of Challenger, Gray & Christmas Inc., discussed in Mary Rowland, "Finding Money to Start a Business," *The New York Times*, May 28, 1991, Sec. 3.)

Once you have realized the value of networking, you will want to take advantage of all the applications. You may have connections from previous jobs or businesses, but they may not suffice if you have now moved into a different industry. One way around this limitation is to bring into your organization someone who already has an extensive network.

As more and more companies downsize, many managers with extensive corporate and networking experience are being released into the job pool. Instead of finding a new job, they may prefer more autonomy, either by starting a business of their own or by joining a small start-up company.

What does this mean for you, the entrepreneur? Mature, experienced people to draw on for staffing your enterprise. In particular, this flood of older, experienced managers into entrepreneurship means networking is an increasingly easy strategy. Experience means contacts, lot of contacts, that can be turned into a network for your business. If you are not well connected in your start-up industry and the financial community, bring one or more of these "downsized" managers onto your board or management team, with the clear understanding that his or her job will be to build your business's network.

Networking to Overcome Objections: the "Influence Network"

Entrepreneurs run into lots of objections. One professor who tracked start-up companies reports that "five of the eight entrepreneurs [he studied] encountered groups or individuals other than competitors who had a vested interest in the failure of the new venture." In other words, you probably have enemies you haven't even thought about. Ask yourself, are there any stakeholders who might see a threat in your planned activities? For instance, if you plan to offer a service to businesses in your area, are there in-house staff whose jobs might be displaced when their companies hire you to do their work? Or perhaps there are community groups who will oppose your plan to manufacture or ship products from the office space you want to rent. Often, home-based businesses are opposed by neighbors, who object to noise, commercial traffic, or frequent visits by clients. Networking can help you overcome the objections of any stakeholders who may object to your activities.

In addition, there are many people and organizations you wish to actively court, from potential investors and customers to the suppliers and other business partners you hope will cooperate with your venture. With these, too, a network can be used to establish credibility and gain influence.

The first step in developing an influence network to target such people is the identification of stakeholders. Stakeholders are those people over whom you need influence because they have a stake in what you do and enough power to influence your ability to do it. Thus the best way to find them is to ask who might care about or be affected by your business and its activities, and who among that group might have enough power to have either a positive or negative influence over the business. You may need to brainstorm with others in the business community or industry to make sure you leave no stones unturned in compiling your list. Once you have a list of names, you are ready to build a special network designed specifically to influence them.

How do you build a network that can help you gain influence over those who might block your activities or fail to cooperate with them? The three-stage model described earlier is generally applicable, but you may also find this more specific model of particular interest. It was developed by the researcher quoted at the start of this section, and here we will quote him again as he describes what he found in studying the networks of entrepreneurs:

To build an influence network:

(Source: Ian C. MacMillan, "The Politics of New Venture Management," in William Sahlman and Howard Stevenson, eds., *The Entrepreneurial Venture*, Harvard Business School Publications, 1992, pp. 164-165.)

1. Identify people and organizations among existing connections who are close to potential stakeholders.
2. Seek criticism, advice, and suggestions on the new venture from these people.
3. Ask them for advice about contacts (at least two) to approach in target organizations and get permission to use their names when doing so.
4. Ask them what preparation is necessary before speaking with the target contacts and do the necessary preparation.
5. Tell existing connections later how they have been particularly helpful, thus cementing useful relationships.
6. Repeat these steps for the new sets of contacts.

five
Form Your Business

(Sources: "Choosing a Form for Your Business," *How to Run a Small Business*, 6th ed., McGraw-Hill Book Company, New York: 1989, p. 39; Richard M. Turitz, Esq, sup. ed., *The Prentice Hall Small Business Survival Guide*, Englewood Cliffs, NJ: Prentice Hall, 1993, pp. 353-377; "Starting a New Business in Massachusetts," Small Business Assistance Packet, Executive Office of Economic Affairs, Massachusetts Office of Business Development-Business Information Service and Arthur Andersen & Co.)

Once you have decided on a type of business, you will need to decide what *form* it will take. Businesses can have one of three basic forms: Sole Proprietorships, Partnerships, or Corporations. There are some variations to each of these basic forms. Each has different taxes, management, liability for the owner, and profit distribution. Some forms can be started easily, with little effort and without legal representation, but for the more complex forms it is a good idea to talk with someone knowledgeable about the particular forms in your state.

Once you select a form for your business, that will dictate what legal steps you must take, how you file documents with your city and state, and so forth.

If you decide at a later date to change the form of the business, it is usually possible, though there may be related tax liabilities, or regulations that govern change of status. In such cases, you will want to be sure to have good legal advice.

Which business form is correct for you? Consider the characteristics of each form, to be discussed, to determine which would be appropriate for your business. Each description includes a list of advantages and disadvantages. At the end of this section, there is a comparison of the forms of business.

Sole Proprietorships

Nearly three quarters of businesses are set up as sole proprietorships. The owner declares that he or she is in business, files any required city or town documents, and runs the business. The owner has full responsibility for all debts and legal liabilities. The income from a proprietorship is reported to the Internal Revenue Service on a personal income tax statement and is taxed as personal income.

Advantages of Proprietorships

- Easiest of the three forms to start and end
- Minimum government restraints
- Lower expenses
- Limited government regulation, but may need state or local license
- Sole management and control
- Tax savings (individual tax rate)
- Credit may be easier to obtain since creditors can attach your personal assets

Disadvantages of Proprietorships

- Greatest personal liability
- May be harder to raise capital
- May need to register with state and collect sales taxes
- Unlimited liability
- Limited growth possibility

- Total responsibility for success or failure
- Death usually ends the business

Partnerships

Partnerships consist of two or more people who share a business. Partnerships may be general or limited. In a *general partnership* all partners are personally liable. This unlimited liability means that personal assets outside the business are liable as well. All partners in a general partnership have voice in management of the partnership, unless specified in the partnership agreement. The partners' contributions are determined by agreement. Each partner pays a pro rata share of income taxes on the net profits of the partnership. The partnership is terminated by agreement, the action of a partner such as a withdrawal, legal action such as death or bankruptcy, or court decree.

A *limited partnership* has at least one general partner, who is fully liable, plus one or a number of limited partners, who are liable only for the amount of money they invest in the partnership. Only the general partners participate in the management of the partnership; limited partners have no voice in management.

To set up a partnership, you should have an agreement drawn up by an experienced lawyer. Note that the Uniform Partnership Act is followed by most states as a guide for legal requirements. You can find a copy of the act in *West's Business Law* (West Publishing, St. Paul, MN), if you want to research legal aspects of partnerships yourself. A key legal assumption of the act is that partners are equal in their rights to profits and responsibility for debt and liability, unless otherwise agreed to in writing.

The partnership agreement, termed *articles of partnership*, typically addresses the following sorts of information:

(Source: Donald Kuratko and Richard Hodgetts, *Entrepreneurship: A Contemporary Approach*, The Dryden Press, 1995, p. 350.)

- Name, purpose, location
- Duration of agreement
- Type of partners (general or limited, active or silent)
- Contributions by partners (at inception, at later date)

- Division of profits and losses
- Draws or salaries
- Rights of continuing partner(s)
- Death of partner
- Release of debts
- Handling of business expenses
- Separate debts
- Authority of partners in conduct of business
- Books, records, and method of accounting
- Sale of partnership interest
- Arbitration
- Settlement of disputes
- Additions, alterations, or modifications of partnership
- Required and prohibited acts
- Absence and disability
- Employee management

Advantages of Partnerships

- Access to more capital through more investors
- Offer of partnership can be used to help keep a top employee
- Higher credit standing
- Access to broader range of knowledge, abilities, skills
- Profits taxed at individual partner level, not partnership level

Disadvantages of Partnerships

- Unlimited liability for all partners (both personal assets and partnership assets are at risk)
- Financing limited to the amount of capital the partners can raise
- Automatic end of business if one partner dies
- Potential for disagreement

Creating Successful Partnerships

(Source: Jakki Mohr and Robert Spekman, "Characteristics of Partnership Success: Partnership Attributes, Communication Behavior, and Conflict Resolution Techniques," *Strategic Management Journal*, Vol. 15 (1994), p. 137.)

There are three factors that are associated with the success of partnerships: attributes of the partnership itself, communication skills of the partners, and ability to resolve conflict.

First, those who wish to be partners must be committed to the partnership. They must be willing to work at the relationship, which will involve the skills we will look at in a moment. The partners must be willing and able to coordinate their efforts in working together. This entails being aware of their interdependence and being willing to trust one another to fulfill their obligations to the partnership.

The second factor, ability to communicate well, is of course important in any business. In a partnership the communication must be open so that the partners are up to date and aware of situations that all need to know about. All must be willing to participate in providing quality information on a timely basis.

Finally, it is inevitable in any group situation that conflict will arise. The important factor here is that the partners have the skills to resolve conflicts. They must be willing and able to solve problems as they arise. This may entail the ability to persuade, to smooth ruffled feathers, to retract harsh words. Some people are more skilled at conflict-resolution methods than others and may find themselves the "peacemakers." In any case, partners need to be willing to resolve problems, even if it means taking the issue to some sort of neutral arbitrator.

S and C Corporations

Corporations are legal entities that have a life separate from their owners'. Corporations must file tax returns, can be sued, and have rights separate from the individuals who work for the corporation. Papers for incorporation have to be drawn up by a lawyer and must be filed with the state.

Corporations are divided into shares or stocks, which are owned by one, several, or many people. The stockholders decide how company profits will be used—whether reinvested or divided among the stockholders. Ownership of the company is based on the percentage of stock owned. Thus, the person with 51 percent of the stock owns 51 percent of the company.

Besides general or "C" corporations, there is another form known as "S" corporations, which are a hybrid of a partnership and a C corporation. We take up S corporations at the end of this segment.

Advantages of a Corporation

- Investment easier to obtain
- Protection from liability
- Ability to sell stock
- Continuity of business if owners change
- Risk limited to what stockholders invest; other assets protected
- Unlimited growth
- Transferability of ownership
- Unlimited life of corporation
- Management can be separate from ownership

Disadvantages of a Corporation

- Heavier taxes
- Higher initial investment
- Higher costs due to fees and other regulations
- Government restrictions, regulations, reports

S Corporations

S corporations combine aspects of both corporations and partnerships. They are like partnerships in the way that they are taxed. That is, individual shareholders must declare profits and losses on their individual tax returns. In the C corporation, profits (earnings, dividends) are taxed at both corporate and private levels. Note that some states do not recognize S corporations in terms of state income tax, so be sure to check the laws in your state.

Like a C corporation, the S corporation provides limited liability. Individual liability is protected because a shareholder is liable only to the extent of his or her investment. However, there are some stipulations. For example, the S Corporation may have no more than 35 shareholders, and each must be a U.S. citizen. This limits merger possibilities and other growth potential.

Note that a new form is emerging, the limited liability corporation, which is designed to offer the simplicity and tax consequences of a partnership with the protection of an S or a C corporation. See the next section for details of this exciting new option.

Limited Liability Corporation

(Sources: Ripley Hotch, "A Liability Shield for Entrepreneurs," *Nation's Business*, August 1994, pp. 36-37; MCLE paper on "Limited Liability Companies and the Operational Differences Among Them, S Corporations and Limited Partnerships," Richard M. Yanofsky, Esq. and Amy J. Mastrobattista, Esq., Sherburne, Powers & Needham, P.C., Boston, MA; Robert P. Cunningham, "Limited Liability Companies Gain Momentum," *BusinessWest,* February 1995, p. 38.)

A Limited Liability Corporation (LLC) is a hybrid of a partnership and a corporation. It is a relatively new form of business, the regulations for which vary from state to state. In some states, you cannot establish an LLC yet. We are based in Massachusetts, and the attorneys and accountants we asked about LLCs looked at us as if we were nuts. But next door in New York we hear there are many of them. However, work is being done to standardize the rules so that there will be consistency across state borders. An LLC can be a good form to use if you want tax benefits and limited liability.

LLCs are becoming a popular business form for real-estate ventures, law partnerships, health and medical practices, and accounting groups. They are also popular with joint ventures, start-up businesses, and personal service businesses. You may want to consider this form because of several of its advantages.

An LLC offers some advantages from both corporations and partnerships. It gives its owners protection from personal liability (like a corporation) and provides tax protection in that profits are taxed only at the personal level (like a partnership) rather than at both corporate and shareholder levels.

Structure

In LLCs, there are two types of partners or "members"—general, and passive or limited. There must be at least one of each. The general partner is liable for the partnership's debts, whereas the passive partners are not liable. This differs from the standard type of partnership, where all partners are liable.

Further, there is no limit to the number of shareholders in a limited liability company. This means that members can be other partnerships, other corporations, and even other LLCs. All members own the business, and contribute capital and/or services. In return, they receive shares in the company. If a partner leaves, he or she can receive the value of his or her partnership interest. Furthermore, the partnership of the LLC does not have to be dissolved and reformulated as members come and go.

Managers of LLCs do not have to hold "stock" in the company; their liability is limited.

The operating agreement for an LLC is much like the bylaws of a corporation or the agreement for a partnership in that it is a source document for operating procedure. But it is much more flexible.

Why the Limited Liability Corporation is Hot

	Owners liable?	Profits taxed as personal income?	Type, number of partners restricted?	Profits taxed as corporate income?
Limited Liability Corporation	No	Yes	No	No
S Corporation	No	Yes	Yes	No
General Partnership	Yes	Yes	No	No
Limited Partnership	Only the general partner	Yes	No	No
Sole Proprietorship	Yes	Yes	Yes	No
Regular Corporation	No	Yes (if distributed)	No	Yes

(Source: Ken Blanchard, Charles Schewe, Robert Nelson and Alexander Hiam, *Exploring the World of Business*, Worth Publishers, 1996, Chap. 5.)

Should You Switch?   Many accountants and lawyers feel that LLCs are best for *new* companies. The cost of converting an existing business form to an LLC may not be worth it.

For example, an LLC is somewhat complex to set up. Most states require that the members draft an agreement about how the company will operate. (Compare this to an S corporation, in which shareholders are not required to make an agreement.)

Further, an LLC is more formal than a partnership. Requirements generally include filing articles with the state and paying a filing fee, plus writing an annual report. However, you need to investigate the laws and fees in your particular state before you decide whether the expense is worth the benefits. The filing fees may not be any greater than those for other forms of business. And while legal fees may vary, depending on the state or the regulations, this may not be enough to prevent your using this form of business if it seems the best form to meet your business's needs.

Many states are recognizing the need for a uniform law and so proposals for such laws are in the works. The IRS has ruled that partnerships may convert to LLCs generally without being taxed either as a partnership or as individuals. But C corporations and S corporations may not convert to LLCs without tax consequences.

If this form interests you, find out whether your state has statutes governing this type of organization, then find a lawyer who is experienced in this type of law to advise you. Be sure to inform yourself as thoroughly as possible first.

Advantages and Disadvantages of Limited Liability Corporations

Consider the pluses and minuses of LLCs, based on your particular situation. If the positives outweigh the negatives for your organization, go for it!

Advantages of an LLC

- Fewer legal restrictions than in corporations
- Limited liability
- Tax advantages

- Flexibility
- Ease of operation
- Liability limited to general partner (not passive partners)

Disadvantages of an LLC

- Tax status may be affected
- Differences among state laws on LLCs
- Complexity of setup
- Requirement of drafted agreement
- Formality greater than for partnership
- Charter required (certificate of organization) (but similar to articles of organization filed by corporation or certificate of limited partnership filed by a partnership)
- Filing fee
- Annual report
- Operating agreement (like corporate by-laws or partnership agreement)

For further reading, see William Bagley's *The Limited Liability Company*, 1994, (James Publishing). Attorney Bagley also publishes a newsletter on LLCs.

Comparing Business Forms

(Source: "Starting a New Business in Massachusetts," Small Business Assistance Packet, Executive Office of Economic Affairs, Massachusetts Office of Business Development-Business Information Service. Compiled with the cooperation and assistance of Arthur Andersen & Co.)

Which business form is best for your business? Consider the aspects for each of the five types of business forms, as follows. See which one makes the most sense for your type of business. Then check with a lawyer in your state for further details on the various forms. Note that legislation is in progress now in many states for the limited liability corporation form.

	Corporation	S Corporation	Partnership	Sole Proprietorship	Limited Liability Corporation
Ownership	stockholders	stockholders (max. 35)	partners	owner	members who contribute capital or services
Setup	governed by law	governed by law	governed by law	simple	complex
Life	unlimited	unlimited	specified term; death terminates	ends with death of owner	limited by contract
Liability	limited	limited	general partners fully liable; limited partners liable up to amount of capital invested	unlimited	limited - general partners liable, passive partners not liable
Transfer	stock is transferable; transfer has no effect on corporation	same as corporation, but could result in unintended termination of S corporation status	may need approval of other partners; may need to create new partnership	ends business and creates new one	depends on agreement
Financing	stocks, bonds	one class of stock allowed; different voting rights	can borrow from partners, outsiders, or add new partners who invest	owner's personal assets, outside borrowing	same as partnership
Management	flexible; can have management team separate from shareholders	similar to C corporation, but more active because max. number of shareholders is 35	general partners usually manage	owner controls	by all or those designated
Taxes	corporation is taxed; dividends taxed for individuals	shareholders taxed on income	partners taxed on income	owner taxed on income	individual taxation only

Earnings	taxable to shareholders	no tax unless distribution is greater than the shareholder's tax basis in the corporation	no tax unless distribution is more than partners' tax basis	no tax effect on owner	same as partnership
Taxability of Salaries	owner/employee salaries are taxable; deductible by the corporation	same as regular corporation	usually considered partial distributions of income; if salary guaranteed, deductible by partnership and regular income to partner	salary is considered a distribution of income	depends on agreement
Membership	no limit	at least one; max. 35	one limited and one general partner, no max. limit	NA	at least 2; no max.
Organizing Document	articles of organization	similar to C corporation	certificate of limited partnership	not required	articles of organization
Operating Document	by-laws, in writing	by-laws	partnership agreement	not required	operating agreement; not necessarily in writing
Liquidation	results in taxable gain at corporate and shareholder level	same as corporation, except not doubly taxed—flows through to shareholders	no tax unless cash is greater than basis in partnership interest	gain or loss declared only when business is sold	declared by court,

(Source: "Starting a New Business in Massachusetts," Small Business Assistance Packet, Executive Office of Economic Affairs, Massachusetts Office of Business Development-Business Information Service. Compiled with the cooperation and assistance of Arthur Andersen & Co.)

Establishing a Board of Directors

(Sources: Justin G. Longenecker, Carlos W. Moore, and J. William Petty, *Small Business Management*, Cincinnati, OH: South-Western Publishing Co., 1994, pp. 289-292; Arthur H. Kuriloff, John M. Hemphill, Jr., and Douglas Cloud, *Starting and Managing the Small Business*, New York: McGraw-Hill, Inc., 1993, pp. 521-522.)

The board of directors is the governing body of the corporation. In the formal corporation, the directors are elected by the stockholders. In a small business, the board might simply consist of the owners and managing officers. A family-owned business might have relatives on its board.

The board elects the firm's officers, who manage the business with the assistance of management specialists if they themselves do not have the requisite skills.

The duties of the board are to set or approve management policies, receive and consider reports on operating results from the officers of the company, and declare dividends as appropriate. The board should meet regularly to discuss and decide on strategy. They should review major policy decisions and be able to advise on external business conditions. As individual problems arise, board members can offer advice.

These are major responsibilities that require strong skills, so it is a good idea to consider carefully just who will be on your board of directors.

Who should be on your board? While it is tempting to ask friends, relatives, and others to be on your board, you will find that you may benefit from selecting those who will take an active role in assisting with the management and growth of your business. You want to look for people with broad experience and extra knowledge who can help you in decision making. And you want people who can be objective. Those with family or other connections may not be able to offer objective opinions and advice.

You want to have a "working board," not just a "rubber stamp" group that will go along with whatever you propose. The members of the board should have strengths in the three major areas of concern for a business: production, marketing, and financing. This is particularly important if your management team is lacking in one of these areas. Board members can help fill in the "holes."

The board can be helpful in scrutinizing the ethical standards of the management team and the company. And board members who have stature in the community, especially the business and financial community, can provide your business with greater credibility.

Talk with your attorney, banker, accountant, or other business executives, and with local management consultants to find out appropriate candidates for your board. You may want to ask some of these people to serve on your board. But remember that an outside board composed of people who do not depend on the corporation for their income can sometimes be more effective. They will not have the conflict of interest that inside board members (management and others employed by the company) would have. Outside directors can be more objective.

Consider carefully the type of business you have and the needs of the company as you make a list of the types of people you need on your board. For example, if your staff is not strong on marketing, then be sure you find a board member with expertise in marketing. Anyone with a high profile in the business community can help, too.

Once you make a list, check (discreetly) before asking people to be on your board.

Compensation

Board members are usually paid for their time, although some small businesses do not offer remuneration. Small firms usually pay $200 to $300 a month, and members are expected to attend one meeting a month for a morning or afternoon. A midsized company with 500 employees might pay a director $400 a month.

An Alternative to the Board of Directors: Advisory Council

You may find that some potential board members are reluctant to join your board because of the legal ramifications. Members of a board may be held liable for decisions they make. And some boards will make recommendations that will not be followed by the CEO or owner.

To avoid this situation, some firms are using instead of a board of directors an advisory council. A council can offer counsel and guidance, but may be less likely to be held liable for lower earnings, for example. And the owner may find a council somewhat less threatening than a board.

Start-up Alternatives: Franchising, Acquisition, and Innovating in Existing Businesses

If you've read Part 1 of this book, you have already put a good deal of thought into starting your own business. You've brainstormed ideas, considered sources and amounts of funding, and reflected on your personal style and needs.

Deciding how to go into business for yourself depends on the level of risk you're willing to tolerate, the amount of capital you can raise, and your confidence and experience. The following discussions will help you understand the pros and cons of various alternatives so you can make a well-researched, informed decision.

six
Invest in a Franchise

General Considerations for Franchising

There are approximately 550,000 franchised businesses in the United States and the rate of opening franchises is estimated to be growing at about 6 percent a year. Franchising is a popular way to have a business of your own without the great start-up costs that would be associated with beginning a small business from scratch.

From the point of view of the franchiser, offering franchises is good business. Even large corporations are finding it lucrative to move into franchising, because franchised outlets allow them to expand in a more cost effective way than they would with company-owned stores. A franchiser such as Boston Chicken does not require layers of management. It does not involve investment in land, buildings, equipment, and inventory. And, perhaps most important, large amounts of working capital are not needed.

It also looks like a good deal on the franchisee side. But, depending on whom you talk to, the failure rate for franchises may be reported as low as 5 percent, or as high as 30 to 50 percent. In any case, it is wise to investigate thoroughly if you are considering a franchise for your business venture.

Do your homework on the type of franchise you want to own and what is available. There are advertisements for all sorts of franchises in newspapers

69

such as the *Wall Street Journal*. Study what is available, make comparisons, and weigh various alternatives. It may help to ask yourself the following questions:

- What are your expectations?
- Do you prefer an established franchise, or a new one, which may be more risky if the franchiser does not have experience?
- Do you prefer a nationwide chain or a local one?
- Is name important—for example, McDonald's or Subway?
- Can you actually see yourself running a franchise?

In your conversations with a potential franchiser, you should ascertain whether the firm is growing fast and how that will fit with your planning. Growth in an existing industry will be different from that in a new one. Other things you need to find out are whether the franchiser offers assistance with promotional activities, financing, and training. Study the service or product. Is the quality of the product or service good?

Before you make any commitments, be sure to talk to current franchisees. (Just asking for the names of franchisees to talk with may be an enlightening experience. The franchisers will tell you a lot by their attitude about sharing such information.) Ask current franchisees whether they felt they had enough training and support. Ask if they are happy or not. If not, why not?

Find out whether the franchiser will offer assistance after your business opens, and what they will do if there are any unusual problems. Do they have specialists to help you with site selection, marketing, and promotion? Will you be taking over for another franchisee, and if so, why is the previous person leaving? Is the franchiser's main purpose selling franchises? Beware of franchises that promise you minimum risk, minimum investment.

As you become more committed to the idea of a franchise, be sure to find out who holds the lease on the property in the case of the termination of the franchising agreement. In addition, ask how termination occurs. Better yet, ask for a copy of the agreement so you can read it carefully.

Before you sign, you will want to have an accountant and/or lawyer check out the company's financials and the agreement. Some franchisers may claim that they cannot show the company's financial records, but you cannot make a decision without the sales and earnings figures. In fact, the Federal Trade Commission (FTC) requires that a franchise seller must give you a detailed disclosure document at least ten business days before you pay any money or legally commit to a purchase. The disclosure document provides information in 20 different areas, such as the following:

- Names, addresses, and telephone numbers of at least ten other franchisees located in your area
- An audited financial statement of the seller for three years
- Detail of background and experience of the business's key executives
- The cost required to start and maintain the business
- Training programs for franchisees
- A summary of any relevant litigation or bankruptcies
- The responsibilities each party will have to the other if you buy.

This document can be very helpful in making comparisons with other businesses.

The Uniform Franchise Offering Circular (UFOC) is a disclosure document required by law in the 14 states that have franchise registration and disclosure laws. These include California, Hawaii, Illinois, Indiana, Maryland, Minnesota, New York, North Dakota, Oregon, Rhode Island, South Dakota, Virginia, Washington, and Wisconsin. The UFOC document is similar, but not identical to, the FTC's disclosure document. In either case, ask for the document and be sure you receive it.

The FTC offers seven points of advice when you are considering buying a franchise or other business.

1. Study the disclosure document carefully.
2. Talk to current owners.
3. Investigate earnings claims.
4. Shop around, comparing possibilities.
5. Listen carefully to the sales presentation.
6. Get the seller's promises in writing.
7. Consider getting professional advice.

There are a number of organizations that can be of help to franchisers and franchisees, including:

- *International Franchise Association* in Washington, D.C.
- *American Association of Franchisees and Dealers (AAFD).* They developed the Franchise Bill of Rights, which is a code of ethics for members. (Not all franchisers belong to this.)
- *American Franchise Association.* This was formed to negotiate better terms and conditions from franchisers.

For further reading, see *The Franchise Fraud*, by Robert L. Purvin, Jr., a franchise attorney and author (John Wiley, 1994).

In addition, the American Bar Association offers a forum on franchising. Look in the telephone book or call information for the number of the American Bar Association nearest you and ask them for information on franchises.

(Sources: Joan Delaney. "10 Danger Signs to Look for When Buying a Franchise," *Black Enterprise*, September 1994, pp. 118-123; Janean Huber, "Changing Times," *Entrepreneur*, January 1995, pp. 84-90; Debra Phillips, "Wish List," *Entrepreneur*, January 1995, p. 92-98; "Franchise and Business Opportunities," *Federal Trade Commission Bureau of Consumer Protection* brochure.)

Franchise Costs

One of your major concerns in deciding whether to buy a franchise will be the level of your initial investment. As you look into various types of franchises, consider not only whether the business is something that interests you, but also how much you can afford. In general, the better known the business, the more it will cost.

Some common types of franchise businesses follow, grouped according to the cost of the initial investment you can expect to make. These amounts may vary according to circumstances, but you can see what various categories will tend to cost. In addition, you will see that some business categories are listed in several cost groupings. This is because of factors such as size and name recognition. For example, in the fast food category, a "Larry's Fast Food" franchise would likely be a lower investment than a McDonald's or a Roy Rogers franchise.

We arbitrarily set up four categories: Low, Medium Low, Medium High, and High.

LOW $350-25,000	MEDIUM LOW $30,000-90,000	MEDIUM HIGH $100,000-200,000	HIGH over $200,000
cleaning services	commercial cleaning	fast food	national fast food
automotive services	residential cleaning	convenience stores	home video rentals
tax services	fast food	postal services	auto maintenance
prefab miniature golf	nutrition services	tire and automotive services	custom framing
car rentals	real estate	travel agencies	automotive services
carpet restoration	weight loss	retail nutrition stores	personnel services
janitorial services	packing and shipping services	real estate	national car rentals
commercial cleaning	auto detailing	weight loss	microbrewery
mobile cleaning	coffeehouse	temporary personnel services	restaurant
windshield repair	collectibles broker	travel agencies	
event-planning service	consulting service	personnel services	
financial aid service	desktop publishing	car rentals	
home computer business	food delivery	auto maintenance	
home inspection service	gift basket service	leak detection	
import/export management	herb farming	auto aftermarket	
information broker	home health agency	printing services	
maid service	mail order business	hair salons	
medical claims processing	mobile frozen yogurt		
private investigator	recycling consulting		
property tax consultant	secretarial service		
wedding planning service	seminar promotion		
personal shopping service	vending machine business		

(Sources: "50 BE Franchise," *Black Enterprise*, September 1993, pp. 53-54; *Small Business Development Catalog*, from EntrepreneurGroup, Boulder, CO 80321.)

Entrepreneur's Franchise 500

Buying a franchise may indeed prove to be a lucrative, professionally reward-ing experience. Other than carefully analyzing the financials and agreements, you should also consider the "softer" side of the deal. For example, can you communicate well with the franchisers? Do they really listen and respond to your concerns or are they just trying to make a sale? Will you be able to dis-cuss problems with them or make suggestions for improvements? As when searching for a job, you want to consider your fit with the company culture to ensure that it is an environment in which you can thrive or at least be pro-ductive.

Do some market research before buying. Nothing fancy but drive around the area. Who is your competition? Where are they located? Buy a coffee, locate yourself near your potential location, and watch the pedestrian and/or automobile traffic. Notice patterns of activity, note age and sex, and try to see what people have purchased. Do a little demographic research by determin-ing your franchise's target market. Now find out who lives in the area and if they are likely to be your customers. How far will people drive to get to you? For demographic and census figures, try the town/city hall or chamber of com-merce.

Ask yourself if the inventory provided by the parent company will sell well in your region. Are you a northener considering purchasing a southern franchise? Does the franchiser have the experience and resources to help you adapt to a new region and make it work? Consider Sue Sapia's story. Sue bought a Formals Etc. bridal and gown rental franchise from franchisers who were new to the business themselves. It was a good deal for her financially, however, and Sue was confident she could make it work.

Sue's was the first Formals Etc. franchise to open in the north, and she soon discovered that the inventory of gowns that appealed to southern women didn't appeal to women in the north. Sue also learned, after the fact, that there wasn't a big demand for bridal gown rentals in the north and that two other rental businesses in her area had recently gone out of business.

The franchisers preferred not to acknowledge regional differences and didn't respond to Sue's requests for assistance. Sue's labor and marketing costs were much higher than the franchiser's estimates because of regional differ-ences in labor costs and costs associated with opening a new market. Finally,

Sue and her franchisers never communicated well. They essentially didn't believe that there was a problem and they didn't support her. Sue was eventually successful in her venture but felt that both she and the franchisers could have done more initially and during the process to ensure success.

Sue's story shouldn't deter you from considering a franchise but should encourage you to go in with both eyes open and with a lot of research to back you up.

(Source: Carol Steinberg, "Grow or Die," *Success,* July/August 1994, pp. 65-73.)

To give you ideas about what franchises are available, *Entrepreneur* magazine publishes its list of the top 500 franchises every year. The recent top 10 were the following:

1. Subway
2. McDonald's
3. Burger King
4. Hardee's
5. 7-Eleven Convenience Stores
6. Dunkin' Donuts
7. Mail Boxes Etc.
8. Choice Hotels International
9. Snap-On Inc.
10. Dairy Queen

Each of the 500 franchises is described in *Entrepreneur.* The categories of franchises included in the survey include the following:

apparel and accessories
automotive
beauty and health
building products and services
business services
business/personnel services
children's products and services

computer-related products and services
food/quick service
food/full-service restaurants
food/retail sales
home-improvement products and services
hotels and motels
maintenance services
pets
photographic services
printing services
publishing businesses
real estate
recreation
retail
service businesses
training services
travel businesses

The broad categories are broken down more specifically: For example, in the *food* category, franchises are subdivided into coffee and tea, cookie, donuts, drinks, fish, frozen yogurt, and so forth. For each franchise the listing shows address, telephone number, year the business began, year the franchising began, where the company is seeking franchises, the number of franchises for each of the last three years, whether it is company owned, the franchise fee, start-up costs, royalty, type of financing, and ranking in the franchise 500. In addition, the magazine lists the overall top 100 franchises, the top 30 fastest-growing franchises, the top 20 low-investment franchises, and the top 30 new franchises. There is even an index.

(Source: "Understanding the Franchise 500," *Entrepreneur*, January 1995, p. 136 + ff.)

Black Enterprise Magazine's Top 50 Franchises

Black Enterprise publishes an annual list of the top 50 franchises for black entrepreneurs. They are listed in order from the greatest to the fewest number of units of a particular franchise (for example, Subway is top on the list, with 1,343 units run by blacks). The listing also shows the total number of units and percent that are run by blacks and the start-up costs for each of the 50 franchises. The range of costs stretches from a few thousand dollars to hundreds of thousands.

Franchises in which a high percentage of blacks have invested include cleaning services, hair salons, and automotive services. The top ten include five fast-food chains (Subway, McDonald's, Burger King, KFC, and Wendy's), two commercial cleaning operations (Coverall North America Inc. and O.P.E.N. Cleaning Systems), personalized books (D&K Enterprises Inc.), mobile soft ice cream (Mister Softee Inc.), and convenience stores (7-Eleven).

The fast-food and convenience stores tend to have medium-high to high start-up costs (anywhere from $50,000 to $1 million). The cleaning businesses have lower start-up costs ($350 to about $4,000). The mobile soft ice cream unit runs about $20,000 to $30,000 for start-up expenses.

Another type of franchise business that appears on the list is automotive services, including retail tires and service (Goodyear Tire & Rubber, King Bear Auto Service Centers, Speedee Oil Change & Tune-Up, Midas International, Meineke Discount Muffler Shops, Inc.) and repairs (Precision Tune Inc.). These tend to be expensive to start up—in the $100,000 range and above.

(Source: "50 BE Franchises," *Black Enterprise*, September 1993, pp. 53-54.)

Steinberg's Franchising Lessons

National franchising expert Carol Steinberg says "Franchising allows you to be in business for yourself, without being *by* yourself." A franchise is an appealing way to have a business of your own. After all, for a small investment (something less than it would cost if you started the business yourself), you can obtain a business with an established following; franchiser-provided training and support; and you can avoid the headaches of start-up. However, before you plunge into a franchise, consider the following story.

Franchises may not be a bed of roses. One franchisee who found it difficult was Rosie Seidelmann of Winston-Salem, North Carolina, who bought into *Deck the Walls*, a custom framing store chain based in Houston, Texas. She and her husband had previous hotel management experience, but not enough capital to start their own business, so the franchise route looked appealing to them.

They struggled financially from the start. For one thing, they started with insufficient inventory. For another, advertising was more expensive than expected. In addition, they used local vendors rather than the national ones with which the franchiser had negotiated discounts, so their costs for materials were higher than anticipated. But because they were able to struggle along and always make their royalty payments, the parent company did not realize that there was a problem until the couple got behind in royalty payments. Only then did the corporation become involved. The company immediately sent a team to audit Seidelman's operation. They set up a plan of payments and offered support to help put the firm on an even keel. Eventually, the business began to move from red to black. Others who try the franchise route are not always so lucky.

To avoid problems such as the Seidelmann's experienced, be sure to use the foregoing checklist for evaluating franchises. If you do invest in a franchise and experience problems, don't wait for the parent company to rescue you. Call them and use their resources to save yourself money and trouble.

While older studies suggested that franchises have a higher success rate than independent businesses, a more recent Woodrow Wilson Center study of 7,000 small businesses started in the 1980s found that 35 percent of the franchises failed within ten years, compared to 28 percent of independent businesses.

In evaluating whether to try the franchise route or to start your own business from scratch, bear in mind the advantages and disadvantages of a franchise. Note that potential disadvantages may outweigh advantages—it will depend on your particular situation and finances.

Potential Advantages

proven operation system
supplier discounts
advertising programs
management team support

marketing support

Potential Disadvantages

risk

start-up costs

royalties

undercapitalization

ineffective marketing

poor location

competition

poor match with franchiser

overhead too great

lack of management skills

regional differences in demand for products (especially if product has not been tried in your area of operation)

(Source: Carol Steinberg, "Grow or Die," *Success,* July/August 1994, pp. 65-73.)

seven
Buy a Small Business

Instead of starting a business from scratch, you may want to consider buying an existing business. The major advantage of this approach is that an ongoing business is already established and you can more or less skip the costs and challenges of start-up.

While you will still need to go through the steps that you would complete in order to start a *new* business, especially in terms of business planning, there will definitely be aspects of buying an existing business that will be easier because someone else has had to think them through already. Necessary equipment used by the business will already have been purchased and some sort of customer base will have been established.

On the other hand, there can be disadvantages that you should take into account. You are not always aware of just what you're buying. Equipment may be obsolete or badly in need of repair. Customers who were faithful to the original owner may not want to do business with you, or you may have to work harder to maintain already established relationships. None of these are insurmountable; just be aware of their possible existence. The objective in your analysis before you decide to buy a business is to discover whether the benefits outweigh the disadvantages. Use the section on business planning as a guide as you explore the possibilities in this section.

See What Is Available

Once you decide that buying a business is an option for you, check the market to see what is available. It is a good idea to scan the market even if you do not plan to buy because you can learn about the other players and about the market value of various businesses. Talk to people who use the kind of business you are considering purchasing. Make sure that the equipment and facilities are in good shape. Consider hiring an expert to evaluate the equipment. Do some investigating—talk to people in the neighborhood, for example, and other business owners. Be a detective and sit someplace where there is a good view of the business such as a coffee shop or your car. Watch the traffic for a week, both pedestrian and vehicle. Find out about the area in general. Is it growing? Are people moving in or away and are those that are there having children or are they older? Are the schools good enough so people will stay? Make the most informed decision possible by learning all you can about the situation *before* you make the investment. This doesn't mean you won't face problems, but you may avoid being blindsided by something you should have known.

Where to Look for Businesses to Buy

There are a number of good sources of information about businesses for sale. First, check the classified advertising in your local and regional newspapers. Read the bankruptcy notices as well. Another good source of information about local businesses is a local or regional business magazine or paper. Use the networking approach. Contact industry and community resources, including the local chamber of commerce, business organizations, and groups organized for particular industries or services. Industry publications will also contain news of current businesses and those looking for buyers.

Talk with suppliers who work in the industry in which you are interested. They may know which businesses are looking to change hands.
Another way to find out about businesses for sale is to work with a broker who functions much like a real estate broker, screening potential buyers and sellers to make appropriate matches. For this work, the broker usually receives a 10 to 15 percent commission, but it may be worth it to work with an experienced person. Brokers sometimes write the sales contract and arrange financ-

ing as well. Other sources include bankers, lawyers, the Small Business Administration and its Small Business Development Centers, management consultants, and mall management offices.

As you do your research and networking, be sure to talk with other people who have bought businesses. They will probably be eager to share with you the advantages and disadvantages from their points of view. One other approach is to keep alert for businesses you would like to own. If there is a business that you've studied, found interesting, and think that the current owners might be willing to sell, make an offer. Sometimes an owner who is contemplating exiting a business, even if the business is not yet up for sale, will welcome an attractive offer. It never hurts to ask.

Advantages of Buying a Going Business

As you will see, there are a number of advantages to buying a business rather than starting one from the ground up.

Shorter learning curve if you are inexperienced.   An established business allows you to plunge right in with somewhat less initial learning than when starting your own business.

On-the-job learning.   A business that is already established can be your teacher. That is, you do not have to learn every part of the business by trial and error, which is a more likely scenario in a start-up situation. Procedures and processes are in place and frequently a prior owner will stay on for awhile to help the new owner.

Less risk.   Established businesses are less risky than new ones. This affects your ability to obtain financing and to conduct business dealings in general (such as obtaining suppliers, customers, etc.)

Simpler financing.   You may be able to arrange with the seller to set up a promissory note to finance your payments. This is usually less expensive than trying to obtain a bank loan. It may also be beneficial to both buyer and seller in terms of taxes, especially if payments are smaller and spaced out over a longer period of time.

Financing easier to obtain.   Even if you have to go to the bank for money, it should be easier to finance the purchase of an established business than it would be to obtain a loan for a startup. And if you need to obtain financing later, you will find banks more interested in businesses that have a financial history.

Existing records serve as a reference.   Existing records can provide you with a guide for making financial and other business decisions. Even if you do not follow the path the previous owner established, you will have historic data to refer to as you carve out your own plan.

Established suppliers, customers, inventory.   Having many of these variables in place already can save you from having to immediately search for suppliers or customers. It saves not only time but money, as the previous owner probably researched the best buys for supplies and materials. If there is an established customer base, you will not have to spend as much time and money advertising and promoting as you would if the business were new. Likewise, established inventory allows you to be up and running right away. In a start-up business, you would have all these issues to deal with immediately and would likely find them time consuming and costly.

Established business and image.   An established business has a reputation, ideally a good one. In fact, "goodwill" may be a part of the purchase contract. A known business with a good reputation usually has less difficulty attracting customers, finding suppliers, and maintaining these relationships. A new business has to work to build up its image and relationships.

Track record.   An ongoing business will have an established record of profits and losses, expenses, and other financial information. With a start-up you can make reasonably good predictions based on market research but you can never be sure how successful a new business will be.

Experienced employees.   Having experienced employees puts you another step ahead of a start-up business. In a start-up situation, employees (and managers) would have to learn together. Having experienced employees reduces the time and costs associated with initial training.

Less planning required. If you are inexperienced in planning and running a business, then a going business may be an easier place to start, provided you have some background in the product or industry. There may be written plans that can give you some direction for planning the future, but the present may be easier to handle if the operation is up and running.

Profitability sooner than a start-up. All the previous advantages of buying a going concern offer you the potential for realizing a profit sooner than you would in a start-up.

Disadvantages of Buying a Going Business

The list of potential disadvantages of buying a business is somewhat longer than the list of advantages. Basically, many of the "cons" are simply the negative side of the advantages discussed earlier. The purpose of this list is primarily to point out that you need to carefully analyze and evaluate key situations to see if they are positive or negative.

Difficulty of changing precedents. If the business has operated in a certain way for a period of time, it may be difficult to change it, especially when people are involved. Employees may resist change, especially if they were loyal to the previous owner and "he (she) always did it that way." Even if you are able to institute changes, you may not be able to make them rapidly enough to respond to the business climate.

Possible internal problems. There may be personality problems among the staff and management or there may be relationships (such as those with suppliers) that have become strained. Such problems may not have surfaced during the research and "honeymoon" period. You need to be on the lookout for clues.

Bad will. The previous ownership may have made decisions or performed actions in the community that created ill will. Or, poor customer service may have created a bad-will situation that you will need to overcome through providing superior customer service.

Customer base. It is possible that no effort has been made to cultivate existing customers or to increase the customer base. This is an even greater problem if the business had relied solely on repeat customers because these customers may decide they want to conduct their business elsewhere.

Poor location. Although a business may start out in a good location, as a community grows and changes the location may lose its value. A good example is downtown stores that lose their clientele when a large mall opens outside of town with well-known anchor stores and the lure of lower prices to draw customers.

Poor image or reputation. The business may have developed a bad reputation over the years. The owner may not realize this, or may not bother to share this information with you. This is a very good reason to be a sleuth before you invest. Even if you are aware of a poor reputation, it's better to know what you're getting into, and the knowledge may give you bargaining power.

Poor employee base. There are several potential problems with inheriting a pool of employees. First, they may not be trained well or properly or according to the way you might train them. Second, they may leave when the owner leaves. Third, they may not leave but may not be fully cooperative.

Hidden costs. There may be costs associated with the business that were not specified or anticipated. For example, if many employees leave with the previous owner, you will have to replace staff. If equipment needs replacing due to age, wear and tear, or obsolescence, you will have additional costs. Anticipate hidden costs when writing your financial plan because even if, for example, you are assured that three out of five employees will stay, things can change very quickly.

May overpay for the business. In your eagerness to buy the business you may offer more than it is worth. If the offer is accepted, you may find that you have compromised your financial position somewhat by spending a lot "up front" and then not having the capital to make necessary changes or investments in new equipment.

Cash flow (and profitability) may be a problem.   Poor cash flow can stem from overpaying for the business or may simply be a function of the type of business. Customers may be slow to pay or vendors may be unwilling to extend payment terms. Many factors can affect cash flow. You need to plan carefully for cash flow which may be difficult to do in a business with which you are unfamiliar. Here again is where prior research can prove invaluable. Find out as much as you can about typical cash flow patterns for the type of business you're exploring. Then you can plan accordingly.

May inherit a difficult landlord.   If you are renting the space for your business, you may find that the landlord is difficult to deal with for a variety of reasons. Always explore the management-landlord relationship *before* you sign the contract.

May need to modernize.   You may need to invest a lot in renovations to improve the location of the business. If you think you will need to do this, be sure to allow for it when you estimate the value of the business and make an offer.

May need to hire new staff.   You may need to hire and train new staff, both of which take investments of time and money. Plan for it and, if possible, factor the costs into the purchase price.

Old inventory.   As part of the business deal, you may inherit inventory that is "stale" or out of date. You may not be able to use it or easily get rid of it. Be sure you check the status of the inventory before you purchase and find out if there is a cost associated with disposing of it if it's unusable.

Personality conflicts in a partnership.   If you are buying out a partner in a partnership, be sure you establish a relationship with the person with whom you will be in business. Partnerships can be problematic because of differences in personalities and work styles. Discuss these issues up front and, if necessary, get your working agreement in writing.

How can you protect yourself against potential problems? Conduct a lot of research on the business before you decide. Ask a lot of questions. Talk with people in comparable businesses. And be sure to meet with your accountant and lawyer for help with financial and legal matters. And always count on spending more money than you initially planned for.

Pursuing the Possibilities

Once you have identified a business which you're interested in owning, call or write to the current owner to obtain whatever selling information he or she is willing to share. When you get further into the process, you will want more detailed information. Your first meeting with the owner will be general. You will probably want to learn why the person is selling and what he or she sees as the future for this business. Try to arrange for a tour of the facility so you can see the operation up close.

Reasons for selling

There are many reasons why an owner may want to sell a business. Some sellers may be totally up front about their reasons; others may not. Consider the following as possibilities:

> age or illness
> desire to retire
> death
> burnout
> relocation
> low profits
> economic conditions
> slow growth or fast growth
> too much competition
> technology outpaced the business
> insufficient capital
> modernization needed—remodeling
> forced liquidation
> no heirs interested
> no managers in line interested in continuing the business

problems with a partner
buying or starting another company
going to work for another company
selling a franchise
changing careers

Bear in mind that if an owner is in a hurry to sell out, you might be able to settle on a lower selling price.

Important Steps in Researching Possibilities

The following suggestions are offered to help guide your thinking as you look into business purchase opportunities. You will see that thorough research is just as important here as it is in other business options such as franchising or starting your own business from scratch.

1. Know thyself. Be aware of the competencies you can bring to a business situation, but also be mindful of your limitations. If you know yourself well, you will be realistic about what you can and cannot do in terms of the demands of a business.

2. Write down your goals and objectives, both personal and financial. You can keep coming back to this list to see if a business proposition fits with these goals.

3. Decide what type of business you want and where you want to be (if possible). You may not be able to make both parts of this step coincide if, for example, you find the perfect business in a poor location. However, trying to be specific now will help you as you discover potential businesses so that you do not jump at just anything that presents itself.

4. Network! We may sound like a broken record but networking and research are critical. They help you become educated about your options and help prevent costly surprises.

5. Make good matches. Look for companies that fit your profile, not only of the type of business you prefer, but of location, goals, and personal characteristics.

6. Look for growth potential and return on investment. This may seem obvious, but be sure the potential is there. If the business is in a saturated market with nowhere to go, you may be buying into a losing battle. Crunch the numbers and convince yourself that a potential buy is going to be a profitable buy.

First meeting with seller or broker

When you have identified a business that you want to scrutinize further, part of your research should include a meeting with the broker or seller. A first meeting will give you an opportunity to learn the history of the business and hear the reasons for the business being offered for sale. Ask about the selling price but don't make an offer until you do further research. Ask for a preliminary financial report from the business. The key at this stage is to listen very carefully to what is being said—and what is not being said. Sometimes information left out or nonverbal signals can give you as much information as the information that is shared. Watch and listen for changes in facial expression or tone of voice. If there is more than one owner, do the partners exchange quick glances or avoid eye contact altogether when certain subjects are mentioned? Be aware of signals and trust your instincts. Probe further until you are satisfied.

Valuing a potential buy

Once you have some information, the next step is to do some valuation and evaluation. First, look at the business's financial statements. If you have the skills to do so, perform an analysis (see Chapter 26 for some basic financial analysis tools). Or have your accountant assist you. The financials will probably be historically accurate, but should be brought up to date. Adjust the numbers accordingly as you receive new information. To value real estate, you may want to pay an appraiser to estimate its worth. To value equipment, talk to people who deal in used equipment to find out the market value. They tend to underprice the value so make allowances.

Another area to check carefully is the bookkeeping. Has it been done well, thoroughly, and correctly? A sloppy job of bookkeeping can result in misleading business figures. If you're not sure, have your accountant look at the books to make sure the owners were using standard accounting procedures.

You should also investigate the customer base to see how large and active it is. If it is not strong, you may be able to lower your offer due to a lack of goodwill.

Look into the business's relationships with its suppliers. Are there enough suppliers to meet the business's needs, at least the current needs? If demand for the product increases, will suppliers be able to meet increased needs? Is there good communication between this business and its suppliers? And is there good feeling between them? (For example, have suppliers been paid on time?)

Bear in mind that a well-managed business will cost more than one that has been managed poorly. Thus, if you are strong in management skills and can turn around a poorly managed company, it may be a bargain; otherwise, you may decide that you prefer to pay the premium for a well-managed business. As you zero in on a value for the business, it may help you to compare it to other similar businesses in the area. Check with the local chamber of commerce to find out about related businesses and their valuations. You may also glean information from the chamber of commerce about the business's stature in the community.

A second meeting with the owner

When you set up a second meeting, the seller will know that you are seriously interested in the business. At this point, you can expect to have a deeper discussion and to obtain more detailed financial information about the business. Ask questions that may have arisen during your research and, as with the first meeting, be sure you listen very carefully.

Try to learn as much as possible about customers, employees, and procedures. You may want to inspect the facilities and observe operations at this time. And remember that the site, location, and marketing plan will all figure into the price you calculate.

Information that you definitely need to have at this stage in order to arrive at an offering price includes:

- At least three years of financial information, including state and federal tax forms

- A list of the business's assets (inventory)
- A description of any pending legal matters
- Leases or mortgages
- A list of suppliers
- A list of stockholders/investors

You may want to schedule a meeting with the landlord and the mortgage holder to inspect the site and ask any pertinent questions related to the physical location. Finally, you need to meet with your accountant and lawyer to resolve any financial or legal concerns before you make an offer.

Setting a price

Your objective in valuing a business is to evaluate its potential to earn money. The best way to do this is to develop pro forma statements for the business, like those described for start-up businesses. For example, create pro forma financial statements, cash-flow analysis, break-even analysis, and profit-and-loss statement. You need to look at this business's potential over the long term, not just next month or next year, because even if you make changes that should increase profitability, you will not see profit increasing immediately. A good rule of thumb is that return on investment (ROI) should increase by about 20 percent a year over five years. Looking at other comparable businesses as benchmarks can also be helpful, bearing in mind that no two businesses are exactly alike.

Calculating the Valuation of a Business

Deciding on the value of a company is not easy or exact. Some sellers misrepresent the numbers on the financial statements so that the business looks more profitable. Some businesses are run very casually with receipts and bank statements tossed into shoe boxes. Our advice is: Be very thorough, critical, and conservative in your analysis. There are four bases for calculating value: assets, market, earnings, and cash flow. Each of these is discussed briefly below.

Assets

This approach to valuation assumes you can determine the value of a business by examining the value of its underlying assets. There are three types of asset-based valuation. First, find out what it would cost to replace such assets as equipment, furniture, and inventory. Second, determine how much money would be received if the firm liquidated its assets. And third, make an estimate of the book value of the business.

The book value is the value of the company as shown on the balance sheets with adjustments made to reflect any differences between the original (historical) cost of an asset and its current value. For example, the book value of your vehicle is the difference between what you paid for it and what it is currently worth on the market. Economic conditions will have an impact on book value; you can't depend on straight depreciation to determine current value.

The asset-based approaches are narrow in their considerations and should be used in conjunction only with other valuation methods.

Market

The market-based approach relies on the market to determine a firm's value. Using this method, sales prices of similar firms are examined relative to their net income and to the book value of equity. Then, the value of a firm is compared to the one being valued, using a price-earnings ratio and/or a market-value-to-book-value ratio. However, good comparisons may be difficult to find. You may be able to obtain them from accounting firms or find them in *Mergerstat Review*, which lists prices of companies sold.

Earnings

Another way to calculate valuation is to value a firm based on its potential future earnings. There are various ways to calculate the value of a company based on its future earnings, but the underlying method is based on normalized earnings (earnings adjusted for unusual, one-time items) and a capitalization rate, which is set according to the riskiness of earnings and expected future growth rate. The more risky the business, the higher the capitalization rate and the higher the potential profits and losses.

The formula is as follows:

Firm's value = normalized earnings divided by capitalization rate

The drawback to this method is that it values a firm based on reported earnings for one period rather than for future cash flows, which are more telling.

Cash Flow

Evaluating a company's value based on future cash flows makes intuitive sense. For example, when you make an investment in a mutual fund, you're interested in future cash flows relative to the money you invested. Using the cash flow method, you compare expected rate of return on your investment to your *required* rate of return. The required rate of return is equal to the risk-free rate plus a risk premium. For example, if the current rate on a savings account is 5 percent and your risk premium for buying a junk bond (or buying a company) is 17 percent, then your required rate of return is 22 percent. The risk premium should be anywhere from 16 to 30 percent depending on the riskiness of the firm.

You use this rate to calculate the current value of the firm's future cash flows. The process is fairly complex and involves significant calculating, but it makes sense and is robust enough a method to pay someone to assist you.

Other Factors to Consider When Setting an Offering Price

There are both external and internal factors that affect the value of a business. External factors are out of the company's direct control, whereas internal factors can be more directly affected by the actions of the business. An external factor might be, for example, whether the property is bordering on wetlands. In this case, you would not be able to expand if that were your intention. An internal factor might be a contract with employees that committed you to periodic raises.

You should be aware of external and internal factors and adjust for them where possible as you complete your valuation of the business.

Competition.   You need to know how much competition there is, where it is located, and how successfully this business has fended off the competition in the past.

Market.   Find out about the market for the business's products or services. Is there enough room for the business in the existing market? Is the market growing? Stable? Shrinking?

Legal issues pending.   It is important to know of any potential legal entanglements such as pending lawsuits, delinquent tax payments, missed payrolls, or overdue rent payments. Resolve these with the seller and your respective lawyers before you make an offer.

Union commitments.   If the business has contracts with a union, find out the details and duration of the contracts. Go over them with your lawyer to make sure you are fully aware of the implications.

Property issues.   You need to know if there is a right of way, common access, or any other property issue that could pose difficulties for you in the future.

Product prices and supplier prices.   Be prepared for changes in prices for raw materials, supplies, and in your competitions' pricing strategies. Research historic trends in relevant prices to give you an idea of what to expect in the future.

Special skills.   If the business requires special skills, you will either need to be trained or hire someone with these skills. Factor this estimated expense into your financial plan.

Goodwill.   Goodwill is the intangible value of a business reputation and/or brand name recognition. It can be an important factor in your estimation of the value of the business. A poor reputation will allow you to lower your offer whereas an excellent reputation or recognizable brand name will necessarily increase your buying price.

Parking. If the business requires space for visiting customers, make sure that there is adequate parking. If not, you may have to pay considerable amounts to develop space or you may have to explore other alternatives, which could be costly. If there isn't adequate parking, make sure there is room for expansion in the immediate area. If not, you might actually lose customers and have to explore other, potentially costly, alternatives such as building a parking garage or acquiring expensive, adjacent real estate on which customers can park.

Patents and trademarks. A business that owns rights to patents, trademarks, or copyrights is generally worth more. You'll need to factor these values into your price.

Future commercial developments. Future commercial developments are an external factor to a going business and can have a direct effect on your decision to buy. Try to find out whether there are any planned zoning changes or expected construction projects or changes in traffic lights or circulation. Does the state, for example, plan to reroute roads? Are there plans for changes in the public transportation system that would affect your potential customers' access to your business? Try your city or town hall for this information. There are typically records of permits granted, blueprints, and other documents on file.

Contingency planning. Though it is hard to calculate for contingencies, look at trends in the economic climate and try to allow for any upcoming radical changes in the supply of labor, supplies, utilities, and other materials and services that your business will need. Read local, national, and international business journals. Find out about possible new utility regulations and/or deregulations and learn about the sources of your raw materials and other supplies. For example, is there a paper shortage, and how will elevated prices affect your cost structure?

Getting Ready to Make an Offer

Before you actually make an offer for a business, be sure to check on your financing to make certain that you can fulfill your end of the bargain. Then make your offer. Usually, you will make your offer somewhat below the value you have calculated, to allow room for negotiation. You can expect the seller to come back with a counteroffer.

Your offer should be in writing, saying something like "I will purchase _____ at _____ price under _____ terms provided that an audit shows inventory, work in process, accounts payable, and accounts receivable are as shown to be."

During negotiation you will discuss, back and forth, the terms of the contract. Both seller and buyer may find that from a tax point of view, they may prefer a smaller down payment and a longer payment period.

When you have come to an agreement, your lawyer should draw up the final contract to be sure all legal points have been covered. The lawyer will include such items as whether the seller can open a competing business and if so, when and in what geographic area; what should be done about unpaid taxes; how to handle customer debts; who is responsible for union contracts; how employee benefits are to be divided; and how to divide up costs such as insurance, taxes, and utilities. It is wise to have a third party, such as your lawyer, close the deal. Before you take over the business, the seller will take a final inventory (if appropriate to the particular business). Be sure that you are present when this is done.

There will be numerous documents, such as a bill of sale, certificate for taxes and other government requirements, and agreements about future payments and guarantees to the seller. When the deal is completed, be sure to apply for a federal ID and a new state ID so that you are a new business entity in the eyes of the government. You do this to disassociate yourself from the old ID numbers so you aren't held responsible for any outstanding obligations.

Service Businesses

It is somewhat more difficult to evaluate a service business because there are fewer tangibles to value. However, the previous discussion can serve as a guide. In addition, there are a few other characteristics unique to service businesses that you should bear in mind.

More intangibles. Intangibles in a service business include such things as the quality of the actual service provided and the value of the service providers. It is difficult, for example, to assign a precise monetary value to someone who provides consulting services. In other words, intangibles are not concrete, like inventory. If possible, compare the intangibles associated with your business with those of other, similar service businesses.

Performance. Performance of the business should be consistently high. Because service businesses are successful only if customer service is excellent, pay particular attention to this aspect of the business. Consider whether customers will remain loyal to your location or if they will take their business to the old owner's new place of business.

Advertising and promotion. A service business has greater need for advertising and promotional activities. Find out what the business has done in the past and be sure to plan for advertising and promotion expenses in your budget.

Price setting. Another extremely important issue is the price at which the service is offered. You will need to research carefully the going rates in the area and compare them with this business's prices. Can the market tolerate higher prices or is this business already charging top dollar?

Location. The location of a service-oriented business is crucial to the success of the business. If customers cannot get there, there is no business. Bear this in mind as you evaluate the location, ease of access, parking, and related factors.

(Sources: Jerry W. Moorman and James W. Halloran, *Entrepreneurship*, Cincinnati, OH: South-Western Publishing Co., 1993, pp. 336-348; Arthur H. Kuriloff, John M. Hemphill, Jr., and Douglas Cloud, *Starting and Managing the Small Business*, New York: McGraw-Hill, Inc., 1993, pp. 441-466; Justin G. Longenecker, Carlos W. Moore, and J. William Petty, *Small Business Management*, Cincinnati, OH: South-Western Publishing Co., 1994, pp. 90-104.)

eight
Innovate to Improve a Small Business

When you think of innovation, you may immediately think of something *new*, such as a new product. However, innovation need not be the creation of a new product or service. It may entail finding a new marketing approach for an existing product, taking advantage of an environmental factor, or enhancing the quality of an existing service or product.

For example, if you sell food products, you will need to adjust your offerings as tastes change. Successful food manufacturers and marketers are aware of the trend toward low-fat, healthful diets and therefore adjust their products to meet those demands.

The selling environment may need to change as styles and preferences change. This is why, for example, restaurant chains periodically redecorate—to keep up with the times, to avoid looking old-fashioned, and to appeal to changing tastes.

When you bring an innovative product to market, it's a given that competitors will imitate your product. To counter the competition, you must be prepared to differentiate your product by making continual improvements, offering more features, charging a higher or lower price relative to your competitors, or providing superior quality or service. If yours is a competitive or price-sensitive market you will need always to be innovating to keep your product or service in demand.

98

You can see that constant innovation is a necessity for success and growth in business. (We touch on innovation in the sections on general management and strategic management as well.) There are four areas in which you can look at innovative possibilities. Each requires that you scan the environment to see opportunities and that you have a good idea of your business's competencies so that you can make an informed choice.

1. An existing product or service in an existing market. If the product market exists, the innovation will occur in some other aspect, such as changing sales techniques; new advertising campaigns; merchandising appeal or updated image; changing the layout, design, or decor of the store; training sales personnel to respond better to customers' needs; or designing new packaging for the product. You may be able to brainstorm other ways to innovate in your particular business.

2. A new product or service in an existing market. In this case, you change the product or service in a market that already exists. For example, change the product by adding new features or add new items to an existing product line. Another innovation is to add improvements or new services to those now being offered. Other improvements and services can be added as you discover which ones customers prefer. Try surveying customers to see what it is they want. Often, sellers think they know what customers want and are surprised by the feedback they receive. If you are marketing a service, you may want to enhance your basic services. For example, a resume service might offer an update for a resume in six months or a year for a reduced price.

3. An existing product or service in a new market. If you want to increase the scope of your business, you may want to take your product(s) into a new market. This means obtaining new customers. Through research, you may find a market niche that is not now being served by your business. For example a popular local product could be marketed regionally, nationally, or internationally. All are big steps and require thorough exploration and planning before plunging in.

4. A new product or service in a new market. Taking a new product or service into a new market is the most risky of the four types of innovation. It also offers the best opportunity for profit, assuming you do your homework. This type of innovation is akin to starting a new business from scratch because everything is new, has to be researched thoroughly, and must be tested. Planning is, of course, key to the success of such operations. The advantage is that you have a business already in place, along with resources and experience, so innovation may not be as risky as pure start-up. (See also the discussion of venturing in the section on strategic management, page 251.)

(Source: Arthur H. Kuriloff, John M. Hemphill, Jr., and Douglas Cloud, *Starting and Managing the Small Business*, New York: McGraw-Hill, Inc., 1993, pp. 60-62.)

Invent New Products or Services Using Drucker's Sources of Innovation

Most business people and entrepreneurs focus on the obvious for product improvement and innovation. They look at their successes and try to repeat them. They imitate other products or services that are successful. They concentrate on new products. But there are other areas where, if you are alert, you will find opportunities for innovation.

One example is in the production process. Improving and innovating how a process is performed (such as service delivery or product manufacturing) can lead to lower costs and, therefore, better products and happier customers.

Because high technology has such a visible profile it is tempting to try to innovate in this area. But beware! High tech is high cost and breakthroughs in this arena are few and far between, made only after great investments of time and money. Most entrepreneurs do not have enough time and money to develop technical breakthroughs.

Peter Drucker, pioneer of management theories and practices, sees the following as sources of innovation. They are presented in order from most useful for entrepreneurs to least useful. Try to invest in the top of this list, not the bottom.

1. Unexpected changes. Unexpected successes—and failures—can provide sources of innovation. It is easy to overlook or discount an unexpected success as a "fluke." But such a change could indicate a shift or trend that could result in a new or large market. Both successes and failures should be considered as opportunities to explore and exploit. In addition, possibilities generated by an outside event may be worth investigating if your company has the resources.

2. Incongruities. When an event does not make sense or fit an expected pattern, look for an underlying change. Recognizing this change can provide another untapped opportunity for innovation. One way to identify incongruities is to take a survey of customer perceptions and compare them with management perceptions. Another way is to look closely at situations that have persisted in spite of repeated attempts to solve them. These incongruities are trying to tell you something, and it could be profitable to pay attention.

3. Process Needs. You may need to alter your work or production processes, but you may not realize it until there is a processing bottleneck or an obvious—and potentially costly—weak link in a process. For example, hand assembly may be sufficient as long as demand for a product is relatively low. But if demand jumps suddenly, you may have trouble getting enough employees to do the assembly, or the process as it exists might be too slow to meet the new demand. Perhaps there is a more efficient assembly method. Go directly to the source for ideas: Ask your assemblers.

Process needs may be the result of demographic changes that cause shifts in demand or become evident when new technologies and innovations appear in the market. If you can take advantage of a new technology, you may be able to solve a process need. In the foregoing example, if a new machine can do the job in less time and will cost you less in the long run, it may well be worth the investment.

Once you are aware that there is a process need, be sure you define and understand it clearly. Next, find out whether the necessary knowledge to solve the need is available. When you implement a solution, make sure it works for those who will be using the process. Train your staff to use the new machinery and include the time and cost in your planning.

4. Industry and Market Structure Changes. Industries or markets in which there are few suppliers or where one firm dominates are perfect settings for innovation. If a stable industry or market changes suddenly, members will need to adapt rapidly and innovations will be required to adjust to the new situation. Many companies are so entrenched that they may not be able to respond rapidly to change. Those that can adjust quickly will be in a better position in the market.

5. Demographic Changes. Changes in population characteristics such as size, level of education, age, or number in an age group may affect markets dramatically. It is important to monitor and anticipate such changes because businesses that don't may miss opportunities to innovate and grow.

6. Perception Changes. People's perceptions of themselves provide possibilities for innovation, especially when those perceptions shift. However, it may be difficult to gauge such shifts. Opinion polls may help in assessing public perception but it is important to avoid innovating based on a fad. For example, people perceive a need to eat healthful, low-fat foods, which has created an enormous demand for such products in the food industry.

7. New knowledge. New knowledge is exciting. It gets people moving, thinking, planning. However, innovations based on new knowledge are hard to manage because the outcomes are unpredictable, production and testing are expensive, and getting a brand new product to market takes considerable time. Innovation based on new knowledge can easily fail. Thus, companies who want to innovate based on knowledge need to exercise caution. They need a solid technical focus and strong research leadership to successfully use knowledge-based innovation.

Remember to concentrate on innovations toward the top of the list rather than near the bottom. Those at the top are easier to institute.

(Source: Alexander Hiam, discussing Drucker's Seven Sources of Innovation in *The Vest-Pocket CEO*, Englewood Cliffs, NJ: Prentice Hall, 1990, pp. 252-257.)

Improve Quality and Cut Costs Using the Malcolm Baldrige National Quality Award Criteria

The Malcolm Baldrige National Quality Award, established by Congress in 1987, is given annually to U.S. companies that have demonstrated excellence in quality management and quality achievement. The three categories for which businesses can apply are manufacturing, service, and small business.

Past recipients of this prestigious award include well-known companies such as Motorola, Xerox Corporation, Cadillac Motor Car Division of General Motors, IBM Rochester, and Federal Express Corporation.

The competition is open to any firm interested in competing for the award and the resulting recognition. According to the brochure describing the award, the purpose of the competition is to promote:

- Awareness of quality as an increasingly important element in competitiveness,
- Understanding of the requirements for quality excellence, and
- Sharing of information on successful quality strategies and the benefits derived from implementation of these strategies

The companies that participate in the competition must strive for constant quality improvement and must be willing to share how they do it. Companies participating in the award competition complete an application package that includes an eligibility form, an overview of their business, and a comprehensive Award Examination plus various supplements for specific industries. In the examination section, applicants provide information and data on their company's improvement processes and their results. Other companies must be allowed and able to replicate or adapt these processes.

The evaluation by a panel of judges is a four-stage process, the third stage of which includes site visits to those companies that have scored well in previous stages. At the end of the process, each company receives a feedback report based on the material submitted and gathered.

Award Criteria

The award criteria are important to those competing in the awards program but are also useful for any company conducting a self-evaluation. Quoting the awards booklet, "The Criteria are designed to help companies enhance their competitiveness through focus on dual, results-oriented goals:

- delivery of ever-improving value to customers, resulting in improved marketplace performance; and
- improvement of overall company operational performance."

Core Values. The values that form the basis for the Baldrige Award Criteria are those seen in the Quality movement: quality based on customer preferences and demands, leadership, continuous improvement, employee participation and development, fast response to changes and needs, quality of design, long-term view, management by fact, development of partnerships, and corporate responsibility and citizenship. These core values are discussed more fully in the Award Criteria booklet published by the U.S. Department of Commerce and the American Society for Quality Control.

Examination Criteria. The areas on which the Award Examination focus are divided into these seven groups that are based on the core values:

- Leadership
- Information and Analysis
- Strategic Quality Planning
- Human Resource Development and Management
- Management of Process Quality
- Quality and Operational Results
- Customer Focus and Satisfaction

In each group are subcategories in which specific concerns are addressed. For example, the Leadership category includes three subcategories: Senior Executive Leadership, Management for Quality, and Public Responsibility and Corporate Citizenship. Each topic and subtopic must be discussed fully by the applicants.

As you can imagine, the application process is thorough and time-consuming. Those who win the award can help other companies get onto the quality track, and they can take full advantage of the publicity. Much can be learned from the application process, even for those who do not win. The self-assessment process underlying the application process will inevitably increase awareness within a company. Some companies, such as Bausch & Lomb, have established their own quality awards based on the Baldrige model. Such awards create an awareness of and impetus for quality improvement efforts. For example, at Bausch & Lomb each division writes a quality plan in June, and the award preparations through the year provide an opportunity for the divisions to review their progress against this plan.

Opinion is divided about whether companies should be encouraged to participate in such competitions. Winning does not mean that a company will be on the competitive cutting edge forever nor does losing mean that a company is a failure. W. Kent Sterett, one of the judges in the Baldrige competition, says, "A winner is any company that applies the tools and techniques of the quality process to improve its competitive position." Or, to look at it another way, "The award is not a destination at all, but simply symbolizes the ultimate destination, which is a truly customer-focused, flexible, innovative, learning organization that is able to renew itself through an ever-accelerating rate of continuous improvement" (Alexander Hiam, *Closing the Quality Gap*, Englewood Cliffs, NJ: Prentice Hall, 1992, p. 192).

To find out more about this competition, to learn about the criteria used for evaluation, or to obtain information about the Annual Quest for Excellence Conference, call the Association for Quality and Participation (AQP) at 800-733-3310. They also offer case studies of the award-winning companies, videos, and other supporting materials. Even if you do not compete in a quality competition such as this, it can be a fruitful exercise for you and your team to look at the Baldrige Award criteria (or others) to see how your company stacks up.

(Sources: Information from the *Malcolm Baldrige National Quality Award 1994 Award Criteria*, U.S. Department of Commerce, Gaithersburg, MD, and American Society for Quality Control, Milwaukee, WI; Alexander Hiam, *Closing the Quality Gap*, The Conference Board, Englewood Cliffs, NJ, Prentice Hall, 1992. p. 206.)

Quality and Manufacturing

The quality movement, started by W. Edwards Deming, has only recently been recognized as important in business. It can have a great effect on the success of your operation. Implementing quality procedures requires scrutiny of all areas of your business, and the results can have a great effect on the success of your operation.

Although everyone in an organization can be brought into the quest for quality, the responsibility for quality ultimately rests with management. If management is not behind the movement for continual improvement, then who is going to be? Quality can affect every nook and cranny of your organization—from the structure of organization to its systems, measurements, tools, customers, design, suppliers, process/manufacturing, field staff, support service, and other involved people, processes, and services.

In manufacturing there are a number of ways to assure a consistent, high quality product. Basically, the methods are all forms of sampling, where you randomly take a number of the items, measure them according to specifications, and record the results.

Measurements can be recorded on paper or entered into a computer. Once you have the basic measurement, you can calculate the mean and standard deviation for the sampling group. After you calculate the z (= Tolerance minus the mean divided by standard deviation) for each sample, you can compare the result with probabilities in a table of standard normal distribution. Obviously, this is much easier with a computer, where you can simply enter the raw data and the computer does the rest of the work.

Another method of calculating quality in manufacturing is the Cumulative Sum Chart in which you calculate the difference between a measured sample and a reference value or specification. You maintain a running total of the differences, plotting the new total on a chart each time a sample is taken. The slope of the line generated indicates when action is needed.

(Source: Alex Hiam, *The Vest-Pocket CEO*, Englewood Cliffs, NJ: Prentice Hall, 1990, pp. 79, 82.)

Garvin's 8 Dimensions of Quality

David Garvin of Harvard Business School offers another way to look at the quality of a product, through eight dimensions.

1. Performance or operating characteristics
2. Features or supplemental characteristics
3. Reliability or probability of failure
4. Conformance or consistency with specifications
5. Durability or expected product life
6. Serviceability or ease, speed, and cost of repair
7. Aesthetics or ability to please
8. Perceived quality or indirect value

(Source: Alex Hiam, *The Vest-Pocket CEO*, Englewood Cliffs, NJ: Prentice Hall, 1990, p. 91.)

The Business Plan

For many entrepreneurs, the fun, invigorating aspect of starting a new business is coming up with the idea or discovering an untapped niche. The brainstorming sessions that follow are exciting, too. However, writing a business plan forces you alone or you and your partners to sit down and grind out a detailed, well-thought-out, written description and step-by-step implementation plan of your idea. For many, this task is approached as the worst kind of chore.

Writing a business plan is a critical exercise. If you can't write a good one, then either your idea isn't feasible or you haven't thought it through well enough. Completing your business plan is a tangible representation of your idea and means that you are really on your way. You might also experience a sense of satisfaction and growing confidence upon writing your business plan. You will undoubtedly learn things about business and you will have that great feeling of accomplishment that is associated with doing something hard.

The following section will describe why you need a business plan, tell you what you need to think about and include, and help you avoid common pitfalls.

nine
Create a Business Plan—Now

A Business Plan Defined

A business plan defines your business in a detailed way. It can help you to scrutinize all aspects of your business and to be very specific about every facet of the business. The business plan also provides you with a written document that can help you sell your idea and your company to others.

A business plan is usually associated with a start-up business, but it can also be useful if you are planning to expand an existing business. In fact, you should look at a business plan as part of a continuous process. It provides a good discipline for establishing and maintaining systematic coverage of all facets of your business.

The document you write should capture the interest of your readers and hold their attention while you describe your business. Since a potential investor or other reader of this document is almost always a skeptic, you need to convince the reader of your qualifications as an entrepreneur, and you can do this in a well-organized business plan.

In defining your business, you will specify the industry, your target market, and the product or service that you plan to provide. You will show how the product or service will benefit the user, that it is readily and widely marketable, and that your staff has the ability to market the product or service efficiently and professionally.

Your business plan will summarize the management capabilities of your proposed staff and will show how you will cover all areas of management expertise, whether through diversity of staff or through training.

The financial aspects of your business will need to be spelled out carefully if you are planning to borrow money. Potential investors, even family and friends who may contribute funding, will want to know how their money will be used. And investors will want specifics of the financial arrangements: who is involved, how much money is needed, what is the minimum investment per investor, how is ownership translated into shares or other forms, what is the price per share of stock, what is the projected compound annual return over the next five or so years.

Even if you do not plan to finance your operations at the beginning, you will need to know, for your own information, what your capital needs will be in the future. The time spent on this section will not be wasted.

(Sources: W. Keith Schilit, "Preparing a Business Plan," *AMA Management Handbook*, John J. Hampton, ed., 1994, New York: AMACOM, American Management Association, pp. 13-6–13-11; Justin G. Longenecker, Carlos W. Moore, and J. William Petty, *Small Business Management*, Cincinnati, OH: South-Western Publishing Co., 1994, pp. 163-173.)

Gumpert's 8 Reasons for Writing a Business Plan

Why is a business plan so important? David E. Gumpert, writing in *The Portable MBA in Entrepreneurship*, gives eight reasons for writing a business plan:

1. To sell yourself on the idea before making a significant financial and personal commitment
2. To obtain a loan from the bank
3. To attract potential investors
4. To convince other firms with whom you may want to build alliances
5. To explain your business to companies with which you would like to establish a long-term contract
6. To attract employees
7. To aid in mergers or acquisitions
8. To assist management in goal-setting and long-range planning

You may find that you want to create two plans, one for planning and controlling your business and the other for marketing and funding your business. The *planning and control document* will be for internal use. It will be the document you use to sell yourself, to attract employees, and to help in goal setting and long-range planning. It can also be used as a reference document to be sure your business is heading in the intended direction. The planning and control document can provide a detailed review of the business if and when you decide to take on a corporate partner. As your business grows, this plan will need to be modified.

The *marketing and funding document* is the plan you will use to attract outside investment, whether through bank loans or investors. You will also need a financial document when discussing alliances or mergers with possible partnering companies.

Some banks may accept a summary business plan (which may be about 10 pages rather than the typical 40) because they require other forms that collect the added information. If you do not intend to seek financing, write a summary plan to help you focus on important issues and goals. If you do decide to seek financing in the future, you still may not need to write an extensive business plan unless it's specifically requested.

(Source: David E. Gumpert, "Creating a Successful Business Plan," *The Portable MBA in Entrepreneurship*, ed., William D. Bygrave, John Wiley & Sons, New York: 1994, pp. 113-122.)

Analyze Setup Costs

As you plan for your business and prepare to write a formal business plan, it is important to take into account all the possible expenses your new business will face. The following is a list of equipment and services, compiled by the editors of *Income Opportunities* magazine, that most businesses will need sooner or later. Depending on the size of your business, you may be able to do without some of these items. If you have the expertise yourself, you may be able to perform some of your own services, such as accounting and advertising. However, sometimes it pays to spend the money on a professional to be sure you are covering all bases, especially the legal and regulatory.

Likewise, to save on initial expenses, you may want to consider buying used equipment rather than new.

Equipment

Computer
Typewriter
Fax
Copier

Furniture

Chairs
Desks
Lamps
Bookcases
Files

Services

Telephone
Electric
Legal
Accounting/bookkeeping
Advertising/promotion

Monthly Expenses

Salaries
Rent
Telephone
Electric
Water
Heat
Advertising
Insurance
Taxes
Maintenance
Legal

(Source: *33 Profitable Part-time Businesses*, Englewood Cliffs, NJ: Prentice Hall, by the editors of *Income Opportunities*, 1992, pp. 31-32.)

The Standard Business Plan

A business plan is usually about 40 pages long, more if you want to be extremely detailed or include lots of exhibits, less if you are using the document to generate some general interest. Although 40 pages sounds like a long document, you may be surprised when you begin to put together all the information.

The most important aspect of writing a business plan is to be concise. The plan should be strong on facts and use good visual formatting, such as bulleted lists, headlines, short paragraphs, and lots of white space on the page. These make the information more accessible and, therefore, easier to read.

The tone of your business plan should convey your enthusiasm for your proposed business. The people who read the plan will need to be convinced to invest money, time, or confidence in your undertaking. This is your arena and opportunity to persuade them.

As you do the calculations and write your plan, be sure you take into consideration the potential risks of your business. Anyone reading a business plan will want to be assured that you have dealt fully with the elements of risk that threaten your start-up business.

Assistance with Writing Your Plan

If you feel hesitant about your writing ability, you may want to find help or counseling on writing the business plan. CPA firms sometimes offer low- or no-cost services to new businesses. There are a number of counseling services, including the federally sponsored SCORE (Service Corps of Retired Executives) and SBDC (Small Business Development Centers). (See the Resources section for details.) Colleges and universities often sponsor programs on small-business topics. There is even software to help you produce a business plan. We discuss software in the section containing business-plan templates.

A Standard Business Plan Format

The basic parts of a traditional business plan are described in texts and other business books. In the following pages, we describe a standard business plan outline. The parts are numbered in our description, and yours should be numbered too although possibly in a slightly different order from the outline shown below. The organization of your plan will be directed to some extent by your type of business and by what you believe to be the natural order and flow of the parts.

Following our basic description of a business plan are several other outlines of business plans to give you an idea of various ways you can organize your document.

In addition, remember that just because the parts are listed and numbered in a particular order, you do not have to *write* them in that order. You may find, for example, that the Executive Summary will be easier to write after all the other parts of your business plan have been written.

Each section of the business plan can be an abbreviated overview or a full-blown description, according to your needs. As we have mentioned, you need to keep in mind the possible pitfalls and risks to the business and be prepared to respond to them. For example, what if your projected customer base doesn't materialize or what if the price appears to be set too high? Be sure to take into consideration any possibilities such as these.

1. Title or Cover Page. The cover page is like the title page of a manuscript or book. It makes the presentation look complete. Items to include on this page are the company name, address, contact person, and phone number. This information is given so that the person reading the plan can contact you if interested in your business.

Both the cover of the business plan and the title page should contain a confidentiality statement to the effect that this is privileged information and must not be copied or transmitted to another party. When you make copies of the completed document, be sure you number each copy so you can track them. Numbering your copies also reinforces the confidentiality statement, showing that you are serious about keeping close track of who has your business plan.

2. Table of Contents. A table of contents is important because your readers will not necessarily read the document in the order in which you have presented it. Some like to start with the summary, others prefer to read the details and then read the summary afterward. The table of contents helps readers find the place they want to start.

3. Executive Summary. The summary is probably the most important part of your business plan, as it may be the only part that some people will read. The summary is often used by readers with limited time to evaluate whether the rest of the document is worth reading. In this section you need to emphasize why you have a good concept and why it will work.

The executive summary is usually about three pages long, and its contents should follow the general structure of your plan. It summarizes briefly and concisely each part of the business plan, covering four areas of competence: technical, marketing, financial, and managerial.

4. Company Description. Here is where you describe your business strategy, objectives, and your visions for the management team. If you or members of the team have a prior reputation or experience, you may want to include details here to show the skills and abilities you can bring to bear on this new venture.

5. Market and Competition. In this section, describe your potential customers—who they are, how many there are, and how you will reach them. You should also cover the presence or absence of competition and how you will handle it. Consider both your advantages and those of the competitors.

6. Product/Service. You must describe your product in close detail from its manufacture from raw materials to pricing and distribution. For a service, describe what you are offering, how you will price it, and how you will market it. You should specify expected demand levels for products or services and how you will meet them.

A description of the product should include its production complexity and special features such as whether it can be produced in an innovative way. Also include if the product can be protected by patent or copyright.

7. Marketing: Sales and Promotions. In this section, describe in detail how you will promote and sell your product or service. For example, what types of advertising and promotions do you expect to use? How will you communicate your product? Will you use surveys? Which media are appropriate for your product or service? Will you use an agency to help in the marketing effort?

8. Financing. This section contains your projected financial information, including cash flow, income/loss, and balance sheet. Include any backers or other financial sources. Financing information should also account for equipment you may need to finance and purchase.

9. Appendix. The appendix can be used for any extra material that does not fit elsewhere in the business plan but is nevertheless useful information. It may include resumes of management team members, letters of endorsement, literature about the product or company, graphs and charts, and other material that you want to include but that does not fit into one of the other headings.

There are a few other topics that you should include if you didn't include them in the preceding sections:

Legal considerations. Any legal issues not addressed in other sections should be put into their own section.

Management. You may want to describe your management structure in the Company section or in a separate section.

Operating plan. This includes details of how the product will be produced. It may be included in the Product section.

This is the basic outline for a business plan. There are also other ways to organize the information, as you will see in the pages that follow.

(Sources: David E. Gumpert, "Creating a Successful Business Plan," *The Portable MBA in Entrepreneurship*, ed., William D. Bygrave, John Wiley & Sons, New York: 1994, pp. 113-122; Jerry W. Moorman and James W. Halloran, *Entrepreneurship*, Cincinnati, OH: South-Western Publishing Co., 1993, pp. 26-27; Arthur H. Kuriloff, John M. Hemphill, Jr., and Douglas Cloud, *Starting and Managing the Small Business*, New York: McGraw-Hill, Inc., 1993, pp. 12-16; Justin G. Longenecker, Carlos W. Moore, and J. William Petty, *Small Business Management*, Cincinnati, OH: South-Western Publishing Co., 1994, p. 173.)

ten
A Business Plan
Writer's Templates and Aids

Business Writing Do's and Don'ts

Although writing 40 pages may seem like a daunting task, there are a few points to remember to make the job a little easier:

- This document will help you sell yourself and your product or service.
- The business plan has multiple uses.
- The plan can be adjusted as necessary.
- It is perfectly acceptable to have someone help you write it.
- Outlines can be useful tools.
- Although good writing will not necessarily sell a poor business plan, bad writing might ruin a good one.

That said, let us now turn to a few basic concepts to keep in mind when you are writing your business plan.

Check List

___ *Think before you start.* Having a clear picture in your mind will help you put your thoughts on paper more clearly.

___ *Keep your audience in mind.* As you write, try to visualize the people you are writing to and write as if you were speaking to them.

___ *Use short, clear sentences.* Long sentences do not necessarily impress the reader and are harder to follow. A rule of thumb for business writing is to limit sentences to between 25 and 30 words.

___ *Avoid the passive voice.* Active verbs are clearer and easier to comprehend. (For those who forget the difference between active and passive voice, passive is saying something like "a vote was taken" instead of using the active form "the group took a vote.")

___ *Use concrete words.* Try not to be vague. Concrete words help to make sentences clear.

___ *Avoid jargon and technical language.* Watch out for words that are industry- or specialty-specific, unless your readers will know what they mean. Lawyers, computer specialists, engineers, and other "specialists" are often guilty of using words that no one outside their profession understands.

___ *Skip unnecessary words.* Do not embroider to impress. It will have the opposite effect.

___ *Get to the point.* Readers with limited time want to know the bottom line. They do not want to have to search to find it, or worse, not find it at all. Consider putting your bottom line on top of each section with supporting information to follow. This way, the reader will immediately know your most important point and can decide whether or not to read on.

___ *Write as you talk.* This may sound surprising, but just "tell it as it is." If you can explain something to someone in words, do the same thing on paper.

When you finish, before you produce a final version of your document, ask someone else to read the document. Almost inevitably a second person will find a typo or other error that escaped your scrutiny.

If you need a good reference for usage, composition, form, and style, we recommend the small paperback that belongs on every desk—*The Elements of Style* by William Strunk, Jr. and E. B. White. It covers the basics with simplicity and humor.

Sample Business Plan Outlines

There are any number of ways to arrange a business plan depending on the material you want to include. The basic information outlined in previous pages should be included, but the sequence of the plan will depend upon what information you want to impart.

In the following pages we offer a few sample outlines to give you some ideas of how you might organize your business plan. To some degree the *type* of business will affect how you organize the plan. For example, Vactek Ltd.'s plan (following) dwells more heavily on technological information because of the nature of the business. One-Hour Photoprocessing's plan attends closely to competitive analysis because it is an innovative entry into an existing market.

Each business plan usually includes exhibits (data in the form of graphs or charts) that provide information to back up the text in the various sections. Exhibits can be incorporated into the text or numbered in an appendix and referred to by number in the body of the text.

Panificio's Bakeries' Strategic Plan

1. Background
2. Concept/Price
3. Product descriptions
4. Market
5. Competitors
6. Staff and Organization
   a. Board of Directors
   b. Management and Staff
7. Operations
   a. Start-up

    b. Ongoing

  8. Forecasts

    a. Income

    b. Cash flow

    c. Pro forma Balance Sheet

  9. Financial requirements

    a. Structure

    b. Proposed terms

    c. Cost projections

  10. Risks and Benefits

    Appendix: Resumes of management, Organization chart

One-Hour Photoprocessing's Proposal

Summary

  1. Retail concept

    a. Product/Service

    b. Store characteristics

  2. Photoprocessing Market Analysis

    a. General

    b. Minilab concept

  3. Competition

    a. Nature

      (1) location

      (2) price

      (3) service

      (4) quality

      (5) advertising and promotion

      (6) selling

      (7) flexibility

    b. Existing competition

   c. Competitive threats
     (1) new competition
     (2) technological changes
4. Economics of Business
5. Management
6. Location of business; associated costs
7. Equipment
8. Operating costs
   a. Variable
   b. Overhead
9. Expected financial performance
10. Capital requirements and Rate of Return

   Exhibits: Profit and Loss, Management, Cost Estimate, Material Costs, Fixed Costs, Cash Flow Forecast, Pro Forma Profit and Loss, Pro Forma Balance Sheet, Debt and Interest Calculation

Vactek Ltd.'s Business Plan for a Technological Firm

1. Product/Technology
   a. Method
   b. Products
2. Market
   a. Existing segments
   b. New segments
3. Competition
   a. Major
   b. Analyzed by market segment
4. Economics
5. Management and Organization
6. Operations
   a. Physical

b. Plant and Equipment

c. Sales and Engineering

d. Assembly

e. Service

f. Suppliers

7. Strategy

a. Marketing

b. Technological innovation

8. Expected financial performance

9. Financial requirements

10. Exhibits: Management team profiles, Organization structure, Expected sales, Orders expected, Projected profits, Projected cash flow, Projected balance sheet

Survival Aids Ltd.'s Proposal for a New Product

1. Objectives

a. Long term

b. Short term

c. Subsidiary (mission, goals)

2. Products/Services

3. Operations

a. Initial structure - employees, responsibilities

b. Development

(1) initial

(2) future

c. Profit sharing

d. Production

e. Supplies, transportation, delivery

f. Sales and marketing

g. Alternatives

h. Administrative

4. Finance

a. General

b. Planning assumptions (optimistic, pessimistic)

Appendix: Resumes, Projections (optimistic and pessimistic)

Note that this last outline is more sketchy than the previous ones. A potential investor will probably be more interested in a completely developed plan.

(Source: *Cases in Strategic Management for the Smaller Business*, ed. Stuart St. P. Slatter. Oxford, England: Basil Blackwell Ltd, 1988, pp. 2-82.)

SBDC Business Plan Template

The following outline is provided by the Small Business Development Center to those who intend to apply to the Women's Pre-Qualification Loan Program. The Pre-Qualification Loan Program, sponsored by the Small Business Administration, allows a small business owned by a woman to apply for loan qualification *before* going to the bank for a loan. It is designed to streamline the loan process for those applying for loans up to $250,000.

Use this outline to review and assemble the information that you will need for *any* loan application.

1. Executive Summary

a. Financial proposal summary

b. Brief description of products/services and industry

c. Brief description of goals and objectives

2. Business History and Overview

a. History of existing business

b. Current status and concerns

c. Future goals and objectives

3. Management Plan

a. Ownership

    b. Organization structure (sole proprietorship, corporation, partnership)

    c. Responsibilities of key personnel

    d. Technical advisors (accountants, lawyers, etc.)

    e. Licenses, permits and insurance

4. Marketing Plan

    a. Overview of industry

        (1). Brief historical perspective

        (2) Current status of industry

        (3) Prospects for industry growth

    b. Description of products and services

        (1) Products and services

        (2) Proprietary position: copyrights, legal, technical considerations

    c. Market

        (1) Target market (demographics, location, etc.)

        (2) Competition (identify at least three)

        (3) Strategic advantage of business

        (4) Estimated market share to be captured

    d. Marketing strategy

        (1) Overall strategy (promotions, advertising, direct mail, etc.)

        (2) Pricing policy

        (3) Sales terms

        (4) Method of selling and distribution

5. Operations Plan

    a. Location and site plan

    b. Staffing plan and number of employees

    c. Job responsibilities and wages

    d. Sources of supply

    e. Production method (if applicable)

    f. Hours of operation

6. The Financial Plan

   a. current financial statements

      (1) Company income/profit and loss year-end statements (past 3 years)

      (2) Company balance sheet year-end (past 3 years)

      (3) Current income statement and balance sheet

   b. Summary financial needs and application of funds

   c. Projected financial statements

      (1) Income/profit and loss statement (2 years by year)

      (2) Cash-flow statement (1 year, by month)

   d. List of available collateral

   e. Uses of loan proceeds

      (1) Individual tax return (past 3 years)

      (2) Personal financial statement

(Source: Adapted from "Business Plan Guide," document provided in packet from Small Business Development Center, Western Massachusetts Regional Office.)

How to Use Software to Help Create a Business Plan

If you are overwhelmed by the thought of creating your own business plan and you like working on a computer, you can get help from software. There are a number of programs on the market that can help you put together a business plan. Some samples: "Bizplan Builder" and "Developing a Successful Business Plan."

"Bizplan Builder" v. 4.0 (1990) ($99.95)

The promotional material on this software product says, "Writing a business plan is easy when you have an outline and most of the typing is already done." It promises also to show you how to raise capital to launch a product, service, or company. You can find this software in a variety of stores, including Staples in the Northeast, where it is listed at $84.99.

Table of Contents for Bizplan Builder

1. Executive summary
2. Present situation
3. Objectives
4. Management
5. Product/Service description
6. Market Analysis
   Customers
   Competition
   Focus Group research
   Risk
7. Marketing strategy
   Pricing and Profitability
   Selling tactics
   Distribution
   Advertising and Promotion
   Public Relations
   Business Relationships
8. Manufacturing
9. Financial projections
   12-month budget
   5-year income statement
   Cash-flow projection
   Pro forma balance sheet
   Break-even analysis
   Sources and uses of funds summary
   Start-up requirements
   Use of funding proceeds
10. Conclusions and Summary
11. Appendix

Perhaps just looking at this outline will give you some ideas for what to include in your plan.

"Developing a Successful Business Plan" ($49.50)

Entrepreneur Magazine Group's *Small Business Development Catalog* advertises "Developing a Successful Business Plan," software that takes you step by step through the process. Request the catalog from Entrepreneur Magazine Group, at the address given in the Resources section.

If software appeals to you, then test drive one or several of these products. Even if you do not buy the software, you can learn about the typical contents for a business plan by looking at the manuals.

Troubleshooting: Abrams' Business Plan Stumbling Blocks

If you are going to use your plan to obtain financing, it goes without saying that your financial information must be complete or the potential investor will reject it. Rhonda M. Abrams, syndicated columnist and author of *The Successful Business Plan: Secrets & Strategies*, cautions that all you need is one error in a business plan to have it rejected. Besides making the plan look perfect (typed, bound), you need to be sure your data are accurate and precise.

In your financial information, you should include a three- to five-year income forecast along with projected balance sheets and cash-flow projections.

Abrams' 10 Stumbling Blocks follow. As you read them, think about how you can show in your business plan that you have considered these points. Then give evidence in your plan that you have taken steps to avoid these pitfalls.

1. Failing to understand the competition. Not only do you need to understand your current competition—and describe it fully—you must anticipate potential new competition. If your product or service is as perfect for the market as you believe, then you are likely to encounter others trying to enter the market in the future, and you need to show that you are prepared.

2. Lacking an understanding of the industry. It is important to know your industry as well as possible. This means that either you or a member of your management or employee teams have had direct experience. Be sure you do not have any blind spots; research thoroughly and learn and consult experts for areas where you lack expertise.

3. Inaccurately estimating income and expenses. It is easy to be optimistic about a new product's potential for success. But it is very important to be realistic about the cash flow. If the market for your product or service already exists, you can research current prices and costs. If you are creating a new market, you need to base your figures on comparable products or make projections that are as realistic as possible. When you estimate expenses, add an additional 5 to 10 percent as a cushion against unexpected expenses.

4. Overestimating the market. If you are offering an innovative product or one based on technical innovations, you may be able to sell at a lower price and so expect that you will have a lot of customers. However, lower prices do not necessarily guarantee you market share. Consumers often prefer to stick with familiar products and services. Therefore, you need to be prepared with a plan for surviving until your product or service catches on and with a plan for getting people to switch to your product.

5. Not detailing management characteristics. Even though enthusiasm is important for a start-up business, what really counts in the long run is experience. Be sure to describe in detail the experience your management team has for running this business.

6. Overestimating the longer-term profit potential. "Mom and Pop" businesses rarely attract investors. However, if you have a larger business that needs infusions of capital, you will have to convince a potential investor that return on investment in your business would be at least as great as return on other investments the investor might otherwise make.

7. Trying to do too many things. You may have a whole menu of ideas you want to try, perhaps all related to a core product or service. And they may all be viable. Although it is tempting to throw yourself into everything at once, it is wiser to start out with one major activity first and then expand slowly.

8. Trying to do it all. If some other firm performs a function that you need for your product, consider outsourcing or making some sort of partnering arrangement such as a strategic alliance. It usually does not pay to reinvent the wheel or spend scarce resources on a process that is already being done efficiently by someone else. (See the discussions of outsourcing in chapter 17 and strategic alliances in Part IV.)

9. Being uninformed about rules, regulations, insurance. Be sure you account for licensing fees, government regulations that relate to your business, and other "necessary evils." Investors need to be assured that you are familiar with the rules that will affect your business and that you are planning for them in your business calculations.

10. Offering an incomplete funding picture. No investor will lay out money for a business with insufficient financial information. Be sure you specify all sources of funding as well as required and anticipated expenditures.

Even if you have a great business idea that sounds good when you talk about it, be sure you scrutinize the idea *on paper* so that you answer all the likely questions from potential investors. While reassuring them of the viability of your plan, you will have also proven to yourself that you can do it.

(Source: Based on Rhonda M. Abrams, "Business Plan Stumbling Blocks," *Working Woman*, October 1994, pp. 45-48.)

eleven
Check and Improve the Plan

Does Your Plan Address Its Audience and Purpose?

Before you finalize your business plan, you should reassess the document to see whether it meets the needs of the people who will be reading it. Does it appear to accomplish your initial objectives such as obtaining investors or getting a loan from the bank?

Check to see whether your business plan sounds appropriate for the audience to whom you are writing. Does it answer the questions that each reader is likely to ask? For example, bankers and investors will want financial information as well as risk analysis; management team members will be concerned that the product and, therefore, the business are viable; suppliers will want to be assured that the product is marketable and will produce income so that they can be paid, and so forth.

Refer back to the section "Templates and Aids" and "Business Writing Do's and Don'ts" (pages 117-119). Use the checklist to evaluate your document. Is it a good quality document, well thought out and presented? Is it clear? Does it make sense? Is your proposal reasonable? And have you been thorough in your analysis and coverage of all the aspects of the plan?

Once you have satisfied yourself that the answers to these questions are "yes," then take a look at the *format* of the document. Appearance is very important. A neat, perfectly spelled, clean copy of the document is essential if you want to be taken seriously.

Be sure you include a table of contents and that the pages are numbered consecutively. Include visual presentations (charts, tables, etc.) where appropriate. It is a nice addition to include tabs to separate the sections of the document.

When you proofread the business plan, be sure to get rid of extra or unnecessary words and check punctuation and spelling. It is also a good idea to have someone else proofread the document, as another eye can frequently catch a mistake you have missed. If the document contains any technical sections, ask someone with the expertise to go over it. This may mean talking with lawyers, marketing specialists, engineering or production specialists, and accountants.

When the entire document is complete, before you copy it, give it one last check. A good proofreading technique is to read the document from end to beginning. Start with the last word and proceed backwards from there. This way, you don't become absorbed in the content but can focus on each word for spelling errors.

Will Your Plan Impress a Banker?

Sooner or later, you will probably have to deal with a bank for financing your business. (We cover financing in Part VII.) Perhaps you will start out with your own financing or you have friends lined up as investors. But eventually the business will start to grow and you will need to talk with lending officers at banks. Your business plan is a tool you can use to convince bankers to help fund your operation. Consider what a few bankers have to say about proposals that are successful and those that are not.

Be concise.   Use bullets. Give facts. The average time spent by a potential lender reviewing a business plan is about 15 minutes, so it is important to make every word count and make the most important information easily accessible.

Bill Holt, vice president of the Wachovia Bank of Reidsville, North Carolina, prefers bullets to a paragraph format. He says "... we want facts, not fluff." Holt's bank, based in Winston Salem, is a leading small-business lender in the Southeast.

The point is to stick to the point. Give precise facts directly related to the business and its niche, not to the whole industry.

Make the summary work for you.   The executive summary is the most important section of the business plan. It can either pique the reader's interest or cause the loan officer to go on to the next application. The summary is usually read first, so include your main points there. Summarize your business plan and tell why it will work. Holt says, "We are looking for a good, concise summary, not a thesis."

Offer projections.   Projections should include not only optimistic expectations but pessimistic as well. Even better, offer a best-case, a worst-case, and a regular projection. Says Brent Priddy, a banker at BB&T in Wilson, North Carolina, "When the projections are too high, I lose confidence in the owner." It is important for the projections to be realistic.

Charles Cannaday, chief lending officer for First South Bank, Burlington, North Carolina, says he usually starts with projections and works backwards. He feels it is a waste of time for him—and for the borrower—to continue if the projections seem unrealistic.

Look at the pluses and minuses.   Be sure to take into consideration the potential problems, not just the positive aspects of your potential business. If you do not deal with the drawbacks, they will surely be attended to by the banker. Along these lines, also consider and address the potential risks.

Include all the components in the loan proposal.   Proposed loan components include the purpose of the loan, the term, the interest rate, and the collateral. Include financial projections to show how you plan to repay the loan. Cash flow and prospective profits are crucial. Be sure the numbers are concrete and realistic and backed up by reasonable assumptions.

Get help if you need it.   According to bankers, having someone help you prepare a business plan is not a disadvantage. They suggest that it indicates a desire to present yourself well and the ability to ask for help when you need it.

Perfect copy.   Finally, if you want the document to be taken seriously, be sure you submit a clean copy, free of errors or erasures. This will help ensure that your proposal is taken seriously.

(Source: Based on J. Tol Broome, Jr., "How to Write a Business Plan," *Nation's Business*, February 1993, pp. 29-30.)

Questions, Caveats, and Musts for a Business Plan

There are many successful entrepreneurs who espouse their own formulas for writing successful business plans. The following advice and guidelines from the experts are grounded in clear thinking and common sense. The overall bottom line appears to be, be practical, thorough, realistic, and well organized in your presentation.

Does Your Plan Answer These Questions?

To attract investors, you need to have a concise business plan, according to Carol Rivchun, vice president of marketing for the Greater Cleveland Growth Association. She suggests that a plan should be able to answer the following questions.

Market and Customers

- How big is the market for your product or service?
- Precisely who is going to buy your product or service?
- Why do these potential customers need your product?
- How will you reach potential customers and persuade them to buy your product?
- How will you get people to realize they need it?

Financing

- How much money will you need?
- How long will you need the money?
- When will you pay back the loan?

(Source: Adapted from a column, "Your Own Account," by Mary Rowland, titled "Finding Money to Start a Business," *The New York Times*, May 28, 1991, Sec. 3.)

Broome's Caveats for a Business Plan

- Prove that you have a vested interest in this business. Why should someone invest in it if you do not really care?
- Support or explain each point you make. Do not assume that people will know what you are saying.
- Be sure you discuss the environment for the business, including the competition.
- Be concise. Make every word count.
- Be sure the data are up to date and accurate.
- Know your facts. Be sure the details you give are clear, not fuzzy. Do not embroider.
- Keep in mind three scenarios for your business: best case, worst case, and most likely. Show that you have considered each of these in your document.
- Be realistic about the loan you are asking for.
- Emphasize cash flow and projected profits rather than collateral.

(Source: Based on J. Tol Broome, Jr., "How to Write a Business Plan," *Nation's Business*, February 1993, pp. 29-30.)

Working Woman's Business Plan "Musts"

Working Woman, together with AT&T and Deloitte & Touche, offered a 1994 Entrepreneurial Grant of $50,000 for the best new-business idea. The magazine's panel of judges reviewed 700 applications from 47 states, from which 16 semifinalists were selected. Each then submitted full business plans and from that group 4 finalists were selected.

The plans of the successful finalists included the following:

- A complete and thorough analysis of the targeted market
- A full description of the specific niche in a market that is growing
- Details of how the concept will be applied in a new market
- Demonstration of the ability to connect with major industry decision makers
- Full exploration of the potential risks and how to minimize them
- Previous sales success
- Realistic financial projections based on concrete data

The competitors who had carefully thought through their potential business and quantified the possibilities made it to the final round of consideration. In the process of fully scrutinizing a product or service idea, you not only satisfy potential investors, you also prove to yourself the viability of your idea.

(Source: Based on a report by Rhonda M. Abrams, *Working Woman*, October 1994, p. 48.)

PART IV
Marketing and Sales

Marketing is one of the fundamental, underlying business concepts. It frames a business and its activities around anticipating and meeting the needs of the customer before and better than competitors do. Some entrepreneurs believe that they have such an excellent product or service that it will market itself. Or they may concentrate on aggressive personal sales rather than trying to increase awareness and desire for their product through more subtle or less direct techniques. Ultimately, most business people realize that their success depends upon the customer: Will they buy or won't they? They find that their business must incorporate the marketing concept, which is synonymous with a customer-service orientation, into their business philosophy and day-to-day activities.

twelve
Improve Your Marketing

Customer Service

As Sam Walton, founder of the Wal-Mart stores chain, said, "There is only one boss: the customer." And this is true—research bears it out—businesses that are customer-driven are successful. Those that ignore customer needs disappear from the market.

Small-business specialist Dick Laird suggests that the only way to be successful is by being attentive to the customer. This includes:

- Making a positive first impression
- Being sure that the customer is satisfied
- Assuring that customers return for repeat business
- Listening to what the customer needs
- Asking what customers want
- Offering a quality product
- Knowing your products
- Being sure employees have sufficient training

- Developing customers' trust
- Showing personal interest in the customer
- Doing the job right the first time
- Underpromising and overdelivering

  (Source: Dick Laird, "Customer Service in Small Businesses," *AMA Management Handbook*, John J. Hampton, ed., 1994, New York: AMACOM, American Management Association, pp. 13-28.)

In their book *Marketing Masters: Secrets of America's Best Companies*, Gene Walden and Edmund Lawler reveal how the pros market their products and services. They enumerate six steps you can take to reinforce your marketing procedures to make them work productively for you.

1. Move quickly to satisfy customer needs. Be responsive to customer complaints, requests, and preferences. Stay tuned to the grapevine, whether through your company's hotline, by reading demographic studies that show coming changes, or by any other method you use to know what the customer prefers. Be able to make changes quickly so you can get a new product to market quickly. Work to keep your customers.

2. Use pricing to differentiate your product or service. Pricing differentiation does not necessarily mean lower prices. For example, you may want to emphasize the quality of your product or service by setting a premium price. If you do set your price low, be sure you know what kind of demand to expect and be sure you can handle the demand the price generates. It is also important to be thoroughly familiar with the competition and the broader market so that you do not price yourself out of business.

3. Pay attention to packaging. While you want your packaging to catch the customer's eye, make sure it fits with your company's image and with other promotions you are creating. Customers tend to be confused when packaging is jarring or out of context. Frequently changed packaging may also confuse customers, with the result being a loss of sales if your customers cannot find your product.

4. Build customer loyalty. A consistently good product, one with responsive customer service, will help you build customer loyalty. This goes hand in hand with meeting customer needs in a timely fashion.

5. Offer samples and demonstrations. People love samples, tastes, and demos. They like to have an opportunity to explore the product or service, even if in a small way. Try to provide potential customers with experiences of your product. Hands-on experience goes a long way toward building customer preference and loyalty. Makers of cosmetics have long been aware of this marketing technique and use it extensively with great success.

6. Educate customers. Help people learn more about your product through seminars, tours of facilities, and other experiences that will help them understand the product. An educational experience that aids a customer in using a product more effectively will help build loyalty. For example, the Samuel Adams brewery in Boston, Massachusetts, gives educational tours of their brewing facility. Not only do consumers learn about the Samuel Adams' brewing technique but they are given fresh beer to drink afterwards.

While these simple suggestions may seem obvious to some, firms often get caught up in the production of the product and forget the bottom line of marketing: the customer. All marketing should revolve around customers and their needs. The company that focuses on customer needs will have a better chance of success in the competitive arena.

(Source: Gene Walden and Edmund Lawler, *Marketing Masters: Secrets of America's Best Companies*, Harper Business, 1993, as itemized in Jenny C. McCune, "Brewing Up Profits," *Management Review*, April 1994, p. 20.)

Customer Analysis

Businesses undertake market research when they want to find out what consumers are interested in or would prefer to see on the market. Market research involves looking at what brands of products customers are currently using and how they could be induced to switch to a different brand. You might also want to construct a profile of your typical customer or establish a list of characteristics of potential customers. Understanding your target market will help you create a specific, tailored marketing strategy.

Before you undertake any sort of research, be sure you define the results or outcomes you are looking for. Then consider the methods available to you for finding the data. Evaluate the cost of a research project against the benefit before you actually begin. Smaller businesses usually use simpler, less expensive research techniques, such as looking through the Yellow Pages for competitors and potential customers; going to the public library and using corporate guides; or getting relevant government statistics. Also, simply watching, listening, and talking to people will provide you with market information.

Steps in Research

The first step in undertaking a market research project is to define the problem. For example, are sales increasing far more slowly than you had anticipated? Are you getting complaints or returns? Is your main competitor stealing
too many of your customers? Next, you need to specify the population that will
be studied, in other words, which people you will look at to find your information. This is why knowing who your target customers are is critical. If you
make your sample too diverse, you won't get relevant, usable data.

Start by looking at "secondary data." If you can find information on this
particular population that is already available, you can save time and money.
Libraries have scores of books and periodicals containing data on all sorts of
populations. Use government statistics from, for example, the Department of
Commerce or the Census Bureau. If yours is a very local business, try your city
or town hall for demographic and commercial information. Just be sure the
information you use is as up to date as possible.

"Primary data" are collected by contacting members of the actual population (or a representative sample of it). Primary data collection methods
include observation, asking direct questions, and surveys sent by mail, telephone surveys, and personal interviews. While mail and phone surveys are
convenient, they often result in a low response rate. Personal interviews, however, cost more and take longer. Formulate your questions for all surveys carefully. If you're going to quantify the responses then you need to use a scale
or rank-order answer format. If you're collecting subjective data then you want
your questions to be open-ended and not elicit "yes" or "no" answers. And
finally, make sure you give your subjects an opportunity to give you feedback
on your service and products and ask them for improvement ideas. Other
research methods include networking (never underestimate the value of networking!), informal polls, focus groups, and location surveys (such as in malls,
for example).

After you have gathered the information you need, then it is time to
interpret the results. This can be a time-consuming, though rewarding,
process. Sophisticated research programs are completed through the use of
computer programs that can analyze large amounts of data, perhaps comparing them to already-existing data bases of information on consumers. The
more complex gathering and evaluating methods are expensive and usually
need to be handled by professionals who have experience with these types

of research. Call some local market research firms for information and esti-mates.

Why Customer Service Is So Important

According to the U.S. Office of Consumer Affairs, one of every four customers is unhappy with the service received on a product. Twenty-five percent is a high percentage of unhappy people. The problem is compounded by the fact that an unhappy customer will complain to *12* other people about the com-pany from which the poor service came. Happy customers, on the other hand, tell only *5* other people. From this we can see that it is preferable to try to keep customers happy.

Do unhappy customers let companies know? Rarely. Only 1 customer out of 20 will complain to a company about a product or service. The other 19 will simply not buy the product anymore. They will obtain it or something like it somewhere else. While we might tend to respond to this with "Good, I don't want to hear about it," no one stays in business that way. And in this case, what you do not know about your customers' satisfaction may indeed hurt you.

What does this mean for your business? You have to stay tuned to your customer base, listen to complaints that you do receive, and do something about them. You also need to take surveys of customer satisfaction from time to time to learn about both positives and negatives. Customer surveys can also be a benefit in that people usually feel good about simply being asked. And, while you do not want customers to dwell on the negative, you may want to invite criticism so that you know where you have to make changes in your product or service.

Customer retention is just as important as customer cultivation. In fact, it actually costs eight times as much to find new customers as it does to keep old ones.

Show customers—through superior service and high-quality products—that you are responsive to their needs.

(See also the discussions of customer service complaint forms on page 144-145 and customer analysis on page 146.)

(Source: Richard M. Turitz, Esq, sup. ed., *The Prentice Hall Small Business Survival Guide*, Englewood Cliffs, NJ: Prentice Hall, 1993, pp. 105-114.)

ECCO's Customer Complaint Tracking System

Electronic Controls Company (ECCO) produces the yellow flashing lights used on service trucks and the beepers that warn when vehicles are moving in reverse. Like other firms, ECCO has its share of customer complaints. The president of the company became concerned that although the customer service staff was handling complaints to customers' satisfaction, they were not tracking the problems and their resolution.

Management felt that there should be a *written* record of problems and their resolutions, for two reasons. First, if a problem recurred, the solution would be on record and thus save time in resolving it. Second, repeat problems could suggest underlying causes that were being overlooked. Tracking problems could help find root causes that could be remedied, and thus the number of customer complaints could be reduced.

How ECCO Handles Customer Complaints

The first stage of handling a complaint was to apologize for the problem, suggest the next step, and outline what actions would be taken. ECCO developed a form on which detailed information about complaints could be recorded. This form, which is adjusted from time to time according to need, was designed primarily by the people who actually take the customer phone calls.

Anyone who might talk with a customer on the phone is provided with a pad of the forms so he or she can take down information as needed. The information (which follows) is filed in a binder to which all the appropriate departments have access. In addition, the complaints are discussed at the company's weekly executive meetings. The three problems that occur most frequently are each assigned to a team (production, sales/marketing, or leadership) for investigation and resolution. There are two or three people on a team and they have the power to make corrections or to ask for further analysis if they think it is warranted.

ECCO's Customer-Complaint Form

ECCO's complaint form collects the following information:

Initial call information

The name of the person taking the call
The date
Invoice number
Purchase order number
Shipping date
Customer name (or company)
Location
Phone
Contact person
Account manager for this customer

Review details

Names or initials of those who reviewed the complaint form (at least one
  from each team)
The date reviewed

The complaint

The category of complaint—product, service, or delivery
Detailed complaint, written out
First response corrective action by the person taking the call

Further steps

Management review response
Suspected root cause
Next step in the process—track it, close the inquiry, or analyze it further
Names of team members assigned to the problem
Root cause corrective action

Resolution

Closed on date, name, etc.

Applying this to your situation

The information collected on a customer-complaint form can be stored in a binder to be used for reference and analysis. ECCO developed a systematic method for analyzing and resolving problems in their effort to improve the quality of their product and service.

Time and staff permitting, the data collected on forms could be entered into a computer to be analyzed and tracked over time. It would also make retrieval of solutions easier. There are software programs designed to be used by service representatives while they take customer service calls. If complaints are entered directly into the computer during the call, time can be saved and the data can be immediately available for analysis and reporting.

Whether you collect the data on printed forms or on the computer, you need to pay attention to them and analyze them to make them work for you.

(Source: Jay Finegan, "The Rigorous Customer-Complaint Form," *Inc.*, March 1994, pp. 101-103. ECCO's form is shown on pp. 145.)

Gordon's Six Steps to Finding Prospective Customers

You know they are out there. You have done demographic research and you know that there are X thousands of people in the range of 25 to 40 who are ripe for your product. But how do you find them? Kim Gordon, author of *Growing Your Home-Based Business,* suggests the following steps for finding customers.

1. Identify the audience. Be specific about this group. You know they are aged 25 to 40, but what industries are they in, what professions? Where do they live? What related products do they buy? How much money do they make? Is your audience primarily male or female?

2. Research. The library is a good starting point for doing research. Look at national directories for the profession or industry you have identified. See if there are local directories as well. Look in trade publications for the identified industry or profession. Look at business publications, including newspapers and magazines and journals for specific professional groups. Find out about national, regional, and local associations. See if you can obtain membership lists for any of these groups. You want to start creating a list of specific groups and then specific people.

3. Edit the list. Scrutinize the list you have made. Make sure the entries are accurate and appropriate. If not, drop the ones that do not belong. Group the data in logical ways to help when you begin to use them. For example, if you are going to send a mailing, group names by state, zip code, and so forth. If you are targeting professional groups, sort by industry. Computer data-base programs can be helpful in maintaining information and can be sorted according to need. There are simple, easy-to-use data-base programs available for small businesses to use on personal computers.

4. Find out who decides. When you call or write to companies, firms, or organizations, try to find out the names of the decision makers. You want to communicate directly with those you will market to and who will be able to purchase your product. Be sure to ask for the correct spelling of any names you obtain. And when you are writing to someone, double-check the spelling of the person's name and title. You could endanger a sale if you cannot spell the name correctly.

5. Network, network, network. Never underestimate the power of networking. As you meet people, you will be able to add to your list. One person will refer you to another, who will mention someone else's name, and so forth. Write down these names so you can add them to your list.

6. Update your list. Update the addresses, names, and other information on the list from time to time. Drop old unused material from the list so you can concentrate on the potentially more productive ones.

(Source: Kim T. Gordon, *Growing Your Home-Based Business*, Englewood Cliffs, NJ: Prentice Hall, 1992. pp. 25-26.)

thirteen
Increase Sales Success

Sales, through promotions and personal selling, are part of every marketing plan. The more elusive of the two strategies is personal selling. What makes a successful salesperson? We've all met someone in our lifetime whom we believe to be a born seller, but what makes us think so? Usually, it's his or her ability to communicate with and influence others. It's a perception of thoughtfulness. A restaurateur might greet regular customers by telling them about a great bottle of wine he or she saved especially for them. Or a salesperson in a clothing boutique might give a customer honest feedback about what looks good and what doesn't, thereby establishing a kind of relationship and trust. No one yet identified the characteristics of the ideal salesperson who will cause sales to skyrocket. However, there are some concrete steps that you can take or keep in mind.

How to Improve Sales

- Sell quality.
- Offer middleman deals.
- Realign to different markets.
- Redesign the packaging. (Be sure to test it.)

- Give more than expected.
- Exploit a cash cow.
- Take advantage of customer loyalty.
- Let customers spread the word.
- Keep current customers.
- Always keep your competition in mind.

(Source: Richard M. Turitz, Esq, sup. ed., *The Prentice Hall Small Business Survival Guide*, Englewood Cliffs, NJ: Prentice Hall, 1993, p. 7.)

Gitomer's Ways to Create an Excellent Sales Staff

In his seminars and training programs on building a strong sales staff, Jeffrey Gitomer, president of Business Marketing Services in Charlotte, North Carolina, offers advice on how to find good sales personnel for your business.

Always be on the lookout. Stay aware of potential candidates for salespeople for your organization, even when you are not hiring. When you are ready to look for a new staff member, you will already have a partial list if you have been keeping track of good candidates.

When you are thinking of hiring, tune up your network. You may find that networking works better than advertising. Call your contacts and ask around. Observe salespeople you encounter in action: You never know when one might be looking for a new job. Advertising tends to pull in lots of applications, but many of them may not be appropriate for your business.

Keep your business attractive. Always be sure that your business is an inviting one, with a good reputation. Keep the physical surroundings clean and well decorated, have an employee dress code for those that deal with the public, and consider developing a telephone-answering script so that service is consistent and of high quality. First impressions count, and with a good one you will have more success attracting staff, and you may even find that people come to you looking for jobs.

Provide information to candidates. It is important to provide applicants with a clear job description. This means that you first have to know exactly what you expect of a salesperson for your business, and then you need to be able to convey that clearly to the applicant. Itemize the specific responsibilities of the job, and be clear about compensation and performance measurement.

Look for these traits. What should you look for in a salesperson? The letter of application, references from others, and your personal interview will give you clues to the character of the candidate. The following are some traits to look for when hiring salespeople. Ascertain whether your candidate has these traits through observation and by asking references.

Personal skills and characteristics

Happy; positive attitude
Good decision-making skills
Strong grammar skills/articulate
Self-motivated
Takes criticism well
Looks professional
Skilled at follow-up
Trustworthy

Interpersonal skills

Good communicator
Demonstrates strong partnering skills with customers
Listening/probing skills help customers clarify needs
Versatile range of people skills

Drive

Hungry
Persistent
Solution or mission oriented
Goal driven
Loves the work
Does not waste time
Wants to serve
Money is not paramount

Personal growth

Always learning
Experienced not just in selling, but also in the field
Shows a willingness to test personal limits
Ability to view self with humor
Reads a lot
Has interests outside of work
Attends training
Solution rather than problem oriented

Some of the characteristics can be observed during a job interview. In particular, pay attention to whether the candidate:

- Asks job- and productivity-related questions
- Talks about goals, career, and values
- Maintains good eye contact
- Presents a professional-looking resume
- Sells him or herself well
- Does not ask about benefits or salary in the first interview

Be a good interviewer

Ask the candidate about his or her

- previous experience
- example of a recent customer experience
- why leaving the other position
- career goals
- personal goals
- sales philosophy
- big success, big failure
- outside interests
- last vacation; was it quiet, restful, adventuresome, innovative

Other sources of information to help you evaluate a candidate are previous customers, references, and sample work. You can ask the person to do a role-play of a sales situation or have the candidate write a sales plan. Your objective should be to try to discover what drives this person and what will make him or her successful.

Evaluate carefully. Try to be realistic in your evaluation of the candidate. For example, do not let yourself be overly impressed by someone's charisma if you know that the person is not good at closing sales. And it always helps to gain some perspective on a situation by asking for input from another person whose judgment you trust. This is a good reason to have several people do short interviews with strong candidates, to make sure you all agree.

Be a good boss. Once you sign on a new sales staff member, be sure you provide the encouragement, support, and training necessary to create an excellent salesperson.

For further reading, see Gitomer's book *The Sales Bible* (William Morrow).

(Sources: Jeffrey Gitomer, "Search for Excellence," *Entrepreneur*, January 1995, pp. 292-295; Phyllis Elnes, "Marketing in the Small Business," *AMA Management Handbook*, John J. Hampton, ed., 1994, New York: AMACOM, American Management Association, p. 13-21—13-22.)

Ladin's Tips for Commercial Success

If you are starting a high-technology business and you have a new product to market, you will likely have an uphill climb. But Lawrence Ladin, chairman of Cimtechnologies Corporation and a director of VayTek Inc. and ASD Inc., feels that this situation is not entirely impossible—if you have the correct sales and marketing plan. Ladin has been there. He was a founder and chairman of Compressor Controls Corporation and has been a consultant to other high-tech firms.

The most important factor to launching a successful high-tech business, says Ladin, is a seasoned board of directors and management team. Next is the sales staff. Although firms often hire independent sales representatives, Ladin believes that it is difficult for independent sales representatives to be able to fully represent a new product from an unknown company. A full sales and technical training program is crucial and may literally take months, at great cost, especially when the product is highly technical. But it is critical for the company's success that the sales staff fully understand the business and the product.

Firms often have more luck hiring direct rather than independent sales personnel. Even though it may be more expensive to make direct hires, it usually turns out to be better in the long run, again because of the technological aspect of the business. High-tech companies should be sure that members of the sales staff have engineering or scientific backgrounds.

In the earlier stages of promotion and sales of a new product, it may be useful to take the inventor along on sales trips, because this person is enthusiastic and more knowledgeable about the product than anyone else. It is also a good idea, in Ladin's experience, for a manager or experienced investor to accompany the inventor/salesperson on the road. The reason for this is to assure prospective clients that the company is financially sound and enduring.

If your company is on a tight budget and has little to spare for advertising, you can write articles about the theories behind the invention and have them published in trade journals. Reprints of the articles can be used for advertising.

Finally, when a business is new, it is of utmost importance that feedback from users be taken seriously and products adjusted, if necessary, to meet their needs. Satisfied customers can help spread the word about new products from unknown companies.

(Source: Lawrence Ladin, "Selling Innovation: Tips for Commercial Success," *The Wall Street Journal*, March 20, 1995, p. A14.)

Turitz's Sales-Planning Guide

Successful marketing and sales of your product or service requires a well-organized sales program that includes goals, both financial and numbers of meetings; training, seminars, and coaching; strategy sessions; and sales support. In your role as chief strategist and coach, one useful tool you can provide is a sales meeting planning guide. This can be a fairly simple checklist or series of questions to help your sales staff focus on the tasks involved in making and completing a sale. The document should be examined frequently during your meetings with your sales staff and updated as necessary. Salespeople out in the field will often find that their improvisations are superior to standard recommendations.

Before filling out the sales-planning guide, salespeople need to do some research and preparation, which ideally would include at least one telephone interview with the prospective customer. The salespeople need to think about and define:

- Objective of the sales call
- Prospect's current situation
- Prospect's goals
- Prospect's stated needs and problems
- Salesperson's objectives
- How decisions are made, and who makes them
- How the product can benefit each constituency
- How to demonstrate the value of the product
- What supporting documents, overheads, slides, videos, or samples to bring
- Competitive pluses and minuses

After the salesperson has given some thought to these issues, the information can be outlined on the sales-planning form. The form is then used to guide the sales presentation.

The following are suggestions for the information that should be included on a sales-planning form. Note that some of this information will have to be filled in after the call.

Sample Sales Form

Company information. Include company (customer) name, type of business, size of business both in dollars and number of employees, division you're dealing with, parent company, subsidiaries, location, phone number, date of contact, person to contact, and contact's title. (These details will help you create a map of your movement within the company. You might be able to use a sale in one division as leverage for a sale in another.)

Background notes. Make notes on your conversations with prospects so you can refer directly to their stated needs or issues both during meetings and in your follow-up letters. Be as detailed as possible and date each set of notes. This type of service will matter to prospects and will make you stand out.

Decision maker. The name of the person who makes the buying decision.

Objectives. Objectives for this call.

Guiding questions.

- How will you influence this person if he or she is not the decision maker?
- How will you demonstrate the value of the product? What will you say? What support materials will you use? What customers could you use as references?
- How will you make the benefits of your product or service relate specifically to the prospect's needs?
- What are potential objections and how will you address them?
- What commitment are you prepared to make in order to get a commitment from the person you are calling on? Will your supervisor support your commitment? Make sure beforehand.

It may be helpful to have the sales staff practice their sales calls by trying out their pitches on each other. The sales guide can then be used to evaluate whether the important issues have been covered.

(Source: Richard M. Turitz, Esq, sup. ed., *The Prentice Hall Small Business Survival Guide*, Englewood Cliffs, NJ: Prentice Hall, 1993, pp. 59-61.)

Gordon's Checklist for Presentations

When you need to make a presentation, whether for a sales meeting, annual meeting, company meeting, or to a group of potential customers, there are three areas to which you should be attentive: content, structure, and style. Kim Gordon, author of *Growing Your Home-Based Business*, offers a checklist enumerating what to watch out for as you prepare, and give, your presentation. The more organized, prepared, and confident you are, the better you will come across and be able to handle any situations that may arise. If you find yourself presenting to a difficult audience, remain calm and centered and focus on what they are saying and not on how they're making you feel. Shift the focus away from yourself by asking them to elaborate or specify or ask them why they feel the way they do.

A rule of thumb for presentations is: Tell the audience what you're going to tell them; tell them; then tell them what you told them. This may sound redundant but it helps you and your audience remain focused and ensures that you get your points across.

Content

Know your topic well.

Cover only what needs to be covered.

Talk about benefits.

Relate to your audience's needs.

Be sure the material is relevant to the audience.

Structure

Organize by grouping ideas and concepts for comprehension.

Make ideas flow from one to the next.

Be sure the points you make are logical.

Promote interaction with the audience if possible.

Style

Use materials appropriate to the topic.

Be sure the presentation is visually appealing.

Make the talk interesting.

Avoid negative behavior.

Communicate clearly.

Practice your presentation at least once before you give it. One helpful tool for rehearsing is the videotape. By watching yourself, you can see how you will appear to an audience. If you do not have access to video equipment, practice your talk on someone who can give you feedback about your presentation, using the foregoing checklist as a guide.

In either case, be sure you are making eye contact and speaking clearly. Watch to see if you have any annoying mannerisms, such as pushing your hair to the side or saying "er" or "ah" between sentences.

Check the pacing of your words and the pitch of your voice. Look at your body movements to see if they appear natural. Do you seem nervous?

Using materials that draw audience attention can be helpful, but be sure you pick an appropriate time to hand them out. While you may want people to have a document or two in hand while you are speaking, you may want to wait until you are finished to hand them out so you do not have to contend with the rustling of paper if you hand them out while you talk. Further, people may not pay attention to what you are saying if they are reading the handouts.

Another way to involve the audience is to ask for questions or comments. People tend to become involved when they are part of the presentation.

Your main objective should be to project a pleasant, likeable personality and instill confidence in your knowledge, professionalism, and ability.

(Source: Kim T. Gordon, *Growing Your Home-Based Business*, Englewood Cliffs, NJ: Prentice Hall, 1992, pp. 110-113.)

Gordon's Guidelines for Successful Sales Meetings

Kim Gordon, a strategic planning consultant for sales and marketing communications, suggests tactics to assure success when meeting with a potential customer. These methods can apply to smaller or larger firms that are selling either products or services. They also apply to telephone sales.

1. Meet with qualified prospects only. It is important to know whether the person is qualified to become a customer. Perhaps the prospect was only making inquiries and has no intention of buying. You need to know whether it is worth spending your time in this situation.

2. Set a goal for every meeting. Have your objectives clearly in mind before you start. Write them down. Stay focused on these goals. After the meeting, look back to see whether you met those goals.

3. Plan the meeting in advance. Be sure your meeting is well planned. Potential customers are impressed when a presenter is prepared, but you can lose your audience if you are disorganized. Since you represent the company, a disorganized presentation will raise questions in the potential customer's mind. The prospect may wonder whether your company is a good organization to deal with. Be sure you understand the industry and type of business so that you come across as knowledgeable. Role plays with a partner who acts the role of the customer can help you prepare for a meeting.

4. Come to the meeting prepared with tools, materials, and "personal polish." Provide hands-on material for the potential customer where possible. This means brochures, exhibits, a slide show, whatever is available and appropriate for this particular customer and the customer's needs. Be ready to use whatever will help you make your points or demonstrate the positive features of the product or service.

As a salesperson, you are going to be associated with your product. Therefore, it is very important to project a positive image to the customer. Your personal characteristics can add to your presentation—or detract. If your style needs polish, get help ahead of time with your presentation skills.

Enthusiasm for the product and for your conversation with a potential customer can be contagious. Even when you are new to selling, it is important to try to appear confident about what you are doing and saying. Customers may misunderstand personal lack of confidence as lack of faith in the product.

At the end of the presentation, leave the customer with material that summarizes your presentation and gives background data on the company, the product, and your business's personnel.

5. Take advantage of site observations. Meeting at a customer site gives you a chance to do more research. Pay attention to the surroundings, staying alert for potential selling points you can make. "I see that you have . . ." or a similar observation will show the customer that you are paying attention to his or her needs.

6. Guide the exchange with open-ended as well as closed questions. Asking questions—and listening to the answers—is beneficial both for you and for the customer. "Closed questions" are of the yes/no variety, or other varieties that have only a single response. "Open-ended" questions leave room for expansion. They are of the type "If you had an unlimited budget, what would be on your wish list?" or "What would you say are your top three priorities for the coming year?"

Meet customers on their turf. Find out their needs and preferences. Do not try to impose your ideas of what they need.

7. Listen carefully; treat objections as opportunities. It is not sufficient just to work through a list of questions. You need to listen to the responses. When you listen carefully to answers and truly hear what the prospect's needs are, you can better make suggestions for solving the prospect's problems.

Listen to what is *not* being said as well as what is being expressed. In other words, pay attention to body language.

Think of objections as challenges that you may be able to turn into benefits or advantages.

8. Be intuitive—probe for spoken and unspoken objections. If you are not clear on a point, ask for further explanation. Trust your intuition when there appear to be unspoken questions or concerns. Be sure that you have taken enough time to get to know the customer.

Expect objections, and be prepared to handle them. If possible, write down all potential objections ahead of time and find concrete ways to respond to them. If the customer voices an objection you have not considered, do your best to show the customer the positive side of the argument.

Potential customers will inevitably be making comparisons of your product with other similar ones. Familiarize yourself with competing products so you can address comparisons directly by pointing out the benefits and strengths of your product. It helps if you can prepare ahead of time for such situations, but if not, stay concentrated on the positive aspects of your product. Do not attack the other product; the customer may be using it now and may feel that you are personally attacking his or her wisdom.

If you can, provide real-life examples of others who use the product or service, to help the potential customer visualize how your product can solve a need.

9. Close by proposing solutions. The point of your presentation is to learn from the prospect what the problem is and to present a way of solving it. Be sure you offer a clearly proposed solution, perhaps by reiterating the problem as you understand it and then showing how your product or service could solve that problem. Your solution should directly address the customer's needs. It should be appropriate, reasonable, and useful.

10. Take positive action. Even when you have offered your closing proposal, you are not finished. Take positive action by stating that you will call (or write) in a few days. Be sure that you *do* follow through!

The basis of a successful presentation is careful research, skillful communication, and timely follow-through.

(Source: Based on Kim T. Gordon, *Growing Your Home-Based Business*, Englewood Cliffs, NJ: Prentice Hall, 1992, pp. 52-73, p. 78.)

Key Medical Supply's One-Minute Sales Presentation

To make an effective sales presentation, you need to get your customer's attention. In some industries, this may be difficult if the potential customer is too busy to take the time to talk with you. Careful study of potential customers and innovative approaches can help. Matt Hession of Key Medical Supply discovered that his best strategy was a one-minute presentation.

Key Medical sells or leases medical equipment such as wheelchairs through independent "corner" drugstores with budgetary constraints. Hession observed that the pharmacists who are his potential customers are extremely busy so he developed a one-minute presentation that gets his point across and results in sales. Hession emphasizes the following:

Don't look like a salesman. Hession speaks with his prospects at the drugstore counter, where the pharmacist (his real target) can hear the discussion but does not have to get drawn into it.

Appeal to the customer's needs (time, money). Hession promises to take only a minute (showing he is considerate of their time) and not cost anything (showing financial consideration). He takes off his watch to make his point.

Skip the nitty-gritty. Just give the broad details. The precise details should be in the brochures you leave. Key Medical's appeal is that everything is taken care of through an 800 number. Emphasize the simplicity and customer focus of what you are offering.

Stay alert to the location. You can assess this potential customer just by looking around at the location of the store, the staffing, and the number of customers that come in and out.

Get the potential customer to visualize your program working. Use real-life examples to illustrate how a program or product will work. Put it into terms that the customer can envision.

Stick to your promise. If you said you would only take a minute, then stop when the minute is up. You can follow through later with a phone call. The potential customer will remember you if your presentation was unique.

One major advantage of this one-minute approach is that it allows you to be succinct, thus keeping the potential customer happy about not taking too much time. In addition, you can complete more sales calls in the course of a day, which allows all parties to win.

(Source: Joshua Hyatt, "The 60-Second Sales Pitch," *Inc.*, October 1994, pp. 87-89.)

fourteen
Write a Marketing Plan

If you have done your research on the market and your product and have written your business plan, you should be all set to go into business, right? Wrong! There is one other document you must have. It is a marketing plan. Although it is tempting to just go ahead with your business, remember that we have stressed the importance of lowering the risk of failure. While a marketing plan will not eliminate the risk, it will provide you with a solid plan of where you are going. Putting the plan in writing helps to crystallize all the research and planning you have done. It can also show you where you may run into problems. (Better to find the problems before you get underway!) Having a good, thorough, well-researched marketing plan is like taking along a map when you make a long, unfamiliar drive. You could do without the map, but would probably make a lot of wrong turns and have to stop and ask directions frequently.

A written marketing plan provides a guide for all those involved in marketing to follow. It directs how the product is produced and sold. All decisions related to the product should be guided by the details of the marketing plan. As the business grows, the marketing plan becomes a measuring stick to evaluate how you are doing. Just as the business plan can show you whether you are meeting your financial, management, and other objectives, the marketing plan provides you with guidelines for comparing your marketing success with your intentions.

And, of course, the marketing plan, like the business plan, is not cast in stone. If you discover that parts of it need fine tuning, you can make changes as needed. In fact, you will probably want to look at the plan annually to make revisions as needed. If you have already written detailed marketing strategy and tactics sections into your business plan, they can provide a starting point for writing your marketing plan.

There are many decisions to make when you are writing a marketing plan. In the following pages we offer tools you can use as you put together your plan. Some will help you analyze your marketing situation. Others will suggest approaches to decisions you must make. In some cases the tools are useful only after you have started your business.

We suggest that you first use the tools to collect the information, then put it together in a format similar to the one that follows. Remember that the marketing plan is an internal document. However, some parts of it may be used in loan proposals (such as the financial statements and spending plans). While it may seem time consuming to create a marketing document, it is an extremely useful tool. If you take time to prepare the initial document well, it will need fine tuning only over time.

Marketing Plan Models

There are many ways to construct a marketing plan, but they all contain the same basic elements. Consider, for example, the following annual marketing plan by Russell S. Winer, writing for the *American Management Association's Handbook*.

Winer's Annual Marketing Plan

I. EXECUTIVE SUMMARY

II. BACKGROUND ASSESSMENT

    A. Historical appraisal

    B. Situation analysis

       • sales

- competition

C. Industry attractiveness analysis

- market size
- market growth
- product life cycle
- sales cycle
- seasonality
- profits
- threat of new entrants
- industry capacity
- technological factors
- political factors
- economic factors
- regulatory factors
- social factors

D. Competitor analysis

- competitors' objectives
- competitors' strategies
- competitors' capabilities
- competitors' future strategies

E. Customer analysis: who, where, when, how, why

F. Planning assumptions

III. STRATEGY FORMULATION

A. Marketing objectives

B. Marketing strategy

C. Marketing programs

IV. CONTROL

A. Financial document

B. Monitors and control

V. CONTINGENCY PLANS

(Source: Russell S. Winer, "The Annual Marketing Plan," *AMA Management Handbook*, John J. Hampton, ed., 1994, New York: AMACOM, American Management Association, pp. 2-42 – 2-48.)

However, as Dwight D. Eisenhower once said, "Plans are nothing, planning is everything," and indeed it is *how* you plan rather than what outline you follow that matters most. In the rest of this chapter, we will examine eight planning activities that are essential to good marketing.

SWOT Analysis

SWOT (*S*trengths, *W*eaknesses, *O*pportunities, *T*hreats) analysis is a helpful tool by which to look at a business's internal strengths and weaknesses and its external opportunities and threats to plan your marketing strategy for the future. This tool is useful for existing businesses to evaluate where they are now and to plan where they are going. By scrutinizing factors that have a major effect on the business, you can develop strategies that will capitalize the pluses and minimize the minuses that you uncover in your analysis.

In SWOT analysis, you look closely at hard data on manufacturing, costs, and other procedures. You consider the strengths and weaknesses of the management team. You may find that some departments have more effective managers than others. Or, you may discover that you are missing a key member of the team and need to fill the gap. You may decide that you have too many layers of management and eventually decide that you need to scale back.

External opportunities and threats arise from factors such as demand for the product or service, extent of the competition, the economy, the political environment, legal considerations, and technological situations. These are also critical components in your analysis.

Your attention should first focus on where the company has been and where it is now, based on the planning you have done in the past. The next step is to project where the company is going with the existing plan. To do this, you need to look at the growth of the industry in which you operate, as well as the company's growth in relation to the industry. You will see that the analysis is a blend of internal and external factors.

As you scan your current environment, you will uncover trends and information to use in your research. You need to ask yourself whether these trends are threats or opportunities, then decide what to do about them. Such environmental scanning should be done not only during an analysis, but on an ongoing basis if you want to stay competitive over the long run.

From your analysis, you should be able to discover what the company does best at the current time. In addition, you should be able to tell where you compete best, for example, in a large market or in a small one. Once you have analyzed the current environment, you should be able to focus on what you *could* be doing and what you *should* be doing in order to be successful. Your long-term objective will be to target growth in strong markets that have a large market share and a great profit potential (and the corollary—to drop the markets where performance is poor).

Once you have a general mission defined, set goals for the various parts of your business. These may apply to a specific department or to a division, if yours is a larger operation. One goal might be to focus on improving quality in order to take advantage of the marketing climate.

Having surveyed the past, present, and future using SWOT analysis, you will be in a better position to design a marketing plan to fit your current circumstances and to move you toward future expectations.

Marketing Segmentation, Targeting, and Positioning

Market segmentation is the grouping of prospective buyers based on similar needs or wants, with the expectation that members of such a group will respond similarly to a particular marketing action that you take.

Members of a market segment are usually homogeneous. One example of a market segment is consumers of sugar-free soft drinks. Another might be those who prefer caffeinated sodas.

By grouping potential buyers into segments, marketers can use a particular marketing tool for all the members of the group, thus saving on marketing costs. Another advantage of segmenting the market is that you can discover the size of potential groups. You may decide that a group you were going to target is too small to spend a lot of effort (time, and money) on.

By identifying market segments, marketers can match their offerings with the groups that are likely to consume them—in other words, to match supply and demand.

The objectives in creating market segments include:

- Maximizing profit and return on investment
- Using the same marketing tools within a segment
- Using fewer segments if appropriate (More segments mean more costs, so you want to be sure revenues will offset costs, or else combine segments into fewer groups.)
- Eliminating segments that are unreachable by marketing tools and strategies
- Making sure there really is a segment (If it is too small, perhaps it can be combined with another.)

How Marketers Segment

There are many ways to segment market groups for products or services such as by:

- Geographical region, such as city, region, density, or even climate
- Demographics, including age, sex, family size, stage of life, ages of children, income, education, race, home ownership
- "Psychographics" or lifestyle preferences, such as activities, interests, politics, personality

From a slightly different angle, you might segment a market by consumer preferences as follows:

- Benefits and features of the product, needs of consumers
- Usage rate, or whether or not the person is a regular user
- Intention to buy, or familiarity with a brand
- Buying condition or kind of store in which the consumer is likely to shop

Industrial products may be segmented by location of purchaser, standard classification code, and number of employees.

One good point to remember is the 80-20 rule: 80 percent of sales come from 20 percent of the customers.

How Should You Segment?

Given that there are different market segments in most markets (except, perhaps, for very specialized, technical products), sellers use *differentiation* to give products separate identities from the point of view of consumers. The idea is to help consumers perceive competing products as different from each other.

While two products may be similar, their producers may focus on different consumer needs or product benefits in order to take advantage of market segments. The sellers will use different marketing techniques to identify the different needs or benefits of their products. Producers thus tend to segment not only customers but also products.

Targeting: Who, When, and Where

The next step in the process is to select your target market segments. The factors to consider as you select your target segments are:

Size of the segment. (Avoid small segments unless you can cover the cost of marketing to this segment.)

Expected growth of the segment. The greater the expected growth, the better.

Competitive position of the segment. If there is already a great deal of competition for this segment, it may be a costly choice.

Cost of reaching the segment. If the cost will overshadow the return in this segment, then it is obviously the wrong place to be focusing your attention. It is also important to consider whether marketing to this segment will be compatible with your organization's objectives and resources.

When you have selected the segments to target, you may want to use a product market grid to evaluate whether your products will fill the needs of the segments you have decided to target. To draw a grid, list your markets down the page and your products across the top of the page. Put x's where they coincide and see how well you have covered your market and its needs.

How to Position the Product to Proper Targets Within Segments

There are two basic ways to position your product: head to head and differentiation. Head to head is, as its name suggests, competing directly with those in the same market with similar products. An example is manufacturers of two different shampoos, two brands of vacuum cleaners, or even two cars.

Differentiation entails selecting a smaller niche for your product, one where there may be considerably less competition—or none. This would be a more or less unique product, for example, a Lexus, which has less competition than a Ford or Chevrolet.

Product Market Grid

Housecleaning Services

Target Markets	Weekly Cleaning	Bi-monthly Cleaning	Monthly, Heavy Cleaning
Working couples with no children		X	
Working couples with children	X	X	X
Young, single, working males/females	X		
Older, single, working males/females		X	X
Elderly			X

The Four P's

The marketing department controls the four aspects of the marketing mix, called the Four P's: Product, Price, Promotion, and Placement. In this section of your plan, you will first summarize your general approach to the Four P's (and then develop it in detail in subsequent sections).

Product is a good or service that can fulfill a consumer's needs. The aspects of a product that can be used in marketing include its features, brand name, packaging, service, warranty, quality, options, styles, sizes, and returns.

Price is what is offered in exchange for the product. Components of price include list price, discounts, allowances, credit terms, and payment period.

Promotion is how the seller communicates with the buyer about the product. Types of promotion include advertising, personal selling, sales promotion, and publicity and other communication.

Placement or distribution is how the product gets into the buyer's hands. Aspects of placement important to marketing include outlets, channels, coverage, transportation, stock level, locations, logistics, and inventory.

These four elements, in some appropriate combination, are the *marketing mix*, which is controlled by the marketing staff. In each category, there are many decisions to be made.

We will look at each of the Four P's—Product, Price, Promotion, and Placement—as they relate to marketing *goods*. At the end of each section we will discuss these elements as they apply to *services*.

Product Tactics

A *product* is a consumer or industrial good. It can be a stand-alone item, or part of a product line. A *product line* is a group of products used together, sold together, in a similar group, distributed in the same outlets, or which fall into a specific price range. An example is a line of hair-care products, including shampoo and conditioner, for dry, normal, and oily hair. If your product could be part of a line, you will need to determine whether consumers need or want a line of such products, and whether you want to provide it.

Bear in mind that each line will have a particular marketing strategy and that different sizes of the product may be considered separate items, for example, different sizes of toothpaste tubes or containers of laundry detergent.

Another aspect of product decision making is *product mix*. This can be a simple, single product, a line, or several product lines. In diverse companies, there may be many product lines in diverse areas. Procter and Gamble, for example, markets a broad product mix of consumer goods.

Products can be tangible or intangible (as a service such as consulting would be). They can be durable or nondurable. If you market a durable product you will have one-time customers; if your product is nondurable, you can expect to have repeat sales.

The type of user of the product may be a consumer or an industrial user. If the user is a consumer, the product may be a convenience good, a shopping good, a specialty good, or even an unsought good. If the user is industrial, the product may be used in production of another product, or in support of production, for example, installations, accessory equipment, supplies, or services.

New Products

If you are marketing a new product, think about how new it is. This will vary depending on your point of view. For example, is it new in comparison to existing products? From the business's perspective, a product may be considered new for a relatively long period because it may take some time for the production process to evolve and stabilize. By then, consumers may not consider it new at all. Likewise, consumers may not view a product as new, even if it says so on the box. They may consider it to be the same "old" product with only a slight change. If you already have a product line to which you are adding a new product, you need to ensure that the new product fits with the existing line.

Another way to look at the newness of a product is how long it will take for a new user to learn to use it. If you are providing a new feature for a product with which a consumer is already familiar, then the learning curve may not be so great. If, however, the product is so new that the customer has to completely learn how to use the product, then marketing will need to be somewhat different. Thus, continuous innovations with little new learning are marketed differently from discontinuous innovations where the consumer has to be taught to use the product.

	NEW	
	Learning	*Examples*
Continuous innovation	no	improved detergent
Dynamically continuous innovation	some	CD player
Discontinuous innovation	yes	VCR

So it is important to look at the level of behavior change that will be required by the potential consumer of a "new" product. If a lot of learning is involved, then you can expect to spend more money and time marketing your product or service. In other words, the larger the behavior change, the larger the expenditure.

Why New Products Fail

New products frequently fail, even for businesses with experience. There are many reasons for a product to fail, some of which are listed below. It is important to be aware of the potential for failure and to plan your product so as to avoid the pitfalls.

- The product is not compatible with the firm's objectives.
- The company's capabilities are not suited to producing the product.
- The competition has been underestimated.
- Management support is not available or sufficient.
- There is not enough money to support the product.
- The market for the product is too small, and therefore the cost of producing the product is too high.
- Marketing features do not set the product apart in customers' minds.
- Quality is lacking.
- There is insufficient shelf space available. (This is especially important if the product is competing with many other similar products.)
- Introduction of the product was poorly timed. Either it was introduced too late, or in the wrong season, or after the demand peaked.

- The marketing mix is inappropriate. Perhaps potential buyers like the idea, but they do not like the packaging, or they do not understand how to put the product to use.

Product Characteristics

Finally, be attuned to the characteristics of the product. If it is complex, it will likely need more hands-on selling to help buyers figure it out. Likewise, if it is a risky concept, it will cost more to market. If the product is likely to require services or support after the sale, it will also be more costly. A complex item is also more likely to need repairs than a simple one.

Product Tactics for Service Firms

Most of the product issues for products also apply to services. In addition to the preceding discussion, sellers of services should be aware of the following:

Exclusivity. Although it is possible to produce an exclusive product that can be patented and then may not be copied exactly, you cannot patent services. Therefore, imitations are likely to occur in the service arena. If you begin to provide a unique or rare service that is successful, others will enter the arena to compete with you. Shopping at home from catalogs or television is an example of a service that has burgeoned in recent years as is the number of companies providing at home, on-line service to the Internet.

Brand name. Since a service is not tangible in the way that a product is, it is important to convey clearly what your service is and what you are providing along with it. The name of the business and the logo thus become extremely important in marketing your service. Consider the names of the top management consulting or Big-Six accounting firms or of AT&T, which is an internationally recognized name and an extremely valuable asset.

Capacity management. One difficulty with providing a service is that demand will be variable, very busy at times and at others, slow. Part of the marketing planning should include a consideration of how to manage these peaks and valleys of demand. To balance seasonal effects, ski areas, for example, may offer other activities such as a water slide or hiking trails in the summer. Hotels offer seasonal rates; travel agencies offer package deals. Airlines offer midweek prices and special rates that can be used if the customer stays over an extra day or travels off-season.

Pricing Tactics

Pricing your product or service is probably the most familiar aspect of marketing. It is also probably the most important. The price you set can influence buyers as to the quality and value of the product and can thus affect your sales. Sales, in turn, affects costs, depending on the efficiency of your production process and your capacity. Low sales, for example, can send your production costs up. And while high sales would seem to be a goal, they may cause problems for new companies that are not ready for them. If demand is higher than production can satisfy, you can run into problems, too.

The basic steps in setting prices are:

- Identify your objectives in pricing, along with any constraints.
- Estimate the demand for the product and the resulting revenue you expect.
- Determine costs, volume, and profits as they relate to one another.
- Select strategies for pricing and related tactics.
- Make special adjustments as needed.

Let us look at each of these steps more closely.

1. Identify objectives and constraints

The *degree of demand* for your product will affect the price at which you can sell it. The *newness* of the product also affects pricing. Generally, the newer the product, the more you can charge for it. *Single products* are usually easier to price than those that are part of a line of products. Appliances are usually purchased singly, whereas lawn-care products might be bought in combination.

Bear in mind also that changing the price of an existing product may be difficult and costly if the product is already widely distributed and advertised.

The *type of market* in which the product is competing will affect the price. For example, in a monopoly there will be pricing regulations. In a purely competitive market, it will be difficult to set a price that is very different from the price that existing competitors charge. A high price will result in decreased or no sales; too low a price may set off price wars. In the case of a low price, it is often set at a point where some profit can be made; to go below this may risk inability to break even.

Legal and regulatory constraints will also affect where a price can be set.

2. Estimate demand and revenue

You will be able to estimate demand for the segment you have targeted based on the market research you have already done. Using the expected demand, plug in the price you have in mind to get an idea of the revenue you will be able to realize. Remember that estimates of demand are often inflated. Avoid the trap of optimistic predictions by making three estimates: best case, worst case, and middle of the road.

3. Determine cost, volume, and profit relationships

Now let us turn to costs to add them into the equation. Bearing in mind that

Profit = Total revenue - Total cost

take a look at costs and how they affect the outcome of your pricing decisions.

There are several types of costs: total cost, fixed cost, variable cost, and marginal cost. *Total cost* is made up of fixed and variable costs, *fixed costs* are those that you will incur no matter how many items you produce, and *variable costs* are based on the number of items you produce. Fixed costs include such items as rent, salaries, and insurance, whereas the raw materials to be used in production are a variable cost. Your price must absolutely cover fixed costs.

Total cost = Fixed cost + Variable cost

Marginal cost is the change in total cost that occurs when you make one more item. The concept of marginal cost is helpful in deciding on production levels. You set the product level (quantity) at the point where the revenue obtained from making one more unit of the product is more than the additional cost of making the unit.

Marginal cost = Change in total cost/Change in quantity

Break-even analysis.   Another way to look at the relationship among costs, quantities, and profits is through a break-even analysis. The break-even point is the quantity at which total revenue and total costs are equal.

Break-even point(quantity) = Fixed cost/(Unit price - Unit variable cost)

This formula allows you to calculate the quantity at which the costs and revenues are equal and above which you will make profit (or under which you will experience a loss). One good approach is to calculate a range of quantities and costs and list it on a grid. Using this visual representation can help you focus on the best combination to use. Break-even analysis can also be a useful tool for testing changes in prices, fixed costs, and variable costs to see how they will affect your profit potential.

4. Select a price

At this point you are ready to set an approximate price. We say approximate, because you may have to adjust it, but for now you want to find a starting place.

In setting a price, you will take into account such factors as return on sales, market share, age categorization, economic breakdown of customer groups, regional location of markets, social aspects of the product, ethnicity of the consumer population, and quality of the product as the customer sees it. But these will hover in the background for the moment.

There are four ways to set a starting point for price: demand-based, cost-based, profit-based, and competition-based. Let us look at each of these.

Demand-based.   This approach to pricing focuses on consumers and aims to base the price of the product or service on their tastes and preferences. Some ways to do this are:

Skimming, where you set the price high initially, then lower it later. This allows you to take advantage of initial high interest in the product. When you have "skimmed" the group of interested buyers, you lower the price somewhat to attract another tier of consumers who may not be willing to pay the highest price, but will be interested when the price moves down somewhat.

Penetration, which is the opposite of skimming. You set the price low in order to attract as many new buyers as possible—you "penetrate" the market. A low offering price may discourage competitors and may allow you to increase production levels (and therefore lower costs).

Prestige pricing means setting the price high for people who are willing to pay for status.

Price lining entails offering a line of goods with special prices within the line. An example might be a line of clothing with a range of prices.

Odd-even pricing puts prices at odd numbers, right below even ones, such as $19.95 or $19.99 instead of $20.00. This is a psychological trick to have consumers perceive that the price is closer to 19 dollars than to 20.

Demand-backward pricing is more complicated to figure out, but can be a useful way to set a price. You start with the final price you want to charge, then work backward through the margins you have to pay to retailers and wholesalers. When you have prices for each of these, then you have to adjust the costs to be able to get the price you require. The drawback here is that adjusting costs may mean sacrificing quality.

Bundle pricing is a way to get consumers to buy a group of related items in a single package. An example would be a computer package consisting of the monitor and central processing unit, software such as an operating system and word processing, a service contract, and perhaps a mouse, modem, or printer.

Cost-based. Another way to approach pricing is to consider your costs. You look at production and marketing costs and add enough to cover expenses and overhead and still make a profit. There are a number of different ways to use the cost-based methods:

Standard markup pricing adds a percentage to the cost of all the items in a product class. Sometimes called absorption costing, this approach sets the price equal to the total cost plus a profit markup. This method will cover all costs and is a good one to use when pricing new products.

Cost plus percentage of cost pricing adds a fixed percentage to the production or construction cost. Architects might use this method for setting a price.

Cost plus fixed fee pricing includes costs plus a fixed fee. This is a standard method used by the government, where the costs are covered—whatever they may be—and then a fixed fee is added.

Experience curve pricing means changing the pricing as the firm's experience grows. This approach is based on the concept that the unit cost declines by 10 to 30 percent each time a firm's experience at producing and selling them doubles. Thus, as your experience grows, you can expect costs to come down somewhat.

Profit-based. Still another way of setting prices is to focus on an annual profit target, either a specific dollar volume of profit or a percentage of sales or investment.

The *target return on sales* involves setting prices such that they will give the firm a profit that is a specified percentage (such as 1 percent) of the sales volume. Food stores typically use this type of pricing.

Another approach is to target *annual return on investment (ROI)* using a specific percentage. A firm might set a target ROI of 15 percent, for example. Setting target rates of return is a common approach for automobile companies, who try to achieve a 15 to 20 percent return on investment, and for regulated firms such as public utilities.

If you want to be able to try different combinations when you are calculating profit-based prices, you will find it easier to use a computer spreadsheet program. You will be able to experiment with different scenarios. For example, you might try several prices in combination with different levels of production, or change the variable cost by altering the elements that go into the product. A spreadsheet can also be helpful if you want to compare last year's or last month's performance with a current planned change.

Competition-based. In competition-based methods of pricing, you set prices based on those of the competition.

Customary prices are those established for traditional products, which are often distributed in a standard way. Candy bars and cans of soda fall into this category, especially when they are sold from a machine, where there is a standard price. The way to get around such pricing is to change the product content instead of the price. Thus, for example, a candy bar might be smaller or contain fewer nuts.

Above, at, or below market are methods based on looking at the competitors' prices and then pricing your product accordingly. If you want consumers to buy your product because of the high price—and, therefore, a perceived higher quality—you would set the price above that charged by your competitors. If your product is about the same as the competitions', you would price it the same and try to win customers using a strategy other than pricing; if you want to undercut the competition, you would price your product below the competitors' price.

A *loss leader* is a product for which the price is purposely set below cost, with hope that it will attract buyers to the store who will then purchase other products as well. Supermarkets use this all the time. They offer either a giveaway or a very low price on one item to lure customers into the store.

Sealed bids are usually used by government agencies. Everyone competing for the sale submits a bid and the lowest bidder wins the contract.

5. Select pricing strategies and tactics

Up until now, you have been working with an approximate price. In this phase you set the actual price based on what you learned as you completed the previous steps. You will need to decide whether you plan to have a one-price policy or a flexible-price policy. A flexible-price policy means that there are different prices for different people. There may be some legal limitations to this approach, but it is used in such businesses as selling cars and houses. You will also find this approach used in volume buying (wholesalers versus retailers), and in such industries as airlines, communications, trucking, and banking.

Promotional Price Adjustments. Although some might prefer to think of coupons, contests, rebates, and other tactics as promotional, we choose to discuss these as price adjustments because they are really variations on pricing. There are numerous ways to attract customers with offers that the customer perceives as a price adjustment. They include coupons, contests, deals, point-of-purchase displays, premiums, rebates, samples, sweepstakes, and trading stamps.

As with other price considerations, you will want to select such adjustments according to a number of factors:

- What the competition is doing
- The size of the market affected
- The cost versus benefits of using such an adjustment
- The ease with which the offering can be carried out
- The popularity of such an adjustment within your target market
- The stage of the product involved—new, familiar, old
- The restrictions to place on the adjustment (such as an expiration date, one to a family, etc.)

6. Adjust prices as needed

From time to time, you will need to adjust prices based on your scanning of the environment and analysis of the current marketing mix and structure. Each time you feel you need to adjust prices, you should run through the process as it has been described. Bear in mind that the process will be somewhat easier as it becomes more familiar and you gain experience.

Note that if you decide to increase the price, you should move it only to the point where you avoid a disproportionate decrease in volume.

Pricing for Service Firms

Although the prices charged by firms for services may have different names, such as fees, charges, fares, or rates, they are nevertheless prices. And much of what was discussed earlier about pricing products also applies to service firms. The following are some of the unique features of pricing for services.

One method of setting a charge for a service is to figure the cost and add a percentage. Professionals such as lawyers, doctors, and counselors usually charge a fee based on a billable rate, which is simply the cost of the professional (salary, benefits, training, overhead) plus a markup. Another method, used by businesses such as airlines and public utilities, is to use a target ROI for setting rates.

Pricing services has two aspects: One has to do with how the value of the service will be perceived, the other has to do with managing capacity, which we have mentioned. When pricing a service, you do not want to set your rate too low, so that the result is a misperception of the value of the service. Although a cheap divorce may be appealing, do customers want to take a chance that it is not airtight? Would you want an appendectomy for under a $100 or a tooth extraction for $25? Potential buyers tend to wonder about a service that is too cheap.

As for managing capacity, movie theaters and restaurants have to deal with peak times and off-peak times, and the way they do this is to offer different rates for different times of day. Movie theaters offer a twilight show for a reduced cost to encourage attendance; restaurants usually offer lunches or early dinners for less than they charge for peak-hour dinners.

Promotion Tactics

Promotion is what the seller does to communicate with the buyer about the product. Types of promotion include advertising, personal selling, sales promotions, and publicity. The intent of these tools is to inform potential consumers about a product and its benefits; persuade them to try it; and to remind users about the benefits they received by using it.

Advertising

Advertising is paid communication, made through the mass media, such as television, radio, magazines, and newspapers. Advertising is not personal; that is, there is no interaction between the potential consumer and the seller of the product. For this reason, it is important that you research your markets carefully to be sure you target them correctly with advertising.

Advertisements are designed to get the attention of the audience and to tell the benefits of the product. Assuming you know your target market, with advertising you have control over *who* receives the message (based on *where* you place your ads) and the message you are sending. Because you are paying for it, you also have control over *when* the message is sent. However, the message will be the same for everyone in the audience.

This means, of course, that you cannot tailor your message to individuals and that you cannot know, other than indirectly through sales figures, whether the advertising you are sending is appropriate and cost-effective.

Personal selling

Personal selling allows contact with potential customers so that the sales message can be tailored to the receiver. Personal selling is usually face to face, except in the case of telemarketing, which is being used more and more for personal selling. In personal selling you have more control over *who* receives the message, but the size of the audience is necessarily reduced because you cannot personally contact as many people in person as you could through an advertisement. An advantage of personal selling over advertising is that you can see how the potential buyer responds to your messages and you can fine tune them as needed. If the prospective buyer has objections, you can respond to them immediately. However, this is a high-cost way to obtain customers, unless your market niche is very small anyway. In addition, you have to contend with the fact that different salespeople will interact with potential customers in different ways, so the message will tend not to be standard.

Sales promotion

Sales promotions are usually carried out on a short-term basis, with the intent of stirring up interest in a product or service. Common sales promotion tools are rebates, samples, and sweepstakes or contests. These can stimulate sales for a while, but sales may still drop off when the deal or contest ends. Therefore, when such promotions are used, every effort must be made to turn the interested prospect into a permanent customer. Generally, it is wise to use sales promotions sparingly.

To summarize types of sales promotions, let us look at a comparison chart:

Type	Purpose	Reasons to Use	Reasons Not to Use
Rebates	Encourage sales	Stimulate demand	Competition can copy; reduces future sales; lowers perceived value of product
Samples	Try new product	No risk for customer	Expensive to company
Sweepstakes	Increase sales; decrease brand switching	Get customer into store to buy product more often	Temporary sales increase; falls after sweepstakes
Contests	Increase purchases	Get customer involved	Need creative thinking to set up
Coupons	Increase demand	Get retailer involved	Changes buying pattern; temporary
Deals	Attract new buyers away from competition	Reduce consumer risk	Same as coupons
Trading stamps	Increase repeat purchases	Create loyalty	Expensive
Displays at point of purchase	Increase trial of product	Improve product visibility	Expensive; need retailer cooperation
Premiums	Build goodwill	Increase sales to get premium	Buy for premium, not product; sales return to previous level after end of premium offer

Publicity

Publicity is "free" advertising in that you do not have to pay for it directly. It may be a press release, a news story or editorial, or a product announcement. Facts about your company and product or service will be made public. Such advertising can be a boon for the small company with a small advertising budget.

However, be aware that news stories and editorials are not always accurate—or flattering. A major disadvantage is that you have little control over the content of the story or when it is published. Even a press release that you have worded carefully may be cut down to fit into a space or may appear on a page farther back in the paper where no one will see it. It may also appear too late to be of help to you.

Promotion Tactics for Service Firms

Service businesses need to emphasize to potential customers the benefits of using the service. Advertising should stress the availability of the service, such as extended or convenient hours; location and ease of parking, quality of the service, courteous service, and so forth. The *image* of the company is especially important for service organizations—perhaps more so than for manufacturers of products.

Publicity can add to the positive image, but remember that publicity as a tool gives you less control. Nevertheless, nonprofit ventures find publicity especially important. Free public-service announcements can help promote a business, too.

Professionals such as accountants, lawyers, dentists, and doctors have traditionally scorned advertising, but this attitude is changing. Ethical standards may influence what and how much advertising is allowed, but even then it is important to consider the image of the organization and what should be conveyed.

Placement Tactics

Place or distribution has to do with how a product gets into the buyers' hands. Aspects of place important to marketing include outlets, channels, coverage, transportation, stock level, locations, and inventory.

Consider *where* the product is going to be sold, *how much* of it will be sold at that location, and *how* it will get there. The "how" of it refers to *channels of distribution*. How many people will be involved in getting the product to market? In a simple one-level channel, the manufacturer sells directly to the buyer. An example of this would be door-to-door sales such as encyclopedias or beauty products. Other direct-marketing techniques include telemarketing, catalog sales, televised and computerized home shopping, and video text. (Experts says that direct marketing will account for about 20 percent of all retail transactions in the late nineties.)

As you add "middlemen" such as retailers and wholesalers, you add levels, and therefore complexity, to the channel. Whatever profit there will be must be divided among the members of the channel. You also increase your product's exposure to outsiders, which you must decide whether or not you want. As the distribution process becomes more complicated, you will have less control over it. In addition, once you set up a system you will find it difficult to change the process quickly if you need to, so it is a good idea to select your channels carefully at the outset, with an eye on the future.

Eventually you will need to decide whether physical distribution will be from one plant to one market, or from one plant to several end points. Rather than using an end point, you could simply ship products directly to customers (as catalog sales operations do). Or, you might have a warehouse to which the products are shipped and from which the product is sent out. If your market coverage is broad, for example, nationwide, then you may need to have several warehouses—or several plants—at strategic locations.

Another placement issue is inventory. You will need to decide what inventory levels are appropriate for meeting the demand.

Placement Tactics for Service Firms

Service firms usually "sell" their services from the location where the staff is located. Therefore, if you expect customers to come to you, select an appropriate location that is easily accessible, with ample parking. If your firm makes "house calls"—such as a cleaning service—location may still need to be convenient to workers, but may not have the requirements that a walk-in business would have.

Making distribution of the service convenient may require having multiple locations, such as banks with branches in strategic locations of a city. Automatic-teller services provide banking even when a bank is not open. Car-repair businesses offer a key-drop box so customers can drop off their cars and car keys the night before they are to be repaired.

Implementation and Controls

Once you implement your marketing program, you want to keep it going and monitor its success. You need to evaluate the actions you planned to see how successful they are. The actual results should be compared with the anticipated outcome from your marketing plan. It is important to know whether you are meeting the goals that you set at the beginning of this whole process. In this part of your plan, describe how you will track progress and make corrections to your strategies and tactics. You will probably want to do some mathematical analysis of your sales and profitability as you prepare to make adjustments. We will turn to analysis in a moment.

As you compare your marketing results to the goals you have set, you will want to do something about the deviations. This may mean making changes if you had negative results, or doing more of the things that were successful.

Close scrutiny might tell you that you need to find ways to cut costs, or that you should simplify the lines you now offer. Perhaps you will decide to offer new products or a line of products, or to try out a new technology. A totally new market may look promising.

You can see that it will be difficult to measure your results unless you have set quantitative goals in the beginning—goals that can be measured in volume, cost, and profit or other concrete characteristics.

Computers can be a great help in performing sophisticated analyses quickly and accurately. Automated programs can gather information for you on a timely basis, as for example, scanning equipment that records purchases and thus lets you know what sells best and what inventory moves slowly. But even if you do not have a computer, you can track figures for comparisons. And you should always be scanning the environment yourself both within and outside of your industry.

Sales Analysis

There are many ways to analyze sales. The best approach is to break sales down into the smallest components, which allows you to look at all the aspects involved in making a sale. You will want to look at the following characteristics in relation to one another. Some of these you will already know from your market research. But stay on your toes, for you may find some surprising information, too.

Customer characteristics include demographics, the size of the customer pool, the reasons customers make the purchase, and the type of store in which they buy.

Product characteristics include model, package size, and color.

Geographic region can be broken down in several ways—either by sales territory, city, state, or region, or by some combination.

Other groupings would include order size, price or discount class, and perhaps commission to the sales representative.

Just knowing these characteristics is not enough to help you plan your marketing; you need to know how the characteristics interact. For example, which models are most popular for various age groups? Or, is the demand for a particular color greater in urban areas than in rural areas?

If you are going to use a computer (and even if not), it is helpful to know ahead of time how you want to break out your data. Computers can give you all sorts of output, but if you do not plan for the numbers you want, that is all that you will get—just numbers. No meaning.

Computers can produce reams of reports, but if they do not pertain directly to you or your business, they are not helpful. Further, if you do produce reports but do not use them, then this, too, is a waste of time and effort.

Profitability Analysis

Another approach to analysis is to look at profitability based on the characteristics already mentioned. This can help you see which products, lines, and models are most, and least, profitable. Then you can shift your attention to the more profitable products and perhaps eliminate the less profitable ones.

Keep in mind the "80-20 principle," in which it is said that 80 percent of your profit comes from 20 percent of your products. Find out which are the profitable 20 percent and concentrate your marketing efforts on them; or identify the 80 percent and phase them out.

(Source: Alex Hiam and Charles Schewe, *The Portable MBA in Marketing*, Wiley, 1992; Alex Hiam, *The Vest-Pocket Marketer*, Englewood Cliffs, NJ: Prentice Hall, 1991.)

Innovative Marketing Ideas: Taking Advantage of the Internet

Claudia Bach, owner of Document Center in Belmont, California, sells copies of standards for building items like microcircuits and hockey sticks—in other words, just about anything. Since she has a lot of competition, she realized that she needed to advertise to reach potential customers for her product. So she hired Marc Fleischmann of Internet Distribution Services (IDS) to help her set up an Internet site on the World Wide Web. There, a potential customer can look through an interactive database to see the history of each product standard that she sells. For a monthly fee, Marc maintains the site and adds updates that Bach delivers to him on magnetic tape. Bach's business is up about 15 percent and includes people from all over the world.

***

NetMarket was a small company, started by four young men, three of them college students. They wrote programs to set up electronic stores on the Web and wrote software to use for browsing the Net. CUC International of Stamford, Connecticut, a giant home-shopping and services company, recently bought out NetMarket. They intend to try marketing home products on the Net. Time will tell how successful this plan is.

***

Laura Fillmore is founder and president of Online BookStore (OBS), located on the Web. The company, physically located in Rockport, Massachusetts, develops on-line versions of books and parts of books. Her company uses hypertext technology to create links from one piece of text to another or to point to backup information. Books can also be ordered online. Fillmore leases space on the Web from Cyberspace Development.

(Source: Monua Janah, "I-Way Entrepreneurs," *Forbes ASAP*, February 27, 1995, pp. 90-91.)

PART V
General Management

Entrepreneurs are ambitious, driven, and independent people. They also have a reputation for making difficult bosses because of the very qualities that make them successful entrepreneurs. Being a good boss entails selecting the right people for the job and then letting them do that job to the best of their abilities. This means you have to let go of some control, and this is a scary proposition for many small-business owners. It's also frustrating to many employees who are either overmanaged or not given the authority and autonomy necessary to do their jobs well.

If you are a small-business owner and boss, seriously consider some management training. Make an effort to get some honest feedback on your style, and consciously work to improve. If you find yourself as a manager of people, it's your job to draw the best from them so your business can be as productive and profitable as possible.

fifteen
Hire and Manage Employees

There are many books in the human resources area that describe how to go about hiring and managing employees. Our discussion here looks at issues more generally related to employee management. You may also want to refer to the section on marketing and sales for a discussion of how to hire an effective salesperson. Many of the issues covered there also apply to employees in general.

Benchmarking to Set Salaries

When you prepare to hire new employees or offer raises to existing employees, you will need to know the appropriate salary range to offer. Setting up a salary structure for your company can be a challenge, especially when you are new to this process.

One method for setting salaries is benchmarking. You use salary figures for other, similar companies or jobs to set the salaries for your operation. Typical salaries are usually easy to find for large businesses, but may be harder to find for smaller ones. Some professional publications list for their members the average salaries, breaking them down by region and experience. Be sure that you take into account the size of companies for which you use statistics, because it is frequently the case that smaller companies pay less well than larger ones. Also take into account the benefits package and whether that is calculated into the figures that are reported for various professions.

Raises

The process of benchmarking can also be used when an employee is asking for a raise. Study the industry figures so you have a basis for comparison. See what the growth pattern in salaries and commissions has been over a period of time. Adjust your benchmark figures to reflect the size of your business and its growth, along with the growth in abilities and skills of the employees who are being considered for raises.

In adjusting salaries for salespeople, you may want to change both the base salary and the total compensation package. Employee compensation is a considerable portion of operating costs and generally includes salaries; benefits such as health insurance, paid vacations, and retirement funds; and training and/or education. Part of the total compensation package for sales people, for example, might be based on reaching sales targets and management's goals for return on investment.

(Source: *Inc.*, June 1994, p. 109.)

SBA's Employee Handbook Topics

As your employee base grows and you find yourself training new employees frequently, you may want to put together an employee handbook containing the general information all employees need. Based on the information given and the questions asked during an employee training session, you can assemble a reference book for when questions arise.

Include in the handbook information on regular work hours, holidays, benefits, and services and make sure you give each new employee a copy; have him or her read it and come to you with any questions. Having your policies in writing will protect both you and your employees from potential misunderstandings. If, for example, an employee is consistently late, you can refer to the working hours section of the handbook. A detailed outline of what you might want to include in a policy handbook follows. It can be tailored to suit the needs of your particular business. The outline is based on material in a brochure published by the Small Business Administration.

Welcome
Company history
Details of employment
    working hours
    reporting to work
    time clock
    rest periods
    absence from work
    how to report absences
    employment record
    pay period
    shift premiums
Safety and accident prevention
Use of telephones
How to present complaints

Employee Benefits

Vacations
Holidays
Health insurance, hospitalization and surgical benefits
Maternity/paternity leave
Parking
Training program
Christmas bonus
Savings plan
Profit-sharing plan
Suggestion awards
Jury duty
Military leave

Old-age benefits

Unemployment compensation

Equal employment opportunity

Special Services

Credit union

Education

Medical dispensary

Employee purchases (e.g., computer)

Company cafeteria

Monthly magazine/newsletter

Annual outings or parties

Bowling league or other team sports

(Source: "Pointers on Preparing an Employee Handbook," *Management Aids No. 197*, (Washington, D.C.: U.S. Small Business Administration, 1975), p. 3., as quoted in *Start & Run Your Own Profitable Service Business*, by Irving Brustiner, Englewood Cliffs, NJ: Prentice Hall, 1993, p. 136.)

Use Alternative Staffing Methods to Save Money

All businesses experience shifting staffing needs from time to time. For new and small businesses such fluctuations in staff requirements can be somewhat difficult to manage, especially if the staff is small and overburdened to begin with. Finding the correct balance of full-time and part-time help to fit season-al needs or changing markets can be a challenge.

What to do? Consider some of the following ways of staffing for your crunch periods.

Part-time staff

The advantages of using part-time staff, especially for fewer than 20 hours (less than half time), is that the costs of benefits and perks are reduced, perhaps eliminated. There are people who prefer to work only part time and who may be willing to work flexible hours, which may be just what your business needs.

If you, in turn, are able to be flexible, you may be able to get just the sort of help you need at a lower cost.

Temporary help

More and more companies are turning to temporary help agencies to fill slots in their companies as the need arises. If you have a large order to fill or if there is a sizable mailing that needs to be done, a "temp" can help you out. One plus is that the temporary agencies pay their workers, so you do not have all the paperwork that you would have if you were employing such workers directly. However, you will probably be paying for the convenience indirectly through the fees you pay to the agency.

Some firms also use temp agencies to screen for workers in particular categories, such as administrative positions. The way this works is that you arrange for a temp, and if the person works out, then you hire the person full time. Most agencies charge a premium for doing this, but some employers find it worth the added cost to be able to try out a worker for a period of time before committing to hiring the person full time.

Older workers

Older workers who may find it more difficult to find a job or who want to work reduced hours can be great resources for the small company with varying staffing needs. Older workers can bring a vast array of skills and experience to the job. They may be more stable and reliable than their younger counterparts.

Places to look for older workers include Temps America, which has a Mature Temps America division, local senior citizen centers, and Forty-plus clubs of older persons looking for work.

SCORE. Another group of older people who can be a valuable resource is the Service Corps of Retired Executives, or SCORE. This group operates in conjunction with the SBA (referenced elsewhere in this book). SCORE counselors provide free management counseling to small business owners and managers and to those who are considering starting a business. SCORE can be an excellent resource, particularly for small businesses that need short-term advice and that, perhaps, cannot afford to hire a professional consultant. To find the phone number for the local chapter of SCORE, look in the phone book under United States Government, Small Business Administration.

Handicapped workers

It pays to hire the handicapped. When disabled workers are compared to nondisabled workers by managers, they are equal or better in reliability, attendance, productivity, desire to work, and ability to lead. Many organizations are willing to help you find handicapped workers. For resources, check your local state employment office or one of the following:

Job Accommodation Network (JAN)
Box 468
Morgantown, WV 26505
800-526-7234

President's Committee on Employment of the Handicapped
1111 20th Street NW
Washington, DC 20036
202-653-5044

Leased workers

Leasing can be a boon if you want to be free of payroll taxes, personnel programs, and benefits. It is a good approach if your company is not strong on the legalities of hiring and firing staff. Leasing companies have expertise in recruiting, hiring, personnel management, and discipline. On the other hand, using leased workers can mean loss of control of the recruiting and hiring process. You will have to decide the best path for your business, depending on the skills you and your management team possess and which activities in the company need your attention the most. Typically, managing personnel is time consuming and will take away time needed for making sales.

One of the largest employee-leasing companies in the United States is National Staff Network.

A slightly different version of leasing is joint employers. An example of this approach is Corporate Management Group, Inc., in New York City. The fees charged by such companies are based on a percent of payroll, usually 3 to 5 percent, or per employee. To find out where there are joint employer organizations in your area, you can call the National Association of Professional Employer Organizations (NAPEO) at 703-524-3636 or write to them at 1735 Lynn Street, #950, Arlington, VA 22209.

In either case, consider the following if you want to try leasing as an alternative approach to staffing:

1. Does the firm offer what you need? Would they adjust to your needs?
2. Ask for banking and credit references to be sure they are a good risk. You need to know whether their taxes and insurance premiums are up to date if they are taking over part of your usual job.
3. Obtain client and professional references and check them.
4. Interview the firm by asking about their administrative competence and experience. Give them a hypothetical situation and ask how they would solve it.
5. Be sure you ask for and get a full explanation of how employee benefits will be funded. Do they insure for the amount? Is there a third-party administrator? Are they licensed or registered in the state if they are required to by state law?
6. Is there a cancellation provision in the contract? What is the lead time for cancellation?

Independent Contractors and Consultants

The advantage of using a contractor or a consultant is that you can specify a certain job or a time frame for the work to be done and thus save the cost of hiring a full-time person when you do not really need one. For example, you might hire a contractor to write a manual for one of your products. Although the project may take three months and cost a large amount, when the project is done, the contractor is done. Your alternative would be to hire a full-time person who would then have to be kept busy for the other nine months of the year.

Another advantage of using an independent contractor or consultant is that these workers are self-employed and thus responsible for their own taxes and benefits, which can be a considerable saving for your small business.

Other Ways to Handle Changing Staffing Needs

You may find that not only do your needs vary, so also do those of the people you employ. It pays to be flexible about employees' needs, because once you have trained someone, it is more cost effective to work with them than to hire a new employee and have to start the training process all over again. This may not be a problem if you need someone with general skills only, but many businesses have specific processes that employees need to learn.

Some areas where you may need to consider being flexible include

Reduced Hours. An employee might want to decrease hours in order to spend more time with family or as retirement approaches. You may be able to accommodate this need by increasing the hours of a part-time person who wants more work, for example.

Job sharing. Job sharing has become a popular option for people who need to work part time but may not be able to find such a job in their field. As an employer, you might be approached to hire two people to fill one job. Although this type of arrangement may take some adjustment and may result in discontinuity at times, it can also benefit you by providing two people who are fresh because they are not tired from a 40-hour week. Mothers with young children are an excellent source of people willing to job share.

Flextime. Unless the nature of the business demands that people be present at certain times of the day, for example, if it is a service-oriented business and employees need to be available to service customers, consider allowing workers to be on flexible time schedules. Knowing that people have different "sharp" times during the day, you might consider letting the "morning" people come earlier, and the "night owls" start later in the day.

(Sources: Richard M. Turitz, Esq, sup. ed., "How to Recruit and Hire a Quality Workforce," *The Prentice Hall Small Business Survival Guide*, Englewood Cliffs, NJ: Prentice Hall, 1993, pp. 190-193; 204-5; "Personnel Hell," Gayle Sato Stodder, *Entrepreneur*, January 1995, p. 57.)

Performance Assessment

Performance assessment or evaluation is one of the least popular functions that managers must perform, yet it can be a valuable learning tool for those involved. Although it may be tempting to skip this process if your business seems to be functioning well, you may be missing an opportunity to exchange valuable information with an employee.

There are a number of strong reasons for performance evaluations. First, it gives the manager an opportunity to spend some time with the employee and to go over the employee's performance. All employees need to know whether they are doing a good job, and this is the time when the strengths and weaknesses of each employee's performance can be spelled out clearly, in private. A good evaluation is a great boost to an employee's morale. Getting constructive feedback on behavior that needs changing helps to motivate and direct an employee to improve.

By evaluating an employee on some established standards, the manager can compare performances in order to distribute, for example, bonuses. Evaluations give the organization an overall picture of its staffing and can provide the business owner with a way of evaluating the managers and the general success (in human terms) of the business. A written evaluation also provides a paper trail for the organization, to cover legal requirements and considerations in the case that an employee has to be fired.

The evaluation should be made on specific points, usually on a form designed to be used for all employees in a particular department or the entire organization. One popular method of evaluation is management by objectives (MBO), in which specific objectives are written for the employee for a specific time period. The manager and employee then look at the objectives together to evaluate the performance. The objectives need to be detailed and measurable, not vague. For example, one objective for a salesperson might be to make a particular number of sales calls in a certain period of time. Needless to say, the objectives should be reasonably achievable and there should be target dates for reaching the goals.

Measurement methods might include comparisons to established standards, observations, ranking or rating scales, or checklists. The person who does the assessment should be one who has been in a position to observe the employee at work. This may not always be the worker's designated manager, but rather a supervisor or some other person. The evaluator should be skilled at assessment, either through experience or training, and be able to provide useful feedback to the employee in order for the evaluation to be useful to both the employee and the organization.

The evaluator should avoid any assessment of the employee's personality or personal characteristics. The focus of any feedback should be on observable behaviors. The quickest way to raise a person's defenses is to say that he or she is lazy or has a bad attitude. Rather, specify a situation in which the employee didn't meet a deadline although he or she appeared to have had plenty of time or when the employee was rude to a customer or co-worker. Negative feedback is difficult to give and to receive but keeping the focus on behavior makes the feedback tangible and the behavior correctable.

The evaluation process should be done at least once a year. Many businesses prefer to evaluate more often when an employee is new, such as every three or six months for the first year. This should be flexible. For example, if an employee is given an important task to complete, it is helpful to have feedback immediately after the completion of the task, not six or twelve months later.

The approach to the evaluation should be one of helping or coaching. The evaluator's attitude should be "How can I help you with this?" Some employees, especially young ones or those lacking confidence, need a lot of encouragement and constructive feedback. It helps you get superior performances from your employees if you aware of their needs and preferred work styles. And the employee should be encouraged to share concerns or difficulties with the idea that manager and employee can solve situations together.

(Source: George T. Milkovich and John W. Boudreau, *Human Resource Management*, 7th edition, Burr Ridge, IL: Irwin, 1994, pp. 165-166, 172.)

sixteen
Control Inventories

Weinstein's Six Tips for Tracking Inventory

Inventory management, also called materials management, is a critical and often overlooked component of any business. All types of organizations require inventory whether it is an elementary school purchasing chalk, erasers, colored paper, and glue or it is a major manufacturer of paper goods. Managing your inventory well will improve your customer service and your profitability.

People running small businesses tend to overstock their inventories because they are eager to meet the demands of each customer, or they get a better deal from vendors when buying larger quantities than they really need. Inevitably, the goods are stored and what isn't sold immediately sits there gathering dust, taking up precious storage space and, most important, tying up capital that could be invested back into the business. In short, tying up your money in inventory that isn't going to move is synonymous to putting your cash into the back storage room and not using it even though you need it. This is something small-business owners, who are often cash poor, need to be aware of. Consider the following. In 1990 the American economy was holding more than $1 trillion in inventory, which was equivalent to having 2.7 months of inventory on hand for all consumers. And, these figures are considered low as compared to inventories held in the 1970s and 1980s. In addition, businesses in the United States invest twice as much in inventory as they invest in, for example, purchasing new plants and equipment. Every dollar tied up in inventory is a dollar that can't be invested in improving technology, developing new products or services, or increasing capacity (Lee J. Krajewski, and Larry P. Ritzman, *Operations Management: Strategy and Analysis*).

Large businesses spend enormous amounts of resources managing inventory, always searching for the optimum balance between having the right amount to meet demand without running out or having too much. Small-business people need to follow some basic inventory management practices such as *frequently* checking inventory levels, tracking sales of all items to calculate optimum amounts to order and store, and figuring out and minimizing ordering, storage, and stock out costs. You can track your inventory by hand or you can use some of the software that has been designed especially for small businesses and that usually costs less than $1,000.

(Sources: Lee J. Krajewski, and Larry P. Ritzman, *Operations Management: Strategy and Analysis*, Reading, MA: Addison-Wesley Publishing Company, 1993; Ronald W. Hilton, *Managerial Accounting*, 2nd ed., New York: McGraw-Hill, Inc., 1994; Justin G. Longenecker, Carlos W. Moore, and J. William Petty. *Small Business Management: An Entrepreneurial Emphasis,* Cincinnati, OH: South-Western Publishing Co., 1994.)

Follow Weinstein's six tips for knowing what you have and how it is working for you.

1. Maintain physical control of stock. Lock it up when it is not in use. Your inventory represents money. Inventory lost or stolen is money lost.

2. Check inventory frequently. Check a few items each day on a regular basis, and your job at the end of the year will be easier. In addition, you will have a better awareness of how inventory moves from day to day and week to week.

3. Concentrate your efforts on marketing the products that sell well. Remember the 80-20 principle—80 percent of profits come from 20 percent of the products. The ones that do not sell well can be "downsized" or eliminated.

4. Work with your key suppliers to take advantage of their capabilities. Help them improve quality and reduce lead times. If they can provide high quality and timely service, then you will be able to do the same for your customers.

5. Use the data you compile to measure inventory performance. Compare your investment in inventory with the revenue it obtains. Pay attention to stock outs so you know where production amounts need to be adjusted. If the costs associated with stock outs are high, then you will want to look at how to adjust inventory levels to resolve this problem. Track the company's record of shipping completed orders on the dates requested to see if you are filling orders in a timely manner. If not, production amounts may need to be changed.

6. Pay close attention to inventory items that cost a lot to maintain, have long lead times, and are costly when out of stock. There are a number of formulas you can use to evaluate your levels of inventory. They include the economic order quantity (EOQ) and reorder point (ROP). You may also want to calculate a level of "safety stock."

EOQ allows you to calculate the least amount of inventory to order to minimize your total annual holding and order costs. Holding costs include transport and storage. Order costs include contacting the supplier and the administrative and labor costs associated with placing and receiving an order. EOQ assumes that demand for the item is constant, that the item is produced or purchased in lots rather than piecemeal, and that supply and lead time are certain and unchanging. These are not terribly realistic assumptions. However, the EOQ model can help you make a good estimate of what inventory you should keep on hand and how frequently you should order so you can keep costs down. For those of you who enjoy a little math, here is the EOQ equation.

EOQ Equation

Step 1: First determine your annual costs

$$\text{Total Annual Cost} = \left(\frac{\text{annual item requirement}}{\text{order quantity}}\right)\left(\frac{\text{cost}}{\text{per order}}\right) + \left(\frac{\text{order quantity}}{2}\right)\left(\frac{\text{annual holding cost}}{\text{per unit}}\right)$$

Step 2: Then determine the least amount of inventory you should order

$$\text{Economic order quantity} = \sqrt{\frac{(2)\,(\text{annual item requirement})\,(\text{cost per order})}{\text{annual holding cost per unit}}}$$

If your EOQ is 500 and you use 3,000 items per year, then you need to order 6 times per year.

The ROP method is based on your consistently monitoring inventory levels. Once your stock gets down to a preset reorder level, you reorder. Your reorder point would ensure that you have enough inventory on hand to cover demand during lead time and a buffer against stock outs. For example, say you own a specialty food shop and have brisk sales for a pesto sauce. Your reorder point is 20—when you get down to 20 jars, you reorder. The 20, you know from experience, will meet demand during the two-week lead time it takes for an order to arrive and includes a few extra jars just in case. Better to store a few more jars than risk irritating one of your hard won, finicky customers.

A good resource for inventory management skills is the American Production and Inventory Control Society. You can call them at 703-237-8344. For more on inventory-control methods, look in any upper-level operations management or managerial accounting text.

(Sources: "Taking Stock," Bob Weinstein, *Entrepreneur,* January 1995, pp. 50-53; Jae K. Shim, Joel G. Siegel, and Abraham J. Simon, *The Vest-Pocket MBA*, Englewood Cliffs, NJ: Prentice Hall, 1986, pp. 282-284.)

seventeen
Outsource

Coopers & Lybrand's Five Good Reasons to Use Outsourcing

Outsourcing is basically "letting the other guy do it." You take a specific task in the production of your product and look to see whether there are other firms doing this process that can do it faster, better, cheaper than you can.

Richard D. Dole, vice chairman of Process Management at Coopers & Lybrand, says that outsourcing is the management technique of the nineties. Why? "Outsourcing keeps companies from having to divert capital from what they do well." He believes firms that outsource can create larger margins and generate more cash flow. Coopers & Lybrand surveyed CEOs of 400 growing firms with $1 to $50 million in sales and found that 66 percent of them use outsourcing in some form. Eighty percent of outsourcers indicated that outsourcing contributed significantly to their growth.

Outsourcing can be a useful tool for the small business that cannot realize the economies of scale that a large manufacturing plant can. You "farm out" the tasks that you can, overseeing them as needed. For example, if you need a particular part that must be built with complicated machinery, you may not be able to afford the machinery and it will therefore pay to have the work done by an outside vendor.

According to the Coopers & Lybrand study, there are five main reasons for outsourcing:

Reasons for Outsourcing:	*Percent of Businesses that say this*
Outsiders are more efficient	70%
You can focus on your own products	45%
You save costs of benefits	42%
Less investment is needed	41%
There is less regulatory burden	21%

Many companies, large and small, are finding that outsourcing is a good management tool. Of course, it takes some research to be successful at outsourcing (see related article on outsourcing), but many have found it to be worthwhile.

(Source: Based on a study by Coopers & Lybrand, reported in Echo Montgomery Garrett, "Innovation + Outsourcing = Big Success," *Management Review*, September 1994, p. 19.)

Keep It Simple: Edmark's Outsourcing Strategy

"I wanted to spend my time doing business rather than managing people." So says Tomima Edmark, founder of TopsyTail Company. This business had $80 million in sales in its third year, a huge sum considering its payroll of only two people! How does she do it? She outsources, hiring other companies to do almost all the work.

How does outsourcing work? Instead of hiring employees to produce your product, you "farm out" or outsource some or many of the tasks that need to be done to get your product to market. This may include any of the following functions:

machining
packaging
design
advertising
photography

printing
shipping
mailings
publicity
distribution

Advantages of Outsourcing

Outsourcing allows you to concentrate on what you do best. You farm out the tasks that are better done externally and retain control of those you can do more efficiently. The vendors to whom you will outsource have usually developed highly efficient ways of doing the tasks that you would need to spend time developing. So you save time and money. Outsourcing is also advantageous for companies that do not have the capital for heavy investment. In addition, you save on the costs of hiring personnel, and you avoid the day-to-day issues of sick days, benefits, and insurance. The money you save can be used for other purposes.

Potential Disadvantages

Although you might expect to lose some control over product quality, delivery, and other performance criteria when you outsource, this does not have to be the case. If you explicitly define your standards and then the vendor does not meet them, you can look for another vendor. This, of course, means you need to define your standards *in writing* and you need to communicate well with the vendor. You will also want to set up a specific time schedule for the vendor to follow. Communication with the vendor does not need to be complicated. A fax machine can facilitate the process.

It may take some time to find the best vendors for the processes you want to outsource. Although this in itself may take time, it is important to be sure you find someone reliable and trustworthy and willing to sign a contract. If you do not research potential partners well, you may find your ideas imitated or stolen. Consider the experience of Mark Thatcher, founder of Teva Sports Sandals, Inc. Mark had no manufacturing experience or facilities so when he first started up his business, he outsourced the production of his sandals. The manufacturer liked the product so much that they decided, since they were in possession of the specifications, to produce and market the sandals themselves, using the Teva name. The legal battle that followed, which Mark eventually won, dragged on for three years and cost considerable money both in lost sales and legal fees.

(Source: Gayle Sato Stodder, "Back in the Sandal," *Entrepreneur*, May 1995, pp.151 - 155.)

Potential vendors also need to be researched as to their financial stability. You want to be sure their financial history indicates skilled planning for economic variability.

Should I Outsource? How Much?

As stated, the most important work in setting up outsourcing is vendor research. Look carefully at potential suppliers. Some may not be interested in working with you if you do not plan high volume, and others may be less than ethical.

Tomina Edmark researches new suppliers for TopsyTail very carefully. She opts for local vendors when possible, in case there are any problems she has to deal with personally. She insists on an interview and references. She uses on-line services, business directories, and magazine articles to learn about the vendor's financial stability, customer-service reputation, and litigation history.

When Edmark started her company in 1991, she was the sole employee and contracted all the functions. Today, there are only two employees, so much of the work is still outsourced to her network of 20 vendors. But she prefers to retain control of new-product development and marketing strategy.

Outsourcing can be an extremely useful tool for the start-up business. As this method grows in popularity, there will likely be more vendors with a particular skill or expertise who are interested in supplying businesses in this manner. Whether you should consider outsourcing depends on the balance of the risks and the benefits for your operation.

Risks of Outsourcing

finding and keeping good partners
loss of control (product quality, delivery time, etc.)
theft/imitation of ideas
financial stability of vendor(s)
breakdown of communication flow

Benefits of Outsourcing

efficiency of operations
focusing on other company functions
savings on costs of benefits
less investment needed
fewer regulations
financial savings, especially if production is capital intensive
provision of needed skills

(Sources: Echo Montgomery Garrett, "Innovation + Outsourcing = Big Success," *Management Review*, September 1994, pp. 17-20.)

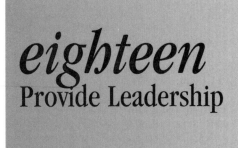

eighteen
Provide Leadership

What does strong leadership entail, and what qualities do good leaders embody? Don E. Marsh, president and CEO of Marsh supermarkets, says "Leading is the process in which a person with power is able to influence the behavior of others in some desired way." But leadership is not simply a matter of wielding power and influence.

Leaders need all the basics that good managers possess: intelligence, commitment, supervisory ability, and people and communication skills. But their abilities and characteristics go beyond what we normally expect from a manager.

Leaders know how to use their power effectively. They are self-assured, authentic, decisive, and focused. They have strong persuasive skills and are consistent. Most of all, leaders have core values and a vision that drives their beliefs, purpose, and mission. And they are able to convey that vision to those with whom they work. They are good at inspiring and influencing others.

Leaders are good at setting priorities and communicating those priorities with everyone else. When they set deadlines, they remain committed to them. Good leaders may also—but not necessarily—manage people well. They manage by walking around. They like to be involved personally. They respect their employees and use positive (not negative) reinforcement and rewards to obtain the desired behavior. This doesn't mean that leaders are good at the day-to-day details of personnel management, but excel more at the social, supportive, inspirational aspects of management.

Good leaders emphasize teamwork and continuous improvement. They share their goals with workers and allow for everyone to speak. They encourage coordination between departments. They support autonomy. They believe in training. Their question is "What can I do for you?"

But perhaps the qualities that most stand out among good leaders are those that reflect an openness to innovation. Good leaders are bold and willing to take risks. They are forward thinking and forward moving. They take action. They are creative and are receptive to ideas. Good leaders are willing to experiment.

Researchers have long tried to isolate the characteristics that make good leaders and have constructed models that describe various types of leaders. Good leaders can emerge from the most unlikely candidates, and different situations can bring out leadership behavior in all sorts of people. The research and models are useful, however, for analyzing and understanding one's own behavior for both self-knowledge and for maximizing employee productivity. Put simply, employees who are satisfied with their work environment and feel well treated will perform better than those who aren't.

Some early research on leader characteristics centered on autocratic versus democratic leaders and the relative performances of their employees. A later refinement of this research put the two styles on a continuum ranging from a boss who makes all the decisions and then announces them, to a boss who allows employees to function within defined limits. Employees working for an autocratic boss performed very well when the boss was present but slacked off when left unsupervised. The democratic boss got an almost equally high performance, the difference being that the employees continued to perform well whether or not the boss was present.

A more recent situational theory of leadership, developed by Paul Hersey and Kenneth Blanchard, focuses on the maturity level of the employees rather than on the characteristics of leaders. This theory postulates that people with a low level of "task maturity," because of little or no training or experience, need a "telling" style of leadership, meaning they need to be told what to do and to be supervised closely. A person with a high level of task maturity exhibits considerable expertise, requiring a leader to act more like a peer and use a delegating style. In between, a coaching style is best.

There are many leadership theories, and the more recent examine a wider range of situational variables rather than trying to identify the innate characteristics present in exceptional leaders. Implicit in these theories is that good leadership behavior can be practiced and learned. Another underlying theme of the theories is, how can managers/leaders maximize performance to improve organizational effectiveness? It might be useful, when considering your own behavior and styles, to think about how you will or do treat the people who work for you. Do you delegate responsibility without checking up or peering over a shoulder? Do you tailor your style to meet the situation and the employee or do your over- or undermanage? Do you give orders and make all the decisions or do you ask for your employees' opinions and involve them in the decision-making process? Are you pleased with how your employees perform or do you feel that you're not getting the best from them?

(Sources: Richard L. Daft, *Understanding Management*, Fort Worth, TX: The Dryden Press, 1995; Robert L. Dilenschneider, *Power and Influence: Mastering the Art of Persuasion*. New York: Prentice Hall Press, 1990.)

We further discuss innovation and leadership qualities in other articles in this section.

(Source: Don E. Marsh, "Management Theories and Practices," pp. 1-15 of *AMA Management Handbook*, John J. Hampton, ed., 1994, New York: AMACOM, American Management Association; Alex Hiam, *The Vest-Pocket CEO*, Englewood Cliffs, NJ: Prentice Hall, 1990, pp. 49, 56-59; James C. Collins and William C. Lazier, *Beyond Entrepreneurship*, Englewood Cliffs, NJ, Prentice-Hall, 1992, pp. 5-6.)

Peters' Eleven Rules for Moving into the Next Century

According to Tom Peters, author, lecturer, consultant, and guru, the rapid innovations in information and communication technology require us to stay on our toes. Many management consulting gurus have proposed "tools" and methods for getting companies going, encouraging innovation, keeping up with the competition, and responding to the customer. But Peters says we need to pay attention to the *basics*. He proposes these basic rules:

1. Build your product now. Speed is of the essence. Tinkering with a product to fine-tune it will leave you behind in the dust. Forge ahead, says Peters, do something. He points to innovation guru Michael Schrage's assertion that hasty prototyping is *the* most important aspect of new-product success.

2. Don't shun failure. Peters stresses the importance of going after something, even if it is risky. This nation was based on entrepreneurship, constant reinvention, and embracing new ideas. You will not move ahead if you are not willing to make errors.

3. Keep your sense of humor. A sense of humor is a necessity, both at work and about your own and others' foibles. Some people even consider sense of humor as an important characteristic in new hires.

4. Value and encourage curiosity. We expect children to be curious, but we do not honor this trait in adults. But spontaneity and even immature behavior may help us through challenging changes.

5.Take and use good ideas. "Lift" anything you can from others and mold it to fit your circumstances. Observation is a good way to get ideas for how you can improve your operation.

6. Hire young people. The ability of young people to assimilate and fully use computer technology illustrates why youth are important.

7. Dare to be different and outrageous. Peters points out that in spite of increased marketing-research, products are not becoming any more interesting. The safe and cautious path does not always result in a winner. Nor does the outrageous always succeed, but you cannot know unless you try.

8. Support blind optimism. An "unrealistic belief in the possibility of success," as opposed to bottom-line evaluation, can result in fascinating new possibilities. While it can also be a stumbling block, sometimes you have to push the limits.

9. Don't have regrets. This is like the adage about not crying over spilled milk. The message here is to pick up and go on, not to remonstrate over what has happened. You can't go back, but you can learn from your mistakes.

10. Respect paradox. Successful people are usually perfectionists and also have a high tolerance for disorder. A paradox, yes, but nevertheless true.

11. Tell the truth. Although politics are a part of all operations, public and private, the basis of a good operation should be telling the truth about situations, whether they are good or bad. Friction is normal. Teasing is acceptable. But large egos are discouraged, and gossipers are dismissed.

If you want to keep up with the constantly changing environment, use these traits as guides when you are hiring. Peters says, "recruit passion and impatience."

(Source: Tom Peters, "Emphasize the Right Stuff," *Forbes ASAP*, February 27, 1995, pp. 108-110.)

nineteen
Encourage Teamwork

Team Building

Teams are one of the modern management tools offered as a solution to improving productivity and quality. In fact, teams have been used successfully in Japan and other places, and they have caught on in some businesses in the United States. Teams can and do improve morale, productivity, and quality of work life. They may reduce costs, increase profitability, and provide better service to customers. However, teams are successful only when the entire organization is committed to helping them accomplish their goals.

Before deciding that using teams is right for your business, try to answer the following questions.

What are your objectives for wanting to implement a team(s)? How do you expect the company, the team members, and yourself to benefit?

- Does your company structure and culture support using teams? For example, are you an autocratic type of boss who needs to have a finger in every pot or can you delegate real responsibility to others? Can you identify processes or areas in which teams can have an impact?

- Do you have the resources to ensure that your team(s) gets the support and training it needs to successfully move through the various stages of team development and become productive, or will it flounder causing productivity to suffer?
- How do your employees respond to the idea? This will give you some idea of how easy or difficult teams will be to implement.

It's important, before implementing a team approach, that you feel confident that it is the best method for achieving your desired results.

Teams do not just "happen" overnight. It is crucial to allow enough time for traditional workers to adjust to the team concept. Even when management is committed to the idea, workers need to understand the reasons for implementing teams. They need to know that the basis of a team is not competition but rather cooperation.

While the objective of using teams is to encourage groups to learn to become autonomous, managers will at first need to coordinate the process and motivate the members of the team.

Sometimes teams are created to accomplish a specific task and are then disbanded when the task is completed. This can be a useful way to introduce and test the concept and use of teams without applying them to all operations in a business. Management will need to be just as committed to a "temporary" team as they would be to a permanent team.

Some cautions on team-building follow.

Define the task clearly. Be sure you know exactly what the team is expected to accomplish.

Consider multifunctional representation on the team. It may be useful to have team members represent different functional areas of the company. This gives the team access to different points of view and to expertise they may need for the project.

Make the first meeting of the team organizational. Someone should be appointed to lead the discussion of the task. From this should come the following activities:

- Write a mission statement.
- Brainstorm a list of success factors and prepare a formal list.

- Identify the business process(es) necessary for each critical success factor; assign someone to be responsible for each.
- Chart the project and priorities.

Management must support the team. There are a number of ways that management can indicate support for the team project:

- Put the team in the same location if they are working on it full time.
- Follow the progress of team members and facilitate communication if needed.
- Make sure necessary resources are available; try to avoid sharing them; that is, give the team their own resources.
- Give the team autonomy.
- Coordinate and motivate team members as needed.
- Provide support for team participants.
- Offer rewards and recognition for a job well done.

The team will need to learn to work together, developing trust through communication. They will have to learn to resolve conflict, again through open communication. Preferably, team members will learn to resolve their own conflicts without intervention of management, unless necessary. One of the goals of using teams, after all, is to foster self-management and autonomy.

The team will also learn to set goals and priorities. If the project is successful, the team may continue with other projects, or may help others put together teams. One issue for the team is their interaction with the rest of the organization. Here again, management can be helpful in smoothing the way for communication.

The makeup of a team will vary with the nature of the task to be performed, the size of the group, and the authority assigned to them. If the team is to learn to continue functioning as a team, they will want to learn multiple skills so they can interchange tasks as needed, particularly if the team is small and the task is fairly large. They will also want to learn support tasks so they are not dependent on others. (This is part of the reason for having their own, rather than shared, resources.)

What a team can learn is an awareness of the process so that they can look for ways to improve it. Sometimes a small team can see what the company as a whole cannot: ways to decrease unit cost or cycle time and to truly affect production costs. The team also learns self-management. In addition, they may be able to monitor customer needs and thus be able to make suggestions for adjusting the process.

Teams, taken to the fullest participation, can learn to do their own performance appraisals, schedule their own vacations, and make selection decisions.

Teamwork Success Stories

John Mackey, founder of the nationwide Whole Foods Market chain based in Austin, Texas, compares his management style to that used by the United Federation of Planets in Star Trek: Both use the team approach. Each Whole Foods Market department, such as dairy, produce, and meats, is run by a team of workers who make their own purchasing decisions, manage portions of their budget, and make decisions about whether or not to keep new employees who are nearing the end of their probation periods. Mr. Mackey believes that these teams know their part of the business and their own customers better than he does and will therefore know what and how much of an item to stock. He also awards bonuses based on a departmental team's gross margin, which is added incentive for them to purchase their stock carefully. Mr. Mackey believes that his use of teams motivates employees to do their best and fosters an environment based on trust. Although skeptics may question Mr. Mackey's philosophy, they can't question his numbers: Whole Foods maintains a 3.7 percent operating margin compared to the average supermarket's 2.6 percent.

Asea Brown Boveri Canada, Inc., the Toronto-based branch of the multinational electrical manufacturer, decided to implement a team-based factory. They assembled a team of seven widely diverse employees and presented them with the challenges to halve production time, increase production by 30 percent, and reduce the work force from 150 to 120 people. They gave the team seven months to have the new factory design implemented and operational. The team put in long hours and, during trips to benchmark other factories, were able to spend leisure time together, which enabled them to bond.

The team came up with and successfully implemented an exceptional design that surpassed even management's expectations. Afterwards, the team disbanded and went their separate ways, but not without agreeing that the experience had been gratifying and educational.

Teams may not be the answer for every business. Good management involves observing and listening to workers' comments on what they need. Sometimes improvements in quality can result from simply providing more training for managers or employees (or both), supplying more information to those who need it, and listening to gripes and committing to resolving them.

(Sources: George T. Milkovich and John W. Boudreau, *Human Resource Management*, 7th ed., Burr Ridge, IL: Irwin, 1994; Howard Bronstein and Darrell Ray, *Teaming Up: Making the Transition to a Self-Directed Team-Based Organization*, McGraw-Hill, 1995; Alex Hiam, *The Vest-Pocket CEO*, Englewood Cliffs, NJ: Prentice Hall, 1990, p. 218; Alex Hiam, "Team Development Success Factors," *The Vest-Pocket Marketer*, Englewood Cliffs, NJ: Prentice Hall, 1991, pp. 125-127, 138-40; *Daily Hampshire Gazette*, February 6, 1995, p. 32.)

twenty
Manage Change

Change is a natural process for any organization. Those who aren't aware of the need to change to adapt to internal and external forces will risk failure. It's true that initiating, implementing, and managing change can be difficult, but not necessarily so. The most difficult changes to implement are those involving cultural or structural changes, in which employees may feel threatened and resist all efforts for what you believe is improvement. However, change can also occur through using new technology, developing new products, or changing the company's processes and procedures to improve productivity and efficiency. It is important to remember that change is inevitable, healthy, potentially profitable both financially and emotionally, confidence-building to those who go through it, and yes, often painful. It shouldn't be avoided, but it also shouldn't be initiated for its own sake. Change for the sake of change is likely a symptom of some underlying issue, for example, dissatisfaction with a business or a lifestyle.

Learning how to recognize the need for change is an obvious first step. Clues to be aware of include watching for trends in performance. For example, did sales dip down after launching your new ad campaign, moving to a new location, hiring a new salesperson, or has there just been a steady downward trend for the last year? Or, has your company and its work processes grown to the degree that efficiency is being hampered by insufficient technology? For example, are you passing along pieces of paper to various employees as part of your work process when using a database with group access and shared files would significantly increase productivity, improve service, and streamline your process? Is it time for your company, in other words, to join the electronic age in a more serious way? Finally, is there a gap between how employees (or one employee) are performing and how you'd like them to perform?

Change doesn't have to be wrenching and major. Buying a new computerized cash register, changing your inventory-control methods, or providing your employees with customer-service training are all changes. However, even these relatively small or benign changes can cause employees to worry or feel threatened. What if your cashier is 60 years old and has computer phobia? It's critical to manage even what you consider small changes.

Once you've identified the need for change, the next step is to develop ideas to solve perceived needs. A logical source for developing ideas is to conduct research. Talk to friends, colleagues, advisers, and consultants. Read relevant literature, take advantage of pro bono consulting if you qualify, and attend trade shows or professional meetings. Also, ask your employees (if appropriate). Discuss with them that you've recognized an area you think needs improvement and brainstorm ideas.

Implementing changes is, of course, the most challenging step because it requires that people change their behavior and routines. This is often where trying to implement change falls apart: Employees resist for reasons management can't understand. Following is a discussion of how people in general react to and cope with change and what you, as a manager, need to be aware of.

Murray's Seven Aspects of Change

Consultant Mike Murray, president of Creative Interchange, cautions those who are dealing with change to heed the following issues that are bound to arise. The underlying message is to include employees in the discussion of change—whether they perceive it to be positive or negative—to hear their concerns, and to make them feel a part of it.

Change can be experienced as a kind of loss, because what has existed is not there anymore, even if it has changed only its form. There are three basic stages that everyone goes through after a loss: shock/denial, anger/depression, and understanding/acceptance. Some people may move through these stages rapidly; others may take longer. But everyone needs to go through them.

1. Be sure you can describe the change clearly so everyone knows what to expect. The shock resulting from change can sometimes be lessened if people are prepared ahead of time. Even if it is a sudden change, open the lines of communication as soon as possible.

2. Acknowledge that the change will cause hardships. Encourage the staff to identify those hardships. Listen to their concerns, but try not to react to them. Give them a chance to vent their anger. It may take some time for them to get used to the change.

3. Have the staff attempt to prioritize the hardships. Then, have them define a method for dealing with each of the expected problems. If you involve the staff in rising to the challenge of the change they will not be able to deny that it is occurring, and they will have to confront what is happening.

4. Acknowledge the grief that people may feel and express. While we normally associate grief with an obvious loss, such as a business closing, there can be a wide range of emotions associated with any change, positive or negative. For example, hiring a new administrator may cause shock, anger, or fear. Merging with another company can cause even greater upheavals. Emotional reactions are normal. Allow people to express how they feel. Some employees may even display physical symptoms such as illness or fatigue.

5. Now focus on turning complaints into goals. If there is a potential problem with this change, given that the change is going to happen, ask what all concerned can do to avoid the problem. This prods people into seeking solutions rather than staying mired in negative reactions.

6. Each employee should be encouraged to identify one personal benefit of the change. This focuses attention on the positive aspects of the change.

7. When everyone has had a chance to gripe and start moving through the emotion to a point where he or she can listen to the positives, present the benefits this change will have on the entire organization. Tell them how you see the company being affected in the long run.

While you will not be able to immediately create "one big happy family," following these steps will go a long way to moving people on toward positive feelings for the change.

(Source: "Smooth Moves," *Entrepreneur*, January 1995, p. 58.)

Case Study: One company's experience with change

Entrepreneur and small-business owner Mimi Smith's company was growing at breakneck speed. Her 12-person company provided innovative customer service training to corporate clients, and they had recently signed a two-year contract with a Fortune 100 company. The work processes that had been developed ten years ago when the business was a one-person operation with two part timers were straining to support the incoming work. Employees were working 15-hour days and there was a high level of stress and tension along with the excitement of the challenge. Mimi, in anticipation of this growth, had hired a manager to oversee general operations and manage the support staff. This person was now telling her that the processes were simply not designed to handle the amount of work and that service and morale would suffer. It was inevitable that the staff couldn't catch every mistake; they were tired, and they knew that company standards, and their standards for their own performance, were extremely high.

Mimi's style was to be cautious about making large capital investments. She was often short on cash and had had to take out a loan from the bank just to cover payroll for the next few months. Still, she realized that unless the company made some changes to improve efficiency, client service would suffer.

Mimi called a company meeting, asking people to prepare by bringing their job descriptions, the forms, sheets, checklists, and other supporting paperwork they used to complete their jobs, and a list of activities they routinely performed. She told her employees that they were going to map the entire process of selling and executing a customer-service workshop, from first contact with a client through to day one of the training. The process would take all day, if necessary, and she would provide lunch for everyone. The employees were intrigued and excited, and everyone came to the meeting armed with folders full of papers.

The process of selling and delivering training to a client was very paper-intensive. The small company wasn't networked, some of the computers were old and incompatible with the new ones, and not everyone had access to the same information even though they all needed it. Several junior employees spent a great deal of time running up and down stairs trying to find the information they needed to complete their jobs.

The mapping process was successful in that the company got to see how the entire process worked and who did what. It was clear that the underlying systems were solid and well thought out but that the volume had increased to the degree that passing paper back and forth as a means for communicating about a particular job was highly inefficient. After some discussion, it became clear that everyone in the company needed access to some of the same information and that networking the computers was the best solution for achieving this.

It took another five years before Mimi made the decision to network the company's personal computers. In the meantime, the company experienced no growth but managed to maintain. During the next two years she experienced a nearly 100 percent turnover in employees.

What went wrong and what could Mimi have done differently? For one, Mimi heightened her employees' expectations by conducting a brainstorming, process-mapping meeting. She led her staff to believe that there would be change when she was unable to provide the necessary resources. Communication was clearly a problem in this situation. Mimi could have defined the company's financial limitations up front, encouraging employees to come up with creative ideas that didn't involve a major capital investment. She could have provided incentives and rewards for employees who stuck with the company through its growth spurt. This story illustrates just one of the millions of scenarios that can occur in a company that is trying to manage change. The one thing that is clear is that honest communication is critical. Then, at least, everyone is operating with the same information and under the same assumptions and can make informed decisions.

(Sources: Richard L. Daft, *Understanding Management*. New York: The Dryden Press, 1995; Lee Sproull and Sara Kiesler, *Connections: New Ways of Working in the Networked Organization*, Cambridge, MA: The MIT Press, 1993.)

twenty-one
Consider Social Responsibility

The social responsibility of an organization is more difficult to define than, perhaps, one would expect. A broad definition is that the management of an organization would make decisions and act in ways that are in the best interest of both society and the organization. The question becomes more complicated when managers need to decide to whom they are most responsible.

As a small-business owner, it's important to establish ties with your community by using local vendors and products when possible, not abusing the environment by overusing natural resources or polluting, and contributing to causes and efforts to improve the community in which you work. More and more entrepreneurs and small-business owners are realizing that you can't run a healthy successful business in an unhealthy community, that the two go hand in hand. However, what if local vendors are too expensive or are of inferior quality? Or, if you're accused of polluting when you're actually operating within the regulations? What if you're a bar or tavern owner and neighbors complain of the noise when people leave your establishment late at night—do you close down the bar at 10 P.M. rather than at 1 A.M.?

There are many stakeholders in an organization, both internal and external, and deciding how and to whom to be responsible can be confusing. Although small-business owners have fewer stakeholders than large ones, take a few minutes to think about who they are. First there is you, the owner, and your family, your community, creditors, investors and stockholders, employees, the local media and chamber of commerce, the local schools, customers, and suppliers such as local office supply stores, as well as vendors from whom you purchase inventory. This may well be an incomplete list but it gives you an idea of the potential responsibility of being a business owner. Clearly, the more you are perceived to be socially responsible, the better your reputation will be in the community, and that is worth some investment.

It's important to consider your internal stakeholders. Joel Makower, author of *Beyond the Bottom Line: Putting Social Responsibility to Work for Your Business and the World*, says that social responsibility should begin in the workplace. Business owners need to support their employees as much as possible through training programs, access to child care, and other programs that boost morale, productivity, and commitment to both the company and the community (Janean Huber, "Social Graces," *Entrepreneur*, December 1994, pp. 121 - 127).

As a profit-making organization, a major concern is economic responsibility. You are in business to produce and/or sell goods or services and make a profit for both yourself and your shareholders. You do this within certain legal boundaries—your legal responsibility—and you maintain certain ethical boundaries, depending on your business practice beliefs. These are the basic social responsibilities that every company must fulfill to some degree.

Then there are discretionary responsibilities. For example, you might decide to contribute time, money, or products to a local food bank, park building, or cleaning effort, or to subsidize your local public radio station. According to business consultant David Calabria, discretionary responsibilities are now becoming market-driven. Investing in your community and in the environment is more and more perceived as valuable in the marketplace. Companies that never much considered social responsibility are now finding that it pays. In addition, says Calabria, consumers are now linking their own social consciences with what they decide to buy. Companies that can appeal to the socially aware consumer will be more competitive.

Organizations, awards, and books have emerged to support this growing trend toward socially responsible business. One visible organization, Business for Social Responsibility, holds an annual conference that gives members a chance to network. Sharing ideas and successes can be inspirational to other entrepreneurs who are just starting out.

(Sources: Richard L. Daft, *Understanding Management*. New York: The Dryden Press, 1995; Janean Huber, "Social Graces," *Entrepreneur,* December 1994, pp. 121 - 127; John F. Steiner, *Industry, Society, and Change: A Casebook*, New York: McGraw-Hill, Inc., 1991.)

And if you are using overseas suppliers for your products, contact *Verité*, a non-profit organization that audits manufacturers to make sure they don't use forced labor, child labor, or unsafe working conditions: Verité Inc., Amherst MA, 413-253-9227.

Murphy's Deadly Sins of Being Socially Conscious

In recent years, companies like Ben & Jerry's, Body Shop, Patagonia, and Smith & Hawken have made names for themselves as "socially responsible" companies. They have demonstrated concern for the environment, responsive management, and "politically correct" philosophies.

Designing your company around a social issue can have definite benefits if consumers see your business as socially responsible. But such a move can also be risky because of the attached and sometimes unexpected costs. "A passion to do the right thing may not translate into a passion for doing things right," says Anne Murphy, who watches small businesses, especially those that have made names for themselves in the social issues arena.

For example, a socially responsible firm can attract a lot of attention in the media for its philosophy and actions. This may provide positive publicity, which can help a new company, but continued close scrutiny by the press may prove irritating and uncomfortable for employees.

Entrepreneurs usually have genius in marketing or design of a product, but rarely have skills in *all* areas. For example, they may be creative or innovative in the product area, but short of skills in management. What starts out as a noble cause can get bogged down in the day-to-day reality of details. Workers in socially responsible firms, attracted to working for a noble cause, may find that their pay is lower, the hours longer, and working conditions more difficult than in other "mainstream" companies.

Supporting a cause may affect hiring practices. For example, if you are promoting a politically liberal cause, could you hire a person who expresses politically conservative views counter to your own? If your company does no animal testing, would you hire someone who wears leather (or fur) to the interview, or reveals that he or she eats meat? While these may be strong examples, you can see the point.

While causes are important, they may distract the management team from attending to the things needed to survive in a competitive market.

The new CEO for Ben & Jerry's Homemade, Inc.—Robert Holland, Jr.—is experienced in turnarounds, and will be expected to get the company growing again. His major talents and abilities are said to lie in leadership, management, and strategic planning. (The search for candidates for CEO was via an essay contest, although Holland came to them through a conservative executive search firm. Before being hired he wrote a poem rather than an essay.)

The message here is that socially conscious companies may have a tougher time at succeeding when they have the multiple goals of accomplishing both a mission and a business success. Frequently, such companies succeed at one but not the other. The problem is that there are still all the mundane tasks of hiring, firing, producing the product or service, manufacturing the product, shipping it, distributing it, making money, and being better than your competition.

We don't think this caution should discourage you from trying to help make your world a better place. As an entrepreneur and manager, you are inevitably going to affect the society in which you operate, so, as the old saying goes, "If you aren't part of the solution, you're part of the problem." But do be careful about *how* you pursue social benefit goals. Look for issues where your firm's interests are parallel to society's. And look for "leverage," areas in which you can make a big difference with minimal effort because of the nature of your business. The most successful efforts are visionary, but also *realistic*!

(Sources: Anne Murphy, "The Seven (Almost) Deadly Sins of High-Minded Entrepreneurs," *Inc.*, July 1994, v. 16, n.7, pp. 47-51; Joseph Pereira and Joann S. Lublin, "A New CEO for Cherry Garcia's Creators," *The Wall Street Journal*, Thursday, February 2, 1995, pp. B1, B11.)

PART VI
Strategic Management For Growth

twenty-two
Do Strategic Planning

One of the difficulties of managing a small business is that you have access to a limited number of specialists, so owners of small businesses frequently find themselves wearing many hats. As the company grows, the organization becomes more complex and more formal, and skill requirements change. Sometimes one or a few persons cannot meet those needs alone. That is where planning becomes important, if you do not want to "stunt" the growth of the company.

As a firm grows, the planning must become more systematic. If a company grows rapidly, productivity can suffer, so planning needs to attend to this factor. And decisions made about the future must always continue to be based on the business's goals and objectives.

While a firm's business plan can shed light on the items on which long-range planning *ought to focus*, the business plan is not in itself a long-range plan. The market niche and product feature you select now may not be the ones to be focusing on in the future.

Planning your strategies for the long term can be one of the most challenging aspects of running a business. Even though your business plan may have led you to successfully plan individual aspects of the business such as pricing, sales strategies, competitive tactics, and the like, in strategic planning, you need to look at the total picture over a period of time, especially if you are aiming to grow your business.

The primary mandate in long-range planning is to set aside time and a place for planning. A good long-range plan cannot be done in a few hours, nor can it be accomplished with phones ringing and other interruptions causing distractions to the business at hand. In addition, long-range planning should not be done solely by management; there should be a place for employee input, too. Further, each department should be represented in one way or another—that is, either by a representative or through written material showing the needs and expectations of the various constituencies of the business. The long-range plan will be a collaboration among all the members of the planning team and should deal with issues such as structure, chain of command, delegation, supervision, and control.

The underpinning of a good long-range plan is a vision that propels everything else. Your planning team will need to take into account the business's strengths and weaknesses, as well as the strengths and weaknesses of the staff. You will need to make realistic projections of what is possible, bearing in mind just what is *un*attainable. And you will need, ultimately, to be sure that all the members of the team are committed to making the plan work.

Both internal and external assessment will be necessary. You may want to refer to the discussion of quality management in Chapter 8, where intensive scrutiny for quality is outlined.

Strategic planning covers the gamut of the processes and people in the business. You must look at all aspects, including:

- Product or service
- Product line
- Manufacturing
- Customer
- Financial aspects, especially cash flow
- People and the organization

Some questions that may help guide your evaluation will be:

- Do we want to foster growth of this company? If so, how much?
- Would it be strategically appropriate to diversify? If so, where, when, and how much?

- Should the company be privately held? Or, do we need to go public in order to raise more money for growth?
- Do we want to be leaders in the market or followers?

In their book, *Beyond Entrepreneurship*, James C. Collins and William C. Lazier offer a strategy formulation example for a fictitious company, an outline of which is given below. We do not include the actual details and content, for that will vary from company to company. But the outline is meant to be thought provoking for those interested in doing some strategic planning.

Corporate Vision

Core values and beliefs
Purpose
Current mission

Internal Assessment

Strengths
Weaknesses
Resources
Innovations

External Assessment

Industry trends
Technology trends
Competitors
Social and regulatory environment
Macro economy and demographics
International
Top three opportunities
Top three threats

Strategy & Strategic Priorities

Overview

Products

Customers

Cash flow

People and Organization

Infrastructure

(Source: James C. Collins and William C. Lazier, *Beyond Entrepreneurship*, Englewood Cliffs, NJ, Prentice Hall, 1992, pp. 95-134.)

Potlatch's Strategic-Planning Guidelines

The hardest part of a project such as writing a strategic plan, is getting started and keeping your focus. Even with an outline, it's easy to get lost in the process. Also, just the thought of writing such a document can be daunting. The outline will help as a guide, and the following list will help you get started and keep focused.

Planning Stage

1. *Do your homework.* Be sure you take into account all affected departments, areas, employees, and so forth. Be thorough so that you do not have to amend the plan later.

2. *Fit the personality of the CEO.* The plan must fit with the vision of the company. And if the CEO is going to be the standard bearer, the plan has to work with that person's personality.

3. *Watch the scale.* In the excitement of planning, it is possible to get carried away with great ideas. Be sure that the plan is not too big to manage and thus doomed to failure from the start.

4. *Decide who will participate.* Be clear about who is affected and will be participating. Sometimes a small-scale change can be instituted in a small way and then enlarged when it has experienced some success.

5. *Keep expectations realistic.* Do not expect that all will welcome changes with open arms. Likewise, do not try to cover too much territory in a short period of time.

Implementation Stage

6. *Give the plan authority.* Plans are better accepted when fully supported at the top. Have the CEO authorize implementation of the plan, explain it to those affected, and support it, along with other members of the management team.

7. *Have planners help implement the program.* The planners, familiar with the plan, are appropriate for helping implement the plan. Those not involved in planning may resist.

8. *Include checks designed to prevent backsliding.* Plan for lapses by incorporating into the plan checks that will show when there are slips.

9. *Update the plan.* As the competition responds to the effects of the plan, expect to update your plan in response to competitive activities.

10. *Be flexible.* Your strategic plan is not cast in concrete. Prepare to be flexible and to adjust as needed if the plan is not working.

(Source: Alex Hiam, *The Vest-Pocket CEO*, Englewood Cliffs, NJ: Prentice Hall, 1990, pp. 422-423.)

Schwenk and Shrader's Meta-Analysis of Strategic Planning

It has long been known that strategic planning is not only useful but necessary for large companies. Current studies show that planning can improve the performance of *small* businesses as well. Charles R. Schwenk and Charles B. Shrader of Baylor University analyzed studies of companies conducted over the last decade and found that the following were positively related to planning:

Return on assets
Return on sales
Sales
Sales per employee
Sales growth
Revenue growth

Percent sales growth

Percent profit growth

Return on investment

Net income growth

Sales revenue

Gross income growth

Planning provides you with a structure to use for looking at and evaluating possible alternatives. This can ultimately help improve performance. Strategic planning moves the attention away from the day-to-day focus and toward long-term thinking and planning.

Planning is particularly important for companies in highly competitive situations, where even minor differences in performance may affect their survival.

(Source: Charles R. Schwenk and Charles B. Shrader, "Effects of Formal Strategic Planning on Financial Performance in Small Firms: A Meta-Analysis," *Entrepreneurship Theory and Practice*, Spring 1993, p. 53.)

Morrison's Five Principles of Planning

Strategic planning is about the future. The planning process is a way to describe and be prepared for anticipated (or unanticipated) events, changes, threats, and opportunities. Futurist Ian Morrison lists the following five areas that he believes businesses must plan for to stay on top in the twenty-first century:

1. Take advantage of global markets.
2. Develop new products.
3. Create vision and leadership in your business.
4. Put people's needs first.
5. Rethink the customers' needs.

Each of these is the subject of other sections in this book, which illustrates nicely that all aspects of business interact and that you must look at the big picture and not focus solely on the individual parts.

(Source: Robert McGarvey, "Back to the Future," *Entrepreneur*, January 1995, p. 240.)

Strategic planning takes place in the context of competitor actions, so it requires careful analysis of the competition—the topic of the final chapter of this section.

twenty-three
Analyze Competitors

According to the Supreme Court, "competition is our fundamental national policy" (Edwin Mansfield, *Managerial Economics: Theory, Application, and Cases*. 2nd ed., New York: W. W. Norton & Company, 1993, pp. 565). Competition is the underlying force that shapes how companies in the United States conduct business and any strategic business plan must be centered around a thorough analysis and understanding of the competitive environment. Models of competition are useful in that they offer a systematic way of researching and analyzing your competitive environment. The industrial organization theory proposes that you conduct your analysis by looking at the market/industry structure, strategy, and performance.

Using the industrial organization model, let's say, for example, that two years ago Jean started a bagel shop. She had tried every bagel within a 20-mile radius of her community and they were all terrible. In fact, very few shops were even offering bagels. Jean's friends were eating more and more of them because the health gurus were touting them as a good, low-fat alternative to other baked goods. She knew there was an unmet demand when she opened her shop, and for the past year and a half it had been doing extremely well. However, in the past six months, things had changed drastically. It seemed that bagels were everywhere. Even Jean's local supermarket was offering them, although they were, in her estimation, simply round pieces of bread.

Her business had dropped off ever since a national bagel franchise opened a shop several blocks down. She decided it was time to revise her strategy by conducting a new competitive analysis and this time she was going to try to anticipate changes in the marketplace so she could plan ahead.

Jean's first step was to take a look at the market *structure* to see how it had changed in two years. She listed all the competitors she could think of including the supermarket, bakeries that offered a variety of goods, the other bagel shops, frozen bagels, and convenience stores. She organized them into categories by size and distribution. Since the supermarket provided fresh baked bagels and frozen bagels, she considered it one of her biggest competitors. She then examined the barriers to entry into the bagel market. There was clearly an increasing demand, and there were a number of franchises available. It would be relatively inexpensive for an existing bakery or food store to start selling bagels, but there was considerable cost involved in opening her own shop or investing in a franchise. There was also increasing competition, and Jean decided that her community could not support more than one or two more players before the market became saturated. So the barriers to entry were somewhat high given the expense and the demographics.

Next, to focus on the *conduct* of her competitors, Jean started buying and eating their bagels to see what the differences were. She also started noting prices, advertising campaigns, special offers, and so forth. She was trying to determine how the bagel sellers were differentiating themselves. The prices were pretty much uniform for a lone bagel. The prices, however, went up considerably depending on the topping. The supermarket won hands down for convenience. For those who weren't true bagel connoisseurs, a supermarket or frozen bagel was just fine, and they could be purchased during the weekly shopping. Jean's competitor down the street offered big bagels, bigger than all the others, although they were airy, not dense and chewy. They also sold travel coffee mugs and offered to fill them for only 30 cents between 6:30 and 8:30 A.M. to get the commuters' business. She also noticed that many convenience stores and local breakfast and lunch restaurants were offering pretty good bagels. After poking around a bit, she discovered that they were being supplied by a relatively large local bread manufacturer located 25 miles north.

Jean realized that in terms of economies of scale, she couldn't compete with the supermarket or the bread manufacturer. She would have had to invest heavily in new equipment and more space if she were going to try to match their capacity. She would also have to hire more people and try to start supplying locally, a step she wasn't sure she wanted to take. She knew that she offered the best, most authentic New York style bagels in town and that her shop was profitable and well run. Now that she had a handle on how her competitors were trying to beat her, she needed to figure out how to beat them.

This scenario illustrates the essential points you should cover when conducting a competitive analysis. All the various models proposed looking at the similar factors:

- Potential opportunities in your market
- The ease of entering the market
- Customers' perceptions about the product. If competing products are perceived as similar, then players must compete on other dimensions such as price and service.
- Economies of scale
- Commitment to the particular market, for example, a bagel shop is more committed than a convenience store with a glass jar full of dried-out bagels

Competitive Intelligence

Another important component in competitive analysis and strategic planning for future growth is conducting ongoing competitive intelligence. Competitive intelligence is a method for discovering your competitors':

Objectives
Comparative strengths and weaknesses
Past performance
Current strategy

In the bagel shop example, the owner became aware of changes in the competitive field very slowly. Had she been methodically gathering intelligence, she would have anticipated the changes in the market rather than recognizing them after they occurred.

Competitive intelligence can be classified into three categories: defensive, in which information is gathered to avoid being caught unaware; passive, in which information is gathered only when a decision needs to be made; and offensive, in which information gathering is conducted on an ongoing basis to identify new opportunities and act upon them before the competition. Obviously, offensive intelligence is the most strategic.

It's important to recognize the difference between data, information, and intelligence. Intelligence is actionable. If you learn through a reliable source that your competitor is experimenting with cranberry bagels and that you have already come up with a good cranberry bagel yourself, then you will push the bagel to market more quickly to beat your competitor. You might even launch a small campaign advertising your new flavor just to make sure that yours is firmly in place first. Data and information are not yet in actionable form, meaning the analysis is not complete and no one yet knows how the data and information will be useful. We all have access to tremendous amounts of data and information: Intelligence is truly valuable.

Your objectives for competitive analysis should be to understand your position and advantages compared to your competitors; to understand your competitors' past, present, and future strategies; and to allow you to create a dynamic strategic plan for your own company's growth and success.

(Sources: Subhash C. Jain, *Marketing Planning & Strategy*, 3rd ed., Cincinnati, OH: South-Western Publishing Co., 1990; Douglas C. Bernhardt, "I Want It Fast, Factual, Actionable—Tailoring Competitive Intelligence to Executives' Needs," *Long Range Planning*, February 1994: 12-24; Donald F. Kuratko and Richard M. Hodgetts, *Entrepreneurship: A Contemporary Approach*, 3rd ed., Fort Worth, TX: The Dryden Press, 1995.)

Zuckerman's Competitive Analysis

There is no doubt that competition makes you stay on your toes. If you ignore the competition, it may pass you by. So you need to know about your competition, in depth. This means that you need to know the same information for your competition that you have collected about your business for your business plan. With the profiles in hand, you can make a comparison of your business and that of your competitors, and then plan your strategy accordingly.

In her book *On Your Own: A Woman's Guide To Building a Business*, Laurie B. Zuckerman recommends keeping a file on your competitors, at least the top five. You should know the following about your competition:

- Number of years in business
- Number of employees
- Dollar sales
- Unit sales
- Market share
- Financial strength
- Profitability
- President and owner of the business
- Outside advisers
- Key employees
- Target markets
- Pricing
- Advertising themes
- Promotion and public relations efforts
- Significant changes
- How competitor competes with you

Zuckerman advocates the use of a comparison sheet on which you list the competitor's price, quality, level of service, location, advertising, and other factors against your own. This can show you quite clearly where the differences lie. Then you need to decide which factors to attend to and compete with. This will be your competitive strategy.

Obtaining information on competitors can be a challenge, particularly because it is important to be ethical in your research. If you have a retail business, one way to obtain information is to shop in the competitor's store, where you can see the operation firsthand. You can observe the products and customer service and obtain a good sense of their target market and strategy.

If you are in manufacturing, purchase supplies and products where they are sold rather than having them delivered, talk with salespeople and suppliers, and obtain a good sense of the business.

Service businesses are somewhat harder to evaluate. You can talk to the competitors' clients, but be sure you are clear about why you are asking about their satisfaction. A somewhat less threatening approach for all concerned is to talk with owners of similar businesses in *other cities or towns*. They will usually not be in direct competition and will thus be more willing to share information.

The strategies that will come out of your research will be some or all of the following:

- Adjust prices if necessary.
- Cultivate your current customers.
- Keep up with technology.
- Maintain a positive image, verbally as well as physically.
- Maintain a strong, well-trained staff.
- Treat employees well.
- Create a new advertising and promotional campaign.
- Shift markets if appropriate.
- Find new outlets for your products.
- Be active in the community, either through fund-raising activities or by supporting employees' involvement.
- Use new management methods as appropriate (quality, teams, etc.)—see discussions of teams in Chapter 9.
- Consider buying a computer if you do not already have one.
- Be sure that whatever you do fits with your corporate philosophy.

(Source: Laurie B. Zuckerman, *On Your Own: A Woman's Guide to Building a Business*, Dover, NH: Upstart Publishing Company, Inc., 1990.)

twenty-four
Plan for Growth and Expansion

Some entrepreneurs don't want to grow their businesses. They like the control and autonomy of running a small concern and are satisfied with their perks. Others want growth and are prepared to commit the substantial time, energy, and capital necessary.

Deciding whether or not to grow your company takes a certain amount of self-knowledge. If you are in the lucky position of having to make a decision about whether or not to grow your company, ask yourself the following types of questions:

- What kind of lifestyle do I want/need?
- How much time do I want to spend with my family?
- Am I a high-enough-energy person who thinks and operates well under pressure or do I prefer my current stress level? Growth can be exciting, challenging, and very profitable and it is wise to try to approach with open eyes.

Lessons from *Fortune*'s 100 Fastest-Growing Companies

Fortune magazine's list of the 100 fastest-growing companies shows a wide array of entrepreneurial activity, from computer companies to health care, from food and beverage services to sports equipment manufacturers. Over several years, these "Fortune 100" firms have shown a very high annual growth rate in sales. In fact, the top 22 are growing at a rate anywhere from 100 percent to 243 percent.

Among the qualities that these entrepreneurial companies demonstrate are innovation and management talent. They are also highly attuned to their customer base. These firms can teach us lessons about how small companies can be run successfully.

For example, the top business on *Fortune*'s list is Wellfleet Communications, which produces computer networking equipment. The founder and CEO of the company, Paul Severino, had prior experience in startups, so he knew he needed to do a lot of careful research and planning before the company started. He also realized that the company could not do everything they wanted to do immediately, so they focused on one segment of the market. Within that segment, the company produced a product that customers wanted and liked.

Outback Steakhouse was founded by a person with prior experience, too. Chris Sullivan had worked at several other restaurant chains before coming up with a new slant for a food business. His Australian theme included red meat, which was contrary to the conventional wisdom that people are eating less red meat. Sullivan's restaurants are thriving. Based on their research, the restaurants serve dinners rather than lunches because lunch is not as good a money-maker. Sullivan prefers to buy land for his restaurants near where people live, rather than near where they work, thus tapping into a dinner market rather than a lunch market.

Ely Callaway had served in senior management of two companies before he launched Callaway Golf. He bought a business that made golf clubs and created a new type of golf club using new technology to meet customer needs. He realized sizable profits because he was attuned to customers' needs and wants.

Howard Schultz of the coffee bar chain Starbucks brought the concept back to the States after a trip to Italy, and the idea is catching on throughout the country. The company's philosophy is that what they sell has to be perfectly fresh. They regularly ask customers for feedback so they can be responsive to changing customer needs and preferences.

Intuit's software Quicken was the result of Scott Cook's frustration with standard financial-planning software. An experienced manager, Cook hired a college student to write a simplified program for him, and then he tested it on people who were not very familiar with computer software. Although the software took some time to catch on, Cook's persistence paid off. Quicken is now practically a household word.

So what do these stories tell us about what it takes to start and grow a company?

- Plan your business carefully, before you start it up.
- Have prior experience with start-up, or get someone on your team who has such experience. Or confer with someone who does.
- Do lots of research before you start. Know your competition. Know your customer pool. Know your potential. Know your limits.
- Select a segment of the industry to target. Do not try to do it all, all at once.
- Be sure you have a well-constructed product that will satisfy your customers.
- Have prior experience in the industry you are targeting. Either have the experience yourself, or get someone on your team who does.
- Take advantage of new technology when appropriate.
- Be sure you and your team have a high awareness of customer satisfaction.
- Try to offer a perfect product.
- Seek out customer comments.
- If appropriate, aim for simplicity of product.
- Stay aware of change or of impending changes that you haven't even anticipated. Constantly scan your environment to try and stay ahead.
- Surround yourself with experts. If you do not have the necessary expertise, be sure your team includes someone who does.

- If you are in a fast-growth industry, stay alert. Do not let others pass you by.
- Watch out for growing too fast as it can result in things being overlooked.

(Source: Andrew E. Serwer, *Fortune*, August 9, 1993, pp. 40-46.)

American Express's Three Key Assets for Business Expansion

A recent American Express study of new businesses found three keys to business growth: outside investors, education, and experience. Here is how you can use these keys in your own business.

Investors

Strong financial backing can make the difference between success and failure, growth and stagnation. In order to expand, you will need to find investors willing to help finance your expansion plans. These may include banks, angels, microlenders, or venture capitalists. (See the entries on these topics in the section on financing your business.) In applying for any of these types of funds, it is to your advantage to have a viable, ongoing operation. In all cases, you will also need to have a solid business plan that enumerates your future plans and projections. (See the section on writing a business plan.)

Education

Education goes a long way in assisting an entrepreneur or small-business owner with a successful operation. Not only do you need to educate yourself about the market you face, but also about the other players in the game (your competition).

Formal education, especially as it pertains to your particular business, can offer an added boost. Technical learning may also make the difference between a so-so operation and a successful one. Studies have shown that education can be a plus to the growing firm.

As your firm grows, you will need to know more about management techniques and financial management. If these are skills you already have, so much the better. If you lack experience or confidence in these areas and you cannot find staff with the requisite skills, investigate the offerings at local colleges and universities. Many offer evening classes that are geared for your situation. The SBA (Small Business Administration) offers seminars for small-business owners, and SCORE (Service Corps of Retired Executives) and SBDCs (Small Business Development Centers) offer business counseling.

It is also wise to learn about new skills and techniques as they arise in business. This means reading extensively to inform yourself about such management tools as team work, total quality management (TQM), time management, customer service methods, strategic alliances, and other methods to improve productivity and performance. (See related entries on these topics in this book.)

Experience and Ideas

Prior experience, particularly if directly related to your product or service, can help your business, especially over the bumpy times. You may find that there are areas in which you do not have the expertise that would help your business grow. The answer to this, of course, is either to get the expertise through further education or to hire someone who has strong skills in that area. You can arrange this on a consulting basis or as a full-time position, according to your needs.

In addition, you or members of your staff may have developed ideas about marketing, product, and so forth, from a previous job or jobs. Brainstorming at crucial moments may help you expand your frame of reference and therefore the possibilities open to you.

(Source: Beverly Wettenstein for American Express, news release October 10, 1989, American Express: New York—to promote "Profiles of Success: An American Express Study of New Business"—commissioned by American Express Small Business Services and the National Federation of Independent Business [NFIB].)

Gordon's 17 Axioms for Growing Your Business

Growing Your Market

If you want to realize growth for your product or service, consider the following:

- Be sure you have a market.
- Quality is important.
- The product or service will not sell itself.
- Customers will not necessarily call when they want to buy.
- Marketing is important.
- Write out your marketing communications plan.
- The phone is a great way to get clients.
- Referrals and cold calls both have merit.
- Prospect meetings may be useful.
- Rehearse your presentations before you make them.
- Watch out for overdoing press releases.
- Advertising works.
- You do not save money by creating your own advertising materials.
- It can pay to run an ad in the same place as your competitors.
- Avoid writing a "quick" brochure, expecting to revise it later.
- No one is an expert.
- Bigger isn't necessarily better.

(Source: Kim T. Gordon, *Growing Your Home-Based Business*, Englewood Cliffs, NJ: Prentice Hall, 1992, pp. 205-214.)

Gordon's 20 Tools for Company Growth

Home-business specialist Kim Gordon recommends the following necessities for "growing" your company:

General

business cards
stationery
mailing labels
forms, contracts, service agreements
brochures
press kits

product packaging/labeling
product instructions/safeguards

Sales

Rolodex™ cards
fold-over cards
price lists
sell/data sheets
sales meeting tools
proposal covers or binders
sales letters on letterhead

Marketing

advertising
direct mail
public relations releases on letterhead
trade show booths/materials

(Source: direct quote from Kim T. Gordon, *Growing Your Home-Based Business*, Englewood Cliffs, NJ: Prentice Hall, 1992, p. 142.)

Collins and Porras's 11 Qualities of Visionary Companies

In their book *Built to Last*, James C. Collins and Jerry I. Porras discuss the qualities found in 18 companies that have lasted over a long period of time. And not just lasted, but have been successful. Their stock performance, compared with competitors that started at the same time, has been better by 6 to 1, and better than the general market by 15 to 1.

The authors say the key is "deeply-held values and purpose, and a relentless urge for progress and change."

So what are the qualities that Collins and Porras identify for these visionary companies?

- Clear core values

- Explicit sense of purpose
- Intuitive rather than mechanical operations
- Focused behaviors
- Mechanisms for progress and change
- "Business practices which foster newness, diversity, entrepreneurship, opportunity, and freedom of action"
- Bold goal setting
- Initiation of "elitist cultures"
- Intense product development
- Heavy investment in recruiting, training, and personal development
- Careful attention to promotion and succession from within
- Built-in practices for renewal

(Sources: Terry O'Keefe, "The Alchemy of Supercompanies," *BusinessWest*, March 1995, p. 44, Review of James C. Collins and Jerry I. Porras, *Built to Last: Successful Habits of Visionary Companies*, Harper Business, 1995)

Block and MacMillan's Venturing

Venturing—encouraging entrepreneurship under the auspices of a large company—is one of the hallmarks of a successful and visionary company. In fact, within a going business venturing is essential if the firm wants to survive in the long run. While venturing usually takes place in a large company, the qualities that foster it and the techniques that go into it can be informative to any company or individual open to innovation.

Zenas Block and Ian C. MacMillan's study of venturing in their book *Corporate Venturing* provides us with clues about how to make a venture or innovative process a successful one.

Corporate venturing allows entrepreneurial activity to occur within the larger context of an organization, with the support of management. This support is one of the keys to success of a venture.

However, you cannot simply decide to create an entrepreneurial situation. The climate of the company must foster innovative activity, and people involved need to have the skills to be successful entrepreneurs.

Since entrepreneurship is risky, venturers need to know how to manage risk. They must be able to assess the risks in a given situation, prepare for them, and thus manage the risk.

An entrepreneurial venture (again, whether under the auspices of a larger company or by itself) will require different skills at different stages. For example, before start-up, business-planning skills will be paramount. After production has begun, day-to-day management of the employee team will become increasingly important. Once the day-to-day operation is stabilized, long-term planning and growth skills will be needed.

One major strategy in venturing is to develop know-how in each of the major phases of the venture: idea generation, evaluation, and selection; planning; monitoring and control; production; marketing; and distribution. These general skills can then be applied to other new products, services, and markets.

In an entrepreneurial situation, a person skilled in start-up planning may not be comfortable with the day-to-day management required as the business begins to show a profit. Or perhaps the long term does not interest the entrepreneur—it is the challenge of conceiving and giving birth to a concept that is more challenging to many. If the operation is to survive, there needs to be a succession plan so that skilled management can be provided at each stage.

It is important that any corporate venture fit with the business's strategy and objectives. If there is no support for venturing, it will be hard to accomplish the intended goals.

Since new ventures are always experimental, tracking is essential. Project-planning methods such as critical path and milestones can be used to help keep track of ventures. This will help the venturers to identify key assumptions, so they can test them. They also have to be willing to make constant adaptations.

Reasons for Failure

Studies have found that unsuccessful ventures were the result of one or more of the following:

- Imperfect market analysis
- Underestimating the competition, the riskiness of the venture, or insufficient funding

- Impatience for results
- Lack of contingency planning
- Lack of experience in technology, products, or markets.

Sound familiar? These reasons are similar to those given for why small businesses fail.

Purposes of Planning

Every venture, no matter what the size or sponsorship, should have a business plan. (Refer to Part III on Business Plans for more detailed information on creating business plans.)

Why is planning so important for a venture, even one that takes place within a corporate setting? Because it is always the case that you need to learn how to conduct a new business. And a perfect way to learn is to design your plan such that you learn what you need to learn. Further, if a new venture is planned carefully, then you will know where you are going and can staff the project appropriately. You will be able to attract the personnel who can best contribute to the implementation of the plan.

The plan should be one that allows you to determine whether the business is feasible and then evolves as you progress.

The plan should specify points along the way that can be used to measure progress and success. It should also show you when the venture is not succeeding and should, if necessary, be abandoned.

Block and MacMillan suggest keeping a detailed document that records information and events. Key players in the venture should be interviewed for their "take" on such details as origin, concept, and testing of the idea; market research; product development; the business plan; organization; assumptions about the market, environment (economy), competition, organizational support, product costs, prices, technology, break-even, economic return, government regulations, distribution. It should include input from the management team as well.

The document should give a chronological history of the venture and should end with conclusions and results, that is, what was learned from the process.

(Sources: Zenas Block and Ian C. MacMillan, *Corporate Venturing*, Boston, MA: Harvard Business School Press, 1993; R. Siegel, E. Siegel, and I. C. MacMillan, "Corporate

Venture Capitalists: Autonomy, Obstacles and Performance," *Journal of Business Venturing 3*, No. 3, Summer 1988, pp. 233-247; I. C. MacMillan, R. Siegel, and P. N. Subbanarasimha, "Criteria Used by Venture Capitalists to Evaluate New Venture Proposals," *Journal of Business Venturing*, No. 1, Winter 1985, pp. 119-128.)

Becoming a Great and Enduring Company

Once you have built an organization, you want to be sure it can sustain its performance and perhaps become a leader in the industry. Enduring organizations can become role models for others, and they can endure for generations.

Building an enduring organization is not without work. According to management consultant James C. Collins and entrepreneur William C. Lazier, "The foundation of greatness is usually laid while the company is still small and malleable enough to be handcrafted into an entity that fully embodies the values of its leaders" (*Beyond Entrepreneurship*, Englewood Cliffs, NJ; Prentice-Hall, 1992. p. vi).

Four characteristics of a great company, according to Collins and Lazier, are performance, impact, reputation, and longevity.

Companies that *perform* well, despite ups and downs, can endure. They meet their objectives on a sustained basis, and in particular, generate the cash flow needed to be self-sustaining. Their operations are highly profitable.

Great companies have an *impact* on their industry. They set standards for others to follow. They may not even be the largest company in the industry, but they may have an impact by virtue of being the most innovative.

Great companies have good *reputations*. They are well respected in the community and in the marketplace.

Longevity is the fourth mark of an enduring company. They are in the game for the long haul. Long after the original management has gone on, future generations of managers are able to continue the business successfully because of strong and competent initial leadership, meaningful corporate vision, effective strategies, innovation, and well-planned tactics.

The management of enduring businesses must be able to continue the vision, purpose, and mission of the company. They must be committed to the objectives. In short, they need to possess the characteristics of a great leader. (See the discussion of leadership in Chapter 18.)

It is also true that a great company is the composite of all its parts, and requires that all the parts function well together. Thus, the importance of teamwork, whatever that may entail within a particular company. It may not mean constituting teams per se, but having the necessary underlying attitude and willingness to do whatever will be most effective in getting the job done.

Another important function for all companies, but one that is especially well-developed in enduring ones, is strategic planning.

Strategy

The basis of strategic planning is vision. If there is no vision, then how can you plan where you are going? Strategic planning is based on internal and external assessment, thus taking advantage of the business's strengths and capabilities to create an ongoing plan, while allowing for constraints that may prevent the accomplishment of goals.

A large part of the success of a strategic plan is having people on board who will make it happen. This is not a simple accomplishment, for many strategies must be coordinated. In the product/service area, for example, the plan must consider product line, manufacturing concerns, customers, and so forth. The financial strategy, which includes cash flow, is crucial. Financial strategy also depends on product pricing, sales, and so forth.

Organizational strategy is important as well. You need to account for the people in the organization—how the organization is set up, and how it will grow and diversify, depending on the success of the product or service. Customer service is also important to strategy, and it in turn depends on the marketing of the product, sales, and so forth.

So you can see that strategies for all the component factors of a business must interact and must therefore be accounted for when you are designing a strategic plan.

Innovation

Another area where enduring businesses do well is in innovation. Success in innovation is due to the support from management that filters down through the organization, thereby encouraging people to be receptive to ideas. They are encouraged to be creative and are thus willing to experiment and to make mistakes. Employees of enduring businesses wear the shoes of the customer, so to speak. All members of the organization are vested in the success of the company and are rewarded for behavior that promotes this attitude.

Creativity

Creativity goes hand in hand with innovation. Where staff are encouraged to be creative—and innovative—there is the catalyst for an enduring company. Collins and Lazier suggest that to encourage and further creativity, management must do the following (pp. 180-185):

1. Encourage, don't nitpick.
2. Don't be judgmental.
3. Help shy people.
4. Stimulate curiosity.
5. Create necessity.
6. Allow time away.
7. Catalyze group problem solving.
8. Require fun.

Of course, creativity cannot stand alone. A great concept will fail if it is poorly carried out.

Finally, it is important to be specific about priorities, including strategic priorities. Annual planning should be concrete, with specific milestones, dates, and designated people to do what needs to be done. You need to be clear to all about what is expected. Be sure the right people with the right skills are doing the right tasks and have freedom and support for doing so. When they accomplish their tasks, they should be appreciated and rewarded. To be able to do this, you have to hire the right people in the first place and make sure they are trained correctly. They need to understand the common goals and then be willing to be evaluated to see if they are accomplishing the objectives.

(Source: James C. Collins and William C. Lazier, *Beyond Entrepreneurship*, Englewood Cliffs, NJ, Prentice Hall, 1992, pp. vi, 166, 180-85, 189, 197.)

PART VII

Funding and Financial Management

Financial management and planning are at the core of the processes you will need to complete to get your business going and to keep it going. Staying on top of finances and making successful financial decisions would seem an obvious part of running a business, but many businesses fail because of poor financial planning.

Financial management and planning are dynamic processes, whereas a financial plan is a collection of documents and is the tangible outcome of these ongoing processes. A financial plan is what you will take to the bank and show prospective investors; it includes financial statements, sales forecasts, cash flow analyses, and break-even analyses.

A good deal of planning and management depends on getting the information you need, and much of this you will already know or have access to simply from knowing your business. The tricky part of financial planning and management is that you will have to make estimates and projections and use them to make decisions. These can be nerve-wracking tasks for anyone, but especially for the inexperienced business person or for someone in an unfamiliar business. It is critical, however, that your projections and estimates are supported by well-substantiated assumptions and explanations. Knowing where to look for information and acquiring experience in your field so that you can anticipate sales cycles and expenses, will help you make more accurate estimates and projections. It will benefit you, though, to be conservative, even pessimistic, in your estimates when using them to secure financing or when forecasting cash inflows.

In addition to financial planning for your own business-planning needs, you must have good financial plans when you are going to banks or other sources for loans. But financial planning has other functions as well. For example, it is used to help support strategic planning. Deciding how you're going to grow your company depends heavily on available financial resources. If your one-year strategic plan includes introducing a new product, you'll want to make sure to plan and manage your finances so that you have the capacity and cash to launch the product. You don't want to later discover that you barely have enough cash to cover your daily operating expenses.

Financial planning also figures into asset management. You need to have the right combination and number of assets, and they must be financed through a combination of resources, not just debt. To achieve this, you need a thorough understanding of the financial aspects of your business and of your financing options.

Financial planning is also an integral part of profit planning. Achieving your short- and long-term profit goals depends upon having financial plans that are in place and functioning properly.

The most important segment of financial planning, often overlooked, is cash-flow planning. Without cash flow, the business cannot exist. A company may be successful on paper but fail because of inadequate cash flow. Cash flow has to be planned for on a monthly basis, because seasonal fluctuations affect sales and also collections. If you make a credit sale this month, even though it may be recorded as income, it is not actually cash in hand until the payment is received, which may not be until next month. The juggling of the inflow and outflow of cash makes running a small business a challenge.

Financial planning and management have become even more important as there have been new developments in financing, reporting, managing, and control. New financial instruments have been developed in recent years, making it more difficult to stay current about ways to finance businesses. Reporting has become more sophisticated, both for external and internal purposes. New laws affect external financial reporting, and internal reporting has become more complex as nonfinancial information has been more often included in the financial reporting picture.

As all businesses struggle with cost containment, they are looking for new and creative ways to create strategies for curtailing costs. Total quality management is another factor with which many firms must deal, and it, too, affects financial planning. In the manufacturing area, especially high-tech, control—the process of measuring progress toward goals specified in the business plan—has become a continuous rather than a periodic function, which means that the structure of planning must change accordingly. The auditing function has found its way from purely financial purposes into the area of management practices as well.

What does all this mean for your business? Knowledge of the financial end of the business is extremely important. If you are not informed or experienced, be sure you have team members who are. Hire an accountant whom you can trust. Take adult education courses, if available. Even if you are not going actually to do the financial end of things, you need to be informed and take an active interest.

(Source: Gordon Cummings, "Finance," *AMA Management Handbook*, John J. Hampton, ed., 1994, New York: AMACOM, American Management Association, p. 6-3; George Willis, "Finance's Increased Role in Management," *AMA Management Handbook*, John J. Hampton, ed., 1994, New York: AMACOM, American Management Association, pp. 6-5 - 6-6.)

twenty-five
Learn to Write and Read Financial Statements

For some people financial matters are a necessary evil, and the concept of having to work with numbers and mathematics evokes anxiety and fear. There is no way around the fact that owning your own business requires some basic understanding of accounting and bookkeeping functions. Purchasing items to run your business, taking out loans, hiring employees, and making sales require a certain amount of bookkeeping. If you remember to save all your receipts, invoices, bills, and statements and keep careful, detailed records of all your financial transactions such as revenues, expenses, payments, purchases, and debts, you will have the necessary data to create financial statements.

There are three main reasons for an entrepreneur or small-business owner to write financial statements. First, chances are good that at some point in your entrepreneurial career you'll want to borrow money from a lending institution and, possibly, get a company credit card. Potential lenders and creditors will want to see your financial statements to determine whether your company is a good lending risk, meaning, will you be able to pay them back. Second, potential investors will want to see if you are running your company efficiently and if they can possibly make a profit if they do decide to invest. And third, you will find financial statements are a powerful tool for your own planning and management activities. There are, of course, other reasons and other interested parties, but for the small business person, getting loans and investors and planning strategically are critical.

A theme throughout this book is that careful financial management will, in the long run, help you succeed. Keeping detailed books and writing concise, accurate financial statements will reflect well on your company. Creditors and investors will feel more secure in knowing they are dealing with a professional who understands the importance of finance.

Writing Financial Statements: The fundamentals

Assets = Liabilities + Owner's equity. This is the fundamental equation in accounting and is the central concept underlying the discipline. The asset side of the equation shows the firm's existing resources and the other side shows how those resources were financed through borrowed and/or contributed capital.

- Assets are all your company's resources that will yield future economic benefits to the company. Examples include cash, equipment, and inventory.
- Liabilities are all your company's obligations to transfer either cash or services to another person or organization at a future time. Examples include short-term loans and orders for goods or services for which you've already received payment.
- Owners' equity is the money given to your company by outside investors who, as a result, have some ownership of the company.

What are financial statements?

The three key financial statements are the balance sheet, income statement, and the statement of cash flows. Typically, a business will produce financial statements one time per year at the end of their fiscal year. For simplicity, it works best if the fiscal year coincides with the calendar year so when we talk about a period of time, we're referring to a fiscal year ending December 31.

The balance sheet. As you can see from Figure 25-1, the balance sheet has two columns or sides, the asset side and the liability and owners' equity side. The totals of each column must be equal. This will always be true. If your balance sheet doesn't balance then you need to recheck your figures.

Figure 25-1

Balance Sheet
Paul's Pizza Parlors Inc.
July 13, 1996

Assets		*Liabilities and Owner's Equity*	
Current:		Current Liabilities:	
Cash	18,765	Salaries	15,665
Inventories	26,006	Bills	8,952
	44,771		24,617
Fixed:		Long-term Liabilities:	
Buildings	425,000	Loans	401,729
Equipment	95,200		
Vehicles	66,722		
	586,922		
Total:	$631,693	Total Liabilities:	$426,346
		Owner's Equity	
		(or Net Worth):	
			$205,347

Premise: Assets = Liabilities + Owner's Equity

Assets are listed by type and can be divided into three categories: current, fixed, and intangible. Liabilities are divided into two categories: current and long-term. Owners' equity is paid-in capital or the amount of money your friends and family gave you to start your business.

The balance sheet is a snapshot of your company's assets and liabilities; it reflects a moment in time. In reality, there is a constant inflow and outflow of resources but the balance sheet gives potential lenders and investors an idea of your company's wealth. If your assets exceed your liabilities, you may be able to borrow against them to fund your acquisition of equipment needed to grow the business, for example.

The income statement.   The income statement, Figure 25-2, reflects the revenues of the period and the expenses associated with earning those revenues. In other words, the income statement shows the results of your company's operations over time. Net income—the bottom line of the income statement—is revenues minus expenses. The link between the balance sheet and the income statement is that net income reflects the amount by which your net assets have changed. Net assets are assets minus liabilities, which according to the fundamental equation leaves owners' equity. So the income statement shows the amount by which owners' equity (also called working capital) changes due to the day-to-day operations of the company.

Figure 25-2

Income Statement
Paul's Pizza Parlors Inc.
June 13-July 13, 1996

Revenues:	
Retail Sales, Store #1	75,063
Retail Sales Store #2	82,080
Catering	9,277
Wholesale Sales	92,859
Total Revenues	259,279
Expenses:	
Materials and Supplies	70,376
Payroll	106,959
Utilities	8,924
Debt Repayment	10,555
Repairs	25,001
Cleaning	3,210
Total Expenses	225,025
Income (or "Net Profit")	$34,254

Premise: Revenues – Expenses + Gains – Losses = Income

The statement of cash flows. The statement of cash flows, Figure 25-3, is a summary of all the transactions that have increased and decreased your cash account over a period of time. These transactions result from business activities that are, on the statement, divided into three groups: operating activities, investing activities, and financing activities, but there was no investing or financing activities in the example illustrated in figure 25-3. The statement of cash flows reflects your company's liquidity (available cash) and shows a potential lender or investor how you used your money over time. Examples of money use include repaying a loan (eliminating a liability), purchasing new equipment (acquiring a new asset), and borrowing funds (acquiring a new liability, perhaps to pay for your new asset). Note that if you buy new equipment, the asset side of your balance sheet will increase and, if you borrowed the money to pay for the equipment, the liability side will increase by the same amount. If you used cash to buy the equipment, the asset side of your balance sheet will both increase and decrease by the same amount because cash is considered an asset. This way, the two sides remain in balance.

Figure 25-3

Statement of Cash Flows
Paul's Pizza Parlors Inc.
June 3–July 13, 1996

Cash Flows from operating activities:		
Net Income		34,254
Adjustments to determine cash provided by operations		
— Prepaid expenses increase	(2,625)	
— Increase in Accounts Payable	(6,105)	
— Decrease in Accounts Receivable	5,627	
— Decrease in Deferred Income Taxes	(4,700)	
Total Adjustments	(26,451)	
		7,803
Net increase in cash		7,803
Beginning cash balance		10,962
Ending cash balance		18,765

Premise: Cash inflows – cash outflows = change in cash
Note: ( ) indicates subtraction.

Laying the groundwork for preparing your financial statements.   This section will provide you with the basic knowledge and tools for keeping your books and preparing financial statements. If you have no background knowledge of bookkeeping or general accounting and you intend to do all your own work, then you may want to read sections of an introductory financial accounting text or take an adult education class. A class on introduction to financial accounting or bookkeeping practices for small business owners, for example, will ground you in the basics. However, the information here will get you started. Even if you hire someone to do your books, it certainly is valuable for you to have some understanding of this side of your business.

Keeping accounts and making journal entries.   It's likely that most of you will use some accounting software for your company bookkeeping. We recommend it if you are comfortable with personal computers, since the software will make it easier to follow correct accounting procedures. In this section, though, we'll go over the how-to's of bookkeeping as though you were keeping old-fashioned ledgers, and you can apply the underlying principles to your electronic version.

Step 1: You need to buy two accounting ledgers into one of which you will record all your day-to-day transactions. For example, if you buy furniture for your shop, record the price of the furniture on the asset or left side of the ledger page. Record the expense of the furniture on the liability or right side of the page. At any time you should be able to total the asset side and the liability side and have them balance. If they don't, you know you've made an error. This is both the pleasure and the pain of bookkeeping. There is always one right answer but getting there requires relentless attention to detail and a devotion to record keeping.

Step 2: The ledger will provide you with the big picture but it won't tell you the balance of each individual account. For example, you can't glance at your ledger and know the balance of your accounts receivable (how much customers owe you). Using the second ledger you bought (and dutifully recorded the purchase of), you will set up, on separate pages, "T-accounts." A "T-account" shows credits and debits in separate columns. Each account should represent a common type of transaction for your business. All businesses have cash, accounts payable, and accounts receivable T-accounts. You might also have accounts for tools and lumber if you own a carpentry business; cleaning solutions if you provide cleaning services; or ledgers and accounting paper if you run a bookkeeping service. Before you begin recording transactions in your separate T-accounts, you first have to determine whether they are asset or liability accounts. Figure 25-4 shows a T-account used for preparing the statement of Cash Flows.

Figure 25-4

Simplified T-account Worksheet for Preparing Statement of Cash Flows

Increases in Cash		Decreases in Cash	
Operating Activities:			
Net income	_____	Increase in prepaid expenses	_____
Depreciation	_____	Decrease in accrued expenses	_____
Increase in accounts payable	_____	Increase in merchandise inventories	_____
Decrease in accounts receivable	_____	Decrease in deferred income taxes	_____
Other	_____	Other	_____
Net cash flow from operating activities	════════		
Investing Activities:			
Sale of securities	_____	Purchase of securities	_____
Sale of property	_____	Purchase of property	_____
Financing Activities:			
Equity issued?	_____	Equity repurchased?	_____
Debt issued?	_____	Debt redemption?	_____
	_____	Dividends paid?	_____
		Decrease in cash and equivalents	════════

How to determine if a company resource is an asset or a liability. Any resource that can be expected to yield cash flows in the future—money that was contributed, equipment, supplies and inventory purchased, and debt incurred for the business—should be included in your assessment of resources. For example, if you provide house cleaning services and you purchased a large quantity of cleaning solutions on sale, this counts as inventory and is considered an asset. You will use these solutions later in your main service to generate revenue. On a blank piece of paper, make a list of all your company resources. If you're not sure, write it down anyway. Next, use the following characteristics to identify and classify everything on your list as an asset or liability. Owner's equity is any capital you received from investors to help start your company. Once you've classified the items, list them under the appropriate heading below.

Assets	Liabilities
Current:	
Noncurrent:	
	Owner's Equity

Characteristics of assets and liabilities *Liquidity or quick cash-generating potential:* Can the asset be sold or transformed into cash within a year? If so, it is a current asset. Can the liability be satisfied within the same time frame? For example, can you within a year pay off the loan you took out to buy vacuum cleaners? If so, these are current assets and liabilities (note that you increased a liability account—the loan—to increase an asset account—the vacuum cleaners). Noncurrent assets and liabilities are harder to transform into cash and are, therefore, less liquid.

Physical form: Is the asset tangible or intangible? In other words, is it a vacuum cleaner or company van or is it a copyright or patent? Tangible assets have a physical form whereas intangible assets are typically characterized by legal rights.

Some examples of current and noncurrent assets and liabilities

Current assets

- Cash, which includes savings and payments received by check or bank transfer

- Stocks, bonds, treasury bills, and other short-term investments
- Accounts receivable, the money you can expect to collect from customers within the current operating cycle. Firms typically deduct a percentage of accounts receivable that they know, from past experience, to be uncollectible so the listed value of this asset is less that percentage.
- Inventories, both items available for sale and raw materials used in production. Items for sale would be finished pieces of pottery for a potter. Raw material inventory would include unused clay and glazes.

Noncurrent or fixed assets

- Property, plant, and equipment including land, buildings, manufacturing facilities, and machinery
- Investments and other assets include amounts you are owed but won't receive for more than a year and amounts you invest in other companies. For example, your 10 percent ownership of your sister-in-law's ice-cream business can be classified as an "other asset."

Current liabilities

- Wages and salaries owed to employees
- Payments owed to suppliers
- Taxes to the government
- Short-term loans and interest payments owed to lenders

Noncurrent liabilities

- Services or products owed a customer for which they have paid but you haven't yet delivered
- Long-terms loans

How to record transactions in your T-accounts.   Accounting rules can seem arbitrary and annoying to anyone not devoted to the discipline. There is one set of rules that seems particularly arbitrary but that must be followed to create successful and accurate financial statements. Here they are:

- An *increase* in an *asset* account is recorded on the *left* side of the T-account; a *decrease* in an *asset* account is recorded on the *right* side.
- An *increase* in a *liability* account is recorded on the *right* side of the T-account; a *decrease* in a *liability* account is recorded on the *left* side.

As you can see, the convention is directly related to the accounting equation:

assets = liabilities + owners' equity

However, a rule of thumb is to not think too hard about the why's of accounting but to follow the rules so that things balance out in the end.

Each transaction will affect more than one T-account. For example, if you buy new vacuum cleaners you will record the decrease in cash on the right side of your cash account (asset) and an increase in equipment on the left side of your equipment account (asset). Or, if you charge the vacuum cleaners on your company Visa, you will increase your accounts payable account (liability) on the right side rather than decreasing your cash account. When you pay your Visa bill, you will decrease your cash account by entering the transaction on the right side of the T-account and you will decrease your accounts payable account by recording the transaction on the left side.

Closing your T-accounts and getting a balance.   Toward the end of your fiscal period or calendar year, you'll be ready to total all your asset, liability, and—if you have them—owners' equity accounts and see if they balance. You can, of course, take a trial balance any time during the year to catch mistakes you may have made along the way. To close your T-accounts, total both sides of each account and then subtract the decrease side form the increase side. For example, for your asset cash account, you'll subtract the right side total from your left side total to get a total for the account. For your accounts payable liability account you'll subtract the left side total from the right side total for a grand total on that account. Next, add the grand totals of all your asset accounts and write down that figure. Add the grand totals of all your liability accounts (including owners' equity accounts if you have them) and compare the two figures. They should be exactly the same. If not, unfortunately you'll have to get your original source documents and go back over your account entries to find your error(s).

Preparing your income statement. Getting the information for your income statement is simply a matter of extracting all your revenue and expense transactions from your individual T-accounts. For example, list all the revenue you made from sales and other sources of income such as rent if you rent out a floor of your building to another business. Then list your expenses such as the cost of goods sold, wages and salary, utilities, interest expense, and depreciation expense on your long-term tangible assets such as buildings, trucks, and any heavy equipment. The difference between your revenues and your expenses is your net income.

Preparing your balance sheet. It may come as a surprise that actually preparing your financial statements is so straightforward. You've done the hardest part already by diligently keeping your records. To prepare your balance sheet, take the separate totals from your T-accounts, making sure to label each total. Organize the account titles and totals into their appropriate classifications: current assets, noncurrent assets, current liabilities, noncurrent liabilities, and owners' equity. Your total assets and total liabilities/owners' equity should, as you already know, balance.

Preparing your statement of cash flows. The statement of cash flows summarizes and classifies each of the entries you made to your cash T-account. If all your cash transactions were from operating activities then the job is made even easier. List all the increases and decreases in cash and a brief explanation of each transaction. If you had transactions stemming from investing or financing activities, then list them under the appropriate heading. Your net increase in cash is the total increase in cash minus the total decrease in cash.

Reading Financial Statements As a small-business owner, you are likely aware of how your company is operating since you are the one making all the decisions and approving all transactions. However, understanding some basic financial analysis techniques will enable you to better understand how potential lenders and investors measure the financial health of your company. When you are talking to your bankers, it will be useful to know how they are evaluating you. In addition, if you are yourself an investor, knowing how to analyze other companys' statements can help you make more profitable choices.

The Basics of Financial Analysis

Trend Analysis

One of the keys to financial analysis is comparison. Numbers by themselves don't tell you much, but comparing one period's numbers to other periods' numbers tells you how the company has performed over time and allows you to spot changes. This targets areas for further, more in-depth analysis. Also, trend analysis provides data that you can then compare with other companies in the same industry or with the economy as a whole. Typically, large companies provide data for trend analysis in their annual reports. Their balance sheets and income statements may show three to five years of data and graphs of some other key data such as earnings per share, revenues, and income.

Ratio analysis

In ratio analysis, two items from the same period's financial statements are compared in the form of percentages or ratios. The ratios can then be compared to the same ratios from other periods or to those of competitors.

An analyst looking at your financial statements is likely to be most concerned with profitability and liquidity ratios. Profitability ratios will give the analyst an idea of how well you are operating your company on a daily basis. Liquidity ratios will help a potential lender or creditor determine your ability to pay your bills—including short-term loan payments, interest payments, and credit card bills—when they come due.

Two other types of ratios that might be important for analyzing a small business are activity ratios— how well a company is managing its assets, such as inventory—and debt ratios, which are measures to determine a company's ability to repay long-term debts.

Profitability ratios.   For the small-business person and entrepreneur, the most relevant profitability ratio is return on sales. There are others such as return on investment and earnings per share, but these require capital investments and issuance of common stock.

Return on sales is: Income before taxes divided by net sales = x percent. It tells an analyst how much your business is making per unit of sales before taxes. Income before taxes is taken directly from your income statement.

Interpretation: If, for example, you operate an ice-cream stand and your income before taxes is $20,000 and your net sales is $230,000, your return on sales ratio is $20,000 / $230,000 = 8.69 percent. This means that nearly 8.7 cents of every dollar earned is profit. When this percentage is compared to the return on sales from other ice-cream stands, it give the analyst a good idea of how efficiently or inefficiently you're running your business. As an ice-cream stand owner, you can be confident that 8.69 percent is a very healthy return on sales and that most in your field make only 2.0 to 3.5 percent.

Liquidity ratios.   The first thing a potential lender or creditor might look at is your working capital, which is simply your current assets minus your current liabilities. This dollar figure will give the analyst a rough idea of the cash you have available after you've paid off all your current debts. However, this dollar amount can be misleading because it might include the value of some slow-moving inventory that can't be readily converted into cash.

There are two ratios that give the analyst a measure of short-term liquidity, and they are the current ratio and the quick ratio.

The current ratio is: Current assets divided by current liabilities = X percent. These numbers can be taken directly from your balance sheet.

Interpretation: Let's look at the ice-cream stand again. If your current assets are $43,000 and your current liabilities are $26,500, then your current ratio is $43,000 / $26, 500 = 1.62 percent. This means that you have $1.62 of current assets to meet every dollar of short-term debts. Again, an analyst would compare this ratio to that of similar ice-cream stands. However, as a rule of thumb a current ratio of at least 2.0 is considered a safe bet for a short-term loan. A ratio of 1.5 or below would stretch a company too far and they might not have a cent left over.

The quick ratio is: Current assets minus inventories divided by current liabilities = X percent. This is a more conservative measure because it leaves out of the equation inventories that, as we have mentioned above, may not be easily converted into cash. Again, these numbers can be taken directly from your balance statement.

Interpretation: Your ice-cream stand has $12,000 in cash, $10,000 in accounts receivable, and $18,000 in current liabilities. Your quick ratio is

$12,000 + $10,000 / $18,000 = 1.22 percent. Generally, a quick ratio of 1 percent is considered reasonable. Even if the business needed cash and inventory were moving slowly, there would still be $1.22 in current assets to meet every dollar of current liabilities.

Activity ratios. One of the most commonly used activity ratios is the inventory turnover ratio. It is used mainly by potential investors to tell them how quickly inventory is being turned into sales. The general rule here is the quicker the turnover, the better.

The inventory turnover ratio is: cost of goods sold divided by the value of inventory at the beginning of the period plus the value of inventory at the end of the period. The average of the period's inventory is taken by dividing the two values in the denominator by two.

Interpretation: Still using our ice-cream stand example, the cost of goods sold was $47,700. The beginning inventory was $3,000 and ending inventory, $3,200. So, $47,700 / $3,000 + $3,200 / 2 is 10.37 percent. This means that the average inventory is turned over into sales approximately once every 35 days (365 divided by 10.37). This information, combined with a ratio for how quickly accounts receivable turns into cash, allows analysts to judge your company's liquidity and your managerial efficiency. Ideal inventory turnover ratios vary depending on the business. For example, a jewelry store may turn over its inventory only two or three times per year.

Debt ratios. The debt-to-total-assets ratio is a measure of a company's ability to shoulder long-term debt. A general rule is that total debt shouldn't exceed 50 percent of the value of total assets.

The debt-to-total-assets ratio is: total liabilities divided by total assets = X percent. You can take these numbers directly from your balance sheet.

Interpretation: Say you are toying with the idea of opening a second ice-cream stand in a nearby town. You've seen an ideal location and are interested in purchasing the building. Before you even approach the bankers, you want to get a more accurate sense of your ability to shoulder the debt. Your debt-to-total-assets ratio is your total liabilities for the period, $38,000, divided by your total assets for the period, $100,000 = 38 percent. This means that for every dollar of assets, your ice-cream company is only 38 cents in debt, which puts you in very good shape, well below the 50 percent guideline.

(Sources: Jerry M. Rosenberg, *Dictionary of Business & Management*, New York: John Wiley & Sons, Inc., 1993; Michael H. Granof and Philip W. Bell, *Financial Accounting Principles and Issues*, 4th ed., Englewood Cliffs, NJ: Prentice Hall, 1991; David J. Rachman et al. *Business Today*, 7th ed., New York: McGraw-Hill, Inc., 1993; Erich A. Helfert, *Techniques of Financial Analysis*, 8th ed., IL: Dow Jones-Irwin, 1994; Leopold A. Bernstein, *Analysis of Financial Statements* rev. ed., IL: Dow Jones-Irwin, 1984; Morton Backer, Pieter T. Elgers, and Richard J. Asebrook, *Financial Accounting Concepts and Practices*, New York: Harcourt Brace Jovanovich, Inc., 1988.)

Finance Terms to Learn Now

To write or read financial statements, you need to master the basic finance and accounting vocabularies. The following terms are essential, so have a quick glance at them. For additional definitions, see the glossary at the back of this book.

Balance sheet - an itemized statement listing total assets and total liabilities of a business to provide information about its net wealth at a specific point in time.

Income statement - reflects revenues, expenses, net gains, and net losses from operations over a period of time.

Statement of cash flows - reflects changes in a firm's liquidity by providing information on cash inflows and outflows from operating, investing, and financing activities.

Liabilities - your company's obligations to transfer either cash or services to another person or organization at a future time. Examples include short-term loans and orders for goods or services for which you've already received payment.

Owners' equity - the financial interest of investors in a business; owners' equity = assets minus liabilities.

Assets - all your company's resources that will yield future economic benefits to the company.

Current assets - also called floating or liquid assets—cash and other items such as short-term investments that can be turned back into cash within one year.

Fixed assets - also called illiquid assets or property, plant, and equipment—are long-term investments required for the normal conduct of a business and that normally are not converted into cash during the period after they were declared fixed.

Intangible assets - have no substance or physical body but are valuable to the owner. Examples are patents, copyrights, and trademarks. Goodwill is an intangible asset that is essentially the value of a company's reputation. The value can be defined as the difference between the price paid for the company and the stated value of its assets.

Depreciation - the process of spreading the expense of a fixed asset over its anticipated useful life. For example, if you buy a new delivery truck for your business and estimate that its useful life is five years, you can spread the expense over five years rather than account for it all in one period.

Liquidity - the ease and speed with which current assets can be converted into cash.

Cost of goods sold - the cost to purchase or produce the goods your company sells, listed as an expense on the income statement.

Fiscal year - an accounting period for which business activities are reported.

Revenues - inflows of cash and/or the settlement of liabilities during a period as a result of the company's main operations.

Expenses - outflows of cash or other assets and/or increases in liabilities during a period as a result of the company's main operations.

Gross - total amount before any deductions.

Net - that which remains after any deductions, such as taxes, from the gross amount.

Earning per share - net income less preferred stock dividends divided by the average number of common stock shares outstanding during a period.

Return on investment - the amount earned in direct proportion to the amount invested.

twenty-six
Budget for Growth

Budgets require that a planner identify key business activities and functions that are sources of revenues or expenses. They are an effective planning tool as they allow planners to set aside resources for future activities, plan for expenditures, and estimate profits. In addition, budgets provide a standard against which actual revenues and expenditures can be measured and so serve as an auditing tool.

Jae K. Shim, Joel G. Siegel, and Abraham J. Simon list, in their book *The Vest-Pocket MBA,* the steps you need to follow for developing a financial plan in general and for budgeting. Use this list as a guide for your own planning, referring to the appropriate discussions in this section.

1. Establish goals
2. Develop strategies
3. Formulate plans of action
4. Evaluate the market
5. Look at economic and political conditions
6. Analyze competition

7. Identify the life cycle of the product
8. Appraise the company's financial strength
9. Take corrective action

(Source: Jae K. Shim, Joel G. Siegel, and Abraham J. Simon, *The Vest-Pocket MBA*, Englewood Cliffs, NJ: Prentice Hall, 1986, p. 75.)

One of the first things you'll want to do when starting up a business is to get capital. Most likely, you'll apply for some loans. Whether applying for loans at your local S&L or from the SBA, you'll need a financial plan, and the following will get you started.

SBA's Borrower Responsibilities

In its brochure on business loans, the U.S. Small Business Administration (SBA) includes a list of the requirements for those businesses applying for loans. This list of five essential parts of a loan application may help you organize your financial material, even if you are not applying for a loan. The basic data will be needed for any financial transaction and are important if only for your own records and planning.

1. Prepare a current business balance sheet. List all your assets, liabilities, and net worth. Start-ups should prepare an *estimated* balance sheet as of the day the business starts. Be sure to list the amount that you will invest in the business. (See chapter 25 for a detailed explanation of how to prepare a balance sheet.)

2. Prepare profit and loss statements (P&Ls). P&Ls should cover the current period and the three most recent fiscal years. Start-ups should project earnings and expenses for at least the first year. Be sure to include monthly cash-flow projections.

3. Prepare a current personal financial statement. You will need a financial statement for each of the following: the owner or each partner and each stockholder with 20 percent or more of corporate stock in the business, as applicable.

4. List collateral to be offered. Tell how you will secure the loan. Estimate the market value of each item and any existing lien balances (the portion of the collateral owned by someone else).

5. State the amount of the loan. You need to specify how much you are requesting and for what purposes it will be used.

For further information, you can find the number for the SBA in the U.S. Government section of the telephone directory, or call the Small Business Answer Desk at 1-800-8-ASK-SBA, or write to the U.S. Small Business Administration at 409 Third Street, S.W., Washington, DC 20416. (There is more on the SBA in the Resources section.)

(Source: "Business Loans & the SBA," U.S. Small Business Administration pamphlet, 9/92.)

Doing the Numbers

To come up with a solid financial plan for your business, you will need to spend some time thinking about your financial objectives. Things to consider include what kind of living you expect to make, how many employees you'll want to hire, and whether you want to grow the business or keep it small. Your objective statement should include the profit you need to gain from the business and from this, the capital you will need to meet your objective.

Calculate your start-up, one-time capital needs, which will include such items as:

- Fixtures, equipment
- Decorating, remodeling
- Installation costs
- Starting inventory
- Utility deposits
- Legal and other fees
- Promotion for opening the business
- Cash

In addition to starting expenses, you will need to calculate monthly expenses, including

- Salaries
- Rent

- Advertising
- Supplies
- Utilities
- Accounting
- Insurance
- Loan repayment (principal and interest)
- Taxes, licensing fees

In each case, be sure to add a line for any additional miscellaneous items that may perhaps be unique to your business—anything that increases your expenses. When you are calculating the totals, you may also want to include a "cushion" by adding a percentage to the expenses. Remember that expenses are usually underestimated and revenues are usually overestimated.

From this expense information, combined with your projected revenues, you should be able to construct an expected income statement and balance sheet for your business.

You will also want to assemble a monthly projection of cash flow that reflects the seasonality of sales. Accounts receivable and inventory will also be affected by the changing business climate. It is important to understand the cycles and dollar amounts involved so you can successfully plan for the ups and downs. One factor that will affect your projections is rapid growth of sales, which may place a burden on your business's cash flow. Cash will be needed for capital investment in such items as equipment, machinery, inventory, raw materials, and supplies. Once your business is underway, it will be easier to obtain short-term borrowing to cover periods when cash is tight. But when you are at start-up, it is more difficult to find outside financing, and cash-flow management is therefore crucial.

Some of the forms you will want to create for budgeting include a balance sheet, forecasted monthly sales, cash-flow analysis, monthly income statement, yearly income statement, and break-even analysis. For examples, see the books listed in the Resources section.

(Source: Jerry W. Moorman and James W. Halloran, *Entrepreneurship*, Cincinnati, OH: South-Western Publishing Co., 1993, pp. 132-149, 162, 165, 174; Arthur H. Kuriloff, John M. Hemphill, Jr., and Douglas Cloud, *Starting and Managing the Small Business*, New York: McGraw-Hill, Inc., 1993, pp. 374, 623-627; Justin G. Longenecker, Carlos W. Moore, and J. William Petty, *Small Business Management*, Cincinnati, OH: South-Western Publishing Co., 1994, pp. 542, 557-558.)

twenty-seven
Find Sources of Financing

There are a number of different reasons you will need to find financing for your business: The first is for the start-up operation, the next is for continuing operations, which include a variety of purposes. Depending on your business's rate of growth, you may need, at some time, to finance growth of the business, and you will surely need, at some point, to replace fixed assets.

In exploring the various sources of financing, you need to consider the *form* of the financing; the *extent*, that is, whether it is sufficient for the need; its *availability* and accessibility; and the *cost* of the particular type of financing.

Creative Financing for Small Businesses

Whether you are just beginning or your business is already underway, there will be times when you need to stretch your cash without going too deeply into debt to finance your operations. Before you go out and try to borrow money, consider using some of the following techniques to extend your financial resources.

1. Credit from suppliers. Once you establish a reputation for your business by consistently paying suppliers/vendors on time, you may be able to get them to extend your credit terms. For example, if you have been paying net 30 consistently, you may be able to get them to extend credit to 45 or 60 days. If you are a large-volume purchaser, you may have an advantage, as they will want to keep your business. Note that small vendors or vendors with small customer bases may not be able to extend your credit very far out in time.

2. Customers. On the customer side, consider requiring a prepayment for part of an order, or requiring a deposit before delivery of the item or service. If you already require a deposit of all customers, try setting it somewhat higher. For unfamiliar customers, request cash on delivery.

When setting up new accounts, screen them carefully. Get credit references. Set credit limits cautiously. Watch out for customers who are in financially unstable industries.

3. Accounts receivable. It is very important to manage accounts receivable, since they are the mainstay of any business. There are a number of areas where you can tighten up receivables, including credit, billing, aging, discounts, and collateral. You can protect yourself through the use of insurance and can use alternate collection methods such as factoring or collection agencies.

First, as we have said, be sure you take on customers with good credit ratings. Check references carefully to screen out "deadbeats."

Be sure you send out bills in a timely manner. Bill large sales immediately. Use cycle billing for uniformity. Mail customer statements within one day of the end of the billing period.

Track the bills you send out to be sure you receive timely payment. If you do not receive timely payments, follow up with the customer to find out when the bill will be paid. Organize your receivables by age to see where you have overdue balances. Compare your receivables to industry norms and to your records of past performance by these accounts. Revise credit limits as necessary to protect yourself from large overdue balances. Require collateral if you think you may have a problem with collections. By doing so you may lose some business but if it is business of uncertain value, then the loss may save you money in the long run.

To stimulate sales, offer delayed payment terms to good accounts that pay on time. To encourage collections, consider offering a discount to accounts that pay within 10 or 15 days of billing.

For the difficult-to-collect accounts, you can factor accounts receivable or use a collection agency. In factoring, another firm takes over your accounts receivable to collect for you, and they take a percentage of what they collect. Or, they may buy your receivables from you and take whatever they can collect. If you do not have the staff or the time to do your own collections, this may be a good route. In either case, these should be a last resort, as they can be an expensive way to gain credit.

One precaution you can take is to buy credit insurance if you think you are going to sustain losses from uncollectible debt ("bad debt").

4. Cash flow. Cash flow is the stream of cash into and out of your business. The objective is to have more cash flowing in, less flowing out, so your goal, basically, is to accelerate cash receipts, and to delay payouts.

Ways to accelerate cash receipts. In the section on Accounts Receivable, we mention cash discounts and billing methods to increase receipts. Other ways include:

- Use a lockbox.
- Transfer funds as necessary to maintain balances.
- Collect accounts personally. It is harder to refuse a person who is standing in front of you than it is to say no to someone on the telephone.
- Ask for cash on delivery.
- Deposit checks promptly.
- Accept postdated customer checks. Even though you cannot immediately deposit them, when they do become current, you can deposit them immediately.

Ways to Delay Cash Payments. Centralize your payables, and be sure you pay them only on the due date. (Or make partial payments.)

Determine how long checks take to clear and write your checks as close as possible to the time they are due, based on the clearing time.

If you can use a computer to transfer funds, you may be able to do so at the last minute because of the immediacy of electronic transfer.

Write a check on a distant bank to slow down the collection time.
Mail your checks from small, out-of-the-way post offices.

5. Inexpensive marketing. There are a number of things you can do to save money in the marketing area. First, you can do your own research. (Refer to the Resources section for suggestions of places to look when you are doing research.)

If there are schools in your area, look for students in a marketing class who might want to do research for you for a lower rate or for free, in return for learning about your business. *Before* you start someone on such a project, be sure you have a good idea of what you want and where such assistants should look for what you need. Be specific about what outcomes you want and expect.

Consumers love to receive samples, so giving potential customers a "taste" of your product is a good way to advertise. Another variation of this approach is to hand out coupons good for one free sample in your store or business.

Instead of a scattershot approach to advertising, it is best, when your budget is limited, to have one good ad and place it in one or two effective places. See how it goes—what the response rate is—then try another locale if appropriate. A good way to test an ad is to offer a discount to anyone bringing an ad into your business. This provides you with a concrete accounting of how well you reached your intended audience. Be sure to carefully track your results. One idea is to code each ad you place so when the ads are redeemed you can assess the relative success of locations.

6. Keep employment costs down. One way to keep down your costs on the employment side is to pay salespeople on a commission basis. (We discuss this in another section, as well as alternative staffing methods, such as using part-time workers, using temporaries, leasing, and so forth.)

Another approach is to use interns or students who are willing to work in exchange for the experience.

7. Alternatives to new equipment. For the very small office, two file drawers with a door across them can suffice for a desk until you have the income to support a larger purchase. To save money, you can buy used office equipment, furniture, and supplies. In used office furniture stores you can often find very serviceable equipment at a much more reasonable cost than it would be for the same items new. Such suppliers often buy whole lots of furniture from businesses that are replacing all their office equipment, so you may even be able to find items that match.

Leasing. As for equipment such as copiers, faxes, and other office tools that are "nice to have" but increasingly "necessary to have," investigate leasing programs offered by major suppliers. Leasing equipment with an option to buy allows you to temporarily avoid the major expenditure that you might have to make for large equipment or other major purchases. You do pay for this privilege in the long run; however, many firms have attractive packages created especially for small firms. You might also want to explore the option of renting or leasing your office furniture so that you save on that initial expenditure as well.

Another alternative is to look in the newspaper or want-ads for sales of used equipment. You may find a small office that is closing and wants to sell off the equipment.

All these possibilities can help keep initial costs down and allow you to function until such time that you have a budget that allows you to invest in new equipment and furniture.

8. Establishing alliances. Networking is an important activity throughout all the business processes. As you continue to network, you'll discover many economic, social, and professional benefits. We discuss networking to make professional contacts in Chapter 4.

In the case of creative financing, networking can help in making contacts with others who purchase similar materials. If you can put together a purchasing group, you can realize better prices in one of several ways. For one, you may be able to get a lower price based on the collective volume that the alliance represents. You may also be able as a group to bargain for discounts. The suppliers would likely welcome the assured volume that an alliance provides and may be willing to give you purchasing breaks.

9. Financing with loans. Financing is dealt with separately in several sections of this book. One suggestion here, however, is to be sure you have someone you can call on to co-sign a loan such as a member of your family or a friend.

Remember, too, that if you have valuable inventory, you may be able to use it as collateral for a loan. Or, you may be able to use your accounts receivable as collateral to obtain a loan, providing that your receivables are good accounts, ones that you expect to collect in a reasonable amount of time.

Venture capital. Venture capital financing is discussed in Chapter 29. Bear in mind that obtaining venture capital is difficult if yours is a fairly new company. Even if you can convince a potential investor that your venture is low risk, venture capital loans are slow to obtain (some may take six months to complete), and the process should be supervised by a lawyer.

10. Family. Although family relations can be difficult at times, family members can also help in a pinch. Small businesses frequently use family members as workers because they can be counted on (especially if they have a stake in the business) to stick with it and to put in long hours.

Other suggestions for creating financing:

- Break the deal into smaller parts. You may be able to financially handle one part of a deal now, another part at a later date.

- Set up a new company to finance a project. You may want to create a separate entity that will handle the financing of smaller projects in the existing company.

- Create a limited partnership. See the section on types of organizations. Partners can bring financial backing to a business, but they bring expectations as well. Research this option thoroughly before you take the plunge.

(Sources: Deaver Brown, *The Entrepreneur's Guide*, New York: MacMillan Publishing Co., Inc., 1980, pp. 116-124; Richard M. Turitz, Esq, sup. ed., *The Prentice Hall Small Business Survival Guide*, Englewood Cliffs, NJ: Prentice Hall, 1993, pp. 398-400; *Step Ahead*, "How Small Companies Bootstrap to Success," December 1994, Nynex, publ. by *Inc.* magazine, Boston, MA, pp. 1, 3; Jae K. Shim, Joel G. Siegel, and Abraham J. Simon, *The Vest-Pocket MBA*, Englewood Cliffs, NJ: Prentice Hall, 1986, p. 193.)

Glink's Sources of Financing for Women

According to Ilyce R. Glink, author and authority on financing for women with small businesses, there are a number of different sources to try when you are looking for financing for your business. For starters, contact the federal Small Business Administration (which offers many different services to the small-business owner). Other sources besides family and friends include microlenders, banks, angel networks, and venture capitalists. Each discussed in some detail below.

Small Business Administration (800-827-5722)

The SBA has taken steps to make it easier for businesses to obtain loans under $50,000. For one thing, the application has been reduced from 50 pages to 1. They have also instituted a "microloan" pilot program for business owners applying for loans of $25,000 or less.

The SBA also licenses private small-business investment companies (SBICs) and specialized small-business investment companies (SSBICs). The focus of the SSBICs is primarily on socially and economically disadvantaged business owners.

(See the Resources section for more on the SBA.)

Microlenders

There is increasing focus on "microenterprises"—small businesses that are either home-based or very small, employing one or two people. Such enterprises have been able to successfully support low-income people or families. As these microenterprises have increased, the demand for funds has also surged, and thus the development of "microlending" businesses and services. One example of a microlender is:

- Women's World Banking, New York (212-768-8513)

This small, nonprofit organization provides small loans (average, $300) to small or home-based businesses. The organization also helps small businesses form local enterprise networks for support and information.

Other Microlending groups include:

- Women's Initiative for Self-Employment, San Francisco (WISE)
- Women's Self-Employment Project, Chicago (WSEP)

- Good Faith Fund, Pine Bluff, Arkansas

Groups such as these offer "lending circles," peer networks where microentrepreneurs meet regularly to discuss, approve, and guarantee loans to one another and to provide personal support and business advice.

Banks

The two banks listed here primarily serve women business owners. They are also local rather than national and are listed as examples of what may be available in your area. Historically, banks have not been particularly responsive to women or minorities, or to small operations, but they are improving—some. You need to network heavily and look carefully for responsive banks. Having a well-thought-out and executed financial plan is critical when networking with bankers. They will definitely want to see some accurate financial information before making a financial commitment.

Women in Business Market, Chicago (312-461-5079). This is a subdivision of Harris Trust and Savings Bank in Chicago. It offers educational programs that teach women how to provide all the financial information the bank needs to analyze a business deal.

Women's Collateral Funding, Philadelphia (215-772-1900). This innovative business helps women business owners develop lending relationships with banks. The group publishes a directory of resources for decision-making women in the Philadelphia area, banks the proceeds, and uses them as collateral for loans made to selected women-owned businesses. Loans are usually in the $10,000 to $25,000 range.

Angel Networks

Angel networks are private and usually nonprofit groups of investors. Some angel networks maintain databases that match businesses with "angels" who might be willing to invest. You just need to submit a one-page summary of your business. Technically, your mother or brother could be considered an "angel." But the larger angels may have greater funding capacity than your family does.

Texas Capital Network (512-794-9398). This angel group maintains a current list of computer-matching services between those offering and those needing investment.

Investors' Circle. This group finds socially responsible businesses that are potential investments for investors.

Capital Circle (fax 708-876-0187). The goal of this group is to increase investment in women-owned businesses. To this end they sponsor activities that promote women-led businesses. To tap into this network, you can fax a request for information, specifying whether you're an entrepreneur looking for investors or an investor looking for entrepreneurs.

Venture Capitalists

Remember that venture capitalists do not usually invest in brand-new businesses, but prefer to fund companies with a strong track record. Nor do they fund extensively. For example, Patricof & Co. Ventures of New York receives 2,000 proposals a year and of those, completes ten business deals.

Also be aware that many venture capitalists have strong preferences for the *types* of companies they fund. For example, New Era Capital Partners invests in information technology and related systems as well as in health care.

Further, venture capital is not so readily available to women (see the section on women- and minority-owned businesses). About 1 percent of venture capital goes to women-owned businesses.

If your proposal is refused and you think you have a viable proposal, do not become discouraged. According to George Kalidonis, managing partner in Chicago Capital Fund, you should seize the opportunity to network by immediately asking for another name. (Also see p. 305.)

National Venture Capital Association (703-351-5269). This association publishes a membership directory (for $25) that lists mainstream venture capital funds.

Capital Rose Perpetual Fund, Malvern, PA (610-644-4212). This national group is gathering funding and plans to finance more women-owned businesses.

Women's Equity Fund, Boulder, CO (303-443-2620). This national group invests up to $50,000 in specialized businesses run by women in Colorado. It may go national in 1995.

Inroads Capital Partners, Chicago, IL (312-902-5347). This group is looking for equity positions in companies with sales in the $10 to $15 million range.

New Era Capital Partners, Los Angeles, CA (310-284-8868). This new venture firm is interested in women-owned companies.

Which Should I Try First?

We have listed the sources of funding more or less in the order in which you will want to investigate them. If you are just starting out, first contact the SBA. Then look first to family and friends for investment. Next, try microlenders, especially if yours is a small operation with only small financing needs. Banks are next on the list, providing you have a strong and well-written business plan (see the section on business plans, pages 107-134.) Finally, look into venture capital.

As small businesses grow in numbers and prove themselves as a viable way of doing business, more financing and networking opportunities will begin to open up. This is an encouraging sign for small-business owners, especially women and minorities.

(Source: Based on an article by Ilyce R. Glink, "Where to Look for Money Now," *Working Woman*, October 1994, pp. 56-62.)

New Sources of Financing

Some of the newer ways to finance include financial futures, EuroCredit, and junk bonds (noninvestment-grade debt). Each of these is complex and should be considered in light of the related tax and accounting implications.

Swaps

Developed in the early 1980s and growing rapidly as a basic tool for lowering costs and adding flexibility to financing, interest rate swaps occur between two parties. The parties meet directly or through an intermediary. One party has access to lower-cost fixed-rate funds but seeks a floating rate obligation, and the other has access to lower-cost floating-rate funds but seeks fixed-rate financing. Again, these are for larger companies.

Advantages of swaps include cost savings, speed, simplicity, minimal disclosure requirements, and low credit risk.

A variation of interest rate swaps is currency swaps in which currency is exchanged, thus allowing a lower-cost loan.

Hedging and options

In hedging, you use the futures market to reduce financial risk. Options are another way to manage risk. "An option contract creates an obligation for one party and a right, but no obligation, for the other to sell or buy at a fixed price for a given period of time" (Robert W. Hiller, "Sources of Financing: Traditional and New," *AMA Management Handbook*, p. 6-32).

Designer products

"Designer products," the newest type of financing, are zero-coupon instruments, debt with warrant instruments, or any such financing that is custom tailored for the individual.

(Source: Robert W. Hiller, "Sources of Financing: Traditional and New," *AMA Management Handbook*, John J. Hampton, ed., 1994, New York: AMACOM, American Management Association, pp. 6-25 - 6-32.)

twenty-eight
Network for Financing

Many generations of people—both those in and outside of business—have said that one key to success is in who you know. Those who are connected to influential people tend to get the most breaks, like it or not. The good news is, you don't have to be born with those good connections: You can forge them yourself. There are two critical tools for building a network: a good business plan and a successful track record. Building a network is really constructing a web of credibility so that when you look for financing, you will be able to call upon your influential acquaintances for references. For example, if an old employer of yours agrees to introduce you to the president of a local bank, you want to be sure to go armed with a very thorough, well-written business plan and a resume that shows you have the skills, knowledge, and background to convince that president that your venture is a good risk. Remember that the premise is simple: You're seeking money and people want to feel somewhat secure about lending it.

According to Ian MacMillan, a professor at the University of Pennsylvania, entrepreneurs can benefit from carefully planning their networking strategy. His advice to speeding up the networking process to get results includes:

- Targeting people and organizations from among your present connections who are close to potential stakeholders
- Soliciting from those identified, criticism, advice, and suggestions on your new venture
- Asking each new contact for at least two other new contacts and permission to use their names by way of introduction
- Getting advice on how to prepare for meetings with the new contacts so that your research and preparation can be tailored
- Following up with your existing connections to cement those relationships
- Repeating all the above steps for every new set of contacts you make.

Once you've made a connection, it's important to nurture it so that you can optimize your benefits. In his research on entrepreneurs and networking, Ian MacMillan found that several strategies worked well. First, point out areas of common interest with those you meet and take time to discuss them. Perhaps you grew up in the same town, went to the same school, or are both avid rock climbers. Second, ask for advice. People love to be asked for their opinion, especially when they are knowledgeable. Try to establish rapport not only by asking but by following up to let them know their advice helped. Finally, offer to help. Try to uncover problems or concerns a contact is having and offer your expertise or others'. This way, you can demonstrate your competence and try to build rapport.

MacMillan found that for some entrepreneurs he studied, networking paid off. For others it didn't. What is certain is that the networking process is time consuming and requires dedication, patience, and some political skill and savvy.

(Source: Ian C. MacMillan, "The Politics of New Venture Management." *The Entrepreneurial Venture.* eds., William A. Sahlman and Howard H. Stevenson, Boston: Harvard Business School Publications, 1992.)

Finance Through Your Network

There are a number of ways to find money to support a new business. The four basic sources are friends, banks, venture capitalists, and angels. Each of these is appropriate in different circumstances, and all require a certain amount of networking to make the connections that will pay off.

The first line of financing for small start-ups frequently is friends, relatives, and business contacts. In fact, these are good sources. They account for five to ten times as much capital as that available from venture capitalists.

Another source of funding is bank loans, which we discuss in more depth in other articles in this chapter.

Venture capitalists are usually not interested in new start-ups. They prefer to invest in a viable business that has a track record of some sort. Generally they are looking for a 20 percent return (or better) on their investment, and start-ups may not be able to produce that rate of return in the first few years.

Another possibility for financing is described by Mary Rowland of *The New York Times* as the "angel network." Angels are wealthy individuals who are interested in investing in start-up companies. One angel network, Venture Capital Network at the Massachusetts Institute of Technology in Cambridge, Massachusetts, lists the names of start-ups for a fee. Then, if an investor is interested, the start-up company will be asked to send a business summary to the prospective investor.

Generally, it is better to be able to start up a business without a venture capitalist or angel, because you usually have to make large monetary or management concessions to obtain that kind of backing. And bankers usually prefer low-risk loaning to companies that have a bit of a track record or can demonstrate strong backing. But of course some businesses require high-risk initial investments, and if you lack the personal wealth to fund them, equity investors may be necessary.

(Source: Mary Rowland, "Finding Money to Start a Business," *The New York Times*, May 28, 1991, Sec. 3.)

Use Outside Members on Your Board

Coopers & Lybrand recently did a study of 300 fast-growing firms looking for expansion capital. What they found is that companies who need financing for growth do better at obtaining it when they have boards composed of outside directors.

	% receiving bank financing
Firms with outside directors	37%
Firms with no outside directors	25%

What is more, the firms with outside boards paid less for their loans.

What this research suggests is that boards composed of outside directors have a greater credibility than those with internal boards.

Where to Look

If you want to find outside members for your board, there are two groups that can be helpful with this effort:

The Executive Committee
5469 Kearney Villa Road
Suite 101
San Diego, CA 92123
1-800-274-2367

The Executive Committee is for CEOs with at least $2 million in sales and 25 or more employees. The Executive Committee organizes forums of advisers nationwide.

The Alternative Board
Suite 317
11330 Olive Blvd
St. Louis, MO 63141
1-800-727-0126

The Alternative Board is for companies with sales from $1 million to $200 million.

(Source: "Outside Directors Can Help Obtain Capital for Growth," *Nation's Business*, February 1993, p. 8.)

twenty-nine
Consider Debt Financing

Once you've tapped all other possible resources for capital, you will undoubtedly turn to debt and/or equity financing. Debt financing involves borrowing money that locks you into a repayment schedule for both the borrowed principle and interest. Equity financing involves selling some of the ownership of your company in the form of stocks. Equity financing avoids the financial burden of debt, but you are also giving up some control of your company. Typically, firms balance the pros and cons by using a combination of debt and equity financing.

Equity (issuing stocks) has traditionally been considered to be permanent capital, whereas debt is used to finance working capital (accounts receivable and inventories) and part of fixed assets (land, buildings, and equipment, as well as goodwill). But this is changing as new financial instruments are being designed to meet changing needs for financing.

The cost of debt capital is usually lower than the cost of equity capital because of the higher risk involved in the value of stock. As a result, the capital structure for a business is usually some *mix* of types of debt that is appropriate for the company and the particular industry it is in. A business in a stable, predictable industry is less risky and can usually support more debt than a company in a volatile industry (for example, in a new technology). A company with tangible assets that are easily liquidated can sustain higher levels of debt. The debt mix may be changed over time.

The main objective for financial planning is to obtain a cash flow that will support the level of debt the business takes on. The goal of lenders is to assure themselves that you have adequate cash flow and asset coverage before agreeing to a loan. Further, management must be able to tolerate the level of risk associated with their chosen debt mix.

Debt financing is more common than equity financing for new, small businesses and includes short-, medium-, and long-term debt financing, as will be described.

Short-Term Debt Financing

In general, it is best to keep working capital to a minimum so as to minimize the amount of external financing that will be required by the business.

Some of the ways of financing debt were discussed previously in the discussion of creative financing. They include adjusting terms of sale, offering incentives for quicker payment or even prepayment, and making aggressive collections on the receivables side. In the inventory area, the focus needs to be on clearing out slow-moving items, offering deals for buying off-season, and using the "Just-in-Time" approach with suppliers and customers to keep inventory at a minimal level—only that which is absolutely necessary. Be aware that just-in-time (JIT) applies more to larger businesses who have the clout to establish JIT relationships with suppliers. Most small businesses don't provide the economic incentives for suppliers to arrange their delivery schedules accordingly.

On the payables side, the business can ask for extended terms, avoid prepayment, and wait until the last minute to pay vendors. Other strategies include adjusting periodic payments or payroll periods to financially more convenient terms (for example, in the former case, paying a small amount monthly rather than a large amount annually).

Establishing a line of credit can be a help to the fledgling business as well as to the longer-lived business. This may be aided by extensive networking.

Medium-Term Debt Financing

Medium-term financing is primarily through a bank or through a savings and loans or commercial finance company. For that reason it is a good idea to establish a good relationship with a bank early on. It may also be to your advantage to find out which banks have programs designed especially for small businesses.

Here again, your networking skills can be invaluable. Find out through your sources which banks can best meet your particular needs and get to know your local bankers.

A medium-term loan is usually in the one- to seven-year range. Lenders usually require that you back your loans with assets.

Long-Term Debt Financing

Long-term financing is any financing that is for a period of more than seven years. Sources for this type of financing include banks, insurance companies, pension funds, and private investors. Large companies also have access to bonds, of which there are two types: mortgage bonds and debentures. Long-term leasing, used for equipment, rolling stock, and building space, can also be considered as a type of long-term debt. Again, you need to have assets to secure this type of financing.

Evaluating financing projects

Capital-budgeting techniques are usually used to evaluate potential long-term financing of projects or investments. Capital-budgeting tools include net present value (NPV), internal rate of return (IRR), payback, and the profitability index (PI). Using these formulas (given in the books listed in the Resources section), you can determine whether it will be financially feasible for your company to replace equipment, expand facilities, refinance debt, enter into a merger or acquisition, add a new product or product line, undertake a large advertising campaign, and such other events that may present themselves to your business.

Strategies for Securing Venture Capital

Perhaps a better place to start before discussing strategies for getting venture capital is to give a brief definition of what are venture capitalists. Unlike other investors, venture capitalists are interested in your *intangible* assets and in how those assets will be able to produce future profits. Venture capitalists use either debt or equity as their vehicle, and the risk is always very high, which, in turn, makes the profit potential very high. Venture capitalists expect very high risk because they expect exceptionally high returns. Since venture capitalists assess intangible rather than tangible assets, it's critical to present your and your partners' expertise, product, invention, or service in the best possible light. Venture capitalists frequently take a long time to decide to fund a venture because they want to explore every possible outcome first. They also back only experienced management teams with proven track records and industry experience. A good idea with no industry experience or managerial ability will not get you anywhere with a venture capitalist.

Although it is difficult for new, small companies to get venture capital, it is not impossible. A typical entrepreneur might see the prospect of winning over a venture capital firm as a challenge. As holds true when seeking any type of financing, you want to have a very thorough, persuasive business plan. Then, according to Gordon Baty, a partner at Zero Stage Capital in Cambridge, Massachusetts, you want to carefully research and evaluate the firm's investment criteria, which may include type of industry, stage of development, geographic location, or the amount of capital the firm typically invests. Says Baty, "Of every 100 business plans we get, 90 of them are irrelevant" (David R. Evanson, "Taking Aim," *Entrepreneur*, November 1994, pp. 32 - 35). To have a chance at succeeding in getting venture capital, you must at least target relevant firms.

Baty describes two strategies for approaching the task: the rifle and the shotgun. The rifle approach is specific and tailored. You concentrate your efforts on a handful of firms on the assumption that a concerted effort in one direction will pay off. The shotgun method is a more widespread effort on the hopes that there will be a hit. The rifle method requires more initial research to find firms that typically invest in your type of venture. Then you call the firm and ask them for a fact sheet or description, which gives you enough information to help you narrow your picks and perhaps even lists partners and their respective areas of expertise. Then you can at least send your executive summary to a specific person. The fact sheet might also list the firm's auditors and attorneys. Scan the names to see if you know anyone. If you can use your networking skills to get a personal referral, you have a much better chance of getting your plan read by the appropriate person.

The shotgun approach is useful in that it increases your chances of success. If you send your business-plan executive summary to 25 firms rather than 5, you might hit on one that is looking to expand in your direction but has been waiting for the right project to come in. Baty's advice is to use a combination of both tactics so that you're not aiming too narrowly or too widely.

(Sources: Bruce Blechman and Jay Conrad Levinson, *Guerrilla Financing: Alternative Techniques to Finance Any Small Business*, Boston: Houghton Mifflin Company, 1991; Donald F. Kuratko and Richard M. Hodgetts, David R. Evanson, "Taking Aim," *Entrepreneur,* November 1994, pp. 32-35; Peter M. Rosenblum, "Creative Debt Financing in the Venture Capital Environment," *Venture Capital Manual*, ed., Steven James Lee, Warren, Gorham & Lamont, 1990.)

Other Sources of Debt Financing

Several other sources can provide financing, provided you have the "right stuff."

Certified development companies (CDCs) offer government-assisted financing under the Small Business Administration's 504 program. The financing is a mixture of bank financing and debentures and can only be used for financing long-term assets such as real estate or equipment with a life of ten years or more.

Small-business investment companies (SBICs), privately operated, have access to federally guaranteed loans for long-term financing of small businesses. The SBIC usually requires an equity interest in the company that receives the loan.

Minority-enterprise small-business investment companies (MESBICs) specialize in helping socially or economically disadvantaged entrepreneurs.

(Source: Alan R. Tubbs, "Sources of Financing for the New Business," *AMA Management Handbook*, John J. Hampton, ed., 1994, New York: AMACOM, American Management Association, pp. 13-12 - 13-15.)

Broome's Pointers for Obtaining Loans

After a dip in the rate of bank loans in the early 1990s, in recent years they have been increasing. From January 1993 to January 1994, total loans by U.S. banks were up 18 percent. In addition, federal regulations have been eased in order to help increase credit for small- and medium-sized businesses.

While the availability of loans is good news for small businesses, the bad news is that rates for small-business loans are usually one or two points above the prime rate.

J. Tol Broome, Jr., a vice president at FirstSouth Bank in Burlington, North Carolina, suggests that you are less likely to be able to obtain a loan if the banker is not familiar with your business or industry. To avert this possibility, invite a potential lender to visit your business to see your operation. It never hurts to network.

And when you prepare a business plan, be sure to include the following elements, to show the potential lender that your business is worth investing in.

- Summary of business plan (Some of the items that follow may be included in your business plan.)
- History of your company (or idea if start-up)
- Resumes of managers
- Description of products, services
- Marketing strategy
- Description of business's day-to-day operation
- Company's goals
- Amount of money required to operate the business
- Cash-flow projections
- Financial projections
- Financial track record. For a going concern, three years of financial statements and current personal financial statements; for a start-up, a financial statement and a business plan

Bankers tend to look at five areas when considering a potential bank loan:

1. Sales trends, which of course should be rising
2. Profitability
3. Liquidity
4. Leverage
5. Cash flow

From the income statement of a going concern, they are interested in the retained earnings. And, the more equity you have the better. The ratio of total liabilities to total equity should not be greater than four to one. (See Chapter 25 for a discussion of financial analysis and ratios.)

Another consideration is collateral. Not only should it be fairly substantial in quantity, but also in quality. Banks will generally loan 65 to 90 percent of the real estate value, or 60 to 80 percent of accounts receivable. They will loan 50 to 80 percent of machinery, equipment, and inventory.

What to Take with You to the Bank

Business plan

Financials

Equity

Collateral

(Source: J. Tol Broome, Jr., "A Loan at Last?" *Nation's Business*, August 1994, pp. 40-43.)

Bankers' 5 C's of Credit

Alan Tubbs, president of the American Bankers Association, describes the loan picture from the banker's point of view. Banks, he says, are in business to make money. They need to be assured that the money they loan will be repaid. So they follow the five C's of credit:

1. Character. The banker will want to know that you are responsible and of good character. Most of all, you need a good credit rating. This means that you pay bills on time, especially your credit cards, and do not overdraw bank accounts. If you have carefully built a sound financial reputation, the banker will be more likely to consider you a reasonable risk.

2. Cash flow. Cash flow is most important and is sometimes considered before any other criterion. You need to prove that you will have sufficient cash flow to repay the loan and to cover expenses. A cash-flow forecast should prove that there will be enough cash to eventually replace assets as well. In addition, having past experience will be important. Either you or a member of your team should have the credentials to reassure the banker that you can manage your planned business, especially on the financial front.

3. Capital. Bankers want to be sure the owner is fully committed to this business, and to this end they require that the owner provide most of the start-up money. When you think about it, this makes sense, for you would not want to own less than half of your business and have someone else running it.

4. Collateral. You must be able to put up collateral to assure the loan. The bank will generally loan up to 75-80 percent of the market value of the real estate, and 50 percent of the value of eligible accounts receivable, inventory, and equipment. (Eligible accounts receivable are those that are current and collectible.)

5. Conditions. The fifth "C" is the conditions in the economy and how your business fits into that picture. Since the banker will be looking at this aspect, you also need to consider the environment when you are putting together your financial plan.

(Source: Alan R. Tubbs, "Sources of Financing for the New Business," *AMA Management Handbook*, John J. Hampton, ed., 1994, New York: AMACOM, American Management Association. pp. 13-12 - 13-15.)

thirty
Consider Equity Financing

Equity financing through the sale of stock offers investors an opportunity to share in the ownership and future growth of the business. The owner benefits by receiving capital without having to pay back the principal amount or pay interest. Equity financing does mean that the owner shares ownership and any future profits of the company. For larger companies, stock is a sizable proportion of the capital structure. The stock may be a combination of preferred and common, with special characteristics attached to each. The stock is marketed by investment bankers, who are experienced in placing it on the market at the appropriate time.

You can raise equity capital through public stock offerings and private placements. Public offerings or "going public" means you are going to sell your securities on the public markets. The benefits of going public include:

- Raising large amounts of capital very quickly
- Improving liquidity since you can sell stock for cash at any time
- Calculating your company's value because the marketplace puts a value on your stock, which in turn lets you place a value on your company
- Enhancing your corporate image because publicly traded companies are often perceived by suppliers, customers, and financiers as stronger

Going public carries with it specific responsibilities and costs. There are significant initial legal and accounting fees plus the cost of underwriting your stock. In addition, you must make public your company's affairs and conform to the Securities and Exchange Commission's requirements. The paperwork required to fulfill the SEC's regulations is considerable and can be a drain on a new company's resources. Finally, once you've sold stock, you are no longer sole owner and must make decisions that keep the best interest of your shareholders in mind. They will want to make a return on their investment in the form of dividends, which might be at odds with your long-term growth plans.

Private placement of securities is a method for raising capital often used by smaller companies. Essentially, private placement involves selling stock to private parties including friends, family and other relatives, customers, and other local professionals. Private placement was adopted by the SEC to ease the strain of public offering regulations. The SEC has different rules and requirements for disclosure for private placement of securities depending on the amount of money that is raised.

Venture capitalists are another source of equity financing. Strategies for securing funds from venture capitalists are discussed in detail in the preceding chapter and in other sections of this book. Keep in mind that although getting venture capital funding is difficult and competitive, there *is* money out there. Securing it involves doing preliminary research into the various funds and their selection criteria before sending off your business plan. It's critical to be well prepared, professional, and targeted to be considered by venture capitalists. If you are being evaluated for funding by venture capitalists, evaluate them as well. You want to make sure that they truly understand your proposal, that they are familiar with your industry, and that the person you're dealing with is someone with whom you can work. If the personality fit isn't good, you should look for another venture capitalist.

How Do You Find (Real) Venture Capitalists?

Warning! The venture capitalists that find *you* are probably scam artists. In most big cities, there are a number of fly-by-night outfits that bill themselves as venture capitalists, and advertise in the newspapers or do telemarketing to find eager but naive entrepreneurs. The scam usually works this way: They ask you for your plan, then contact you with the good news that it "fits the requirements of their partners perfectly." You are 99% certain to receive funding. But of course, there is the "standard" due diligence on their part—their staff must spend a week or two analyzing your plan and industry. And *you* will have to foot the bill for their work! Often the entrepreneur does not realize there is anything wrong with this picture—the venture capital firm may have leased up-scale offices in a big downtown building for the month—and signs over a check for anywhere from $1 to $5 thousand for the review. Only later, when nobody will return their calls and the sign has changed on the office door, do they realize their money is gone for good.

Remember, it's not a real venture capital firm if your money funds it, rather than it funding you. Don't ever write a check to a venture capital firm and you will be sure to avoid falling for the fakes. But how do you find a real venture capital firm? Your network of advisors may know the right people, but we doubt it. Unless you are working with law firms and accountants that do V.C. deals regularly, they won't be much help. And it is hard to find these experts outside of Silicon Valley and other hot spots that have hundreds of high-tech start-ups. You may have to build a new network, and the best place to start is the nearest venture capital association or V.C. firm. Associations sometimes stage monthly or quarterly "meet the V.C.'s" events where entrepreneurs can sign up for a half-hour of presentation time. If you can find a few firms to talk to, they will know about any associations in your area—or might just ask you to come directly to their offices to meet them. So the best place to begin is probably your telephone. Here is a sampling of venture capital firms around the country to get you started. Be sure you have at least a short draft of a business plan, complete with financial projections for several years out, before you bother calling them. If they like your concept, the first thing they'll ask is to see your plan. (Also see p. 288-289.)

Contact List of Venture Capital Firms

ABS Ventures, Baltimore, MD, 401-783-3263
Accel Partners, Princeton, NJ, 609-683-4500
Advanced Technology Ventures, Menlo Park, CA, 415-321-8601
Allstate Insurance Co. Venture Capital Div., Northbrook, IL, 708-402-5681
Atlantic Venture Partners, Winston-Salem, NC 910-725-2961

Bain Capital, Boston, MA, 617-572-3000

Baird, Robert W. & Co., Milwaukee, WI, 414-765-3500

Bay Partners, Cupertino, CA, 408-725-2444

Campbell Venture Management, Palo Alto, CA, 415-853-0766

Citicorp Venture Capital Ltd., New York, NY, 212-559-1127

Columbine Venture Funds, Englewood, CO, 303-694-3222

Continental Capital Ventures, San Francisco, CA, 415-989-2020

Cornerstone Ventures, Menlo Park, CA, 415-854-2576

Development Corp. of Montana, Helena, MT, 406-422-3850

Eastech Development Corp., Boston, MA, 617-423-1096

Equity Dynamics, Des Moines, IA, 515-244-5176

Founders Equity Inc., New York, NY, 212-953-0100

Institutional Venture Partners, Menlo Park, CA, 415-854-0132

Jafco American Ventures, San Francisco, CA, 415-788-0706

Kleiner Perkins Caufield & Byers, San Francisco, CA, 415-421-3110

Landmark Ventures, Inc., Simsbury, CT, 203-651-5681

Lehman, T.H., & Co., Houston TX, 713-621-2693

Madison Dearborn Partners, Chicago, IL, 312-732-5400

Manhattan Venture Co., New York, NY, 212-688-4445

Massey Burch Investment Group, Nashville, TN, 615-329-9448

Morgan Stanley Venture Capital Fund, New York, NY, 212-703-6981

Morganthaler Ventures, Cleveland, OH, 216-621-3070

NEPA Venture Fund, Bethlehem, PA, 610-865-6550

New Enterprise Association, Baltimore, MD, 410-244-0115

North American Business Development Co. Ltd., Fort Lauderdale, FL, 305-463-0681

Peregrine Ventures, Cupertino, CA, 408-966-7212

Raytheon Ventures, Lexington, MA, 617-860-2274

Signma Partners, Menlo Park, CA, 415-854-1300

Southwest Venture Partnerships, San Antonio, TX, 210-227-1010

Sutter Hill Ventures, Palo Alto, CA, 415-493-5600

Venture Founders Corp., Lexington, MA, 617-863-0900

Wind Point Partners, Chicago, IL, 312-649-4000

A wonderful source of up-to-date information and listings on the venture capital industry is called the *Venture Capital Yearbook*. It is published yearly by Venture Economics Inc., 1180 Raymond Blvd., Newark, NJ 07102; telephone them at 201-622-4500 to order the latest copy and to see if they have other publications or services that might be of help in your search. And you can also use your local library to see if venture capitalists are active in your industry. Just use the PC-based key-term search capabilities of most libraries to look for relevant articles in any database of business or general newspaper and magazine stories. Try a search using "venture capital" and the name of your industry. It may reveal some articles mentioning firms that have made investments in business plans similar to yours.

Selecting Your Strategy

When you designed your original business plan, you may have planned for growth through various forms of financing. Or, perhaps you are just beginning to see growth potential in your business and you want to explore methods of financing.

There are a number of ways to finance the growth of a business. One way is to use debt—loans from banks, investors, venture capitalists. Another is through equity financing—selling shares of stock in your company. Some firms choose to use a combination of these methods.

It pays to look carefully at the various options before you decide which path to take. Some investors want a high percentage of the profit for their investment. Consider the equity financing discussed in this section, and also investigate the other entries on financing—loans, venture capital, and so forth—in this section to see which is the best mix for your business.

How to Arrange a Private Placement

The Securities and Exchange Commission made it easier to sell securities to private parties in 1982 when it adopted Regulation D—but it is still a complex process. Under Regulation D, you may sell equity shares in your business to friends, customers, employees, relatives, and professionals, without the full disclosure requirements of a public stock offering (which we will describe in the next section). Specifically, the SEC permits three exceptions to standard procedures of public sale of securities:

1. When raising less than $500,000 (Rule 504), you are not constrained by any specific disclosure requirements and there are no limits on who can purchase stock, or how many people you can sell it to. Basically, the SEC decided to stop regulating private placements under the half-a-million-dollar level. However, remember that many other laws may apply! For example, an offering that defrauds investors will probably land you in court. So hire a lawyer experienced in small-scale private placements—on a straight fee basis, not on a percent-of-funds-raised basis, as the latter might bias the lawyer toward risks you don't want to take! And even though there are no formal SEC requirements concerning disclosure, you will find it best in the long run to provide honest and full statements of what your business is and does.

2. When raising between $500,000 and $5 million, you are limited by the SEC (Rule 505) to a maximum of 35 "nonaccredited purchasers," who are, basically, people who do not have the experience, expertise, and excess money to make high-risk investments. For instance, if you sell $10,000 worth of securities to each of fifty friends and relatives, and then your business fails, they might get together and sue you using the argument that they were nonaccredited, and you should not have sold them securities in the first place. If, on the other hand, you comply with this rule, then their case is much weaker—the courts are liable to decide that they should have known better. Accredited purchasers of securities include institutional investors (a venture capital firm, small business investment company, or bank, for example), anyone buying at least $150,000 of the security whose net worth is at least five times the amount of their investment, anyone with a net worth of at least $1 million, anyone with an annual net income that is consistently above $200,000, and directors, officers or partners in your firm. There are some SEC information disclosure requirements at this level of financing, so be sure to work with a lawyer or professional underwriting firm that is familiar with them.

3. When raising more than $5 million, you are still required to limit the placement to 35 nonaccredited purchasers (or an unlimited number of accredited purchasers), and the disclosure requirements are even higher. So again, be sure to work with a firm that is experienced in such placements—either a larger, full-service venture capital firm or the same sort of underwriting firm that would handle a full-scale public placement.

Warning! So far, we have just covered SEC requirements, but there are a variety of regulations over private placements at the state level as well. So when you seek legal advice for your private placement, be sure to work with an individual or firm experienced in the state in which you are raising capital.

(Sources: Kenneth Clarkson, et al., *West's Business Law*, 5th ed., West Publishing, 1992, pp. 819-838. Donald Kuratko and Richard Hodgetts, *Entrepreneurship: A Contemporary Approach*, Third Edition, The Dryden Press, 1995, pp. 410-411.)

Who invests in private placements? If you knew that, you could raise all the funds you'd ever need. But finding willing investors is an up-hill battle for most entrepreneurs and small business owners. The most common sources, at least statistically, are wealthy professionals within your own community or industry. They either know you, or your markets, well enough that they are willing to risk a small portion of their savings on your business. But they *will* view it as a big risk, so be prepared to go through a lengthy disclosure process, often involving examination of your books and plan by their accountants and lawyers. And be prepared to offer them at least a 30% return on their investment, because if they have any savvy at all they will know that roughly half of such investments turn sour. That means they will discount your projected returns by half, and still want to make a decent amount of money. For example, if your plan permits an investor to be bought out at the end of one year, assume you will have to offer her at least 130% of her initial investment in order to buy the stock back from her.

Successful entrepreneurs are another common source of informal equity. Someone who started a computer company fifteen years ago, took it public five years ago, made twenty million, and retired from management three years ago, is now extremely likely to invest in several new computer startups. They too will look for opportunities that offer the potential of a high return on investment, which means you have to have some reasonable way to grow your business using their money. For other ideas on how to find such individuals, see William Bryant Logan, "Finding Your Angel," *Venture*, Vol. 8, No. 3, March 1986, p. 39.

An essential, but little-known, requirement for successful private placements is that your plan provide one or more easy ways for the investors to *cash out*. Can the business be sold to a bigger competitor in a few years? Is a second-round private placement realistic in a couple of years, at which time the initial investors could be bought out? Can the company be taken public within three to five years? Can its inventions be licensed at such a profitable rate that high dividends can be paid to the investors? Might you make enough money from the business that you would be in a position to buy out your investors in a few years? Are you purchasing assets that can be sold on the general market, such as trucks, land, leases, or equipment that might be of value to businesses other than your own? The more "yes" answers you can give, the easier it will be for an investor to get money out of your business at some point in the future. If the answers are all "no," then the investor will not be able to profit from your success.

How to Go Public

If you are seriously considering going public, we hope you know you will need a great deal more information and assistance than this book can provide! But here is a brief overview of the process to help you get a feel for when and how public offerings take place.

First, are you a likely candidate for a public offering? According to a group of experts from the accounting firm Coopers & Lybrand, you need to ask the following questions in order to find out if you are a good candidate for going public:

1. Has your company demonstrated a sustained or increasing growth rate high enough to attract investors? (It helps to be growing faster than typical businesses.)

2. Has the company reached the point where prospects for maintaining strong sales and earnings growth are pretty good? (Don't bother if you are losing money!)

3. Are your products/services visible and interesting to the public? (Otherwise, it will be harder to explain who you are and what you do.)

4. Do you think you can meet the difficult SEC disclosure and financial reporting requirements? You will need to provide audited financial statements every quarter, plus lengthy annual SEC filings and an annual report, for example. And you will need a higher level of management information and control systems than you probably have right now. All this is easy—if you are big enough to hire professional managers and the

right accounting and law firms. But it is a big transition. And managing in the "fish bowl" atmosphere of a public company is an even bigger transition for some entrepreneurs. Do you want the public and a potentially hostile board of directors examining your expense account and second-guessing your strategies?

(Source: Seymour Jones, Bruce Cohen, and Victor Coppola, "Going Public," in William Sahlman and Howard Stevenson, *The Entrepreneurial Venture*, Harvard Business School Publications, 1992.)

If, after reviewing these issues, you still think a public offering is feasible, then you will need to prepare a registration statement for the SEC, and also to find an underwriter to handle the public sale of stock in your company. In practice, the underwriter generally helps with the filing, or at least brings in an expert law firm to do it, so the first thing is to find an underwriter. Also, the underwriter generally finds buyers for your public stock offering, by picking an appropriate stock exchange to list it on, and by enlisting brokers to sell the offering to investors. That makes the underwriter the key to a successful public offering. But (to reiterate our initial question), how do you find an underwriter?

How to Find an Underwriter to Handle Your Public or Private Placement

In practice, underwriters are often found through referrals provided by accountants, attorneys, venture capitalists or bankers. They may know which firms are active in the kind of equity financing you require at the moment. So the first thing to do is to "milk your network" and ask professionals familiar with your business if they have contacts who specialize in taking companies public. They may not, or even if they do, you may want to evaluate a number of alternatives before choosing one firm. Therefore, you should also try calling a number of investment banking firms, small business investment companies, and venture capital firms on your own to enquire whether they could provide underwriting services for taking your firm public. If they can, they will probably have someone who evaluates opportunities. Get this person's name, and talk to them by phone or have them visit your company to see if there is a potential match.

As we wrote this chapter, we assumed we could look up "underwriters" in the index of one of the dozens of specialized texts and references on our overloaded bookshelves, and quickly find a list of firms for you to call. Amazingly, we could find no book that provided even a single name and phone number! And since *Yellow Pages* listings do not cover this category either, it is extremely difficult to find such firms. Perhaps they try to keep a low profile? Anyway, to make up for the past invisibility of these firms, we are herewith providing a list of firms that may be able to help you. Some we know do underwriting for public offerings on a routine basis, others are apparently in the business but we have not verified the nature of their work, and still others handle at least some aspect of the process and so might be able to provide referrals or partial support. We can't guarantee that every number will still work when you try it, or that all these firms will be interested in helping you, but at least this provides a place to start your search for underwriters. And remember the cardinal rule of telephone research: Don't hang up until you get a "Yes," or *another phone number* to try! The people at these firms are much more likely than you are to know which companies are currently active in underwriting initial public offerings for firms in your size range and industry. So ask them!

Contact List for Entrepreneurs Seeking Underwriters

Acorn Ventures Inc., Houston, TX, 713-622-9595

Alimansky Capital Group Inc., New York, NY, 212-832-7300

American Commercial Capital Corp., New York NY, 212-986-3305

Banc One Capital Partners Corp., Dallas, TX, 214-979-4361

Banc One Venture Corp., Milwaukee, WI, 414-765-2274

BankAmerica Capital Corp., Costa Mesa, CA, 714-556-1964

Bergstrom Capital Corp, Seattle, WA, 206-623-7302

BMI Capital Corp., New York, NY, 212-476-0774

Boca Raton Capital Corp., Boca Raton, FL, 407-394-3066

California Capital Investors, Los Angeles, CA, 310-820-7222

Capital Group Inc., Los Angeles CA, 213-486-9200

Capital Southwest Corp., Dallas, TX, 214-233-8242

Central Securities Corp., New York, NY 212-688-3011

Chase Manhattan Capital Corp., New York, NY 212-552-6257

Chemical Venture Partners, New York, NY, 212-270-3220

CIGNA Investments Inc., Bloomfield, CT, 203-726-6000

Eaton Vance Corp., Boston, MA, 617-482-8260

First Jersey Securities Inc., New York, NY 212-269-5500

Fleet Equity Partners, Providence, RI, 401-278-6770

John Hancock Income Securities, Boston, MA, 617-375-1715

NationsBanc Capital Corp., Dallas, TX, 214-508-0900

New York Business Development Corp., Albany, NY, 518-463-2268

Northland Venture Partnership, Duluth, MN, 218-722-0545

Pierce Investment Banking, Arlington, VA, 703-516-7000

Prudential Asset Management Co. Inc., Newark, NJ, 201-802-7804

Smith Affiliated Capital, New York, NY, 212-644-9440

Sterling Capital Corp., New York, NY, 212-980-3360

Ventures Group Inc., Hancock, MI 906-487-2970

In addition, you might try calling the *Association of Publicly Traded Companies*, Washington DC, at 202-857-1114. It lobbies on behalf of public companies, but one of its staffers might be able to give you some ideas or referrals on the question of how to find an underwriter who will take your company public.

Assessment

If you decide to sell stock you will need to decide how much you are willing to offer for the investment each shareholder will make. To set the stock price, you first need to know how much your company is worth to you.

Armed with your business plan, financial projections, and a concrete dollar figure that you know you are going to need for this expansion, the next step is to consider your personal goals and those of key people in your organization. One way to zero in on your goals is to ask yourself where you see yourself in five or ten years. Do you expect to stay with this business for the rest of your life, or just get it going and then move on to something else?

Another way to assess your business's value is to calculate what you would like to make if you were to sell it, say, five years from now. The equity value of your business will also depend on your market niche and how popular your type of business is. The microbrewing industry, for example, is new and growing. It is currently a popular one for people to invest in. On the other hand, a traditional business such as a clothing store may not appear to prospective stockholders as having growth and profit potential.

One way to learn the value of your business is to have a professional valuation. An investment banker familiar with your industry or an accountant in a firm that deals with small businesses may be helpful in setting an accurate dollar figure.

Comparison

After you have evaluated your own business, compare it with other similar businesses in the industry. If others are public, get their prospectuses to learn about their stock issues and valuation. For a fee, organizations such as Washington Watch or Disclosure Inc. will provide financial information on public companies. Calculate the market value for each of the comparable firms. Also calculate the ratios for each business so you can use them for comparison to the financials of your company.

Definition

Finally, decide which qualities of your company are unique or special or set your company apart from the others. These may include location, reputation, distribution techniques, name, special contracts, and management, to name a few.

Your valuation of your company needs to be as accurate as possible. When you are ready to sell stock you need to be able to explain why the price you have set is appropriate. Here is another point where your comparison with other similar companies will be helpful.

Reassurance

Prospective investors will want to be reassured about your company's growth potential. They will also ask around about your company, so reputation is important—not only for the first round of equity financing, but for potential later releases of shares of stock. If you distribute your product or services to a small area and your investors tend to be local, be sure they are happy, or you may find that the next time you want to sell stock, the pool of investment has dried up.

(Additional Sources: Cathy Ewing, "How Green Is My Beer?" *The New Brewer*, September-October 1994, pp. 10-14; Bruce Blechman and Jay Conrad Levinson, *Guerrilla Financing: Alternative Techniques to Finance Any Small Business*, Boston: Houghton Mifflin Company, 1991; Donald F. Kuratko, and Richard M. Hodgetts, *Entrepreneurship: A Contemporary Approach*, 3rd ed., Fort Worth: The Dryden Press, 1995. John Kerr, "The 100-Day Makeover: What's the difference between the company you run now and the one you'll take public?", *Inc.*, May 1996, pp. 54-63. This article is a "must-read" if you are seriously considering a public offering!)

PART VIII

Resources

This section provides you with resources to help you in planning, starting, or managing a small business. Material is grouped into the following areas: Educational programs and information, Financial, Franchising, General and government information, Magazines/books/publishers, Management and organizations.

When you are looking for information or connections, consider the following general resources:

- Business and trade publications
- Newspapers
- Newsletters
- Magazines
- Radio stations
- Banks
- Colleges, universities
- Federal government—Government Printing Office; business service checklist, population census, census of housing, national business patterns

- Surveys of current business
- State and local government
- Public utility and transportation companies
- Business directories—Dun & Bradstreet, Moody's Manual, Thomas' Register of American Manufacturers
- Market research services
- Chambers of commerce
- Rotary Clubs
- Leads clubs
- Professional organizations
- Barter associations

One of the best resources for addresses and phone numbers of business, professional, and trade associations is *Gale Encyclopedia of Business and Professional Associations*, which you will find in most libraries. It lists more than 8,000 business, professional, and trade organizations (800-877-4253).

Also,

Economic and Demographic Statistics
Bureau of the Census
U.S. Dept. of Commerce
Data User Service Division, Customer Service
Washington, DC 20233
(301-763-4100)

Another general resource is the *Information Please Business Almanac and Sourcebook*, published every year by Houghton Mifflin Company, Seth Godin, editor.

Educational Programs and Resources

The Entrepreneurial Edge

This small business produces educational conferences nationwide. EE's four-hour workshops cost $95, and treat a variety of topics, such as management, marketing, and sales for new and growing businesses. The training staff are themselves entrepreneurs.

The group also produces a quarterly how-to magazine for entrepreneurs, called EDGE.

Entrepreneurial Edge will soon be offering a line of motivational audio cassettes on which entrepreneurs give business advice and step-by-step instruction. The 120 modules will range in price from $4 to $10.

The Small Business Administration (SBA) chose The Entrepreneurial Edge as one of two national initiatives to provide information to small businesses. For this work, the SBA underwrites part of the costs The Entrepreneurial Edge incurs.

American Management Association (AMA) Extension Institute

In cooperation with community colleges and other institutions, the AMA offers noncredit extension courses that can be applied toward the AMA Certificate in Management. To earn a certificate, you need only complete any six AMA courses.

Topics taught in AMA courses include negotiation, delegation, leadership, time management, customer management, managing stress, supervision, and conflict management.

Check with the community colleges in your area for availability and a listing of AMA extension courses.

Entrepreneur Group

This organization offers an Entrepreneur's Incorporation Kit, start-up business guides, books, tapes, and software on small business topics. Contact them at P.O. Box 50370, Boulder, CO 80321-0370.

Higher Education

Community colleges.   Community colleges throughout the nation offer continuing education courses in topics of interest to small-business owners, including computers, small-business marketing, and other business topics. Look under Schools in the Yellow Pages of your telephone directory.

Institutions where courses in *entrepreneurship* are offered include:

New York University, which has a Center for Entrepreneurial Studies

University of Pennsylvania (Wharton) has the Sol C. Snider Entrepreneurial Center and Entrepreneurial Studies department. The director of the Center is Ian MacMillan.

University of California/Berkeley offers courses in Entrepreneurship. Contact Professor John Freeman.

Georgia State University in Atlanta has courses in family entrepreneurship. Contact Leslie W. Rue.

FasTrac (Midwest and West).   FasTrac is an intensive course to help individuals research the feasibility of a business concept.

U.S. West Communications, which serves the states of Arizona, Colorado, Iowa, Idaho, Minnesota, Montana, North Dakota, Nebraska, New Mexico, Oregon, South Dakota, Utah, Washington, and Wyoming, offers training grants to nonprofit coalitions in each state.

There is also a FasTrac Two, which is for existing business owners who want to expand. It can help them create a business plan. Fees for this program range from $125 to $300.

U.S. West Foundation also sponsors one-day training for rural businesses who want to start a tourism business.

For more information, call the Western Entrepreneurial Network at 1-800-873-9378.

CareerTrack Publications
3085 Center Green Drive
P.O. Box 18778
Boulder, CO 80308-1778
(800-334-1018)

This company provides on-site seminars as well as video and audio cassettes on such topics as:

Management - customers, leadership, delegating, interviewing, performance appraisals, work teams, team building, quality, total quality management

Professional development - finance, training, negotiating, presentation

Customer service - phone skills, retaining customers

Communication - conflict, listening, assertive

Time management - project management

Writing Skills

Computer Skills - all the popular software

Self-Esteem

Achievement and Motivation - goal setting, sales

Stress Management

Financial Resources

Regional Investment Bankers

Look into second-tier, regional investment banking groups, such as *Regional Investment Bankers Association* (RIBA), which is based in Highland Park, Illinois. Members of such groups may be willing to finance established as well as growth companies.

Taking Your Company Public see Chapter 30 for underwriters of public and private equity offerings.

Venture Clubs

Consider contacting venture clubs. Get a list of these from the *Association of Venture Clubs*, 265 E. 100 South, #300, Salt Lake City, UT 84110.

Financial networking for women

Connect wtih *Women's World Banking*, 8 W. 40th Street, 10th floor, New York, NY 10018 (212-768-8513).

Check out the book *Guerrilla Financing* by Bruce Blechman and Jay Conrad Levinson (Houghton Mifflin). Ask your local bookstore to look it up, and order the latest edition if it is not already in stock.

The National Association of Small Business Investment Companies, 1199 N. Fairfax Street, Suite 200, Alexandria, VA 22314 (703-683-1601) puts out a directory of the membership of the Small Business Administration-sponsored small-business investment companies (SBICs) and specialized small business investment companies (SSBICs). The focus of the SSBICs is primarily on socially and economically disadvantaged business owners. (See more about the Small Business Administration (SBA) in the government section.) The directory is called *Venture Capital: Where to Find It.* It can be ordered for $10 from NASBIC Directory, POB 2039, Merrifield, VA 22116.

Credit Reports

How to obtain TRW credit reports. Need a credit report to use in a loan application? Here's how to obtain TRW credit reports, according to the SBA: Send a written request to TRW, P.O. Box 2350, Chatsworth, CA 91313-2350. (800-682-7654). Their Business Services Credit national hotline is 800-344-0603. Be sure to include all of the following:

- Full name
- Full current address
- Each previous address for previous five years
- Social Security number
- Date of birth
- Verification of your current address (use a utility bill, a copy of your license, or something containing your address)

You may obtain one complimentary copy of a TRW credit report per year.

Another group to contact is *The National Association of Credit Management*, 8815 Centre Park Drive, Suite 200, Columbia, MD 21045 (410-740-5560).

Government Programs

Small Business Administration (800-827-5722)

The U.S. Small Business Administration (SBA) is another route to go when you are looking for financing. Consider the information and programs we list below (and refer also to the more general information on the SBA in the Government Resources section on p. 327). The SBA has recently been increasing its loans to small businesses. In Massachusetts, for example, the SBA District Office approved 953 loans totaling $132 million between October 1994 and May 1995. This was nearly three times the total for the same period one year ago.

Small-Business Loans

Recently, the SBA has made efforts to make it easier for businesses to obtain loans under $50,000. For one thing, the application has been reduced from 50 pages to 1. They have also instituted a "microloan" pilot program for business owners applying for loans of $25,000 or less.

Business loans for manufacturing, wholesaling, services, retailing, general construction, special trade construction, and agriculture are available through the SBA. The loans are guaranteed up to 90 percent by the SBA. There are various eligibility standards. Congress has increased its annual authorization for the SBA's guaranteed loan program as follows:

to $9.15 billion in 1995
10.5 in 1996
$13.1 billion in 1997.

LOWDOC Program

LOWDOC is a loan program for entrepreneurs starting a new business or for businesses with average annual sales for the prior three years of $5 million or less and with fewer than 100 employees. As the program has gained momentum, more and more loans have been offered to minorities, women, veterans, and start-up businesses.

The loans granted through this program are $100,000 or less, and the SBA guarantees up to 90 percent of the loan. The compelling features of LOWDOC include a one-page application and a quick turnaround time (sometimes a matter of days).

Some additional information may be required of applicants. For example, for loans over $50,000, applicants have to include a copy of their federal income tax Schedule C or the front page of the corporate or partnership returns for the past three years.

In the state of Massachusetts, 20 percent of the LOWDOC loans were for businesses owned by women; 8 percent were awarded to businesses owned by minorities.

Through the local branch of the SBA you can obtain a list of banks in your area that participate in these loan programs.

Women's Prequalification Pilot Loan Program

The SBA's Women's Prequalification Pilot Loan Program is designed for women business owners who want to receive prequalification from the SBA for a loan guaranty before they go to a bank for a loan. There is a streamlined application process and a quick response to loan requests of $250,000 or less. Qualification criteria for applicants include character, credit, experience, and reliability.

The SBA can guarantee up to 90 percent of loans up to $155,000 and up to 85 percent of loans between $155,000 and $250,000.

To be eligible, the business must be at least 51 percent owned, operated, and managed by women; it must have average annual sales for the preceding three years that do not exceed $5 million; and it must employ fewer than 100 people.

The Women's Prequalification Pilot Loan Program is available through the following SBA offices:

SBA OFFICE	PHONE
San Francisco, CA	415-744-8490
Chicago, IL	312-353-5429

New Orleans, LA 504-589-6685
Buffalo, NY 716-846-4517
Columbus, OH 614-469-6860
Louisville, KY 502-582-5971
Charlotte, NC 704-344-6563

The program is also available statewide in the following five pilot states:

STATE	SBA OFFICE	PHONE
Colorado	Denver	303-844-3461
Maine	Augusta	207-622-8242
Montana	Helena	406-449-5381
New Mexico	Albuquerque	505-766-1879
Utah	Salt Lake City	801-524-6831

Franchising Resources

Request disclosure of background information on a franchisor (according to state regulations) from the state Office of Investor Protection. Use the freedom of request form.

Or, obtain the Uniform Franchise Offering Circular (UFOC) in the states that use it. (See Chapter 6)

There are also franchise consulting firms such as Francorp Inc., in Olympia Fields, Illinois, but these will cost money.

Organizations

International Franchise Association, 1350 New York Avenue, NW, Suite 900, Washington, DC 20005 (202-628-8000) offers a Franchise Opportunities Guide for $15.

There is a *Franchising & Licensing World Center* (FLWC) in Chicago, Illinois, that boasts showrooms, museum, auditorium, video production center, library, and dining room.

Federal Trade Commission (FTC)

The FTC will provide a free package of information about the FTC Franchise and Business Opportunity Disclosure Rule. Write to the Division of Marketing Practices, Federal Trade Commission, Washington, DC 20580 or call 202-326-3128.

The FTC has regional offices in Atlanta, Boston, Chicago, Cleveland, Dallas, Denver, Los Angeles, New York, San Francisco, and Seattle.

American Business Opportunity Institute Inc.

3 Bethesda Metro Center, #700, Bethesda, MD 20814 advertises books and a newsletter. ABOII is a national information clearinghouse and seminar company that specializes in business opportunity and franchise investment and regulation. For information on their publications, programs, and services, send them a business-sized stamped envelope.

General Business

City and Local Resources

Chambers of Commerce. City chambers of commerce can be useful resources for the new business owner. Although the services offered vary from chamber to chamber, these organizations are designed for the small-business person. The dues are reasonable and provide access to a number of services as well as to networking.

Members can obtain, for example, discounts on long-distance telephone service and group health insurance; they can make valuable business contacts through chamber activities and networking; they have access to business expertise through seminars, workshops, and individual counseling.

Some chambers have affiliations with local SBDCs (see the section on the SBA) and can arrange for consultations on business questions. They can provide you with listings of financial resources, information about the economic climate, and demographics of the area. Chambers can help with finding commercial space and learning about local permits and zoning.

Many chambers provide a packet of information about doing business in the state, including the legal, financial, and regulatory requirements of that state.

State Programs

State Economic Development Program. Economic development programs will vary from state to state, as they are funded by individual states, sometimes with federal assistance. They can help people who want to expand their business, as into exporting, for example. Areas of support include requests for proposals and subcontracting.

State governments can be good sources of listings or directories of large companies in the state or region.

In addition, some states have minority- or women-owned business certification if you are qualified.

Look under the state listings in your telephone book.

Federal Programs

Federal government resources. Contact the offices in your state (capital) for

Small Business Administration
Department of Labor
Internal Revenue Service
U.S. Department of Commerce
U.S. Government Book Store

Or contact the Federal Information Center, P.O. Box 600, Cumberland, MD 21502 (800-347-1997) or U.S. Small Business Administration (SBA) 409 Third Street, S.W., Washington, DC 20416.

The U.S. Small Business Administration (SBA) is a federal agency that offers many services to small businesses. Through their state and regional offices they offer loan programs, counseling, training, and referrals. They publish a directory of publications and guides that can be ordered for a nominal fee. They sponsor SCORE, the Service Corps of Retired Executives. Much of the work is done through state and local offices that are a part of the SBA's Business Development Service Network.

Local Branches.   Most states have regional offices that direct the work of the SBA. For example, in Massachusetts there is the Massachusetts Small Business Development Center, whose purpose is to help new and existing small businesses to succeed. They offer specialized services in international trade, minority business assistance, and capital formation. Through the regional centers (there are four in western Massachusetts, in each of the four major cities there), you can obtain counseling, training, referral, software training, and other resources. Some local offices have connections with area colleges and universities to enhance their offerings.

In most cases, services are free. Seminars may be offered for a nominal fee.

For further information, look for "Small Business Administration" under "U.S. Government" in the telephone directory, or call the Small Business Answer Desk at 800-8-ASK-SBA (800-827-5722) or write the U.S. Small Business Administration at 409 Third Street, S.W., Washington, DC 20416. The Office of Public Communications can be reached at 202-205-6743.

Small Business Development Centers (SBDCs).   SBDCs are sponsored by the SBA in partnership with state and local governments, the educational community, and the private sector. They are usually found at local colleges or universities. Their purpose is to provide high-quality, low-cost counseling to prospective and existing business owners. They can offer training, advice, help in writing a business plan, advice on financial assistance, and marketing advice. There are 500 SBDC service locations in 42 states.

Small Business Institutes (SBIs).   Small Business Institutes are organized through the SBA on almost 500 college campuses nationwide. The SBIs offer counseling by students and faculty to small business clients.

Office of Women's Business Ownership (OWBO).   The Office of Women's Business Ownership (OWBO) is part of the U.S. Small Business Administration. It has its own office at 1441 L Street, N.W., Room 414, Washington, DC 20416 (202-653-8000).

Active Corps of Executives (ACE).   This is another SBA program in which currently employed executives work with small businesses on a volunteer basis.

Service Corps of Retired Executives (SCORE). Another service of the SBA is SCORE. This is a volunteer group of retired men and women with diverse backgrounds and expertise in business. SCORE counselors provide free management counseling to small business owners and managers and those who are considering starting a business.

One New England SCORE chapter is presenting a three-hour workshop at a local bank. The main focus of the event is a video presentation by *INC.* magazine. At the end of the session, SCORE members will be on hand to field questions and answers. The fee for this workshop is $20. Topics include the idea, testing the idea, protecting the idea, finding good people, structuring the business, understanding cash flow, finding the money, the business plan, starting out on the right foot, and looking ahead.

You can reach a SCORE counselor in most large cities by contacting the SBA office near you.

IRS Hotline (800-829-1040). The Internal Revenue Service has a hotline to which you can turn to have tax questions answered. They also offer free publications to help you prepare your taxes. Call 800-829-3676.

Magazines, Books, and Publications

There are many publications that can be of assistance to small business owners, from general newsletters to professional association journals and on a wide range of business topics.

Booklets on almost any business topic can be obtained through the Government Publishing Office, Washington, DC 20402.

Small-business directory

The Small Business Association (SBA) offers publications and videotapes containing information on starting and managing a successful small business. These are listed in a directory published by the SBA.

Videotapes include such topics as marketing, customers, business planning, advertising, public relations, and direct mail. Publications discuss products, financial management, planning, marketing, crime prevention, and personnel management. Most are obtainable for a minimal fee (usually 50 cents or $1).

One example of an SBA publication ($1) is "Selling by Mail Order," written by William A. Cohen, professor of marketing and chairman of the Department of Marketing at California State University, Los Angeles. The publication is six pages long and includes such topics as Mail Order Successes, What Qualities Are Required, Product Selection, Pricing Structure, Forecasting Sales, Testing —Mail Order's Secret Weapon, Advertising (including a copywriting checklist), What Cost, Keep Good Records, Repeat Business—Key to Maximum Profits.

These SBA publications can provide good resources for entrepreneurs and small business owners and can be useful in combination with counseling and the other resources of the SBA.

For a free copy of the *Directory of Business Development Publications*, write to: Publications, P.O. Box 1000, Fort Worth, TX 76119 or contact your local SBA office.

Magazines

Entrepreneur Magazine, Subscription Department, P.O. Box 50368, Boulder, CO 80321-0368. Address general inquiries to Entrepreneur Group, 2392 Morse Avenue, Irvine, CA 92714 (714-261-2325). This magazine runs an issue on franchises every January.

Business Start-Ups Magazine, Subscription Department, P.O. Box 50347, Boulder, CO 80321-0347.

Executive Female, published by the National Association for Female Executives (NAFE) New York, NY (212-477-2200).

Working Woman, Subscriptions, P.O. Box 3276, Harlan, IA 51593-2456.

I.B. (Independent Business, America's Small Business magazine), 125 Auburn Court, Thousand Oaks, CA 91362-3617.

Income Opportunities, IO Publications, 1500 Broadway, New York, NY 10036-0600.

Owner-Manager, P.O. Box 1521, Wall Street Station, New York, NY 10268-1521.

Inc.Magazine, 38 Commercial Wharf, Boston, MA 02110.

Sales and Marketing Management magazine, 355 Park Avenue S., New York, NY 10010-1789.

Business Marketing magazine, 740 N. Rush Street, Chicago, IL 60611.

Home-Office Computing, 730 Broadway, New York, NY, 10003.

Journal of Business Venturing, 655 Avenue of the Americas, New York, NY 10010.

Books

Jeffrey Gitomer, *The Sales Bible: The Ultimate Sales Resource*, New York: William Morrow, 1994.

James C. Collins and Jerry I. Porras, *Built to Last: Successful Habits of Visionary Companies*, New York: Harper Collins, 1994.

Laurie B. Zucherman, *On Your Own: A Woman's Guide to Building a Business,* Dover, NH: Upstart Publishing Company, Inc., 1990.

Geraldine A. Larkin, *Woman to Woman: Street Smarts for Women Entrepreneurs*, Englewood Cliffs, NJ: Prentice Hall, 1993.

Ronald E. Merrill and Henry D. Sedgwick, *The New Venture Handbook: Everything You Need to Know to Start and Run Your Own Business*, AMACOM, 1995.

Staff of Entrepreneur magazine, *Entrepreneur Small Business Advisor and Desk Reference*, Wiley, 1995.

Earl Naumann, *Creating Customer Value*, Southwestern Pub., May 1995.

Earl Naumann and Kathleen Giel, *Customer Satisfaction Measurement and Management*, Van Nostrand Rheinhold, April 1995.

Jill Ellsworth and Matthew V. Ellsworth, *Marketing on the Internet*, Wiley, 1995.

The Upstart *Owning and Managing* Series: Chicago, IL: Dearborn Trade. Owning and managing a resume service, desktop publishing service, bar or tavern, bed and breakfast, antiques business. Upstart Publishing Company, Inc., November 1995.

Paul and Sarah Edwards, *The Best Home Businesses for the Nineties*, Jeremy Tarcher, publisher, 1992.

American Business Opportunity Institute, Inc., 3 Bethesda Metro Center, #700, Bethesda, MD 20814. Offers books and a quarterly newsletter.

The Entrepreneur's Business Success Resource Guide. Published by the Aegis Publishing Group, this bulletin lists numerous books for small businesses, on topics such as: working at home; business start-up; business management; information resources; marketing and publicity; telecommunications and computers; mail order and direct marketing; arts, crafts, creative skills; and writing and self-publishing. Write to: Aegis Publishing Group, 796 Aquidneck Avenue, Newport, RI 02840 for a current issue of the booklist and order form.

Communication Services in Rochester, New York publishes job-skills booklets for individuals and small businesses. They have a catalog of 25 booklets designed for small businesses, covering such topics as hiring, networking, writing issues, direct marketing, and training. To order the catalog, write to David R. Young, Publisher, Communication Services, 210 Glen Ellyn Way, Rochester, NY 14618-1617.

Wiley Professional Books-by-Mail, John Wiley & Sons, Inc., Somerset, NY 08875-9977. Write for a book list.

Management

Blue Chip Enterprise Initiative. *Nation's Business* co-sponsors with Connecticut Mutual Life Insurance Company and the U.S. Chamber of Commerce the Blue Chip Enterprise Initiative. Its purpose is to recognize businesses that have been able to overcome difficulties and that have grown in strength as a result.

Malcolm Baldrige National Quality Award. This award and the process involved in applying for it are discussed in Chapter 8. To obtain a copy of the Award Criteria and application forms and instructions for the Malcolm Baldrige Quality Award competition, write Malcolm Baldrige National Quality Award, National Institute of Standards and Technology, Route 270 and Quince Orchard Road., Administration Building, Room A537, Gaithersburg, MD 20899 (301-975-2036).

American Society for Quality Control. Customer Service Department, P.O. Box 3066, Milwaukee, WI 53201, 800-248-1946. Call or write for information on the ASQC.

Printed materials. For printed materials at low cost, use professional looking papers from Paper Direct, 800-272-7377, or Queblo, 800-523-9080.

Customer service. Consider providing an 800 number for orders and information and customer service. You don't need a new line. It's $5 to $10 a month.

Telephone services. Office Depot Communications, 800-800-5243, offers a flat rate of 15 cents per minute for interstate calls, with no installation charge and no monthly service charge.

Temporary help. For inexpensive employment help, consider using college students as interns.

Business Organizations

American Business Women's Association (ABWA), 9100 Ward Parkway, P.O. Box 8728, Kansas City, MO 64114-0728 (816-361-6621).

American Entrepreneur's Association. Membership in this organization is $29.95, or $10 when purchased with a business guide from *Entrepreneur* magazine (800-421-2300).

Association of Black Women Entrepreneurs, Corita Communications, P.O. Box 49368, Los Angeles, CA 90049, 213-559-2375.

Business and Professional Women's Foundation, 2012 Massachusetts Avenue, NW, Washington, DC 20036.

Coalition of Women in National and International Business, 1900 L Street, NW, Washington, DC 20036.

Federation of Organizations for Professional Women, 2001 S Street, NW, Suite 540, Washington, DC 20009 (202-328-1415).

International Resource Network on Disabilities (IRND). The IRND offers business assistance and information on the Americans with Disabilities Act of 1990 (ADA), as well as consulting services on ADA compliance, workshops and seminars, and publications. Contact them at IRND,

2706 Alt. US 19 North, Palm Harbor, FL 34683, 800-877-IRND or 800-877-4763 voice, or 813-787-8465.

National Association for Female Executives (NAFE), 127 W. 24th Street, New York, NY 10011 (212-645-0770).

National Association of Black Women Entrepreneurs, P.O. Box 1375, Detroit, MI 48231 (313-341-7400).

National Association of Women Business Owners, 600 S. Federal Street, Suite 400, Chicago, IL 60605 (312-922-0465).

National Council of Career Women, 3222 N Street, NW, Washington, DC 20007 (202-333-8578).

National Federation of Business & Professional Women's Clubs, 2012 Massachusetts Avenue, NW, Washington, DC, 20036 (202-293-1100).

National Federation of Independent Business (NFIB), 53 Century Blvd., Suite 300, Nashville, TN 37214 (615-872-5800).

Glossary of Business Terms

accounting Measuring, interpreting and distributing financial information for internal and external decision-making.

accounting equation Basic principle that assets are equal to liabilities plus owners' equity.

accounts payable Obligations incurred by a business not yet paid.

accounts receivable Credit sales not yet paid by customers.

accounts receivable financing Short-term financing based on pledging receivables as collateral for a loan, or the direct sale of receivables.

accounts receivable turnover The number of times accounts receivable turns over during a year; to calculate, divide annual credit sales by average accounts receivable.

acid-test (quick) ratio Measures the ability of a firm to meet its current debt on short notice; to calculate, subtract current inventory from current assets and divide by current liabilities.

acquisition Process by which one firm takes over the property and assumes the obligations of another firm.

activity ratios Measure the efficiency of a firm's use of its resources. Includes inventory turnover, average collection period, and total assets turnover.

advertising; institutional advertising Sales message directed at a target audience, usually through impersonal media; promotion of a concept, idea or philosophy of a corporation or organization.

advisory council A group, usually from outside the company, that serves in an advisory capacity rather than a governing one.

agents Distributors who do not take title to the goods they distribute.

amortize To write off capital equipment expenses by prorating the costs over a fixed period of time.

angel financing Investments in new ventures by wealthy individuals known as "business angels."

appraisal An evaluation of individual job performance; an estimate of the value of assets.

assembly line Manufacturing technique in which the product passes through workstations, each with a specialized task.

asset-based valuation A method of evaluating the value of a business based on the value of its assets.

assets Items of value owned by a company and shown on the balance sheet, including cash, accounts receivable, equipment, inventory, and the like.

bait and switch advertising Attracting customers to a business by promoting discounted goods, then selling them full-priced equivalents.

balance sheet A statement of the assets of a business and the claims against them (liabilities), including any claims by its owners (equity).

board of directors By state law, a governing body of a corporation elected by its stockholders to provide management oversight.

bond Certificate of indebtedness sold to collect long-term funds for corporations or government agencies.

book value The value of a business calculated by subtracting total liabilities (adjusted for intangible assets) from total assets.

brand Name, term, sign, symbol or design used to identify a firm's goods or services.

brand name Words or letters that uniquely identify a firm's product.

brand preference Degree to which a consumer will select one brand over competitive brands when the preferred brand is available.

brand recognition Degree to which a consumer is aware of a brand.

breakeven point Dollar value of sales that will cover but not exceed all of the company's costs, both fixed and variable. Can apply to a particular project or a period of time.

broker An agent who receives a fee for selling real estate or a business.

business plan A written document detailing a proposed venture, covering current status, expected needs, and projected results for the enterprise.

buyout The purchase of an existing business.

C corporation A business form which is considered to be a separate legal entity for tax purposes.

capital, circulating Monies which finance the operation of a business.

capitalization rate Used in assessing the value of a business; this rate is based on risk of current earnings and their expected growth rate.

carrier See common carrier and contract carrier.

cash budget A budget strictly concerned with the inflow and outflow of cash.

cash flow A measure of money taken in versus money paid out on a periodic basis.

cash flow statement A financial statement setting out the amount and timing of actual and/or anticipated cash inflow and outflow.

cash-flow-based valuation Used in assessing the value of a business, this method compares expected and required rates of return on investment.

certified public accountant (CPA) Accountant who has completed education and experience requirements and passed an examination.

channel of distribution The steps by which a product moves from producer to ultimate consumer. A direct channel contains no intermediaries; an indirect channel has one or more intermediaries.

charter A document that describes the business and its mission, goals, strategy and values.

commercial bank A profit-making business that holds the deposits of individual and business customers in the form of checking or savings accounts, using these funds to make loans to individuals and businesses.

common carriers Transportation firms that provide services within a particular line of business for the general public.

common stock See stock

comparable worth Philosophy seeking compensation equity for men and women holding jobs requiring similar levels of education, training, and skills.

comparative advertising Effective advertising approach in which direct comparisons are made with competing goods or services.

competition Struggle among businesses for consumer acceptance.

computer-aided manufacturing (CAM) Computer analysis of a product design to determine the steps for producing the design, and electronic transmission of instructions to production equipment used in producing the product.

conglomerate merger Merger of unrelated businesses.

contingency planning Having a strategy to be used in case of unexpected events.

continuous process Manufacturing operations whose production runs last months or years.

contract carriers Transportation firms carrying goods for hire by individual contract and not for the general public.

convenience products Products consumers desire to purchase often, immediately and with a minimum of effort.

cooperative advertising Sharing of local advertising costs between the manufacturer and the marketing agent.

copyright By federal legislation, legal protection of literary or artistic work by granting exclusive rights to the work's creator.

corporate culture An organization's value system.

corporation / public / closely-held Legal entity having authority to act, with liability separate and apart from its creators. A public corporation's stock is held by the public, while a closely-held corporation's stock is family-owned.

corrective maintenance Major and minor repairs that keep equipment in good working order.

cost of capital Rate of return a firm needs to earn to satisfy investors and owners.

credit The decrease in an asset, increase in a liability, or an increase in owners' equity; agreement to delay receipt of payment for goods or services, usually thirty to ninety days.

critical path Sequence of operations in PERT diagram requiring the longest time to complete.

current assets Cash and other assets that can or will be converted to cash or used within a year.

current liabilities Claims of creditors that must be repaid within one year.

current ratio Ratio which measures a company's ability to pay its current debts as they mature; calculated by dividing current assets by current liabilities.

customer service Competitive strategy based on how a business treats its customers.

data Statistics, opinions, facts or predictions categorized by some criteria for storage and retrieval. *Primary data* is new, while *secondary data* is obtained indirectly from data already collected.

database Integrated collection of an organization's data resources, organized to meet various business needs.

debit An increase in an asset, decrease in a liability or a decrease in owner's equity.

debt ratio Ratio which measures the extent to which a firm relies on debt financing for its operations. Calculated by dividing total debt by total assets.

debt to owners' equity ratio Ratio which measures the extent to which company operations are financed by borrowed funds; calculated by dividing total liabilities by owners' equity.

decline stage The fourth stage in a product's life cycle during which demand falls at an increasing rate.

demand Consumers' willingness and ability to purchase products.

demand deposits Checking accounts for which the institution promises to pay immediately to the depositor any amount of money requested if not in excess of the account balance.

demographic variables Characteristics of a given population such as average age, sex, family makeup, income and ethnic background that can be considered when developing markets.

depreciation Decrease in the value of assets over their expected life by an accepted accounting method, such as allocating the cost of an asset over the years in which it is used.

disclosure document Financial information which by law must be made available to potential investors.

discount rate Interest rate charged by the Federal Reserve System on loans to its member banks.

discounts Price considerations offered as an incentive to a consumer to buy a product or service.

discretionary income Consumer funds available for spending after basic living costs have been met.

distribution channels Pathways by which goods are moved from producer to consumer, sometimes through intermediate channels.

dividends Payments of a corporation's profits to its stockholders.

double-entry system A method of bookkeeping in which entries are made in two places in order to be sure they balance.

drop shipper Limited-function merchant-wholesaler who takes legal title to products but never physically handles them.

earnings per share Profits earned by a corporation for each outstanding common stock share; calculated by dividing net income after taxes by the number of common shares outstanding.

earnings-based valuation approach A method of assessing the value of a business by looking at its potential future income.

economic opportunity Ability to earn profits by marketing a product or service in a particular market segment.

effectiveness The quality of the managerial act of doing the right things, in which the payoff is the greatest for the time, money and effort expended.

efficiency In a given process, the measure of the value of output divided by input.

E-mail - electronic mail System of sending, receiving and storing written messages through computers.

employee benefits Employee rewards such as pension plans, insurance, sick-leave pay and paid vacation, given at all or part of the expense of the company.

employment at will Right of employers to retain or discharge personnel as they wish.

entrepreneur One who starts, manages and assumes the risks and rewards of a new business enterprise.

equity Claims against the assets of a business, including owners' invested capital plus earnings retained by the business; perceived fairness in resolving disputes, decisions, granting raises, and the like.

equity capital Funds provided by the firm's owners by reinvesting earnings or making additional contributions, by stock issues to the public or by contributions from venture capitalists.

ergonomics Work environment design based on human factors.

evaluation See performance appraisal

executive summary Concise overview of major points in a longer business report or study.

exporting Selling domestic goods and services abroad.

facsimile machine (fax) Telecommunications device which allows for the transmission of documents electronically.

factor A financial organization or individual who purchases a firm's accounts receivable at a discount.

fax see facsimile machine

feedback Data or information reporting on the level of performance of managerial effort, such as profitability, productivity, or reduction in absenteeism.

finance Business function of effectively obtaining and managing funds.

financial control Process of periodically checking actual revenues, costs, and expenses against forecasts.

financial plan Document that specifies the funds needed by a firm for a period of time, charts inflows and outflows, and details the most appropriate uses of the funds.

finder An agent who for a fee brings together a businessperson seeking funding and a wealthy investor searching for a promising business investment.

fixed asset turnover A means by which to measure the turnover of plant and equipment, calculated by dividing sales by fixed assets.

fixed assets Assets expected to be used for periods longer than one year, such as machinery.

fixed costs Costs that remain constant over a given period of time regardless of the level of production, for example, the cost of leasing machinery to make a product.

flexible manufacturing system (FMS) Facility that allows production to be modified quickly for the manufacture of different products.

flextime Work-scheduling system which allows employees to set work hours within constraints specified by management.

float Time delay between writing a check and the transfer of funds to the recipient.

focus-group A selected group who are asked for their responses to aspects of a new product such as pricing or features.

franchise An agreement between a producer of a product or service and a retailer that permits the retailer to supply and market these products or services for a fee.

franchisee Retailer who enters into an agreement with a supplier to sell that supplier's goods or services for a fee.

franchisor Supplier of goods and services who enters into an agreement with a retailer to sell those products or services for a fee.

fringe benefits See employee benefits.

general partner A member of a partnership in which all partners are equally liable for business debts. See also *limited partnership.*

generally accepted accounting principles (GAAP) Standards that provide consistency in the conventions, rules and procedures in accounting practices.

goodwill The value of a business in patronage and reputation which exceeds its tangible net worth.

gross domestic product (GDP) Sum of all goods and services produced within a country's boundaries.

growth stage Second stage of product development, when it has overcome its initial hurdles and is now providing a flow of return and sales are growing.

human resource management Process of acquiring, training, developing, motivating and appraising a sufficient quantity of employees to perform necessary activities.

human resource planning Developing programs and an organizational climate fostering maximum efficiency and worker satisfaction, including comprehensive strategies to meet future staffing needs.

income statement Financial record of revenues, expenses and profits over a period of time, usually a year.

inside directors Members of a corporation's board of directors who are also employees.

installment account A consumer payment method in which a down payment towards the purchase price is made, with the balance of payments made over a specified time period.

insurance Transfer of risk from an individual or business to a group which shares any losses, up to specified limits, on a fairly distributed basis among the group's members.

intangible assets Items of value that have no tangible physical properties, such as ideas.

interest expense The interest amounts owed to lenders on borrowed dollars.

intermittent process Manufacturing operation with short production runs that allows machines to be shut down or changed to make other products.

internal rate of return (IRR) Capital-budgeting technique involving discounting future cash flows to the present at a rate that makes the net present value of the project equal to zero.

inventory control Balancing the cost of holding raw materials, work in progress and inventory against the costs involved in carrying the inventory.

inventory turnover ratio Ratio which measures the number of times merchandise moves through a business; calculated by dividing the cost of goods sold by the average amount of inventory.

job description Describes job objectives, work tasks, responsibilities, skill requirements, working conditions, and the relationship of the job to other jobs.

job evaluation Determination of wage level for a job based on skill requirements, education requirements, responsibilities, and physical requirements.

job rotation Process of familiarizing junior executives or workers with the various operations and contributions of each department through temporary assignments to each department.

job sharing Division of one job among two or more employees.

just-in-time (JIT) inventory system Management philosophy aimed at improving profits and return on investment by reducing inventory levels to absolute minimums.

leasing employees Leasing personnel from a firm that administers the paperwork and benefits.

leverage Technique of increasing the rate of return on investment through the use of borrowed money.

leveraged buyout (LBO) Use of borrowed funds to purchase a company or division.

liabilities Debts a business owes, including accounts payable, taxes, bank loans and other obligations. *Short term liabilities* are due within a year, *long-term liabilities* are for a period of more than a year.

limited partnership Organizational arrangement allowing investors to put money into a partnership without assuming liability for any losses beyond this initial investment.

line activities Business functions that contribute directly to the primary objectives of a firm, such as sales.

line manager Manager who forms part of the main line of authority in a business.

line of credit An agreement between a commercial bank and a business firm that states the amount of unsecured short-term credit the bank will make available to the borrower.

liquidation value A method of valuing a firm in which the value of all assets is determined on the basis of their current sale value.

liquidity Speed at which objects can be converted to cash.

liquidity ratio Ratio measuring a business's ability to meet its short-term obligations.Includes current ratio and quick ratio or acid test.

long-range planning A firm's strategies for the long-term future (also called strategic planning).

long-term debt Liabilities with a repayment term of one year or longer.

management The planning, leading, organizing, and controlling of a firm's operations.

management by objectives (MBO) A program designed to improve employee motivation through their participation in goal setting and by informing them in advance of factors used in performance evaluations.

management information system (MIS) Organized method of providing decision-making information, such as sales activity or productivity levels.

management plan A section of the business plan describing a firm's key players including investors, management and directors, and their experience and qualifications.

management team The managers and other key persons who provide a firm's general direction and execute its business plan.

market Customers or potential customers with need, authority and purchasing power.

market segmentation Process of dividing a total market into groups differentiated by specific sets of characteristics.

market share Percentage of a market controlled by a company or product.

market value A method of valuing a business, good or service that involves an estimation based on prices recently paid for similar enterprises or items as well as on the methods of sale; the current price at which a security is selling.

market-penetration price An introductory low price for a new product or service, intended to achieve a quick, high volume of sales in order to gain a good share of the market.

marketing A system of getting goods or services to the customer, using research, product development, promotion, advertising, distribution, pricing and selling.

marketing mix Combination of a firm's product, pricing, distribution, and promotional strategies focused on certain consumer segments.

marketing plan A document describing a firm's potential customers and a comprehensive strategy to sell them goods and services.

marketing research Information function that matches the marketer with the marketplace.

mass production Manufacture of goods in large volume as a result of standardization, specialized labor and mechanization.

maturity stage The third stage of product or service sales, in which rate of volume and profitability decline while competition increases.

me-too pricing Pricing strategy that is similar to that of the competition.

median The middle value of a sequenced set of values.

merchant middlemen Independent wholesalers that take legal title to goods they distribute.

merger Two or more firms combine to form one entity.

microcomputer Desktop, laptop, and pocket-size portable computers used by one person at a time.

missionary selling Form of indirect selling in which a sales representative markets the goodwill of a company and provides technical or operational assistance.

modem An electronic device that converts digital data to analog and vice versa, used in computer communication over telephone lines.

monopoly Market situation in which a firm has no direct competitors and thus controls the market.

NOW (negotiable order of withdrawal) account Interest-bearing checking account.

net income Profit or loss incurred over a specific period, calculated by subtracting all expenses from revenues.

net present value (NPV) The present value of future cash flows from an investment minus the initial investment outlay.

net profits after taxes Income that can be divided among the owners of a company or else reinvested in the company.

networking Process of developing and engaging in mutually beneficial relationships with professional peers.

niche marketing Identifying and targeting markets not adequately served by competitors.

Occupational Safety and Health Administration (OSHA) Federal legislation requiring implementation of procedures to ensure employee health and safety in the workplace.

odd lots Purchase or sale of shares of stock in amounts fewer than 100.

on-the-job training Training employees in new job tasks by having them perform under the guidance of an experienced employee.

operating expenses All business costs not included in the cost of goods sold.

operating income Profits before interest and taxes are paid (also called earnings before taxes and interest).

operating plan Section of the business plan describing the facilities, labor, raw materials, and processing requirements of a business.

operational planning Short range or functional planning consisting of specific practices intended to carry out the objectives set forth in the strategic plan.

operations management Planning and control of the production process.

opportunity cost The rate of return that could be otherwise earned on monies invested in an enterprise.

order processing Sales task of receiving and handling an order; function of preparing an order for shipment.

organization Structured group of people working in concert to achieve business objectives.

organization chart Diagram showing the chain of command, division of tasks, and departmentalization of an organization.

outside directors Board members who are not employed by the organization.

outsourcing Contracting of all or parts of production to an outside vendor.

owners' equity Claims of the proprietor, the partners, or the stockholders against the firm's assets; the excess of assets over liabilities.

par value Value printed on some companies' stock certificates.

partner One of two or more persons co-owning a business for profit. Active partners are involved in day-to-day business functions, while passive partners act as advisors or investors only.

partnership An association of two or more persons owning and running a business for profit; limited partnerships give investors special tax advantages and shielding from liability in exchange for forfeiting any management control.

performance appraisal A system of defining acceptable employee performance levels and evaluating actual performance on a scheduled basis in comparison to stated goals; used to determine training, compensation, promotion, transfers or terminations.

perpetual inventory system Maintaining an ongoing, current update of items in inventory.

PERT Program Evaluation and Review Technique. A method for scheduling that coordinates all aspects of a process so as to minimize production delays.

physical inventory system Program of periodic counting of inventory items.

piggyback franchising The operation of a retail franchise within a host store.

point-of-purchase (POP) advertising Sales promotion technique that displays and demonstrates an item at the location where the actual purchase decision is made.

point-of-purchase display A fixture showing, promoting and offering goods for sale, usually at the cash register or checkout counter.

point-of-sale (POS) terminals Machines linked to a bank's computers that allow funds to be transferred from a purchaser's account to the seller's account when a purchase is made.

positioning Marketing strategy used to differentiate a good or service from its competitors in the mind of a prospective buyer.

preferred stock See stock

premium Fee paid by an insured party to an insurer for coverage against losses. A reward or prize used to encourage sales.

preventive maintenance Inspections and other activities meant to prevent machine breakdowns.

price Exchange value of a good or service.

price line A firm's offering of a range of several distinct prices at which goods or services are sold.

price-earnings ratio Current market price of a stock divided by annual earnings per share.

pricing strategy Part of marketing decision making that deals with setting profitable and justifiable prices. *Prestige pricing* strategy involves setting a high price to convey a unique or fine quality image. *Penetration* is a strategy of pricing a new product relatively low to encourage wide market acceptance that will allow a price increase later on. *Skimming* strategy is setting the price of a new product relatively high, then gradually lowering it.

private carriers Companies that use their own vehicle to transport their own goods.

product A package of physical, service and symbolic qualities designed to meet consumer needs. *Industrial* products are purchased for use in the manufacture of other goods or for resale. *Specialty* products are those perceived to be so desirable that customers make extra efforts to obtain them.

pro formas Projected financial statements for a business.

product development Formulation of new or improved products for current markets in order to increase sales.

product life cycle The four stages of a successful product: introduction, growth, maturity and decline.

product line Series of related products offered by one firm.

product line pricing Offering merchandise at a limited number of prices rather than pricing each item individually.

product mix Group of products offered by a firm.

product strategy Aspects of marketing decision making dealing with developing goods and services, package design, trademarks, warranties and product life cycles.

production Use of people and machinery to transform materials into finished goods or services.

production control Well-defined set of procedures for coordinating people, materials and machinery to provide optimal production efficiency.

production planning Aspect of production control that determines the amount and type of resources needed to produce a certain quantity of goods or services.

profit Difference between a firm's revenues and expenses.

profit margin The net profit after taxes divided by sales.

profit maximization Pricing strategy in which management sets increasing levels of profitability as its objective.

profit sharing A process of distributing company profits to employees who participated in producing those profits.

profitability ratio Ratio that measures the overall financial performance of the firm. Includes profit margin on sales, return on total assets, and return on net worth.

promissory note Traditional bank loan for which the borrower signs a note stating the terms of the loan, including its date of repayment and interest rate.

promotion A planned, ongoing program of communications with customers in an effort to encourage their acceptance and purchase of a product or service. A change in job which increases an employee's authority, responsibility and salary.

promotional mix Firm's mix of both personal and non-personal sales strategies to achieve sales objectives.

promotional strategy Element of marketing decision making involving the blending of personal selling, advertising, sales promotion and public relations to create effective communications between a firm and the market-place; the function of informing, persuading and influencing consumer decision making.

proprietorship See sole proprietorship

prospecting Sales task of identifying likely customers.

public accountant See certified public accountant

public relations An organization's communications with its various audiences.

publicity Free advertising gained by communicating newsworthy items about a business via newspapers, radio, television or other media.

purchase order A written order issued to a vendor to buy goods or services.

purchasing Function of obtaining materials, merchandise, equipment and services needed to meet production and sales goals.

qualifying Sales task of identifying most likely customers with authority and ability to buy.

quality Features and characteristics of a product or service which enable it to satisfy customer needs.

quality control Measurement of goods and services produced against established quality standards.

quick ratio See acid-test ratio.

rack jobber Full-function merchant wholesaler that sets up and services a section of a retail store.

ratio analysis Analysis designed to measure business performance by analyzing relationships between financial statement accounts.

reciprocal buying A firm's policy of selling to businesses from which it also buys.

reorder point Level at which more merchandise should be ordered.

repetitive manufacturing Producing a large quantity of a standard product using long production runs.

replacement value approach A method of assessing the value of a business based on the current cost to replace each of the firm's assets.

research and development Scientific process of development of new commercial products and services.

retail inventory valuation method Inventory control system by which retailers can estimate inventory cost from marked selling prices.

retailers Distribution channel members who sell goods and services to individuals for their own use rather than for resale.

return on equity A ratio measuring a firm's profitability by comparing net income and total owners' equity to assess the returns owners receive for their overall investment.

return on investment (ROI) Net profit divided by funds invested equals the percent return on investment.

return on sales Ratio that measures company profitability by comparing net income and net sales.

revenues Monies received from sales of products and services and from interest payments, dividends, royalties and rents.

reverse technology Adapting an obsolete method, process, mechanism, or device for current use.

risk Uncertainty.

risk-return trade-off Balance between the risk of an investment and its potential gain or return.

risk management Efforts to preserve assets and the earning power of a firm.

round lots Stock bought or sold in multiples of 100 shares.

S corporation Corporation which retains some of the advantages of a corporate form while being taxed similarly to a partnership.

sales forecast Prediction of how much of a good or service will be purchased by a market in a defined time period.

sales promotion See promotion.

seasonal discounts See discounts.

seed money Initial capital secured to start a business.

segmentation strategy Grouping prospective buyers based on similar needs or wants so that members of a group can be targeted with a particular marketing action.

selling expenses Costs incurred in marketing and distributing goods and services.

service mark Words or designs or a combination of these used to advertise a specific service.

SCORE (Service Corps of Retired Executives) Federal government program utilizing retired executives as consultants to small businesses.

short-range plan Action plans governing business operations for a specified time period.

short-term debt Borrowed funds that must be repaid within twelve months.

site analysis Process of finding the optimal location for a business through the study of the various factors that determine the suitability of the location.

skimming price Practice of setting very high prices over a limited time period for goods or services before reducing them to competitive levels.

Small Business Administration (SBA) Federal government agency concerned with small US firms.

Small Business Development Center (SBDCs) SBA program using university faculty and others to assist small businesses through research and consulting activities.

Small Business Investment Companies (SBICs) Federally-funded investment group making loans to small businesses.

software Applications programs, languages, operating systems or utilities used in a computer, including documentation to explain use of these tools.

sole proprietorship A business form in which ownership is invested in a single individual.

spreadsheet A display presenting a rectangular grid of horizontal rows and vertical columns for showing data and the relationships among this data.

statistical process control (SPC) Process of gathering, plotting and analyzing data to determine problem areas in production.

staff manager Manager who provides support to line manager in the form of information technological assistance or advice.

stock certificate Document issued to a stockholder itemizing the number of shares owned.

stock Share of ownership in a company. *Common* stock owners have voting rights in the corporation; *preferred stock* owners have first claim to the corporation's assets after all debts have been paid, but usually do not have voting rights.

stock out Running out of an item needed for manufacturing production.

stock turnover Number of times average level of inventory has been replaced within a given period, typically a year, measured by retail dollar value of merchandise.

stock-to-sales ratio see Stock turnover.

stockholders People who own the shares of and therefore own a corporation.

stocks The shares of ownership in a corporation.

strategic planning Process of setting organizational objectives, then establishing the strategy and resource allocations necessary to reach these objectives.

supplies Expense items needed in a firm's daily operations that are not part of the final product.

system A group of parts functioning together to achieve a central purpose.

tactical planning The planning of short-term tactics or activities and allocation of resources to accomplish them.

tangibles Products with physical substance that can be seen, heard, smelled, touched and/or tasted.

target market (niche market) An identified market segment not adequately served by the competition towards which a firm directs marketing efforts.

target return Pricing strategy in which a desired profitable outcome is stated in terms of particular sales goals.

telemarketing Use of electronic technology such as the telephone or fax to directly contact and sell merchandise to consumers.

tender offer Offer to purchase all or part of a corporation's stock at a premium over its current price.

test marketing New product development stage in which the product is sold in a limited area under close scrutiny.

time study Measure of the time taken by a worker to complete a task.

total asset turnover Measurement of the efficiency with which a firm's assets are used to produce sales. To calculate, divide sales by total assets.

total cost Total fixed cost plus total variable cost.

total quality management (TQM) Systematic promotion of quality as a crucial strategic objective for the entire company.

trade credit Credit given by a vendor to customers who are also vendors. Short-term sources of capital resulting from purchases made on credit or open accounts. See also Credit.

trade discounts Price reductions given to intermediaries in the distribution channel as payment for services provided.

trademark A word, name, symbol, device or a combination of these used to identify and create an image for a specific firm and/or its products, and which has been given legal protection as exclusive to its owner.

Universal Product Code (UPC) Bar code imprinted on or affixed to merchandise to be read by an optical scanner, which prints out the item and price on a receipt.

unlimited liability Liability which extends beyond the assets of a firm.

unsecured loan Short-term source of borrowed capital for which the borrower does not pledge any assets as collateral.

variable costs Costs that vary as the amount produced or sold varies.

vendor A supplier of goods, raw materials, components, services and the like.

venture capital Funds invested by outside investors in emerging, small or struggling businesses with potential for rapid growth in exchange for an ownership share in the business.

voice mail A computerized system for recording, storing and retrieving telephone messages.

warehousing Storage of raw materials or finished goods.

warranty Firm's guarantee to repair, replace or refund purchase price if an item proves unsatisfactory within a specified time period.

wholesaling intermediaries or wholesaler Distribution channel participants selling primarily to retailers, other wholesalers, or industrial users.

word processing Use of computers and software systems to write, store, edit, retrieve, electronically transfer and print text materials.

work sampling A method of work measurement that estimates the ratio of working to idle time.

working capital Difference between current assets (cash, accounts receivable and inventories) and current liabilities (accounts payable and short-term notes).

working-capital management Management of current assets and current liabilities.

yield Income derived from securities, calculated by dividing dividends by market price.

zoning ordinance Local laws regulating land use.

Index